THE UNCERTAIN RETIREMENT

THE UNCERTAIN RETIREMENT

Securing Pension Promises in a World of Risk

James H. Smalhout

IRWIN
Professional Publishing®
Chicago • London • Singapore

Times Mirror
Higher Education Group

Library of Congress Cataloging-in-Publication Data

Smalhout, James H.
    The uncertain retirement : securing pension promises in a world of
risk / James H. Smalhout.
        p.   cm.
    Includes index.
    ISBN 0-78630-799-4
    1. Retirement income—Planning.   2. Old age pensions.
3. Pensions.   4. Finance. Personal.   5. Suretyship and guaranty,
6. Insurance.   I. Title.
HD7105.S58   1996
332.024'01—dc20   95–47695

Printed in the United States of America
1 2 3 4 5 6 7 8 9 0 B 2 1 0 9 8 7 6 5

For my parents,
Mary M. Smalhout
and
John J. Smalhout

CONTENTS

Chapter 3

The Dynamics of Defunding   99

Chapter 7

Alternatives for Reform 303

Chapter 8

A Roadmap into the Future 339

Index 363

PREFACE

Safe and secure pensions come at a price. Our public debate about retirement issues all too often overlooks this simple fact. Yet, no one can have confidence in the future without a belief that the resources will be there when we can no longer work. That confidence today seems to be almost completely lacking. A recent public opinion survey revealed that more young people apparently believe in flying saucers than in the possibility that social security will pay them any benefits.

The aging of America's population will intensify interest in the country's retirement system. If this book had been written 30 years ago, the story of workers losing pensions they believed they had paid for would have been relatively simple. No backup system existed to protect private pensions when employers went out of business and left large unfunded retirement promises behind. Since then, much has changed; but those changes were not always for the better, and they created some new problems with equally serious effects.

This book provides an extensive review of the issues involved with how to guarantee private retirement promises and what that security is worth. My search for answers took me from Stockholm to Santiago and from Chicago to Cologne. The result, *The Uncertain Retirement,* is addressed to policymakers, participants in the public debate, commentators, academics, members of the pension and financial communities, and other interested observers. Today, government programs—like the pension guarantee considered in this study—are being reexamined as never before. To justify their existence in this period of tight budgets and political conservatism, they must compete for scarce resources and demonstrate that the private sector is not able to do the same work or not able to do it better. Similarly, I need to justify to you, the reader, why this issue deserves serious thought.

Private defined-benefit pension plans remain important despite the well-known trend in favor of other forms of retirement saving. They still cover almost 40 million workers and retirees. Yet, our political institutions have clearly demonstrated that they are poorly designed to manage financial guarantees in systems of this scale and magnitude. The savings and loan debacle proved that; but America still has not significantly changed the terms of these arrangements. As the debate about what should be done rages on among the experts, there is widespread confusion about what to believe in other circles. For their part, advocacy groups have no reason to provide objective information, and government itself is anything but a disinterested bystander. Yet, these two groups represent the principal sources of information available to the public.

This project is one attempt to meet the resulting need. The book is divided into eight chapters. Chapter 1 examines the risks to workers that led to the Employee Retirement Income Security Act of 1974, and how they were and were not addressed by that legislation. Chapter 2 focuses on the tricky question of what it means for a pension plan to be adequately funded in an actuarial sense and the available data about the condition of the defined-benefit system as measured on this basis. Chapter 3 draws the important distinction between the financial solvency of a pension plan and actuarial definitions of full funding. Chapter 4 considers yet another essential measure: the value of government insurance provided by the Pension Benefit Guaranty Corporation. Chapter 5 reviews the many useful lessons that the experience of other countries can teach in this area. Chapter 6 examines the ethical dilemmas involved with creating a pension guarantee system and how policymakers should approach them. Chapter 7 discusses the very extensive array of reform alternatives. Chapter 8 reviews how a privatized system of pension guarantees could operate in the United States.

To ensure essential objectivity, the project relied on financial support from independent philanthropic foundations and, to a much lesser extent, the World Bank.

James H. Smalhout

ACKNOWLEDGMENTS

I am indebted to many for the comments, support, suggestions, guidance, and encouragement that were essential in bringing this book to fruition. Edward Cowan, then the president of the National Economists Club, started the process by suggesting that I address the Club about potential taxpayer losses from the ERISA pension termination insurance program.

Robert Litan, then a senior fellow at the Brookings Institution, urged me to think in terms of writing a book to expand on that speech. Special thanks are due to Henry Aaron, Philip Bagnoli, Barry Bosworth, Gary Burtless, Robert Crandall, William Gale, Linda Gianessi, Sylvia Okala, and Greg Pentecost for everything they did to make my year as a guest scholar at Brookings a productive one.

The book itself was not completed until later, when I was a visiting fellow at the Hudson Institute. Hudson did many things that enabled me to reach that point. I feel deeply grateful to Leslie Lenkowsky, Hudson's president, as well as to Neil Pickett, Peter Pitts, and Sam Karnick for their help and encouragement along the way.

The quantitative chapters benefited in major ways from the advice and comments of Professors John Miller and Clifton Sutton at George Mason University as well as from Phillip Kott. Paul Jackson,

Peter Hardcastle, and Joseph Applebaum clarified some of the more esoteric actuarial issues. In this context, the formidable programming skills of Ross Merlin also deserve mention.

Numerous others were generous with their time and their willingness to review my drafts: Thomas Donlan of *Barron's,* Professor Stewart Myers of M.I.T., Professor Zvi Bodie of Boston University, Professor Norman Daniels of Tufts University, Professor Edward Altman of New York University, David Lindeman of the Social Security Administration, Richard Jackson, and several Washington attorneys who shared their unique experience with our complex pension laws. Henry Rose, Diane Burkley, Edward Mackiewicz, Donald Myers, and Michael S. Gordon all contributed major insights concerning the policies that lie behind ERISA and why the PBGC operates as it does.

At the U.S. Department of Labor, Dan Beller cheerfully responded to my frequent questions about the official pension data. John Turner, also at that Department, was helpful with comments and referrals about the international issues discussed in Chapter 5. However, no individual was more essential for the success of that chapter than private consultant Lorna Dailey.

I owe much to many in Europe who shared their views about pension guarantees and provided valuable comments about my drafts: Peter Lindblad and his staff at the FPG/AMFK Pensionsgaranti organization in Stockholm; Matti Uimonen, Managing Director of Finland's Central Pension Security Institute, and his staff; Lauri Koivusalo, General Manager of Finland's newly privatized pension guarantee organization (known as Garantia), and his staff; Risto Tanner; Professor Roy Goode of St. John's College, Oxford; Stuart James of Row & Maw in London; Paul Johnson and Jane Falkingham of the London School of Economics; E. Philip Davis of the Bank of England and the European Monetary Institute; David Hill and Philip Morgan of the Department of Social Security in the United Kingdom; and Duncan Ferguson, together with his associates, Richard Whitelam and Penny Webster, of Bacon & Woodrow in London.

In Germany, Klaus Heubeck and Peter Ahrend, both consulting actuaries, were generous with their time, hospitality, and comments.

Martin Hoppenrath and Jürgen Paulsdorff of the firm Pensions-Sicherungs-Verein generously defrayed the cost of my travel to an international conference on pension guarantees held in Cologne.

In Switzerland, I wish to thank Claude Chuard, a consulting actuary, Peter Senn of ATAG Ernst & Young in Bern, Werner Nussbaum of the Bundesamt für Sozialversicherung, and Jacob Van Dam of the Hochschule St. Gallen, for their considerable help and interest.

In the Netherlands, I am indebted to P.J.C. Keizer and Rob Bakker of the Verzekeringskamer for sharing their perspectives on how to secure pension promises without guarantees from the State. Pieter de Lange of the Beheer Life Insurance Company also contributed valuable views about the Dutch system.

The Pension Fund Association of Japan and two members of the Actuarial Division there, Naoyuki Tsuru and Yasukazu Yoshizawa, clarified many of my questions about the guarantee provided by their organization.

At the World Bank, I wish to thank Dimitri Vittas, Anita Schwarz, Robert Palacios, and Estelle James for their interest, comments, and collegiality. The World Bank provided the resources necessary to study pension guarantees used by Chile. In Chile, thanks go to many who were helpful and interested in the project: Julio Bustamante and his staff at the Superintendencia de Administradoras de Fondos de Pensiones; Augusto Iglesias; Salvador Zurita; Salvador Valdés-Prieto; Gert Wagner; Jorge Tarzijan; Mario Marcel and Alvaro Clarke of the Ministerio de Hacienda, and José Piñera of the International Center for Pension Reform and the chief architect of Chile's restructured social security system. Robert Myers, an American social security specialist knowledgeable about Chile's new system, provided useful background prior to my trip there.

In the United States, the following companies in the steel and auto industries contributed their pension data going back for many years: Armco, Bethlehem Steel, Inland Steel Industries, U.S. Steel, Chrysler Corporation, Ford Motor Company, and General Motors. The United Steelworkers Union and the Air Line Pilots Association also provided historical data for specific pension plans.

Neil Howe provided essential advice about launching the project. David Keating and Paul Hewitt at the National Taxpayers

Union encouraged me to begin writing about the subject. William Duncan helped me place my first op-ed about pension insurance. Harry Moody of the Brookdale Center on Aging provided many insights about the ethical dilemmas in this area.

The reform proposal in Chapter 8 could not have been developed without extensive discussions with executives and analysts working in the financial guarantee industry. Judith Radasch, Christopher Tilley, and Robert Godfrey at MBIA, Inc., as well as Mark Cohen and Renwick Paige at FGIC, Inc., were particularly helpful. Leo O'Neill, president of the Standard & Poor's Ratings Group, made a very important contribution to this project: computer files of corporate credit ratings going back to 1980. This information was indispensable for estimating the value of PBGC insurance in Chapter 4. I am also indebted to Scott Sprinzen, Richard Smith, Arthur Grisi, and Andy Rosado at Standard & Poor's; to Alan Backman and James Schmidbauer at Moody's Investors Service; to David Litvack of Fitch Investors Service; and, finally, to Martin S. Fridson at Merrill Lynch & Co.

A valued friend, John F. Wilson at the International Monetary Fund, read drafts, made comments, and even arranged for some key appointments. Lorenzo Figliuoli at the IMF also provided helpful comments about risk preferences and the moral hazard problem.

In addition, I wish to thank my able research assistant, Jeffrey Santos, at the Brookings Institution.

This project relied on private philanthropic foundations for financial support to assure that the result would be completely impartial and objective. Resources provided by the Retirement Research Foundation are gratefully acknowledged. Completion of this project simply would not have been possible without the continuing interest of Marilyn Hennessy, president of the Retirement Research Foundation, and her trustees.

1

THE UNCERTAIN RETIREMENT
Groping for a Response

Tremors race back and forth across the country in a rhythm set by the terminal cases among America's once-familiar companies, whenever one of them closes its doors for the last time. These are the shock waves of economic progress. Studebaker, Rath Packing, Allis-Chalmers, White Motors, White Farm Equipment, Raybestos-Manhattan, Braniff Airlines, Eastern Airlines, and Pan Am[1]—all have made their final exit, along with many of the steel companies. Continental Steel, Wisconsin Steel, and Phoenix Steel are just a few among the mighty that have fallen. The lives of those who worked for these firms changed abruptly. For some, there was a transition period and then new jobs. Others faced idleness and lengthy unemployment.

This process never ends. Tomorrow, more companies will liquidate. Their passing will clear the way for newer, more nimble producers, capable of meeting the needs of a constantly changing marketplace. As Schumpeter taught, capitalism is an evolutionary process of creative destruction. Today's companies will either transform themselves beyond recognition or fall by the wayside.[2] Yet, most of today's declining firms are sponsoring pension plans designed for yesterday's labor force—one in which changing jobs was rare if not taboo. As a result, only a handful of workers at these dying firms can escape the fate of a less prosperous retirement.

THE PROBLEM:
GROWING RISKS AND PAINFUL LOSSES

This book focuses on an important subset of the many issues related to securing an adequate retirement income: the traditional American pension plan. The traditional plan, which promises a monthly income based on preretirement earnings and length of service to a single employer, involves major risks for workers. People covered by these arrangements can lose most of their pension wealth as a result of inadequate funding by sponsors that liquidate before making all of the promised pension payments. Many of these same long-service workers also have firm-specific skills that they cannot readily transfer to another employer. Much of their wealth depends on the survival of just one company, and this risk cannot be diversified.

Yet even without bankruptcy of the employer, most working people today experience routine job changes that can result in substantial losses. These losses can drastically alter the prospects for workers to live out their retirement years without depending on relatives for support, turning to charity, or becoming wards of the state. Two issues are apparent here. First, job mobility of all sorts reduces benefits. Second, the demise of an employer results both in involuntary career changes on the part of workers and in termination of any defined-benefit pension plans sponsored by the company.

In the traditional defined-benefit plan, workers are placed at risk of losing much of their accumulated retirement wealth, because these arrangements usually base pension benefits on the worker's last three to five years of earnings.[3] Workers therefore need to stay in the same pension plan until retirement and end their careers at salary levels that at least reflect previous inflation-adjusted earnings. Otherwise, they are unlikely to receive full value for benefits earned when they were younger. The risks of these arrangements become clear in cases where earnings fall just before retirement as the result of poor health or deteriorating business conditions. When changing jobs for whatever reason, workers lose; this is because pension promises are *backloaded,* meaning that the value of additional earned benefits increases with age and time in service. However, that value is heavily dependent on the pension benefits accumulated previously; and those benefits almost invariably cannot be transferred from one plan to another.[4]

To understand the important principle of backloading, consider the case of a 50-year-old worker employed by the same company for 15 years and earning a salary of $50,000 in 1995. The worker has earned vested benefits in a defined-benefit pension plan that provides a retirement annuity equivalent to 1.5 percent of final salary multiplied by years of service. Looking to the future, this particular worker expects to live until an actuarially estimated age of 78, after having worked for the same employer for another 15 years (i.e., until the normal retirement age of 65) and spending 13 years in retirement. He assumes that his salary will increase at an average rate of 5 percent between 1995 and 2010, with the increase reflecting 3 percent inflation as well as additional merit and seniority-based raises of 2 percent per year. Between 1995 and 2023, both the pension plan and this worker are capable of earning a 7 percent pretax return on investments. With this background, consider the following:

I. Expected salary upon retirement in 2010
   = Current salary ($50,000) × 2.079 (future value of $1,
      15 years later, accumulating at 5%)
   = $103,946

II. Expected annual retirement benefit commencing in 2010
   = 1.5% × (30 years of service) × $103,946 (final salary)
   = $46,776

III. Lump-sum value of annuity in 2010
   = $46,776 (annuity) × 8.358 (present value of an annuity
      for 13 years, discounted at 7%)
   = $390,937

IV. Real expected pension benefit
   = $390,937 (lump sum value in 2010) × .362 (present
      value of $1 15 years later, discounted at 7%)
   = $141,694

In other words, the company's implicit commitment to provide an annual retirement income of $46,776, beginning in 2010, is equivalent to granting this employee $141,694 in 1995. This valuation assumes that those funds could have been invested in an Individual Retirement Account or some other tax-deferred arrangement during the 15 years in question. However, these results would have been very different if the pension plan had been terminated in 1995. In that case, the worker's loss can be estimated as follows:

    V. Reduced annual retirement benefit starting in 2010
        = 1.5% × 15 (years of service in 1995) × $50,000 (salary in 1995)
        = $11,250

    VI. Lump-sum value of reduced annuity in 2010
        = $11,250 (reduced annuity) × 8.358 (present value of an annuity for 13 years discounted at 7%)
        = $94,024

    VII. Terminated pension benefit in 1995
        = $94,024 (lump-sum value in 2010) × .362 (present value of $1 15 years later, discounted at 7%)
        = $34,079

    VIII. Capital loss for pension plan participant
        = $141,694 (real expected pension benefit) − $34,079 (terminated pension benefit)
        = $107,615

As another study concluded, these losses—even with federal insurance—can represent as much as 90 percent of expected benefits, depending on the age of the employee and the interest rate assumption.[5] For the worker described here, the losses exceed 75 percent of expected benefits at age 36 and fall to about 5 percent one year before the normal retirement age. Another way of thinking about these losses involves the distinction between two accounting concepts: the Accumulated Benefit Obligation (ABO) and the Projected Benefit Obligation (PBO). The ABO represents the present value of benefits. It does not consider the effect of future salary increases. The PBO represents the present value of the same benefits but it assumes future salary increases. For an entire pension plan, the ABO is one measure of the total liability, assuming that the plan terminates. On the other hand, the PBO reflects the pension costs of a going concern.[6] Figure 1–1 depicts the pattern of change in pension losses as an individual worker ages.

Some might question whether it is appropriate to use a single discount rate—as in Figure 1–1—to compute the present value of

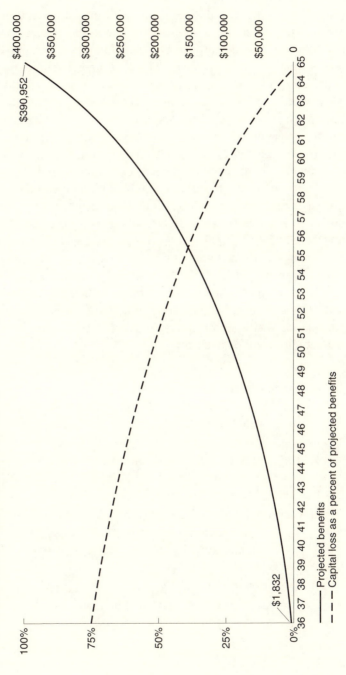

FIGURE 1-1

Projected Benefits and Capital Losses by Age

—— Projected benefits

--- Capital loss as a percent of projected benefits

$400,000

$350,000

$300,000

$250,000

$200,000

$150,000

$100,000

$50,000

0

$390,952

$1,832

100%

75%

50%

25%

0%

36 37 38 39 40 41 42 43 44 45 46 47 48 49 50 51 52 53 54 55 56 57 58 59 60 61 62 63 64 65

projected benefits for all ages. Younger workers may be more risk averse with respect to future benefits, due to the greater uncertainty that those benefits actually will be paid. On the other hand, the pure rate of time preference probably is higher among the old; thus, these two factors would seem to offset each other at an intuitive level. Meanwhile, individuals of all ages face the same market rates of return. Market rates, in effect, represent a collective judgment concerning the appropriate extent of discounting at any given time. The case for a single rate is therefore a plausible one.[7]

Of course, the extent of benefit loss could be reduced, depending on the characteristics of any plan that might cover the worker in his or her next job and on whether that worker ultimately vests in the other pension plan. To see that job mobility itself is penalized by current benefit accrual and vesting practices, consider the case of a worker in slightly different circumstances. This worker also leaves the pension plan at age 50, but moves on to another job with no change in current or projected earnings. This second worker then stays in the second job until retiring at age 65 and is covered by a pension plan with identical benefit provisions. In this situation, the worker's loss will be determined by:

IX. Expected benefit from Plan #2 in 2010
   = 1.5% × 15 (years of additional service) × $103,946
      (final salary)
   = $23,388

X. Total expected annual pension benefits in 2010
   = $11,250 (from Plan #1) + $23,388 (from Plan #2)
   = $34,638

XI. Lump sum value of combined benefits in 2010
   = $34,638 (annual benefits) × 8.358 (present value of an
      annuity for 13 years discounted at 7%)
   = $289,504

XII. Real combined benefits at time of job change
   = $289,504 (lump sum value in 2010) × .362 (present
      value of $1 15 years later discounted at 7%)
   = $104,801

XIII. Capital loss at time of job change
    = $141,694 (original real expected benefit) – $104,801
        (real expected benefit after job change)
    = $36,893

Some commentators argue that the most important goal for full vesting, and even pension finance in general, is a simple one: Once acquired, a benefit should not be subject to devaluation through a change in employment or a change in the pension fund.[8] Yet this priority has so far been overlooked in the development of our private retirement system. As a result, the campaign to safeguard benefits has fallen woefully short of the mark.[9] This book therefore assumes that any effort aimed at controlling the risk of pension losses facing workers needs to address inequities resulting from the erosion of benefit values by inflation subsequent to a change in employment or a change in the pension plan.[10]

As the calculation indicates, the worker described above would lose 26 percent of expected pension wealth, all other things being equal, due to the effect of the job change. The fact that benefits are frozen in nominal terms on the date of such a change, or on the plan termination date, imposes the greatest losses on younger workers. Inflation erodes the value of their benefits between the date in question and retirement. Expected benefits are based, in part, on the assumption that pre-retirement earnings will grow by at least the rate of inflation. Most defined-benefit plans link pension income either to the participant's final salary, just as in the calculation above, or to some measure of average earnings that would rise with inflation. In other cases, labor unions negotiate benefits to reflect some fraction of wage levels prevailing at the time of retirement. For their part, retirees tend to receive only partial inflation adjustments that are voluntarily granted by the sponsor.

THE ERISA STOPGAP

A corporate bankruptcy and the resulting termination of seriously underfunded pension plans can represent the most dramatic and extreme circumstance preventing workers from receiving the full value of their retirement benefits. The need for more secure pensions first became conspicuous in this country as the result of major business disasters during the 1960s. Widespread public sympathy for the workers who lost their pensions, not to mention their jobs, eventually led to the establishment of the termination insurance program currently administered by the Pension Benefit Guaranty Corporation (PBGC). The growing concern over pension rights produced this new federal program by 1974. This problem in labor relations, however, was hardly restricted to our shores. Subsequently, Canada, Germany, Japan, and Switzerland all created special "insurance" funds to take over poorly funded plans in bankruptcy. Finland and Sweden had acted earlier, setting up their systems in the 1960s.

Despite the PBGC's many shortcomings, the case for improved benefit security was compelling. During the early 1970s, the savviest and most forward-looking observers of the economic scene anticipated massive dislocation in America's industrial heartland. True to their predictions, during the next two decades hundreds of plants from Massachusetts to Michigan would downsize or close, throwing millions out of work as manufacturing moved elsewhere. In the 1980s alone, 20 million workers lost jobs because of plant closings or permanent layoffs.[11] An entire region was transformed into a virtual ghost of its former self, becoming known throughout the country as the "Rust Belt." This loss of comparative advantage in manufacturing represented a direct threat to the retirement hopes of a generation of workers who, in many cases, already had spent decades serving a single employer. With less stability in the labor market, the terms of their old-style defined-benefit pension plans suddenly became poorly suited to their needs. Suddenly, portable retirement benefits were much more valuable to workers.

Momentum for change first began to build when the Studebaker Company liquidated in 1964. In that bankruptcy, pension plan participants under the age of 50 lost all of their benefits. Studebaker, along with the other automakers, had used funding methods that implied even more backloading than most others. Meanwhile, the company had negotiated a labor contract with the United Auto Workers Union that included allocation rules for pension assets upon termination of the plan. As a result, assets had not been accumulated to back the pensions promised to many workers who had served Studebaker for as long as 30 years in some cases. The bankruptcy courts made matters worse by confirming that the workers had no pension rights. Yet many of these people had virtually no hope of finding another steady job, much less one in which they eventually could earn a full pension. Studebaker's workers between the ages of 50 and 60 were more fortunate: they lost only some of their pension benefits. Those over the age of 60, on the other hand, were left completely unscathed. Distribution rules like these were typical in scores of bankruptcies that followed. Without new legislation, the bankruptcy claims of pension participants could not extend to assets of the sponsor or its affiliates.

Despite these results, other more politically compelling events would be required to bring together the forces necessary to produce federal legislation. Almost 10 years later, one such event took place when the Raybestos-Manhattan Company shut down a plant in Passaic, New Jersey, with the same unfortunate effects as in the Studebaker case.[12] The Raybestos-Manhattan case was different, however, because one of New Jersey's U.S. senators, Harrison A. Williams, Jr.,[13] served as chairman of the Senate Labor Committee. Ballentine's (a Newark dairy company) also was on the brink of closing. As a result of losses to unionized workers at Raybestos-Manhattan and Ballentine's, Senator Jacob Javits, together with Williams's allies in the labor movement, persuaded Williams to push for a federal backup guarantee to protect participants in poorly funded defined-benefit plans. This provision later became part of a landmark bill known as the Employee Retirement Income Security Act of 1974 (ERISA).

Signed into law on Labor Day 1974, ERISA's principal significance was attributed to the *minimum funding standard* and liberalized vesting requirements. The chief intent of the legislation was to make sure that pension plan participants received their promised benefits. However, ERISA was also drafted to serve important secondary goals.[14] The authors of the legislation hoped to prevent private pension plans from being nationalized as part of a greatly expanded social security system. ERISA was enacted shortly after substantial increases in social security benefits in 1968 and 1973. Social security expansionists of the day argued that the pension system should aim to provide much more than a retirement income floor. There was little reason to rely on private plans, in their view, when large numbers of workers did not vest and when the funds might not be sufficient to pay for promised benefits in cases where workers did vest. With some justification based on the record, they saw the private pension system as unreliable.[15] ERISA was also inspired by concern that employers could deliberately evade their responsibility to workers who had provided labor in exchange for pension promises. Unfortunately, the law's success in accomplishing these objectives has been doubtful at best.

For its part, the minimum funding standard has been notoriously ineffective in halting the growth of unfunded liabilities. The standard took aim first at the *normal cost* of a pension plan: the cost of new benefit obligations arising from employee service in a given year. It required that normal costs be completely funded during the year incurred. However, this simple approach overlooked large differences in assumptions and funding methods that can cause the actuarial measure of normal cost to diverge greatly across plans. The normal cost reported by many plans often bears little relation to the economic value of benefit promises made in connection with a given year's work.

It was clear from the start that the amortization periods specified in the ERISA standard were much too long and would aggravate the problem of deliberate underfunding, particularly among collectively bargained plans. The minimum funding standard required that the cost of past service credits be amortized over 40 years and liabilities for benefit improvements be amortized over a 30-year period. The problem here is that benefits for unionized workers typically are renegotiated and improved during each round of collective bargaining, which occurs every three years or so. The plan amendments that result from this process, at a minimum, usually reflect the effects of the inflation that has occurred since the last contract was signed. A succession of these plan amendments almost inevitably leads to the buildup of large unfunded liabilities, because these additional costs are unfunded and could still be amortized over a 30-year period. Finally, the standard also required that "experience" gains and losses (i.e., the amount by which subsequent performance differs from earlier assumptions) be amortized over 15 years. However, even amortization over 15 years can lead to dangerous instability.[16]

In a more positive vein, liberalized vesting made it possible for some workers to qualify for a pension after 10 years.[17] Prior to ERISA, workers frequently needed 25 years of service in order to vest. During congressional hearings, one man testified that he had been fired after 24 years of working for a particular company and could not qualify for a pension because the plan required 25 years of continuous service. Another man spent 40 years with one company only to discover that he also did not qualify for a pension. He had moved several times between different plants and divisions, each with its own separate pension plan, and had not accumulated enough continuous service to vest in any of the plans. In other cases, people who had worked 30 years or more for the same employer found that they were unable to collect retirement benefits because they had been laid off at some point. Each layoff was considered a "break in service" that disqualified the worker from receiving credit for benefits previously earned.[18]

ERISA also gave plan participants the right to reach beyond the assets of the pension plan to recover the value of their benefits when plans terminated with insufficient funds. The employer, together with its controlled affiliates, became liable to the PBGC for any shortfall up to a maximum of 30 percent of net worth.[19] The PBGC, in effect, now serves as the agent for pension plan participants. ERISA therefore converted pension promises from mere gratuities to legally enforceable corporate liabilities. Yet, these new rights frequently resulted in little additional recovery, because corporate net worth often eroded so severely before any bankruptcy or before the termination of an underfunded plan outside of bankruptcy. Subsequently, amendments to ERISA gave the PBGC additional recourse, but the average recovery has remained in the 15 percent range.[20] Each attempt to strengthen or defend the PBGC's position in bankruptcy has made other lenders less willing to extend credit to financially ailing companies. As a result, difficult tradeoffs almost always confront those caught between the immediate need to preserve jobs and the less urgent, yet still compelling, interest in preserving assets available to pay pension benefits.

There have been other tradeoffs as well. ERISA's initial complexity, together with its thousands of pages of amendments and regulations, made the arrangement a paradise for lawyers—but few others. Ongoing administrative costs for a sample of defined-benefit plans with 15 participants rose to $445 per participant by the early 1990s and one-time costs associated with accommodating to frequent legislation and regulatory changes averaged $5,500 per participant for plans of the same size. As a result of this and other factors, large numbers of defined-benefit pension plans were terminated in favor of defined-contribution plans or no replacement plan at all.[21]

The authors of ERISA regarded the PBGC termination insurance program as only a peripheral aspect of the new law. Nevertheless, a number of financial experts warned almost from the start that the consequences of applying a federal guarantee to the defined-benefit system would be extremely costly over the long term. Quite apart from its social significance, ERISA's behavioral incentives spelled profound change for the nation's financial system. By creating the PBGC, ERISA provided plan sponsors with the opportunity to borrow (i.e., by deferring compensation) from their employees on the assumption that, if the company failed, the additional debt would be repaid by the U.S. government. This opportunity has become known in the financial literature as the *pension put,* and in many cases it represents a significant portion of the company's value to shareholders.[22] Private pension promises, of course, also became much more valuable to workers with the PBGC standing behind them. As early as 1976 Treynor, et al., pointed out that:

> . . . the plan beneficiary has an asset which is equal to the employer's pension liability. ERISA . . . has made this claim a real liability for the PBGC. In addition, there is an additional one, the pension put. Since it is a financial asset for the employer corporation, it is a financial liability for the PBGC. The combination of these two liabilities for the PBGC absolutely dwarfs its assets . . . In short, using this descriptive framework, the PBGC is insolvent.[23]

The program has consequences that go far beyond its stated purpose. In particular, it provides a massive subsidy to depressed and dying industries, and it has tilted the playing field in favor of defined-benefit plans at the expense of other forms of retirement saving.

The scale of this risk shifting was nothing less than monumental.[24] At one time, the PBGC guaranteed the obligations of approximately 98,000 defined-benefit pension plans covering more than 40 million participants. Today, those totals have declined somewhat, but they remain large. PBGC officials believe that the agency now insures 65,000 plans covering 32 million workers and retirees. But coverage is not entitlement: people who work for a firm that sponsors one of these plans must be covered for at least five years before earning the right to receive any benefits. As a result, a much smaller proportion of American workers gained additional benefit security than the public should have expected from this watershed legislation. Figure 1–2 shows that 42.4 million workers had private pension coverage of some sort by 1990.[25] Of this number, 26.3 million were covered by defined-benefit plans, but only 21.4 million had vested in at least one defined-benefit plan.[26] As a result, only 16.9 percent of the total labor force received greater benefit security as a result of the ERISA termination insurance program.[27]

Be that as it may, this relatively small share of the labor force still represents a significant number of people. For them, the defined-benefit system remains important and offers major advantages. This book therefore does not attempt to make a case for

FIGURE 1-2

Benefit Security and the Labor Force (Workers in thousands)

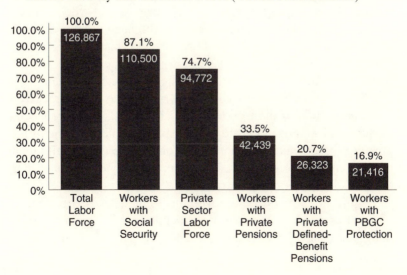

sweeping change of the sort that would abolish this form of retirement saving. Nor does it suggest that the goal of further reducing the
scale of this system should motivate future policy changes. Instead,
it argues that the defined-benefit plans now offered in the United
States need to be modified in major ways in order to meet the needs
of today's labor force and that those plans should be put on a sound
financial footing.

For individual pension plan participants, the value of the
backup guarantee is directly related to the vested benefits they have
accumulated in one or more pension plans. Based on this factor, as
well as on recent trends in earnings and pension coverage, it is possible to describe the type of worker most likely to gain significantly
from the program. More often than not, that worker is male, over 50,
working in a relatively high-paying job for an employer he has
served for a long time,[28] and probably living somewhere in the north
central or northeastern part of the country. These survey results, together with the amply documented trend in favor of defined-contribution plans, suggest that perhaps only a third of all workers actually
covered by PBGC-insured pension plans can ever expect to have
substantial guaranteed benefits.

In strictly operational terms, the PBGC's mission is to provide
timely payment of pension benefits, up to the maximum guaranteed
amount, when a company goes out of business and when, under a
limited set of other circumstances, it terminates a defined-benefit
pension plan that is underfunded. So far the agency has taken over
more than 1,971 underfunded pension plans that covered 372,200
participants. But if the ERISA termination insurance program disap-
points by providing improved benefit security to only a relatively
small proportion of the working population, it also accentuates the
inequities of America's pension system by guaranteeing benefits that
greatly exceed available benchmarks for average and socially minimal retirement income. In 1993, the maximum benefit guaranteed by
the PBGC stood at $2,420 a month, or $29,250 a year.[29] As Figure
1–3 shows, this produced a government-guaranteed retirement income of as much as $42,796 in that same year.[30] Combined maxi-
mum guaranteed benefits amounted to 316 percent of the average

FIGURE 1-3

Annual Benefits Guaranteed by the PBGC Compared with Social
Security and Private Pension Levels

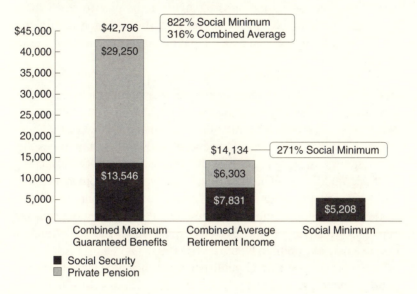

level of private pension income[31] and social security benefits combined.[32] The same combined maximum was 822 percent of the minimum retirement income provided by the federal government under
the Supplemental Security Income (SSI) program.[33]

Does the relatively high maximum guaranteed level prohibit
the PBGC from disbursing benefits that exceed even this amount?
Widespread misunderstanding exists concerning this feature of the
program. Participants in terminated underfunded plans can receive
more than the maximum guaranteed benefit because ERISA directs
the agency to "allocate" remaining plan assets according to priorities
that favor some of the highly paid (e.g., former airline pilots and senior executives). The maximum guaranteed amount only applies
after all plan assets have been allocated to cover voluntary employee
contributions and mandatory employee contributions. Before the
maximum limit can be applied, remaining plan assets must also be

used to pay benefits that have been in effect under the terms of the plan for at least five years and that are owed to participants who have been retired for at least three years when the pension plan terminates.[34] As long as enough assets remain in the plan to cover these three categories of benefits when an underfunded plan terminates, the PBGC does not reduce pension payments to the maximum guaranteed amount.

Originally, companies paid an annual premium of $1 per covered worker. Congress later increased this premium twice before authorizing a "risk-adjusted" supplement in 1988. But even at current levels it can bear little relation to the market value of the guarantee. Federal pension insurance can be worth many times the PBGC premium to financially weak companies.[35] Notwithstanding ERISA's fabled "prudent man rule,"[36] as well as its other fiduciary standards, this disparity creates a "moral hazard"[37] that encourages riskier investment policies and systematic underfunding of promised benefits.[38] According to the U.S. Government estimate, underfunding rose to a hefty $71 billion by the end of 1993.

Each year, the PBGC publishes a list of the country's 50 most poorly funded pension plans. The "Top 50" accounted for unfunded liabilities of $39.7 billion in 1993, compared with a $14.2 billion shortfall in 1990.[39] Yet the agency was in no immediate danger of running out of cash because most underfunded plans—while risky—were not going to be terminated anytime soon. The PBGC had accumulated $7.9 billion in investments and cash, and government officials believed that premium revenues would rise to $1.6 billion annually in the wake of the Retirement Protection Act of 1994 (RPA '94). Meanwhile, benefit payments to the participants of previously terminated plans remain below $750 million per year. The agency has, as a result, become a cash cow for the government. Under budget agreements since 1990, this positive cash flow makes additional spending possible for programs within the jurisdiction of congressional labor and education committees. A constituency therefore has emerged that seeks to increase PBGC premiums as a means of financing other government activities. In fact, many Washington observers believe that the principal motivation for passing RPA '94 was to offset the revenue losses resulting from the GATT legislation.[40]

Despite this cushion, the Single-Employer Fund reported a deficit of $1.2 billion in unfunded liabilities of plans that have already terminated or were considered likely to terminate as of September 30, 1994. In addition, the PBGC estimated "reasonably possible future losses" of $18 billion in connection with unfunded liabilities associated with other single-employer plans. The PBGC has therefore been cast in the unlikely role of deficit reducer, and it apparently will be contributing in a very perverse way to deficit reduction efforts for some time to come. The agency's deteriorating financial position actually threatens to increase federal indebtedness while the federal budgeting conventions create exactly the opposite impression.

Even without these other defects, inflation alone has periodically driven the program deeply into the red. The maximum benefit originally was set at $9,000 a year. However, it was indexed to rise with inflation by the same factors used for Social Security. For its part, the annual premium had no corresponding indexation feature. Claims under the program quickly exceeded projected revenues as a result. Compare this with the approach taken by the Province of Ontario. Ontario's pension guarantee fund was established in 1980 when the maximum guaranteed benefit was set at C$1,000 per year. That maximum guaranteed amount has never been indexed or otherwise increased.

Nobody really knows the amount by which future claims will exceed premium revenues. Companies can use actuarial assumptions that greatly understate the cost of retirement benefits, and even the limited information required by the PBGC becomes available only after long delays. Not surprisingly, the agency has discovered that unfunded liabilities accumulated by terminating plans tend to be much larger than plan sponsors previously reported. However, the PBGC and its 700 employees simply lack the ability to monitor a system of more than 65,000 different pension plans. Dr. Alicia Munnell summarized the problem in 1982 as follows:

> The PBGC's vulnerability stems from its inability to control the actions of plan sponsors. Often it does not have access to detailed information about a pension plan until the company decides to terminate. Hence, the PBGC will always remain financially vulnerable and the federal government may well end up as the insurer of the nation's private pension system.[41]

In matters of financial regulation, it's not "what you see is what you get," it's what you don't see that gets you.[42] This story hasn't changed. According to economists at the Federal Reserve Bank of New York writing in 1990:

> We have estimated the funding status of the PBGC to be significantly worse than its financial statements would indicate. If net liabilities arising from future terminations are taken into account, its total funding deficiency is more than $16 billion. This funding deficiency derives from plans that are currently overfunded as well as those that are in an underfunded state. Thus, if the coverage of the insurance is to remain at current levels, additional funding is necessary. Since a deficit has already developed, the problem is particularly pressing.[43]

Official forecasts of PBGC claims have been far too optimistic from the beginning because they were based on the assumption that only the program's direct costs matter, and because they did not adequately consider the influence of ERISA's financial incentives.[44] The original forecasts suffered from the fact that no insurance of this sort had been offered before ERISA and, as a result, there was a complete lack of appropriate data for estimating future claims. Furthermore, it is impossible even today to project future costs of a program with only 18 years of claims experience for the simple reason that accepted statistical methods do not support estimation based on such a small amount of data.[45] Recently, the pitfalls of such forecasting have been underscored by the failure of official estimates to reflect the eventual size of the savings and loan disaster, even with 50 years of available data.

Government efforts to examine possible costs of pension insurance began when the Department of Labor and the U.S. Treasury released a report entitled *Study of Pension Plan Terminations, 1972*.[46] The study was based on the assumption that the $40 million in losses incurred by plan participants during that year would indicate the level of termination activity following ERISA. The interagency group therefore concluded that an annual premium of $1.75 would be sufficient to cover the cost of the program. Instead, Congress chose to set the premium at $1.00 per participant.

By 1977, the new agency had already accumulated a deficit of $41 million. At that point, the PBGC recommended an annual premium in the neighborhood of $2.25 to amortize the deficit. Otherwise, the claims expectations were consistent with those outlined in the first report. In response, Congress chose to raise the premium somewhat—to $2.60.

The subsequent record has been remarkably consistent. By 1981, the agency's deficit had reached $188 million and the PBGC recommended that the premium be increased to $6.00. For its part, Congress delayed further action until 1986, when it raised the premium to $8.50. Shortly thereafter, the agency released its most recent premium study, entitled *Pension Promises at Risk*. Based on the program's first 12 years, the study estimated that it would require a flat premium of $54.05 to match expected direct costs over the subsequent 30-year period. True to form, claims under the program now exceed even the most pessimistic scenario considered as part of the effort.

Following the severe problems caused by several large bankruptcies in the steel industry, Congress adopted a risk-related premium in 1988. More recently, the Bush Administration opposed the latest premium increase enacted by Congress in 1990. At that time, Congress raised the basic charge to $19.00 per participant and increased the risk-related supplement to $9.00 per year for every $1,000 in unfunded vested benefits. In addition, the new upper limit for the risk-related supplement became $53.00. Shortly after the Clinton Administration took office, a task force was assembled to recommend new legislation to reform the ERISA insurance program. The group proposed to phase out the $53-per-participant cap on the variable rate element. Adopted without modification in late 1994,[47] this change will require some of the most seriously underfunded plans to pay premiums that substantially exceed the previous levels.

The problem of inadequate information in setting PBGC premiums pales in comparison with the problem of the linkage between the plan sponsor's incentive to fund a defined-benefit pension plan and the product life cycle that affects the company's core businesses. At the level of the individual firm, the most direct influence on pension plan funding and management is corporate profitability.[48] Profitable companies in mature markets with the heaviest tax burdens have greater incentive to use the tax deductions available for pension contributions.[49] As a result, they will prefer actuarial assumptions that justify larger pension contributions, thus enabling the sponsor to build up "financial slack" in the plan. As long as the firm remains profitable, it will also have an incentive to invest its pension portfolio in less risky assets (i.e., to emphasize bonds rather than stocks).

A firm will adopt a very different approach when it enters a period of long-term decline. Companies with little or no taxable income have an incentive to "defund" their defined-benefit pension plans. Accordingly, sponsors will use the considerable latitude available to them to understate the value of future benefits so that the level of required contributions can be reduced. This type of sponsor will prefer a riskier portfolio for the pension plan. Such behavioral incentives have in fact contributed to the recent erosion, much of which has yet to be recognized under current federal budgeting practices.

Nor does the private pension system represent an efficient instrument for stimulating growth in depressed industries and regions. In fact, it could do so only at substantial unnecessary cost. However, exactly this type of motivation appears to have dominated as lawmakers crafted Title IV of ERISA.[50] The termination insurance guarantee—combined with fictitious actuarial and accounting practices that are widespread in this area—gives managers, owners, and unions the incentive to bankrupt their companies for a profit. These conditions trigger a process that extracts more dividends, inflated salaries, and other emoluments from these firms than they are worth.[51] The Internal Revenue Service even encourages these excesses, perhaps unawares, by requiring that many pension obligations be undervalued or not reported at all.

Federal pension insurance reinforces firms' incentives to underfund a pension plan, because workers place much greater faith in otherwise hollow pension promises when the U.S. Treasury stands behind them. Systematic underfunding has been particularly noticeable in collectively bargained pension plans. Benefits provided by these plans are renegotiated upward roughly every three years. Although the increases are predictable, they cannot be funded in advance under current law and are not reflected beforehand in the sponsor's financial reports. This pattern of behavior represents another example of the classic insurance problem known as *moral hazard*.

The ERISA termination insurance program suffers from another insurance problem known as adverse selection. Adverse selection occurs in systems where premiums are not completely adjusted to reflect risk. Mispriced insurance provides high-risk firms with the incentive to stay in the system while low-risk firms will leave unless participation is compulsory. Concern about adverse selection was clearly evident when two noted financial economists observed:

> Ultimately, the United States could be left only with bankrupt defined-benefit plans with the benefits financed directly by taxpayers.[52]

For its part, the nonpartisan Congressional Budget Office reported that

> far-sighted, fiscally sound premium payers will not voluntarily subsidize the pension costs of their competitors indefinitely. Instead, they will terminate their plans and avoid paying these overpriced premiums. A voluntary federal insurance system that relies heavily on subsidies from one insured firm to another is probably destined for a federal bailout.[53]

The growing popularity of defined-contribution plans coupled with the simultaneous decline of defined-benefit plans over more than a decade is consistent with the impression that healthy plan–sponsor combinations have been deserting the program.

The nation's recent experience with deposit insurance has demonstrated beyond any doubt that misguided federal policies affecting the financial system can impose an awesome burden on the economy. Without significant change in the pension area, the adverse effects could be felt for a very long time. Trends beginning in the early 1970s suggest that future retirees will be far less likely to benefit from the current pension insurance program. Not only is a declining proportion of today's younger workers covered by defined-benefit pension plans, but this same group also can expect lower lifetime earnings than people retiring in the 1980s and 90s. Meanwhile, workers who are now young will be exposed, as taxpayers, to large contingent liabilities attributable to the PBGC for many years. In terms of social equity, a deplorable imbalance has emerged, which threatens to produce a large intergenerational transfer of wealth from the less well-off to their relatively more prosperous predecessors.

How large is that transfer likely to be? There are many indicators of the ultimate size of this problem. Unfortunately, none of them is very precise or capable of providing conclusive evidence. A subsequent chapter will examine one such indicator in considerable detail: the very substantial gap between premiums that have been charged by the PBGC and the actual value of the insurance. Another useful indicator is the proportion of that insurance value that has been recognized in the accounts of the PBGC. The interest rate risk implied by the relationship between the duration of pension assets and liabilities also provides some insight.[54] Finally, the size of the pension system itself serves as a reminder of the stakes involved should conditions deteriorate seriously.

When comparing the cost of providing federal insurance to S&Ls and banks as well as to pension plans, it is important to recognize that these institutions play very different roles in U.S. capital markets. As a result, the structure of their respective assets and liabilities is quite different as well. A review of tabulations compiled by the Office of Thrift Supervision,[55] showed that the duration of S&L deposits appeared to be less than a year while the duration of the assets in their portfolios (e.g., 30-year mortgages) is probably about 10 years.[56] In periods of interest rate volatility, this mismatch becomes the principal source of risk to the insurance fund. The same mismatch also can represent an important profit opportunity for the S&Ls.

It is interesting to note that the mismatch at commercial banks, while in the same direction (i.e., long assets and short liabilities), tends to be much less severe. Bank deposits appear to have a duration of between one and two years while assets seem to run for five or six years. In part, this closer match between asset and liability duration at the commercial banks explains why the cost of providing deposit insurance to such banks has so far been less than providing the same level of insurance to S&Ls.

Defined-benefit pension plans have a different mismatch altogether. In effect, plan sponsors borrow from workers over very long terms while investing with much shorter time horizons. This suggests a severe mismatch between asset and liability duration at most defined-benefit plans, and in a direction that is consistent with the belief that the condition of a typical defined-benefit plan will erode as interest rates decline. This risk will persist regardless of the value of unfunded liabilities at any particular moment and regardless of the current state of the economy.

In terms of size, perhaps the most useful measures for comparing these systems are the liabilities that banks and S&Ls issue as opposed to the assets held by pension plans. For its part, the commercial banking system reports liabilities in excess of $2.5 trillion, while S&Ls have taken on liabilities of approximately $1 trillion. With about $1 trillion in assets, the defined-benefit pension system therefore appears to be roughly as large as the S&L system.

The express goal of ERISA was to end the uncertainty about whether an employee would receive his or her promised retirement benefits. However well-intentioned, that objective has not been reached. Far from it; younger participants remain exposed to huge losses whenever a defined-benefit plan terminates, even with a massive federal guarantee. Noting this outcome, legal scholars have concluded that ERISA has failed to protect workers' pension rights in situations where it was expected to be most successful.[57] A conspicuous example of regulatory failure under ERISA involved the wave of "terminations for reversion" during the 1980s.[58] A result of this wave was that many workers were left without compensation for the lost opportunity to accumulate benefits at the end of their careers. These final years of work are when the backloading described above produces the largest increases in pension wealth.

Reversions involve the voluntary termination of a defined-benefit pension plan by the sponsor and, upon termination, the recovery of assets beyond those needed to cover benefit promises made previously. In some cases, the sponsor then replaced the first defined-benefit plan with one that provided similar or identical benefits and granted substantial past service credits. The principal effect in these situations was to increase the risk to the insurance program. However, for many plan participants in other cases, the phenomenon painfully underscored major weaknesses in ERISA's ability to secure benefits. Frequently, the past service credits weren't granted or didn't offset the workers' termination losses described at the beginning of this chapter. The old defined-benefit plan was often replaced with a defined-contribution plan, or it was not replaced at all. These outcomes produced windfalls for many companies and losses for workers, because the cost of funding benefits in a terminating defined-benefit plan usually is much less than the cost of providing benefits to the same participants in an ongoing defined-benefit plan.

More than 2,300 of these transactions occurred—a sufficient number to produce a political outcry. In 1986, Congress levied an excise tax on the net proceeds and then raised it twice until it reached 50 percent. The burden of these taxes brought direct reversions virtually to a halt. Nevertheless, terminations continue apace. Employers today are still able to extract the value of "surplus" pension assets by taking a contribution holiday for several years and then terminating the plan just as benefit obligations approach the value of pension assets. In this way, no surplus funds are recovered by the sponsor and no excise tax is paid, but benefit security for workers is seriously eroded anyway. Since 1989, employers have also been able to remove "surplus" pension assets—which, in most cases, are not surplus at all—to pay for retiree healthcare benefits. These outcomes amount to reversion on the installment plan.

The original reversion movement ended with a scandal that called into question the conduct of regulators in protecting workers from a new source of harm. In 1991, the collapse of the Executive Life Insurance Company resulted in a 30 percent reduction in annuity payments to policyholders of that company. Among them were many participants in pension plans that had been terminated for reversion. Policymakers completely overlooked the fact that an insurance annuity of doubtful credit quality is not a fair substitute for a financially secure pension.

This particularly applied in cases where companies used the reversion proceeds to finance a leveraged buyout arranged by the now-defunct junk bond firm of Drexel Burnham Lambert. For example, Revlon used a $50 million surplus in its pension plan in this way. At the same time, the company converted the benefits into Executive Life annuities. That, however, wasn't the end of the story. Executive Life then turned around and bought $400 million of the Revlon junk bonds. Milken's group repeated this gambit many times, creating not only new risks for pension plan participants, but also substantial bailout costs for insurance commissions in several states.

In no sense did the ERISA statute rely on sound financial or insurance principles to achieve what little improvement in benefit security it made possible. Risk shifting instead of risk pooling became a means of providing selected groups in the labor force with hidden transfers. Complicating this picture, other groups with relatively little or even no claim on guaranteed benefits have also been able to extract value from this arrangement. One effect of providing subsidized guarantees for pension debt is to prolong the life of dying firms. Among the constituencies that gain from these subsidies are shareholders in financially declining companies and the management of those same firms. Their gains generally come at the expense not only of taxpayers but also of bondholders and other creditors. Over time, the financial aspect of this system will become increasingly unstable, and political support for it seems bound to diminish.[59] As a result of the well-documented shift to defined-contribution plans, the number of those who benefit from PBGC insurance will decline relative to those who are left exposed to large contingent liabilities. A recent study by the Congressional Research Service observed:

> Coming on the heels of the S&L collapse and the massive taxpayer bailout, the situation causes alarm. Unless significant changes are made in the way pension insurance is priced and benefits are funded, it may be necessary to curtail the portion of the pension promise that Government can guarantee.[60]

PROFILE OF CHAPTERS

This book argues that most collective systems of backup pension guarantees have adverse effects so undesirable that other means should be found for securing the retirement obligations of private companies. Chapter 2 examines the condition of the defined-benefit pension system during the period 1981–87, when detailed sample data about actuarial practices were collected. Data for a reasonably thorough assessment did not exist for any other period. Chapter 2 demonstrates that, at the time this study was conducted, the actual condition of the system was quite different from its reported condition if asset and liability data are adjusted to reflect market values. That the reported pension data can be so terribly misleading represents a major problem in its own right. Chapter 2 also shows that the actual condition of a typical defined-benefit plan deteriorates as interest rates fall. In fact, the PBGC's exposure to interest rate risk is so large that this factor alone represents a significant long-term threat to federal taxpayers.

In view of the substantial subsidies available from the pension termination insurance system, sponsors of private defined-benefit pension plans that do not avail themselves of these resources will, sooner or later, be criticized for failing to maximize shareholder value. This problem goes beyond simple moral hazard to create a costly and wasteful imperative with far-reaching, destructive consequences. For plan sponsors to take full advantage of the PBGC subsidy involves adopting practices that otherwise would be considered unsound. Chapter 3 therefore draws the distinction between the financial solvency of a pension plan and the quite different actuarial measures of funding that are considered in Chapter 2. The discussion covers the methods that private companies intentionally use to increase risks to the insurance fund. In addition, Chapter 3 examines the effect that these incentives have had since ERISA was adopted in 1974. It also reviews changes in the condition of substantial pension plans sponsored by major airlines, automakers, and steel producers during this period. These are the industries where the risks to the PBGC are thought to be concentrated.

The existence of unfunded liabilities per se has become something of a red herring in the continuing policy debate about pension insurance. Even the somewhat broader concept of pension plan financial solvency introduced in Chapter 3 doesn't encompass the more pivotal concern existing both before ERISA, when there was no federal guarantee, as well as subsequently. That concern is with the proper valuation of the sponsor's option to "put" unfunded pension obligations to other parties: pension plan participants, creditors, and, since 1974, the PBGC insurance fund. A third fundamental concept, the value of PBGC insurance, therefore provides a focal point for discussion in Chapter 4. On an intuitive level, PBGC insurance represents the difference in the expected values of one series of benefit payments coming directly from the U.S. Treasury, and an alternative series of benefit payments coming from a private employer. A series of payments from the U.S. Treasury is worth more, because the U.S. Treasury won't default or go bankrupt. By contrast, some probability always exists that an otherwise identical series of benefit payments from a private employer will be interrupted or ended altogether by a bankruptcy or liquidation.

Current actuarial practice ignores fundamental principles of corporate finance as they apply to the valuation of risky debt, as future benefit payments are discounted using the expected rate of return on pension assets. When workers focus on the pension plan's *reported condition* to determine the tradeoff between higher earnings and additional contributions to the pension plan, the issue becomes one of correcting nonrational assessments made by workers and their representatives. To the extent that labor ignores proper discounting to reflect the possibility that some fraction of vested benefits might be forfeited as a result of an employer's insolvency, policymakers are bound to become concerned about inadequate benefit security.[61] When these concerns produce a collective pension guarantee system, that system will probably become subject to political influence, if not outright control. In such an arrangement, pricing will not reflect the risks to the insurance fund. This breeds instability, usually accompanied by suboptimal transfers among different groups in the economy.

Chapter 5 compares systems from nine other countries that in some respects resemble the PBGC. Some of these arrangements are based on insurance contracts that manage to avoid the moral hazard and adverse selection problems we observe in the context of the ERISA program. Other systems ignore these issues at considerable peril. Finland's system of pension-linked credit insurance completely collapsed in 1992, despite precautionary reserves that were built up methodically for 28 years. The Province of Ontario imported the defective PBGC model almost completely intact, and already some of the consequences have been costly. On the other hand, systems in Chile, Japan, and Switzerland insure mandatory benefits or some notion of socially minimal retirement income. These contrast sharply with the ERISA concept, which targets pension benefits promised to only a minority of workers, without regard to some universal or mandatory level coordinated with other government retirement programs such as social security and medicare. We can learn much from the ways that public and private pension guarantees interact elsewhere that will help guide America toward providing its workers with adequate and more secure retirement income.

Chapter 6 considers the ethical framework within which alternative pension insurance systems and their modification should be considered. Without adequate attention to this aspect, public policy concerning pension insurance will inevitably sink into a deep morass of problems. A socially viable system of secure pensions must somehow accommodate a variety of values and concerns that may not be entirely compatible. Furthermore, the problem of defining legitimate and fair levels of retirement income security should not be addressed only in a one-period framework. One needs to consider what rate of time preference can be justified in making policy and to take into account the difficult ethical question of defining duties and obligations between different generations of workers. These concerns seem to have been all but overlooked in the development of the PBGC concept. As a result, that concept rests on a shaky ethical foundation.

Chapter 7 weighs the competing interests of workers, consumers, taxpayers, shareholders, and creditors by examining the question of how much benefit security should be provided in terms of alternative approaches to reform. By providing subsidized insurance, ERISA acts to impede the mobility of resources in the economy, making it less responsive to changing needs and preferences. To rectify this situation, the goal for public policy should be to ensure that workers receive the value of their marginal product. In competitive markets, profit-maximizing firms will hire more labor until the wage rate exceeds the value of additional production. ERISA insurance, by way of its hidden subsidy, reduces the cost of labor but by differing amounts. The most creditworthy and financially strong private employers clearly derive the least value from the program. In many cases, that value is entirely offset—and more—by other costs associated with offering a traditional defined-benefit pension plan. Hence, the trend in favor of defined-contribution plans.

Be that as it may, the weakest firms remain positioned to extract substantial value from the program. This enables them to retain workers that they otherwise could not afford to employ. At the same time, the additional demand for labor on the part of weak and failing companies gives more successful firms less incentive to hire in the face of increased costs. Financially weak firms with products poorly suited to market needs therefore will produce more while stronger firms with products that are in demand will produce less. Inefficiencies can also be introduced as subsidized labor is substituted for other production inputs. Under these conditions, consumers find themselves less well-off and taxpayers are placed at risk.

After considering this unfortunate result, it is tempting to ask whether unrestrained market forces should simply be left to determine benefits, and whether government can play any constructive role in protecting workers from abuses in this area. Fortunately, other insurance markets and other pension systems have demonstrated that market forces can be harnessed to provide perfectly adequate levels of benefit security. At the same time, these private alternatives have avoided many of the efficiency costs described above. By way of a conclusion then, Chapter 8 discusses how a restructured and privatized approach to ERISA termination insurance would operate in practice.

SUMMARY

Much of the retirement income promised to workers in the context of traditional defined-benefit pension plans is placed at risk when a company's pension plan terminates or whenever a worker changes jobs. Depending on a worker's age, length of service to the current employer, and prevailing interest rates, losses can range as high as 90 percent of projected benefits, even with federal insurance provided by the PBGC. Problems resulting from these losses can be particularly severe during and after major structural change in the economy.

The current pension insurance program in the United States was established by the Employee Retirement Income Security Act of 1974, following a spate of business disasters including the Studebaker bankruptcy. The authors of ERISA correctly identified many problems involved with the transition to a postindustrial economy. Unfortunately, ERISA's remedies failed to match its rhetoric. Before ERISA, when companies liquidated, workers under the age of 50 typically lost not only their jobs but also their entire pension wealth. ERISA gave plan participants the right to reach beyond the assets of the pension plan to recover the value of their benefits when plans terminated with insufficient funds. Despite these new rights, however, many workers remain vulnerable to catastrophic pension losses. The new law also set up a minimum funding standard, which has subsequently failed to prevent the growth of unfunded pension liabilities. And, though it liberalized vesting requirements to a degree, those requirements are considerably more restrictive today than vesting standards in most other industrialized countries.

Given that corporate net worth can vanish altogether before a plan sponsor liquidates, ERISA provided firms with the opportunity to borrow from their employees (i.e., by deferring compensation) on the assumption that, if the company failed, the additional debt would be repaid by the U.S. government. As a result, pension promises became much more valuable and have been used as a means of providing hidden subsidies to depressed and dying industries. The resulting costs were then shifted to other groups that will be unable to escape them in the future. The classic insurance problems of adverse selection and moral hazard have been central to repeated criticism of the program. The PBGC's predicament is made worse by the agency's practical inability to restrict companies with no future from making empty retirement promises to their workers or from gambling for redemption by taking excessive risks with pension investments. These structural problems suggest that the ultimate cost of the program could be substantial. Such costs will become increasingly difficult to justify in view of the declining proportion of workers that qualifies for the pension benefits the program guarantees.

ENDNOTES

1. A group of entrepreneurs purchased the right to use the Pan Am trademarks during the bankruptcy proceedings. They plan to begin operating a charter service and other ventures. However, the old company has been liquidated entirely.

2. See Josef P. Schumpeter, *Capitalism, Socialism and Democracy* (New York: Harper & Row, 1950), pp. 81–86.

3. Many sponsors have recently changed to benefit formulas based on average career earnings. Such changes usually produce lower benefit levels and hence lower pension costs as well. For workers, job mobility still is penalized in "career average" plans, because most employers periodically update the career-average base to adjust for inflation. See Hay/Huggins Company, Inc., and Mathematica Policy Research, "The Effect of Job Mobility on Pension Benefits" (Washington, DC: U.S. Department of Labor, July 1988), pp. 15–17.

4. This occurs even though the Employee Retirement Income Security Act prohibited certain types of benefit formulas that resulted in backloading. See ERISA §204b.

5. See Richard A. Ippolito, *The Economics of Pension Insurance* (Philadelphia: Pension Research Council of the Wharton School at the University of Pennsylvania, 1989), p. 10.

6. See Financial Accounting Standards Board, *Statement of Financial Accounting Standards No. 87,* 1985.

7. However, subjective judgments about time preference and risk aversion clearly vary even within cohorts. The effect of using higher discount rates for younger workers would be to reduce the capital losses as a percentage of projected benefits for those people. The use of multiple rates therefore could produce similar termination losses for younger and older workers alike. A belief that significantly higher discount rates should be used for the young could imply that workers of all ages should be provided with accrued benefits and no more when leaving the firm.

8. For example, see Markus Nievergelt, "Security of Pension Rights." Paper presented at the European Actuarial Consultancy Services Pensions in Europe Workshop/Symposium, Maastricht, The Netherlands, October 28–29, 1993.

9. Other countries currently offer workers much better protection in this area. For example, the U. K. Social Security Act of 1985 provides

"early leavers" with inflation protection at levels determined by that country's Retail Prices Index. However, the statute caps increases in deferred benefits at 5 percent annually.

10. Some have argued that it is appropriate to impose so-called quit losses on workers. For example, Dorsey has suggested that such losses serve as a penalty to workers for breaking an implicit contract with their employers. Subsequent research has shown, however, that implicit contract theories are most applicable to temporary layoffs and that other theories better explain labor mobility resulting from job creation and destruction, and the movement of workers from one continuing position to another. See Stuart Dorsey, "Pension Portability and Labor Market Efficiency" (Washington, DC: U.S. Department of Labor, September 1990); and Bruce D. Meyer and Patricia M. Anderson, "The Extent and Consequences of Job Turnover," in *Brookings Papers on Economic Activity: Microeconomics 1994,* pp. 177–248.

11. See Congressional Budget Office, *Displaced Workers: Trends in the 1980s and Implications for the Future* (Washington, DC: U.S. Government Printing Office, 1993).

12. See Thomas G. Donlan, "Keep the Faith: And End the Fraud in U.S. Pension Benefit Insurance," *Barron's,* July 1, 1991, p. 10.

13. Senator Williams was later sent to prison as a result of his role in the so-called Abscam scandal.

14. See Jack L. Treynor, Patrick J. Regan, and William W. Priest, Jr., *The Financial Reality of Pension Funding under ERISA,* (Homewood, IL: Dow Jones-Irwin, 1976), p. 85.

15. See Michael S. Gordon, "Introduction: The Social Policy Origins of ERISA," in American Bar Association Section of Labor and Employment Law, eds., *Employee Benefits Law* (Washington, DC: Bureau of National Affairs, 1991), p. lxxii.

16. This 15-year amortization period was modeled on Canadian practice and was considered to be the generally accepted standard at the time. The Omnibus Budget Reconciliation Act of 1987 (OBRA '87) subsequently reduced several of the amortization periods used in determining the ERISA minimum funding requirement. Unfunded liabilities grew, despite these changes, as a result of other provisions adopted at the same time.

17. The Tax Reform Act of 1986 subsequently reduced the minimum period for partial vesting to five years. Most defined contribution plans vest in five years or less.

18. See Treynor, Regan, and Priest, *Financial Reality,* p. 6.

19. This particular claim is more valuable when a pension plan is terminated before the sponsor files for bankruptcy protection. In these rare cases, the PBGC has a secured claim. There have also been cases—like LTV—where the controlled group had significant net worth even after entering bankruptcy. Congress stipulated in ERISA that this claim for employer liability would be treated as a tax due to the United States with priority over general unsecured claims. However, this priority has been challenged and remains subject to some ambiguity. See David C. Lindeman, "Pensions' Plagues and the PBGC," *American Enterprise,* March–April 1993, p. 78.

20. According to Moody's Investors Service, the average recovery rate for senior unsecured debt from 1970 to 1993 was 48.38 percent. See Jerome S. Fons, "Default Risk and the Term Structure of Credit Risk," *Financial Analysts Journal,* September–October 1994, p. 28.

21. See Hay Huggins, Inc., *Pension Plan Expense Study for the Pension Benefit Guaranty Corporation,* September 1990, p. 2.

22. Before ERISA, the pension put existed, but the unfunded liabilities were "put" to plan participants instead of the government insurance fund. A similar put was created by deposit insurance. For the deposit insurance background, see Lawrence J. White, *The S&L Debacle* (New York: Oxford University Press, 1991), p. 39.

23. For example, see Treynor, Regan, and Priest, *Financial Reality,* p. 62; and Alicia H. Munnell, "Guaranteeing Private Pension Benefits: A Potentially Expensive Business," *New England Economic Review,* March–April 1982, pp. 24–47.

24. For a discussion of the politics of risk shifting, see Yair Aharoni, *The No-Risk Society* (Chatham, NJ: Chatham House, 1981).

25. See U.S. Department of Labor, Table A2 "Total Covered Workers," *Private Pension Plan Bulletin: Abstract of 1990 Form 5500 Annual Reports 2* (Summer 1993), p. 6.

26. The 26.3 million private-sector workers covered by a defined-benefit plan consist of workers covered only by a defined-benefit plan as well as workers covered by both a defined-benefit plan and a defined-contribution plan during the 1990 fiscal plan year. The 21.4 million workers with PBGC protection include active participants who were either fully or partially vested, plus the number of separated participants with a vested right to benefits. It should be noted that the total number of workers with PBGC protection includes double counting of workers

vested and/or covered by plans sponsored by more than one employer. It is not possible to determine the extent of double counting. See U.S. Department of Labor, *Private Pension Plan Bulletin,* pp. 6–7.

27. For labor force data reported in Figure 1–2, see Table II, United States, in *Labor Force Statistics, 1971–1991* (Paris: OECD, 1993); and Table 3.B1 in *Social Security Bulletin: Annual Statistical Supplement, 1992,* p. 121, and U.S. Department of Labor, *Private Pension Plan Bulletin,* p. 6.

28. For background on pension coverage rates by age, gender, company size, industry, etc., see United States Department of Labor, Social Security Administration, United States Small Business Administration and the Pension Board Guaranty Corporation, *Pension and Health Benefits of American Workers: New Findings from the Current Population Survey,* pp. B1–B23.

29. The maximum guaranteed benefit is increased every year by the same factor that applies to Social Security benefits. In 1995, the maximum benefit guaranteed by the PBGC stood at $2,573.86 per month or $30,886.32 annually.

30. The maximum social security benefit of $13,546 in 1993 assumed that the worker earned the maximum taxable wage for an entire 35-year career and retired at age 65 in that same year. See Table 2.A28 in *Social Security Bulletin: Annual Statistical Supplement, 1993,* p. 58.

31. See Table 10.10 in John A. Turner and Daniel J. Beller, eds., *Trends in Pensions 1992* (Washington, DC: U.S. Government Printing Office, 1992), p. 247.

32. See Table 1.B2 in *Social Security Bulletin,* Fall 1993, p. 114.

33. SSI is a means-tested supplement to social security financed from general revenue. A single person, age 65, with *no* "countable income" and with "countable" assets of less than $2,000 is entitled to the full, federal SSI payment of $5,208 per year. Individual states may supplement the federal amount. See Social Security Administration, *Social Security Handbook 1993,* 11th ed. (Washington, DC: U.S. Government Printing Office, 1993), pp. 356–7, 392–94.

34. This little-known aspect of ERISA is based on a concept adopted from state trust law, which states that those with the most settled expectations are entitled to the most protection. See ERISA §4044.

35. The value of PBGC insurance is a central issue in the debate about the program's future. It is examined in depth later in this volume.

36. The ERISA prudent man rule requires pension plan trustees and other fiduciaries to perform their duties with "the care, skill, prudence, and

diligence that a prudent man acting in a like capacity and familiar with such matters would use . . ." See ERISA §404.

37. Moral hazard is a classic insurance problem whereby the buyer of insurance adopts riskier modes of behavior as an undesirable response to the financial protection provided by the insurance carrier.Without countervailing incentives in the insurance contract or elsewhere, insured people tend not to protect themselves from risk as much as they would in the absence of insurance.

38. Despite published empirical results, PBGC officials have the impression that investment policies of terminated underfunded pension plans seem to approximate those of better-funded plans. The author is indebted to David C. Lindeman for sharing this observation. Also see Zvi Bodie, Jay O. Light, Randall Morck, and Robert A. Taggart, Jr., "Corporate Pension Policy: An Empirical Investigation," *Financial Analysts Journal,* September–October 1985, pp. 10–16.

39. These steep increases reversed in 1994 for temporary and potentially misleading reasons. As this book went to press, the PBGC estimated that total unfunded liabilities had fallen to $31 billion in 1994 with the Top 50 accounting for $13.5 billion of that amount. The rapid increase in interest rates during 1994 appears to explain most of the improvement. However, rates fell again in 1995 suggesting that these estimates may not be as rosy next year. The Clinton Administration also permitted General Motors to contribute $6 billion of company stock to one of its pension plans. That transaction made the condition of the plan appear better than it really was. Equity in the company was the only asset—apart from the government guarantee—standing behind the unfunded liability to begin with.

40. RPA '94 actually was passed as part of the GATT legislation.

41. See Munnell, "Guaranteeing Private Pension Benefits," p. 47.

42. See Ricardo Hausmann and Michael Gavin, "The Roots of Banking Crises: The Macroeconomic Context," Paper presented at the Conference on Banking Crises in Latin America organized by the Inter-American Development Bank and the Group of Thirty, October 1995. p. 5.

43. See Beverly Hirtle and Arturo Estrella, "Alternatives for Correcting the Funding Gap of the Pension Benefit Guaranty Corporation," Mimeograph 1990, p. 30.

44. Both indirect and opportunity costs also have major incentive effects in the context of government guarantee programs. For example, see John B. Shoven, Scott B. Smart, and Joel Waldfogel, "Real Interest

Rates and the Savings and Loan Crisis: The Moral Hazard Problem," Working Paper #3754, (Cambridge, MA: The National Bureau of Economic Research, June 1991). The authors estimated that raising deposit insurance coverage from $20,000 to $100,000 per account led to increased borrowing costs to the Treasury of about $100 billion. This amount was in addition to direct budgetary outlays associated with deposit insurance guarantees.

45. Analyzing a time series that is stable in the statistical sense would require at least 30 years of data. Some researchers would insist on 50 years of data. Unfortunately, the limited data from 18 years of PBGC claims experience appear to lack even the desirable characteristics of a stable time series.

46. For a more extensive chronology of premium studies, see Richard A. Ippolito, *The Economics of Pension Insurance* (Philadelphia: The Pension Research Council, 1989), pp. 50–65.

47. However, many other aspects of the Clinton Administration's PBGC proposal were substantially revised before this legislation was enacted.

48. See Bodie, Light, Morck, and Taggart, "Corporate Pension Policy," pp. 10–16; and Mary Stone, "A Financing Explanation for Overfunded Pension Plan Terminations," *Journal of Accounting Research,* Autumn 1987, pp. 317–26.

49. See Robert S. Kemp, Jr., "Firm Evolution and Pension Funding," *Benefits Quarterly* 3 (1985), pp. 43–59.

50. The dissenting comments by Michael Gordon, a former aide to Senator Jacob Javits who helped draft many sections of ERISA, concerning a previous book provide evidence of this. See Ippolito, *The Economics of Pension Insurance,* pp. 263–65.

51. See George A. Akerlof and Paul M. Romer, "Looting: The Economic Underworld of Bankruptcy for Profit," in *Brookings Papers on Economic Activity* 2 (1993), pp. 1–73.

52. Zvi Bodie and Robert C. Merton, "Pension Benefit Guarantees in the United States: A Functional Analysis," in *The Future of Pensions in the United States,* R. Schmitt, ed. (Philadelphia: Pension Research Council at the University of Pennsylvania, 1993), p. 208.

53. See Congressional Budget Office, *Controlling Losses of the Pension Benefit Guaranty Corporation* (Washington, DC: U.S. Congress, 1993), p. 5.

54. *Duration* is a measure developed to indicate the interest rate risk of fixed-income investments. It represents the average time required for the investor to receive the investment principal as well as the interest on the principal. It is similar to maturity, except that maturity only considers the timing of the final payment of a bond. The significance of duration is that as it increases, the volatility of investment returns also increases with respect to changes in the general level of interest rates. See Arthur Williams III, "Performance Evaluation in Fixed Income Securities," in Frank J. Fabozzi and Irving M. Pollack, eds., *The Handbook of Fixed Income Securities,* 2d ed. (Homewood, IL: Dow Jones-Irwin, 1987), p. 773.

55. At the time of the saving and loan crisis these data were published as the "Quarterly Thrift Aggregates." Currently they are available in unpublished form as the *Consolidated Maturity Rate (CMR) Report.*

56. The duration of a cash flow stream is the weighted average of the time that the cash flows are due. Each flow's weight is determined by its present value as a percentage of the present value of the stream as a whole.

57. See Gordon L. Clark, *Pensions and Corporate Restructuring in American Industry: A Crisis of Regulation* (Baltimore: Johns Hopkins University Press, 1993), p. 15.

58. High interest rates played a major role in motivating the reversion movement. Federal regulators permitted these transactions in part out of fear that more defined-benefit plans would otherwise have been terminated in favor of defined-contribution plans.

59. See Yair Aharoni, *The No-Risk Society* (Chatham, NJ: Chatham House, 1981).

60. Ray Schmitt, "Pension Benefit Guaranty Corporation: Proposals to Shore Up the Single-Employer Program" (Washington, DC: Congressional Research Service, November 24, 1993), p. 1.

61. James E. Pesando, *Issues Regarding the Reform of Canada's Private Pensions System* (Ottawa, Ont.: Policy Research, Analysis and Liaison Directorate, Bureau of Policy Coordination, Consumer and Corporate Affairs of Canada, 1983), p. 50.

ANALYZING MORAL HAZARD

The Government of Chile provides several pension-related guarantees in connection with its privatized social security system. Only Chile's minimum pension guarantee will be considered here. In 1981, Chile replaced its traditional pay-as-you-go social security program with individual investment accounts. Workers in the formal sector must contribute at least 10 percent of covered earnings to fund these arrangements. The State currently guarantees a minimum pension that amounts to 25 percent of the average wage and 75 percent of the minimum wage for any participant retiring with 20 years of credited contributions. Consider the following thought experiment based on this example.

Figure 1–4 depicts the individual retirement outcome distribution in this type of situation. It plots outcomes for the individual account balance at retirement, or $V(A)$, as a standard normal distribution with a mean value of zero and a standard deviation of one. Figure 1–4 assumes a simplified world in which contributions are set aside so that $EV(A)$ [i.e., the expected or mean value of $V(A)$] will match the goal for an individual's retirement income. However, the ultimate amount of accumulated assets will depend on market valuations, as distinct from prior assumptions. Uncertainty about the worker's future participation in the labor force, wage growth during the balance of the career, inflation, and the mortality age also contribute to uncertainty concerning the ultimate cost of a pension. In Figure 1–4, society defines V_{min} to be the hardship level. Figure 1–5 portrays the same outcomes as a discrete case by loading the proba-

FIGURE 1-4

Individual Retirement Outcome Distribution

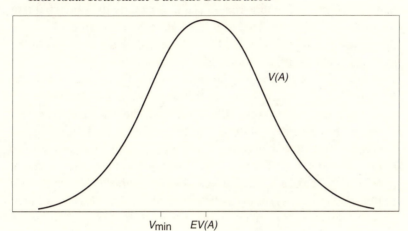

Note: This is a standard normal distribution with mean = 0 and standard deviation = 1.

FIGURE 1-5

Discrete Case: Individual Retirement Outcomes

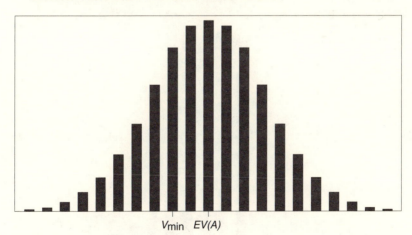

Note: This is a density corresponding to the standard normal distribution.

bility mass onto 21 points between –3 and 3. The mean, median, and standard deviation all remain unchanged.

Figure 1–6 shows the effect of imposing a guarantee that eliminates the lowest one-third of retirement outcome probabilities. Note
that the median value of zero still remains exactly the same, but that
the expected value, at .16, has shifted slightly to the right. The new
distribution therefore is skewed (i.e., the mean lies to the right of the
median). This change is quite different from the wealth effect that
would occur in a general equilibrium framework. The entire distribution in Figure 1–5 simply would shift to the right in that case.

Figure 1–7 shows the effect of setting the guarantee to correspond with the central point of the original distribution in Figures
1–4 and 1–5. Here, skewness has risen to its peak. The median has
remained fixed at what now has become the guaranteed level and, at
.39, the expected value has shifted slightly farther to the right. The
retiree in Figure 1–7 is protected from all downside risk, and the
standard deviation has fallen by more as a result.

Figure 1–8 represents a case in which the minimum pension is
set—either by accident or design—above the actual contribution
target. This distribution is less skewed than the one in Figure 1–7.

FIGURE 1-6

The Minimum Pension Guarantee

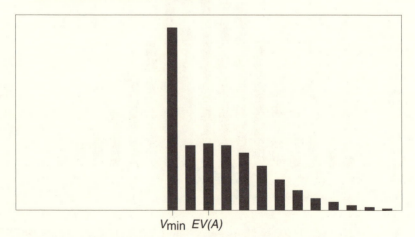

V_{min} $EV(A)$

Note: This is a mixed distribution with $P(V_{min})$ = .33, median = 0, mean = .16, and s.d. = .77.

FIGURE 1-7

A Midpoint Pension Guarantee

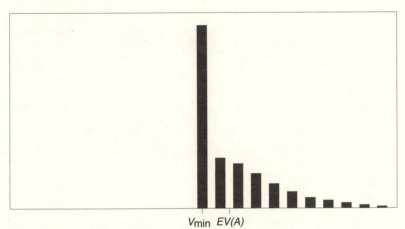

Note: This is a mixed distribution with $P(V_{min})$ = .56, median = 0, mean = .39, and s.d. = .58.

FIGURE 1-8

A Skewed Pension Guarantee

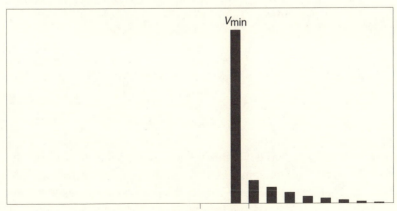

Note: This is a mixed distribution with $P(V_{min})$ = .77, median = .6, mean = .77, and s.d. = .38.

TABLE 1-1

Probability Distributions

Outcome	Figure 1–5 No Guarantee	Figure 1–6 Minimum Guarantee	Figure 1–7 Midpoint Guarantee	Figure 1–8 Skewed Guarantee
–3	.0014	0	0	0
–2.7	.0032	0	0	0
–2.4	.0068	0	0	0
–2.1	.0134	0	0	0
–1.8	.0239	0	0	0
–1.5	.0390	0	0	0
–1.2	.0584	0	0	0
–.9	.0787	0	0	0
–.6	.0998	.3246	0	0
–.3	.1140	.1140	0	0
0	.1179	.1179	.5578	0
.3	.1140	.1140	.1140	0
.6	.0998	.0998	.0998	.7716
.9	.0787	.0787	.0787	.0787
1.2	.0584	.0584	.0584	.0584
1.5	.0390	.0390	.0390	.0390
1.8	.0239	.0239	.0239	.0239
2.1	.0134	.0134	.0134	.0134
2.4	.0068	.0068	.0068	.0068
2.7	.0032	.0032	.0032	.0032
3	.0014	.0014	.0014	.0014
Median	0	0	0	.6
m	0	.16	.39	.77
s	1	.77	.58	.38

However, the standard deviation has collapsed. Table 1–1 reports the probabilities for all outcomes considered in Figures 1–5 through 1–8.

In what sense will these guarantees motivate changes in behavior? Most people are risk averse, but they tend to become less so as they accumulate wealth. Figure 1–9 shows utility functions for three generic individuals: risk seekers, risk-neutral personalities, and risk-averse personalities. Table 1–2 reports a set of utility values for these

FIGURE 1-9

Three Personal Utility Functions

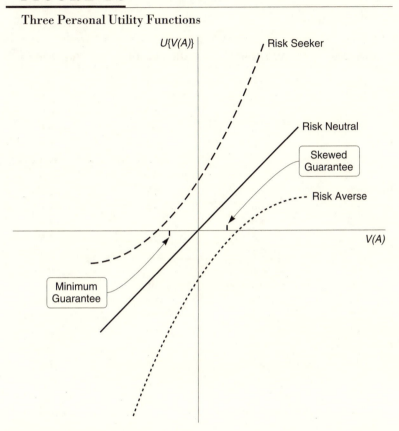

Note: V(A) = retirement account balance.

three profiles. Table 1–3 reports the improvement in expected utility from each of the three guarantees compared with the case of no guarantee. Expected utility is defined as

$$E\{U[V(A)]\} = \sum \pi_i U[V(A_i)]$$

where π_i is the probability of outcome $V(A_i)$, and $U[V(A_i)]$ is the utility value of the same outcome.

Not surprisingly, the risk-averse personality shows the largest utility gain relative to the case with no guarantee at every level of insurance protection. Table 1–3 also suggests why the minimum

TABLE 1-2

Utility Values

Outcome	Risk Seeker	Risk Neutral	Risk Averse
-3	-1	-3	-8
-2.7	-.9	-2.7	-7.2
-2.4	-.78	-2.4	-6.5
-2.1	-.56	-2.1	-5.8
-1.8	-.43	-1.8	-5.1
-1.5	-.3	-1.5	-4.5
-1.2	-.1	-1.2	-3.9
-.9	.2	-.9	-3.3
-.6	.55	-.6	-2.7
-.3	1.0	-.3	-2.1
0	1.5	0	-1.5
.3	2.1	.3	-1
.6	2.7	.6	-.55
.9	3.3	.9	-.2
1.2	3.9	1.2	.1
1.5	4.5	1.5	.3
1.8	5.1	1.8	.43
2.1	5.8	2.1	.56
2.4	6.5	2.4	.78
2.7	7.2	2.7	.9
3	8	3	1

TABLE 1-3

Expected Utility Differences[1,2]

	Figure 1–6 Minimum Guarantee	Figure 1–7 Midpoint Guarantee	Figure 1–8 Skewed Guarantee
Risk seeker	.15	.58	1.26
Risk neutral	.16	.39	.76
Risk averse	.33	.79	1.37

[1]Expected utility is: $E\{U[V(A)]\} = \Sigma \pi_i U[V(Ai)]$, where π_i equals the probability of outcome $V(A_i)$ and $U[V(A_i)]$ represents the utility value of the same outcome.

[2]All differences reported in this table refer to the case with no guarantee.

guarantee in Figure 1–6 probably would have little effect on behavior. Risk seekers derive minimal gains from the imposition of a guarantee at this level, particularly if they are wealthy. The more numerous members of the risk-averse group will remain sensitive to the possibility of loss in this region, primarily due to lower personal income and net worth. The marginal value of the extreme outcomes to the right in Figure 1–6 also matters little to them.

The case of the midpoint guarantee in Figure 1–7 tells a somewhat different story. Depending on the shape and location of the actual utility curves, it seems plausible that both risk seekers and risk averters could feel substantially better off with a guarantee for the expected value of contributions. Will this lead to greater risk taking at the expense of the guarantee fund? It could. People who were originally risk averse would be unlikely to remain so when $V(A)$ equaled or exceeded zero in this case, because all downside risk has been eliminated below that level. Their utility curve therefore could change in the presence of a guarantee for $EV(A)$. Furthermore, it is possible—and even likely—for one person to be *both* risk averse and risk seeking at the same time in a situation like this.

Consider the case of someone who buys fire insurance when the cost of the premium is more than the expected monetary value of the loss. This clearly is risk-averse behavior. Now, suppose that the same person simultaneously buys a lottery ticket when the cost of that ticket is greater than the expected monetary value of the lottery. This clearly involves risk-seeking behavior. In classic work many years ago, Milton Friedman and a coauthor showed that a person even can maximize utility by simultaneously buying insurance and engaging in lotteries.[62] Exactly this type of utility function is shown in Figure 1–10.

The type of utility function shown in Figure 1–10 is cubic, and the expected utility would be computed as follows:

$$E\left\{U\left[V(A)\right]\right\} = U(V_{\min}) \cdot \pi_{V_{\min}} + \frac{1}{2\pi}\left\{\int_{V_{\min}}^{\infty}[V(A)]^3 e^{-\frac{[V(A)]^2}{2}}\, dV(A)\right\}$$

Note that the integral doesn't have a closed form solution. However, it can easily be solved by symmetry for the interval between negative and positive infinity. For the lesser intervals in Figures 1–6

FIGURE 1-10

A Personal Utility Function with Two Ranges: The Case of
Decreasing and Increasing Marginal Utility

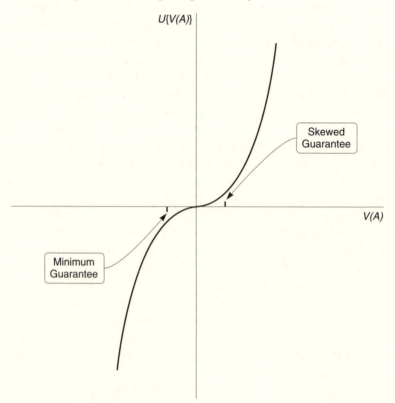

Note: $V(A)$ = retirement account balance.

through 1–8, it could be estimated using Simpson's Rule for numeri-
cal approximation. Figure 1–10 merely illustrates that some people
are willing to spend a small amount of money to protect themselves
from the small probability of a catastrophic loss while at the same
time also spending a small amount of money to obtain the small
probability of a very large gain.

The point of these analytics is simply this: Any guarantee that
sets the level of insurance protection in a region where the marginal

utility of wealth is *not* decreasing creates a moral hazard problem. In such a region, each unit of additional wealth becomes more valuable than the last one—at least to the person covered by the guarantee. The minimum pension guarantee in Figure 1–6 avoids this pitfall. The case of the midpoint guarantee in Figure 1–7 would not.

Figure 1–8, the case of the skewed guarantee, is even more problematic. The skewed guarantee represents a risk seeker's paradise, with V_{min} set toward the right of these utility curves. As noted in Table 1–4, risk seekers experience their highest marginal utility when insurance protection is increased from the midpoint guarantee in Figure 1–7 to the skewed guarantee in Figure 1–8 and even further to the right of the skewed guarantee. A skewed guarantee will provide an added incentive for this group to gamble on low probability outcomes. Risk seekers will do so not only when the rewards are actuarially fair but also when the "deck is stacked" against them. Of course, the difference between the expected value of these gambles and the individual's certainty equivalent (i.e., the level of wealth that the person would accept without the opportunity to gamble) eventually will be paid by the guarantee fund.

Figure 1–8 characterizes the minimum pension guarantee provided to most workers in Chile. In fact, the minimum pension in Chile—with its relatively lenient requirement of 20 years of credited contributions—was set above projected retirement outcomes at virtually every income level based on plausible economic assumptions.

TABLE 1–4

Expected Utility Cross Comparisons

	Minimum Guarantee versus No Guarantee	Midpoint Guarantee versus Minimum Guarantee	Skewed Guarantee versus Midpoint Guarantee	Skewed Guarantee versus Minimum Guarantee
Risk seeker	.15	.37	.74	1.10
Risk neutral	.16	.23	.37	.60
Risk averse	.33	.46	.58	1.04

The median worker in Chile earned about U.S. $235 per month in 1993. That same worker would be eligible for a minimum pension of $1,457 per year upon retirement (at age 65) in 2013. About $535 or 37 percent of the minimum pension would be subsidized by the State. This projection assumes: continuous contributions for 20 years until age 65; 5 percent real returns on the accumulating assets; 2 percent real growth in wages; and the minimum pension remaining steady in relative terms at about 20 percent of the average wage. The minimum wage worker meanwhile would expect a much higher subsidy. In fact, the minimum wage worker's subsidy would amount to about $1,030 per year, that is, 71 percent of the minimum pension.[63]

Is Chile's minimum pension guarantee too generous? The answer is subjective. Chile's minimum pension isn't high by international standards. Real returns have also averaged 14 percent—not 5 percent as in the example above—since the new system became operational more than 13 years ago. Most workers will undoubtedly contribute for more than the minimum requirement of 20 years and others will begin contributing earlier, before the last 20 years of a normal career. Some economists in Chile also argue that the redistributional aspect of the minimum pension guarantee is appropriate in the absence of a pay-as-you-go, "first pillar" social security program. Still, critics persist in the view that Chile's minimum pension guarantee has created a potentially large contingent liability for the State, and they could be right. Such a threat, however, is not imminent, because most workers participating in Chile's privatized system are young.

The cost to the state of Chile's minimum pension subsidy is highly sensitive to the number of years (i.e., beyond the minimum requirement of 20 years) in the contribution period and whether those contributions occur early or late in the career. Strategic behavior concerning these factors represents the dominant form of moral hazard created by Chile's minimum pension guarantee. Regardless of the individual income level, both of these threats could be addressed by a properly designed rate-of-return guarantee.

One variation on a rate-of-return guarantee would grant some rate of accrual for each year of credited contributions. For example, workers could receive minimum pension rights amounting to 75 percent of Chile's average wage for each year of service. This would encourage more workers to participate beyond the current minimum of 20 years. An accrual rate of less than one percent would have another important advantage. It would reduce the intergenerational subsidies that would otherwise result even with Chile's high real rates of return so far. Unfortunately, such a guarantee would not automatically assure that all workers could escape poverty during retirement.

Implications for the OECD Countries

Most pension guarantee systems operating today are found in the OECD countries. They also apply more often than not to defined benefit plans. These guarantees are not designed to protect against the type of hardship just discussed in connection with Chile's minimum pension guarantee. Private pension plans in most OECD countries instead deliver "second pillar" benefits designed to replace pre-retirement income at much higher levels. Pension costs in these systems may or may not be funded in advance. However, most observers consider that the employer is obligated to honor all vested benefits, even if the funds set aside in a separate pension trust are not sufficient to cover them.

The moral hazard problem in this type of environment is completely different from the one discussed in connection with Chile. In any rational defined-benefit system, economic assets—in the form of the sponsor's net worth, or pension fund investments, or both—will overcollateralize pension promises from the moment they are made. From the point of view of the guarantee fund, the most serious moral hazard problem therefore involves excessive risk-taking with those assets. The minimum rate-of-return guarantee that seemed well-suited to the example from Chile would only accentuate it. A better generic approach for defined benefit systems therefore would involve a minimum pension guarantee or some variation on it.

In reality, every pension guarantee gives rise to some form of moral hazard. The challenge is to find effective ways of controlling it. No single method is perfect. More often than not, some combination of approaches will work best in terms of the needs and circumstances of specific retirement systems.

APPENDIX ENDNOTES

62. Milton Friedman and L. J. Savage, "The Utility Analysis of Choices Involving Risk," *Journal of Political Economy* 56 (August 1948), pp. 279–304.

63. By way of background, personal income in Chile appears to be distributed lognormally, with many workers grouped just above the minimum wage of about U.S.$108.50 as of 1993.

2

PRIVATE DEFINED-BENEFIT PENSION PLANS IN THE 1980S
How Well Funded Were They?

What does it mean for a pension plan to report that it is fully funded? The obligation to pay retirement benefits in the future is not like a bank loan for a specific amount. Instead, it represents only an estimate based on assumptions about a variety of factors that will determine ultimate pension costs. Among these factors are retirement age, employee turnover, disability rates, mortality patterns, and investment returns. Long ago, William F. Marples recognized that the challenge of estimating the financial strength of a pension plan could be truly formidable:

> The peculiar difficulty in judging the condition of a pension plan is that its assets may be growing even as it is becoming more and more insolvent actuarially, and the reason is that the full measure of its outgo may take many years to develop.[1]

Rising asset prices during the 1980s subsequently allowed the sponsors of private defined-benefit pension plans to justify more liberal actuarial assumptions and thereby reduce the minimum cash contributions required by ERISA.[2] Was this reduction justified? Or did the funding standards governing the reduction provide yet another example of fictitious accounting similar to that which for so long concealed the ultimate cost of the savings and loan debacle?

This chapter responds to these concerns by examining Form 5500[3] pension asset and liability data from samples that the U.S. Department of Labor collected for the years 1981, 1986, and 1987.[4] In view of the considerable latitude that was accorded to plan sponsors and their actuaries, we rely on several adjustments to mark reported pension data to market values.

The chapter begins with a brief summary of essential findings. Second, it provides a background discussion of the alternative ways of measuring a pension obligation and the suitability of each for indicating the condition of the defined-benefit system. Third, it reviews trends in pension funding and actuarial assumptions during the 1981–87 period as well as more recently. Fourth, it discusses the need for the specific adjustments used in this study. Fifth, it reports universe estimates of the aggregate surplus and deficit positions of all single-employer, defined-benefit plans. Sixth, it presents statistical testing results that summarize patterns of association between changes in the funded condition, both actual and reported, and three plan characteristics of interest: union affiliation; an indicator of the relative burden for supporting current retirees; and, industry group. Seventh, it examines the results of a sensitivity analysis. Finally, it discusses caveats concerning the interpretation of this statistical evidence and reviews the implications for public policy. Two appendices appear at the end of the chapter documenting the asset and liability adjustment algorithms.

KEY FINDINGS

At the beginning of the 1980s, the overall condition of the pension system was considerably better than plan sponsors were reporting, because interest rates had risen to unprecedented levels. Actuaries were slow in changing the assumptions used to estimate the value of pension liabilities. Low actuarial discount rates therefore inflated reported pension obligations far beyond their economic value at the time.[5] Simultaneously, these interest rates were also depressing the value of most financial assets held in pension portfolios. The official Form 5500 reports indicated that an estimated 21.8 percent of all plans were underfunded. In fact, less than a third of that same 21.8 percent of all plans was underfunded after adjusting asset and liability data to market values.

This situation had reversed itself by the middle of the decade. Market interest rates had declined, thereby producing substantial and well-publicized gains in the value of pension portfolios.[6] Meanwhile, plan actuaries gradually relaxed their discount rate assumptions to the point where the latter exceeded benchmark rates from the annuity markets. In contrast with the situation in the early 1980s, the condition of plans that were underfunded on an economic basis had eroded to the point where funding fell to much lower levels than sponsors were reporting. The aggregate shortfall for plans that were underfunded on a PBGC termination basis stood at $48 billion by the end of the period. The sponsors of these same underfunded plans nevertheless were reporting an aggregate *surplus* of approximately $1 billion on the Form 5500. With respect to adequately funded plans, there was less difference on both an absolute and a proportional basis between the aggregate surplus of $230 billion reported and the adjusted surplus of $188 billion. However, the direction was the same. Adequately funded plans were reporting a surplus of $230 billion, but their adjusted surplus amounted to only $188 billion.

The conditions one year earlier, in 1986, when interest rates were 75 basis points lower, are also worth noting. Even though the total unfunded liability appears to have exceeded $100 billion, sponsors of the underfunded plans that year were reporting an aggregate *surplus* of $40 billion. Sponsors of adequately funded plans meanwhile reported an aggregate surplus of approximately $230 billion when their assets actually exceeded liabilities by only $164 billion. The larger unfunded liability for 1986 was consistent with the widely held belief that the condition of a defined-benefit pension plan will improve as interest rates rise, even though approximately half of the difference in total unfunded liabilities between 1986 and 1987 appeared to be related to differences in the composition of the two samples.[7] The mismatch between pension asset and liability duration also leads to an erosion in funded condition as interest rates fall. Such high volatility on the part of the aggregate shortfall underscores the government's exposure to interest rate risk through the termination insurance program administered by the Pension Benefit Guaranty Corporation.

Between 1981 and 1986, an estimated 14.21 percent of all plans slipped from adequately funded status to underfunded status relative to vested benefits. This slippage amounted to 10.37 percent between 1981 and 1987. Meanwhile, the ratio of plan assets to vested benefits declined from an estimated 1.45 to 1.10 between 1981 and 1986. The data for 1987 also show statistically significant erosion by this same measure. However, the erosion was less than that detected at the end of 1986, as a result of a temporary rise in interest rates to levels that have not been experienced since.

The subset of plans that was included both in the 1981 and 1987 samples provide additional evidence of change—in opposite directions—in both the adjusted and reported condition. On an adjusted basis, more of the adequately funded plans became underfunded during the period than the opposite. However, the reported data told a very different story: that the defined-benefit system was in robust and improving health by virtually every measure. These patterns of change extended to union and nonunion plans alike, and to plans in both the manufacturing and service sectors.

ALTERNATIVE LIABILITY MEASURES

Before examining the available pension data, it is important to clarify some essential concepts. First, a *pension liability* represents an actuarial reserve for the estimated present value of benefits promised to workers. A *defined-benefit pension plan,* used as the vehicle to satisfy those promises, is a legal entity separate from the sponsoring employer, although the sponsor funds it and the sponsor's appointees administer it. Usually, the plan makes regular monthly payments to retired workers based on their previous earnings and length of service. The ultimate cost of these benefits cannot be known with certainty until after they have all been paid. The level of contributions therefore does not define the level of benefits. Any shortfall between plan assets relative to liabilities represents a claim on the sponsor as well as a contingent claim on the PBGC.

Vested benefits are entitlements that workers retain in the event that their employment by the sponsor ends or the sponsor voluntarily terminates an adequately funded plan. In most cases, the *vested-benefit obligation* closely approximates the liability that the federal government guarantees under the PBGC termination insurance program for underfunded plans. However, the guaranteed obligation can exceed the reported liability for vested benefits in the event of a plant shutdown or the liquidation of the sponsor. Often, special early retirement provisions take effect in these cases, which involve costs that are not recognized beforehand under current actuarial and accounting practices.

A slightly broader liability measure would include vested benefits as well as additional contingent obligations. These obligations are not yet vested because the participant has not accumulated an adequate period of continuous service to the sponsor as of the valuation date. At least five years of continuous service are usually required even for partial vesting. In terms of comparability across plans and years, this *accrued-benefit obligation* (ABO) appears to be the best single liability measure when adjusted to a common set of actuarial assumptions. However, it suffers from one weakness relative to the needs of this study: the ABO tends to overstate the liability guaranteed at any one moment by the PBGC.

Another important liability measure is the *projected-benefit obligation* (PBO). The PBO includes vested benefits, but it also reflects the effect of assumptions about future inflation and salary growth. Over time, even the projected benefits for a vested worker will grow as he or she accumulates credit for additional service to the sponsor. In virtually all cases involving a continuing plan, estimates of the PBO will exceed the other liability measures. However, the various "actuarial cost methods" used to value these benefits assume very different approaches when it comes to spreading the cost of a given dollar of benefits across the expected working life of a plan participant. For this reason, analysis of data available for this period will not yield comparable estimates of the projected liability.

Another central issue in liability measurement involves the choice of an appropriate *discount rate*. Depending on the point of view, the value of a pension obligation, even when using the same liability measure, can be quite different as a result of differences in the appropriate discount rate. The appropriate rate for both plan participants and the PBGC is the risk-free rate with respect to those benefits that have been vested and that are guaranteed by the U.S. government. The risk-free rate yields a relatively large estimate of the liability, because it is lower. On the other hand, plan sponsors don't attribute nearly as much economic value to these obligations. For them, the value of these pension promises is determined by the opportunity cost of capital facing the firm.[8] The cost of capital for any private firm will exceed the risk-free rate by the amount of the appropriate risk premium. The sponsor's higher discount rate therefore will reduce the value imputed to the pension promise.

Actuaries have viewed the choice of a discount rate in terms of the return that can be expected on plan assets over an extended time. Unfortunately, they have based their estimates of expected returns on past data that are misleading.[9] This approach has provided great latitude in selecting a discount rate tailored to suit the preferences of plan sponsors. Firms whose products are profitable will prefer a low discount rate to maximize the allowable tax-deductible contributions. On the other hand, declining firms with weak and erratic earnings prospects will prefer high discount rates in order to reduce the minimum required pension contributions.[10] More generally, the linkage between pension plan portfolio returns and the choice of a discount rate to value benefit obligations is unsatisfying, because it fails to consider the pension plan as an integrated part of the sponsor's corporate financial structure.

Finally, there is the official PBGC *rate set*. By regulation, the agency sets its interest rates in a manner intended to replicate private-sector annuity prices. However, private insurers, quoting the single-premium nonparticipating group annuity contracts covered in the monthly PBGC surveys, increasingly have shifted away from mortality tables similar to the one used by the agency.[11] The PBGC interest rate assumptions were therefore set lower than they otherwise would have been under more current mortality assumptions. Adjustments for mortality table assumptions meanwhile can produce differences in liability estimates by as much as 15 percent. For this reason, the official PBGC rate set should be used only in conjunction with appropriate mortality table adjustments to replicate private-sector annuity prices during the period covered by this study.[12]

To summarize, each method for estimating the condition of a specific pension plan suffers from distinct limitations. However, estimates based on a standardized measure of accrued vested benefits appear to be the most suitable ones for this study. Implicit in this choice is a recognized tradeoff between the greater realism associated with some measure of projected obligations and the comparability of a measure that more closely approximates the current PBGC liability. When based on market interest rates, any of the measures will exhibit substantial volatility from year to year. Accordingly, no immediate and direct link is implied between the measure chosen for evaluating plan condition and a prospective standard for setting current funding requirements. The principal advantage of using the accrued vested-benefit measure in conjunction with the market value of plan assets is that it represents the best feasible approximation of a consistent indicator suitable for comparisons across time periods as well as across different pension plans, companies, and industries.

On a fundamental level, this selection assumes that plan assets and liabilities are essentially frozen on the valuation date, but that potentially large additional costs associated with plant shutdowns and corporate liquidations have not accrued at that point. For this reason, the measure chosen should be considered as one very specific and limited indicator of the PBGC's exposure to unfunded liabilities. Its motivation is to facilitate comparisons across time and selected categories of pension plans. It does so by standardizing and enhancing the available data as much as possible. Future experience of the insurance fund could differ substantially from losses suggested by these estimates. Such differences could result from changes in market interest rates, subsequent funding, and investment choices, as well as material potential costs associated with downsizing various companies that sponsor defined-benefit pension plans.

TRENDS IN FUNDING
AND ACTUARIAL ASSUMPTIONS

Since at least 1981, contributions to defined-benefit pension plans
have been on a downward spiral, falling from a total of almost $47
billion in that year to just $23 billion in 1990. The latest available
tabulation for 1991 indicates an improvement for that year alone,
when the total apparently rose to $30.1 billion. As noted in Table
2–1, however, the number of participants in these plans remained
relatively stable—moving from a low of 38.6 million in 1982 to a
high of almost 41 million in 1984. Contributions per participant fell
by more than 36 percent in nominal terms and by about 57 percent in
constant 1987 dollars as a result. On average, employers were contributing only $772 per participant to their defined-benefit pension
plans by 1991. In spite of this decline, assets in these plans rose from
$444.4 billion in 1981 to approximately $1.1 trillion in 1991 (as

TABLE 2-1

Contributions to Private Defined-Benefit Pension Plans

Year (1)	Contributions (in millions) (2)	Participants (in thousands) (3)	Contributions per Participant (4)	(4) in 1987 Dollars
1981	$46,985	38,903	$1,208	$1,531
1982	48,438	38,633	1,254	1,496
1983	46,313	40,025	1,157	1,327
1984	47,197	40,980	1,152	1,266
1985	41,996	39,692	1,058	1,121
1986	33,161	39,989	829	856
1987	29,793	39,958	746	746
1988	26,300	40,722	646	622
1989	24,898	39,958	623	574
1990	23,026	38,832	593	523
1991	30,146	39,027	772	656

Sources: The Council of Economic Advisors, *The Economic Report of the President 1994*, Washington, D.C., p.
272; and U.S. Department of Labor, *Private Pension Plan Bulletin: Abstract of 1991 Form 5500 Annual Reports*,
no. 4, Winter 1995, Washington, D.C., pp. 64, 73.

noted in Table 2–3). This represented an increase of almost 66 percent per participant in constant dollars. The magnitude of these capital gains allowed many plan sponsors to satisfy the ERISA minimum funding requirement during the 1980s without making any additional contributions. Other sponsors found themselves prohibited from making further contributions without penalty after Congress adopted a new and misguided definition of full funding as part of the Omnibus Budget Reconciliation Act in 1987. The decline in contributions resulting from these and other factors played a major role in the disappointing level of personal saving observed during this period.[13] On average, defined-benefit pension plans had accumulated asset balances of $28,237 per participant by 1991.

However, the same trends were not evident among private defined-contribution plans.[14] Simply by way of additional background, Table 2–2 indicates that in both nominal and real terms contributions per participant showed sizable increases at the same time

T A B L E 2–2

Contributions to Private Defined-Contribution Pension Plans

Year (1)	Contributions (in millions) (2)	Participants (in thousands) (3)	Contributions per Participant (4)	(4) in 1987 Dollars
1981	$28,384	21,661	$1,311	$1,661
1982	31,064	24,610	1,262	1,506
1983	36,134	29,122	1,241	1,423
1984	43,428	32,915	1,319	1,450
1985	53,192	34,973	1,521	1,611
1986	58,342	36,682	1,590	1,641
1987	62,277	38,265	1,628	1,628
1988	64,948	36,963	1,757	1,691
1989	80,143	36,447	2,199	2,027
1990	75,766	38,091	1,989	1,756
1991	80,978	38,634	2,096	1,782

Sources: The Council of Economic Advisors, *The Economic Report of the President 1994*. Washington, D.C., p. 272; and U.S. Department of Labor, *Private Pension Plan Bulletin: Abstract of 1991 Form 5500 Annual Reports*, no. 4, Winter 1995, Washington, D.C., pp. 64, 73.

that the number of participants grew by 78 percent, or almost 17 million people. As with defined-benefit plans, a booming stock market and rising bond prices helped fuel a large increase in asset balances.[15] Tables 2–3 and 2–4 provide summary asset data for private defined-benefit and defined-contribution plans, respectively.

But the more important questions are whether Americans are accumulating enough through these arrangements to meet their retirement needs, and whether these levels of saving will be adequate to protect the PBGC and other entitlement programs from additional claims that may be difficult to honor. For the defined-benefit system, we can obtain some insight into the latter concern by comparing asset values with a proper measure of liabilities.

Regular surveys of actuarial practices report that some of the assumptions that tend to have very large effects on the present value of pension liabilities, particularly for chronically underfunded plans, have been relaxed since 1980 to reduce required contributions even

T A B L E 2–3

Assets in Private Defined-Benefit Pension Plans

Year (1)	Assets (in millions) (2)	Participants (in thousands) (3)	Assets per Participant (4)	(4) in 1987 Dollars
1981	$444,376	38,903	$11,427	$14,477
1982	553,419	38,663	14,314	17,081
1983	642,359	40,025	16,049	18,405
1984	700,669	40,980	17,098	18,789
1985	826,117	39,692	20,813	22,048
1986	895,073	39,989	22,383	23,099
1987	877,269	39,958	21,955	21,955
1988	911,982	40,722	22,395	21,544
1989	987,971	39,958	24,725	22,788
1990	961,904	38,832	24,771	21,863
1991	1,101,987	39,027	28,237	24,001

Sources: The Council of Economic Advisors, *The Economic Report of the President 1994.* Washington, D.C., p. 272; and U.S. Department of Labor, *Private Pension Plan Bulletin: Abstract of 1991 Form 5500 Annual Reports,* no. 4, Winter 1995, Washington, D.C., pp. 64, 70.

TABLE 2-4

Assets in Private Defined-Contribution Pension Plans

Year (1)	Assets (in millions) (2)	Participants (in thousands) (3)	Assets per Participant (4)	(4) in 1987 Dollars
1981	$184,540	21,661	$8,519	$10,798
1982	235,567	24,610	9,572	11,422
1983	281,111	29,122	9,653	11,070
1984	343,922	32,915	10,449	11,482
1985	426,622	34,973	12,199	12,922
1986	487,837	36,682	13,299	13,724
1987	525,219	38,265	13,726	13,726
1988	591,653	36,963	16,007	15,406
1989	687,626	36,447	18,866	17,388
1990	712,236	38,091	18,698	16,503
1991	834,284	38,634	21,595	18,363

Sources: The Council of Economic Advisors, *The Economic Report of the President 1994,* Washington, D.C., p. 272; and U.S. Department of Labor, *Private Pension Plan Bulletin: Abstract of 1991 Form 5500 Annual Reports,* no. 4, Winter 1995, Washington, D.C., pp. 64, 70.

further. For example, average assumed discount rates, used to esti-mate the value of pension liabilities for large ongoing plans, rose consistently from an average of 6.1 percent in 1980 to 8.3 percent in 1991.[16] At the same time, the choice of cost methods that actuaries use to determine the pattern of funding appears to have shifted in the direction of those methods that load less of the cost of a given dollar of benefits onto the early years of a participant's working life; that is, there is less frontloading. The effect of this change is to delay fund-ing of benefits until later, when the sponsor may be weaker and less able to bear the cost.

On the other hand, the salary increase assumption rose from a level of about 5 percent per year to 6 percent by the mid-1980s and then held steady until 1991 when it appears to have declined slightly.[17] Although a higher rate of salary increase will add to the funding requirement, changes in this assumption did not have a major effect on the many seriously underfunded plans that are collectively bargained.[18] As for other actuarial assumptions, the evidence concerning any changes is much less developed for such factors as retirement age, employee turnover rates, the mortality table assumption, and separate discount rates used to value lump sum payments to retiring workers.

The discount rate assumption appeared to matter most in terms of underfunded plans, and it was moving in the opposite direction from market-based indicators during the period covered in this study. The set of discount rates that the PBGC uses for valuing the obligations of terminating underfunded pension plans provides one reference point with respect to just how much these trends have diverged.[19] (Table 2–5 reports these rates as of the end of each calendar year following 1981.) While interest rates assumed for funding purposes have been steadily moving up, the PBGC's benchmark

T A B L E 2–5

PBGC Interest Rates for Selected Dates

Date (End of Year)	Immediate Rate	Deferred K1[1]	Deferred K2
1981	11.00	10.25	9.00
1982	10.25	9.50	8.25
1983	9.50	8.75	7.50
1984	10.00	9.25	8.00
1985	9.00	8.25	7.00
1986	7.50	6.75	5.50
1987	8.25	7.50	6.25
1988	7.75	7.00	5.75
1989	7.25	6.50	5.25
1990	7.50	6.75	5.50
1991	6.75	6.00	4.75
1992	6.00	5.25	4.00
1993	4.25	4.00	4.00
1994	6.25	4.25	4.00

[1]All interest rates are reported here as percentages. However, the PBGC's K1 and K2 rates are published in the format of 1 plus the standard decimal notation (e.g., the K1 rate at the end of 1981 would be expressed as 1.1025). Adjustment algorithms documented in Appendix 2 assume the original format for all PBGC interest rates.

immediate rate declined from a high of 11 percent in 1981 to 8.25 percent at the end of 1987, to just 4.25 percent by the end of 1993. As market annuity rates decline, the present value of any obligation to pay a stream of regular benefits in the future goes up, suggesting the need for additional funding. Unfortunately, the actuarial practices favored between 1981 and 1987, as well as public policies adopted subsequently, seem to ignore this basic fact.

One additional caveat should be noted concerning the use of Form 5500 pension data from this period. The reported liabilities attributable to retirees in certain plans sponsored by airlines, among other companies, were covered by annuities purchased from insurance companies. A common practice in such cases even today is to report the present value for those liabilities as the cost of the annuities. In turn, the insurance companies may use an entirely different set of actuarial assumptions for calculating that cost. But these assumptions go unreported on Form 5500, and they differ substantially from the official assumptions reported for the plan. Hence, large disparities may develop between the reported value of vested benefits and their actual value upon actual termination.

ADJUSTMENTS TO PENSION DATA

The goal here in adjusting Form 5500 pension data is to produce a realistic set of estimates—as measured on a PBGC termination basis[20]—of changes in the actual condition of these plans as well as to achieve greater comparability across plans and categories of plans. The source of these data was the official U.S. Department of Labor Research Tapes that were prepared for the years 1981–1987. The separate tapes for each of these years include a stratified random sample of Form 5500 reports. Plan size, as measured by the number of participants in each plan, determined the probability of selection.

The "base case" results reported in Tables 2–6 through 2–12 represent estimates of the condition of the plans in the sample. Those estimates reflect adjustments to asset values in cases where Form 5500 was not reported on a calendar-year basis.[21] A detailed model was used to estimate end-of-calendar-year balances. It

TABLE 2-6

The Private Defined-Benefit Pension System: Actual and Reported Condition[1]

	1981		1986				1987			
			Base Case		Scenario B[2]		Base Case		Scenario B	
	Under-funded	Funded	Under-funded	Funded	Under-funded	Funded	Under-funded	Funded	Under-funded	Funded
Adjusted position[3]	−30,116 (7,767)[4]	166,355 (24,040)	−100,803 (28,198)	164,219 (17,348)	−66,241 (19,946)	202,925 (20,872)	−47,976 (7,345)	188,303 (17,064)	−32,014 (5,204)	231,394 (19,955)
Reported position	−32,868 (13,692)	101,653 (16,973)	40,357 (17,509)	229,057 (23,747)	17,693 (10,759)	251,502 (27,405)	1,043 (3,601)	230,079 (19,140)	−7,564 (3,128)	238,658 (19,190)
Percent plans underfunded (adjusted basis)	6.31 (.72)		20.52 (1.12)		14.72 (.98)		16.68 (.95)		11.72 (.82)	
Percent plans underfunded (reported basis)		21.80 (1.47)		9.81 (.85)				12.34 (.88)		
Reported less adjusted	15.59 (1.42)		−10.71 (.91)		−4.91 (.79)		−4.34 (.76)		.62 (.73)	
Adjusted vested benefit security ratio	1.45 (.08)		1.10 (.06)		1.25 (.07)		1.28 (.04)		1.45 (.04)	
Reported vested benefit security ratio		1.19 (.06)		1.64 (.04)				1.56 (.03)		
Adjusted less reported VBSR	.26 (.04)		−.54 (.04)		−.39 (.05)		−.28 (.01)		−.11 (.02)	

[1]Includes single-employer, defined-benefit plans with more than 100 participants.

[2]Scenario B assumes interest rates 100 basis points higher than the official PBGC rate set.

[3]Adjusted and reported positions are expressed in millions (000,000s) of dollars.

[4]Numbers in parentheses denote standard errors.

TABLE 2-7

Differences in Funding Status Across Years[1]

	1986 versus 1981[2]		1987 versus 1981	
	Base Case	Scenario B[3]	Base Case	Scenario B
Adjusted Unfunded Liability	−70,687,000[4] (22,634,700)[5]	−36,125,500 (14,486,800)	−17,859,700 (8,241,390)	−1,898,260 (7,401,870)
Adjusted Surplus	−2,133,790 (24,076,500)	36,571,900 (25,433,100)	21,948,800 (24,473,600)	65,039,300 (25,560,700)
Reported Unfunded Liability	73,225,000 (26,538,600)	50,560,500 (22,662,600)	33,910,400 (14,073,200)	25,304,000 (13,896,400)
Reported Surplus	127,404,000 (25,543,000)	149,849,000 (28,981,700)	128,424,000 (22,543,800)	137,003,000 (22,478,100)
Percent Plans Fully Funded (Adjusted Basis)	−14.21 (1.29)	−8.41 (1.17)	−10.37 (1.16)	−5.41 (1.04)
Percent Plans Fully Funded (Reported Basis)	12.00 (1.81)		9.46 (1.80)	
Adjusted Vested Benefit Security Ratio	−.35 (.05)	−.20 (.05)	−.17 (.07)	.00 (.07)
Reported Vested Benefit Security Ratio	.45 (.04)		.36 (.06)	

[1]Includes single-employer, defined-benefit plans with more than 100 participants.

[2]Monetary amounts expressed in thousands (000s) of dollars.

[3]Scenario B assumes interest rates 100 basis points higher than the official PBGC rate set.

[4]A negative sign indicates deterioration.

[5]Numbers in parentheses denote standard errors.

TABLE 2-8A

McNemar's Test for Symmetric Change in Adjusted Pension Funding Condition (Scenario A)

Union	Retiree Burden	Industry	Observations	Percent Underfunded 1981	Percent Underfunded 1987	z_c[1]	P-value
Yes	Light	Services	82	8.54	13.41	−1.11	.172
"	"	Manufacturing	128	10.16	16.41	−1.68	.058
"	Heavy	Services	56	21.43	37.50	−1.81	.011
"	"	Manufacturing	174	37.93	60.92	−5.10	.000
No	Light	Services	598	2.34	5.35	−3.31	.000
"	"	Manufacturing	341	3.52	9.68	−3.57	.000
"	Heavy	Services	101	14.85	26.73	−2.35	.011
"	"	Manufacturing	144	15.97	27.78	−3.18	.001
	All plans		1,624	9.98	17.92	−8.76	.000

[1]The z-scores (corrected for continuity) are reported for the convenience of the reader. The P-values were computed using the one-sided exact binomial test.

TABLE 2-8B

McNemar's Test for Symmetric Change in Adjusted Pension Funding Condition (Scenario B)

Union	Retiree Burden	Industry	Observations	Percent Underfunded 1981	Percent Underfunded 1987	z_c[1]	P-value
Yes	Light	Services	82	8.54	10.98	-.53	.363
"	"	Manufacturing	128	10.16	10.16	-.13	.605
"	Heavy	Services	56	21.43	21.43	-.20	.656
"	"	Manufacturing	174	37.93	48.85	-2.76	.003
No	Light	Services	598	2.34	3.34	-1.17	.143
"	"	Manufacturing	341	3.52	5.57	-1.42	.095
"	Heavy	Services	101	14.85	16.83	-.35	.407
"	"	Manufacturing	144	15.97	20.14	-1.23	.132
	All plans		1,624	9.98	12.56	-3.34	.000

[1]The z-scores (corrected for continuity) are reported for the convenience of the reader. The P-values were computed using the one-sided exact binomial test.

TABLE 2-9

McNemar's Test for Symmetric Change in Reported Pension Funding Condition

Union	Retiree Burden	Industry	Observations	Percent Underfunded 1981	Percent Underfunded 1987	z_c[1]	P-value
Yes	Light	Services	82	14.63	9.76	.94	.363
"	"	Manufacturing	128	32.81	13.28	4.55	.605
"	Heavy	Services	56	46.43	21.43	3.61	.656
"	"	Manufacturing	174	62.64	37.36	5.81	.003
No	Light	Services	598	7.20	3.18	3.46	.143
"	"	Manufacturing	341	9.09	5.28	2.18	.095
"	Heavy	Services	101	30.69	6.93	4.61	.407
"	"	Manufacturing	144	29.86	13.19	4.29	.132
	All plans		1,624	20.75	10.16	11.05	.000

[1]The z-scores (corrected for continuity) are reported for the convenience of the reader. The P-values were computed using the one-sided exact binomial test.

TABLE 2-10

Sample Design and Stratum-Level Estimates: 1981[1]

Stratum Number	(1) 1,000 or More Participants	(2) 500–999 Participants	(3) 250–499 Participants	(4) 100–249 Participants
Number of plans	4,043	3,285	5,293	10,515
Number of participants	22,414,000	2,303,000	1,875,000	1,590,000
Sample plans	1,812	267	189	230
Participants in sample plans	11,791,329	189,277	68,271	36,086
Percent plans underfunded (reported basis)	20.97 (.96)[2]	23.22 (2.59)	21.69 (3.01)	21.74 (2.73)
Percent plans underfunded (adjusted basis)	11.04 (.74)	9.74 (1.82)	7.94 (1.97)	2.61 (1.05)
Aggregate shortfall (adjusted)[3]	−29,284,900 (7,763,090)	−574,835 (216,175)	−169,631 (67,141)	−86,612 (64,530)
Aggregate surplus (adjusted)	140,422,000 (24,011,700)	10,624,800 (800,963)	7,900,540 (709,684)	7,407,340 (442,582)

[1]Includes single-employer, defined-benefit plans with more than 100 participants. An additional 175,099 plans with a total of 2,148,000 participants were in stratum 5. They were not processed because Form 5500 Schedule B is optional for plans with less than 100 participants.

[2]Numbers in parentheses denote standard errors.

[3]Aggregate shortfall (adjusted) and aggregate surplus (adjusted) are expressed in thousands (000s) of dollars.

TABLE 2-11

Sample Design and Stratum-Level Estimates: 1986[1]

Stratum Number	(1) 1,000 or More Participants		(2) 500–999 Participants		(3) 250–499 Participants		(4) 100–249 Participants	
Number of plans	4,331		3,302		4,995		9,797	
Number of participants	23,816,000		2,487,000		1,771,000		1,594,000	
Sample plans	2,061		368		291		373	
Participants in sample plans	11,811,521		276,794		104,911		64,082	
Percent plans underfunded (reported basis)	7.04 (.56)[2]		11.68 (1.68)		5.50 (1.34)		12.60 (1.72)	
	Base Case	Scenario B[3]	Base Case	Scenario B	Base Case	Scenario B	Base Case	Scenario B
Percent plans underfunded (adjusted basis)	19.55 (.87)	15.19 (.79)	22.28 (2.17)	15.49 (1.89)	18.90 (2.30)	12.71 (1.96)	21.18 (2.12)	15.28 (1.87)
Aggregate shortfall (adjusted)[4]	-91,768,500 (28,111,100)	-59,789,400 (19,863,100)	-4,950,070 (2,016,180)	-3,675,730 (1,647,240)	-2,102,070 (803,078)	-1,380,780 (690,210)	-1,982,330 (416,526)	-1,395,370 (320,624)
Aggregate surplus (adjusted)	133,424,000 (17,275,000)	166,332,000 (20,796,400)	12,509,200 (971,558)	14,741,100 (1,049,670)	9,639,200 (101,896)	11,500,300 (1,160,050)	8,647,360 (725,611)	10,351,500 (835,261)

[1]Includes single-employer, defined-benefit plans with more than 100 participants. An additional 136,965 plans with a total of 2,033,000 participants were in stratum 5. They were not processed because Form 5500 Schedule B is optional for plans with less than 100 participants.

[2]Numbers in parentheses denote standard errors.

[3]Scenario B assumes interest rates 100 basis points higher than the official PBGC rate set.

[4]Aggregate shortfall (adjusted) and aggregate surplus (adjusted) are expressed in thousands (000s) of dollars.

TABLE 2-12

Sample Design and Stratum-Level Estimates: 1987[1]

Stratum Number	(1) 1,000 or More Participants		(2) 500–999 Participants		(3) 250–499 Participants		(4) 100–249 Participants	
Number of plans	4,359		3,219		4,806		9,055	
Number of participants	24,504,000		2,417,000		1,689,000		1,490,000	
Sample plans	2,715		439		327		382	
Participants in sample plans	14,761,125		330,385		115,838		66,304	
Percent plans underfunded (reported basis)	10.24 (.58)[2]		15.26 (1.72)		10.40 (1.61)		13.35 (1.74)	
	Base Case	Scenario B[3]	Base Case	Scenario B	Base Case	Scenario B	Base Case	Scenario B
Percent plans underfunded (adjusted basis)	19.15 (.76)	14.15 (.67)	19.36 (1.89)	13.67 (1.64)	14.98 (1.98)	10.09 (1.69)	15.45 (1.85)	10.73 (1.59)
Aggregate shortfall (adjusted)[4]	-42,724,800 (7,215,490)	-28,357,000 (5,083,210)	-3,647,790 (1,348,160)	-2,674,970 (1,094,390)	-617,941 (149,609)	-339,558 (111,643)	-985,213 (221,717)	-642,564 (168,752)
Aggregate surplus (adjusted)	158,614,000 (17,019,100)	195,593,000 (19,906,800)	11,772,900 (755,684)	14,057,300 (841,439)	8,555,440 (711,010)	10,211,200 (783,201)	9,361,220 (681,840)	11,172,600 (778,916)

[1]Includes single-employer, defined-benefit plans with more than 100 participants. An additional 127,048 plans with a total of 1,830,000 participants were in Stratum 5. They were not processed because Form 5500 Schedule B is optional for plans with less than 100 participants.

[2]Numbers in parentheses denote standard errors.

[3]Scenario B assumes interest rates 100 basis points higher than the official PBGC rate set.

[4]Aggregate shortfall (adjusted) and aggregate surplus (adjusted) are expressed in thousands (000s) of dollars.

reflected the returns to four principal categories of pension assets (i.e., equities, fixed-income securities, cash equivalents, and other assets); the flow of funds between those categories; new pension contributions; and benefit payments.[22] To ensure greater consistency among the data, this adjustment was made to asset values for all noncalendar-year filers. Estimates for the so-called reported condition of these plans, as well as for the adjusted condition, reflect the resulting differences.[23]

The base case estimates also reduced total reported asset values by the amount of any receivables for employer contributions. In addition, they reflected changes on the liability side that were designed to reexpress the value of vested benefits as an approximation of the official PBGC termination liability. The adjustments to the liability side also reflect the date of the actuarial valuation (i.e., the effect of the passage of time); the benefit accruals between the valuation date and the end of the calendar year in question; a common early retirement age; the use of dedicated bond portfolios;[24] the mortality table assumption; and most importantly, a common discount rate. Table 2–13 reports the proportion of plans using dedication according to annual surveys conducted by Greenwich Associates. Table 2–14 shows the discount rates assumed in this adjustment. No previous study has based universe estimates on such extensive adjustments to the U.S. Department of Labor Form 5500 sample data.[25] Appendix 2 includes a detailed description of liability adjustments.

ESTIMATED FUNDING LEVELS

Table 2–6 reports universe estimates for the aggregate surplus and unfunded liability of the single-employer, defined-benefit pension system for 1981, 1986, and 1987.[26] The period began with plans that were actually underfunded on an economic basis reporting an estimated unfunded liability of almost $33 billion. At that time, the base case adjusted shortfall was slightly less, at $30.1 billion, for these same underfunded plans when asset and liability values were marked to market. However, the baseline estimates of the unfunded

TABLE 2-13

Use of Dedicated Portfolios by Plan Size[1]

Total Plan Assets	1981	1982	1983	1984	1985	1986	1987
Over $1 billion	14%	17%	28%	21%	37%	39%	33%
$501–1,000 million	11	24	19	30	50	40	30
$351–500 million	16	27	29	30	39	35	25
$251–350 million			20	17	28	33	41
$201–250 million	23	22	17	27	34	40	25
$151–200 million	22	13	19	19	27	22	22
$101–150 million	10	16	20	13	29	30	29
$ 76–100 million	17	11	21	25	26	25	15
$ 51–75 million	6	14	9	14	24	15	12
$ 41–50 million	14	9	13	17	13	16	23
$ 31–40 million	11	9	11	6	10	11	9
$ 21–30 million	11	10	19	6	14	12	15
$ 16–20 million	9	16	19	7	11	20	9
$ 11–15 million	4	11	15				
$ 5–10 million	1	7	14				
Under $5 million	0	0					

[1]From annual surveys conducted by Greenwich Associates, Inc. In some years, reported percentages also include immunized portfolios.

TABLE 2-14

Assumed Discount Rates Used for Dedicated Portfolio Adjustment[1]

1981	15.06
1982	14.94
1983	12.78
1984	13.49
1985	12.05
1986	9.71
1987	9.91

[1]This adjustment assumed the Moody's average rate for corporate bonds. See U.S. Department of Commerce, *Business Statistics, 1961–88*, (26th ed.), p. 74.

liability showed substantial changes in 1986, rising to approximately
$101 billion before falling to $48 billion in 1987.[27]

Figure 2–1 depicts 95 percent confidence intervals[28] for these
estimates and plots the course of the PBGC's benchmark immediate
annuity rate, which was used to discount the value of adjusted benefits attributable to retired lives. A simple visual inspection of the
chart reveals the strong negative correlation between the size of the
unfunded liability and the discount rate. Another striking feature of
the base case unfunded liability estimates in Table 2–6 concerns the
difference between the adjusted value of $101 billion for 1986 and
the $40.4 billion surplus that the sponsors of these same plans
reported for that year. By 1987, this difference had narrowed substantially, but the actual unfunded liability after these adjustments
remained almost $48 billion higher than the reported values.

Table 2–6 also reports the estimated proportion of plans that
were underfunded on both an adjusted basis and reported basis.
Here, the base case story is even more compelling. The proportion of

FIGURE 2-1

**Confidence Intervals for Total Unfunded Pension Liabilities
(Based on Sample Data for 1981, 1986, and 1987)**

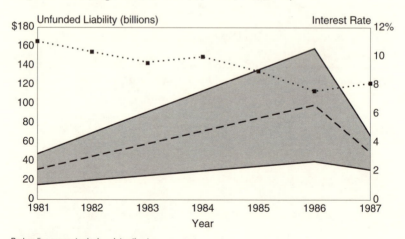

Broken line connects single point estimates.

Solid lines indicate boundaries of the 95% confidence interval.

Dotted line reflects changes in the PBGC immediate annuity rate.

plans which were fully funded on an adjusted basis fell by 14.21 percent between 1981 and 1986 and by 10.37 percent between 1981 and 1987. The standard errors in Table 2–7 indicate that both of these differences were statistically significant at the 1 percent level. The data reported by plan sponsors meanwhile gave the opposite impression, but also at extremely high levels of statistical significance.

In addition, Table 2–7 reports the estimated differences between several other indicators of funding status across years. Differences in the base case adjusted unfunded liability are more than two standard errors for the two comparisons across the period: between 1981 and 1986, and between 1981 and 1987.[29] On the other hand, the differences in the reported data create exactly the opposite impression—that is, that there were statistically significant improvements at the 5 percent level. These large divergences between changes in the actual and reported condition of underfunded plans call into question the actuarial and accounting practices that were in widespread use at the time.

With respect to the highly publicized growth of the surplus assets, the evidence that such improvement really occurred is not persuasive, either for the period 1981–1986 or the period 1981–1987. Nevertheless, sponsors of plans that were adequately funded reported improvements, compared to their position in 1981, of more than $127 billion for both periods. Tables 2–10, 2–11, and 2–12 report stratum-level estimates for the three years covered in the study. A striking feature of the base case results here is the relatively larger increase in the proportion of underfunded plans with 250 participants or less, in the face of deterioration across the board.

IMPLICATIONS FOR BENEFIT SECURITY

Another indicator of the health of defined-benefit pension plans is the *vested-benefit security ratio* (VBSR). This measure is simply the ratio of plan assets to vested benefits.[30] Estimates of the VBSR are also reported in Tables 2–6 and 2–7. Of course, the VBSR in most cases will be higher than the *benefit security ratio* (BSR). The BSR is a broader measure reflecting the extent to which all accrued benefits are secured by plan assets. Neither measure taken by itself, however, is an appropriate or revealing indicator of benefit security when plans are simply grouped for an average. Still, they can be very useful for comparing different formulations of that ratio (e.g., the actual versus the reported benefit security ratio) as well as the averages for groups of plans across years.

An essential feature of the VBSR is that it reflects the nominal value of benefits as of a given valuation date. Even in the presence of pension insurance such as that currently provided by the PBGC, the VBSR ignores the large economic losses that workers sustain when a plan is terminated. Participants often pay for and expect some post-retirement inflation protection,[31] only to find their benefits frozen at levels determined by the amount of the guarantee upon termination. Moreover, the amount of coinsurance (i.e., the losses workers absorb as a result of plan termination) is also quite volatile and extremely sensitive to changes in market interest rates.[32] To summarize, the implications of these calculations for benefit security are, from the plan participant's point of view, quite limited. The VBSR is much more useful as an indicator of the ultimate risk to taxpayers and as a tool for policymakers as they consider problems confronting the insurance program.

From Table 2–6, we note that the adjusted base case VBSR stood at a robust 1.45 in 1981. It fell substantially to 1.10 in 1986, and it remained far below the 1981 level in 1987 as well. The standard errors for these differences reported on Table 2–7 indicate that the declines between 1981 and 1986, as well as those occurring those between 1981 and 1987, were significant at the 1 percent level. Meanwhile, a similar measure based on unadjusted data reports highly significant improvements for both periods.

MEASURING CHANGE AMONG SUBSAMPLES

Seven dichotomous indicator variables extend the above analysis to overlapping subsamples of interest. These were either taken directly from Form 5500 or constructed from data reported on the form. First, a union affiliation variable identified those plans that were subject to collective bargaining on behalf of blue-collar workers. Second, a retiree burden indicator revealed whether the ratio of current retirees to other participants fell in the top quartile of the sample. Third, the four-digit standard industrial classification code indentified the line of business as either manufacturing or service. Fourth and fifth, the adjustments to reported Form 5500 data discussed above provided classification of plans as either underfunded or not on December 31, 1981 and 1987. Sixth and seventh, the unadjusted data provided classification of plans as underfunded or not on these same dates.

With respect to repeated measures on the same sample relative to the adequacy of plan assets, McNemar's test offers the advantage of greater precision compared to a test using independent samples.[33] In this case, McNemar's test determined the equality of the binary response (i.e., a change in the funded status of the plan) from two populations: underfunded and adequately funded plans in 1981. Basically, it measured the rate at which adequately funded plans deteriorated to the point of becoming underfunded, and whether this equaled the rate at which underfunded plans improved to become adequately funded.[34] Corrected for continuity, the test statistic used here can be expressed as

$$z_c = \frac{\left(\left|n_{21} - n_{12}\right| - .5\right) \times \text{sign}\left(n_{21} - n_{12}\right)}{\sqrt{\left(n_{21} + n_{12}\right)}}$$

where

n_{21} = Plans underfunded in 1981 but adequately funded in 1987.

n_{12} = Plans underfunded in 1987 but adequately funded in 1981.

$\text{sign}(n_{21} - n_{12})$ = 1 when $n_{21} > n_{12}$ and -1 when $n_{21} < n_{12}$

The distribution of the statistic z_c can be approximated by a normal distribution and then used to indicate the direction of change—as well as the significance of that direction—between the beginning and end of the period.

Tables 2–8A, 2–8B, and 2–9 clearly indicate that union plans were underfunded in much higher proportions than nonunion plans in both 1981 and 1987. The results strongly suggest, however, that union affiliation was not a determinant of the observed deterioration. The direction of change was uniformly negative and highly significant both for the sample as a whole and for those plans in every subsample except two that involved union plans with a relatively light burden for current retirees. This trend stands in stark contrast with conditions that plan sponsors were reporting as shown in Table 2–9. Here, the story is simple. Unadjusted data show highly significant improvement in every subsample except those for unionized plans in service industries that did not have the burden of a relatively high proportion of current retirees.

SENSITIVITY ANALYSIS

To examine the sensitivity of these trends to discount rate assumptions used in 1986 and 1987, 100 basis points were added to the PBGC rate set for those years. The estimates then were recomputed. Tables 2–6, 2–7, 2–8B, 2–11, and 2–12 report these "Scenario B" results. In this scenario, aggregate unfunded liabilities remain considerably larger than plan sponsors were reporting in both years but not as large as those estimated in the base case.[35] However, the total surplus attributable to adequately funded plans increased by considerable amounts. Compared to the base case in 1981, the total unfunded liability rose in both years. This deterioration was significant at the 1 percent level in 1986, but not significant even at the 10 percent level in 1987. Meanwhile, the adjusted surplus grew in both years but by amounts that were significant at the 5 percent level only in 1987. Consistent with these shifts, the adjusted VBSR continued to show a deterioration that was significant at the 1 percent level in 1986. However, we cannot reject the hypothesis that there was no change in this indicator between 1981 and 1987 under the Scenario B assumptions.

The proportion of plans that were fully funded continued to show highly significant declines for both years, according to Table 2–7. The results at the subsample level, on the other hand, were not quite as robust. The deterioration was highly significant only for union plans in the manufacturing sector with a heavy burden for current retirees. Still, the test statistics reported in Table 2.8B retained the same negative sign observed in the baseline estimates.

INTERPRETATION

The evidence presented here demonstrates that, by several key measures, the actual condition of the single-employer, defined-benefit pension system experienced significant deterioration between 1981 and 1987. In some respects, the adjusted estimates of both the unfunded liability and the aggregate surplus are understated, given the exclusion of plans with less than 100 participants and the partial omission of the additional cost of maintaining all defined-benefit plans on an ongoing basis. These findings are at odds with previous assessments disclosed by government and other sources regarding conditions during this period.[36] For example, only in 1992 did the PBGC raise its own estimate of the *current* unfunded liability by 28 percent to $51 billion. Two years later the Agency's estimate had risen further to $71 billion. On the other hand, some find consolation in the growth of surplus pension assets held in adequately funded plans. Even here, the improvement was considerably less than advertised. This growth was statistically significant at the 5 percent level only under the Scenario B assumptions at the end of 1987.

Subsequent developments are not encouraging. The mismatch between the duration of pension assets and liabilities typically leads to an erosion in funded condition as interest rates fall. As noted in Table 2.5, interest rates declined during the seven years following 1987 by as much as they did during the period covered in the study. However, the Department of Labor has not compiled sample tapes for any year subsequent to 1987. Alternative data sources available at the time of this study reveal far less and cannot be adjusted at the same level of detail. So, we are left to ask: was this system in serious trouble then, and just how stable is it today? Many believe that the answer is relative. As recently as 1983, only 16.3 percent of all Savings & Loan associations were insolvent as well.[37]

Others emphasize that a pension plan is not directly analogous to a savings and loan because the plan's most important asset is the ability of the sponsor to provide additional funding in the future. Unlike a pension plan, most savings and loans were organized as stand-alone operations. Notwithstanding that well-taken point, many of America's largest employers would be insolvent if the true value of their pension liabilities was recognized on corporate balance sheets.[38]

In fact, the parallels between recent trends in the defined-benefit pension system and the initial stages of the savings and loan disaster are striking in several other respects. At its peak, the S&L system held approximately $1 trillion in assets guaranteed by the Federal Savings and Loan Insurance Corporation. Today, private defined-benefit pension plans appear to have incurred roughly the same amount in benefit obligations insured by the PBGC. In both cases, a severe mismatch between the duration of assets and liabilities exposed the government insurance fund to substantial interest rate risk. In another similarity, the process of financial regulation became heavily politicized, with high attendant costs resulting from interference by political figures. The fact that this study itself was forced to rely on sample data ending in 1987 provides compelling testimony that the information essential for effective regulation is almost totally lacking.

In both cases, government authorities tolerated and even encouraged the use of fictitious reporting practices. Federal policies that were intended to protect the insurance fund from imminent losses or to increase federal tax revenues in the short term also worked to increase risks facing both insurance programs.[39] Finally, the classic insurance problem of moral hazard encouraged risk taking on the part of both types of institutions at the expense of their respective insurance funds.[40]

CAVEATS AND QUALIFICATIONS

A serious potential shortcoming of the aggregate surplus and unfunded liability estimates reported above is the impression they sometimes create that surplus pension assets in one plan can be used to offset the unfunded liabilities of another. This is clearly not the case. In fact, sponsors of adequately funded pension plans object vigorously to suggestions that such transfers should be made through the pension insurance system. Taking this approach to reforming the pension insurance system would constitute one of the most perverse industrial policies imaginable, since it would involve potentially massive subsidies to declining sectors of the economy and the least efficient economic performers.

Another shortcoming is that the categorical data analysis presented in Tables 2–8A, 2–8B, and 2–9 ignores the stratified sampling design. Since the Department of Labor stratified the pension data used here according to the number of participants in each plan and assigned very different probabilities of selection to each stratum, readers should treat these unweighted results with caution.[41] Unfortunately, the limited size of the eight subsamples of interest does not permit the use of tests and models capable of analyzing cross-classified data that arise from more complex sample designs (e.g., those relying on stratification). Still, it is possible to draw tentative inferences from the unweighted results despite this shortcoming. At the time of the study, they were based on the best data available and are therefore reported here.[42]

An additional caveat that deserves mention stems from the unusually high incidence of nonresponse. In this case, nonresponse resulted from reporting omissions. U.S. Department of Labor employees involved with the preparation of the sample tapes attribute many of these omissions to plan sponsors as they completed the Form 5500. Further omissions occurred later when government contractors converted the reported data into machine-readable form. The adjustment algorithms used for this project depended altogether on a dozen liability-side variables that therefore had a high joint probability of either being missing or containing characters the computer interpreted as errors or omissions. Furthermore, the asset-side adjustments for noncalendar-year filers depended on valid data for up to 59 additional variables. As a result, only about 40 percent of the observations in the sample could be processed.

While this may seem to be an unusually severe level of nonresponse, no systematic problem could be identified as a contributing source among the four sampling strata studied here.[43] It therefore seems reasonable to assume that plans included in the processed samples were underfunded in the same proportion as plans that could not be processed.[44] If this issue becomes a major concern, users of the study can improve estimates derived from the sample by consulting more carefully edited data for plans and their participant counts on Department of Labor "Universe Tapes" and then by incorporating the appropriate regression techniques.[45] Finally, the use of data collected directly from companies in the sample—particularly with respect to the dedicated bond portfolios—undoubtedly would enhance the estimates of unfunded liabilities reported above.

PUBLIC POLICY IMPLICATIONS

The fact that the actual condition of the private defined-benefit pension system appears to have deteriorated and probably was much worse than the reported data indicate does not necessarily argue for more stringent minimum funding requirements. Such a change would presume that reducing unfunded liabilities also reduces the value of federal pension insurance and, at the same time, the attendant risks to taxpayers. The unfunded pension liability is just one measure of risk to the insurance system. Unfortunately, the probability of firm bankruptcy also increases when weak companies finance additional contribution requirements with corporate debt or working capital. Given the inextricable link between the health of a pension plan and the creditworthiness of its sponsor, the resources and prospects of the combined enterprise must be taken into account when evaluating this problem. We will examine this link more thoroughly in Chapters 3 and 4.

With respect to those plans that were fully funded on a PBGC termination basis, the fact that the growth of surplus pension assets was considerably less than advertised calls into question the wisdom of the congressional action reducing the maximum funding limit in the Omnibus Budget Reconciliation Act of 1987. Before the new law was enacted, plan sponsors established a well-documented trend of relaxing actuarial assumptions in response to major investment gains during the 1980s. This, in turn, permitted lower contributions that helped produce the erosion detected in the data. Coming on the heels of all of this, OBRA '87 then restricted the ability of sponsors to contribute to their defined-benefit pension plans while at the same time making the range of permissible contributions far less predictable. Some actuaries even concluded that the law could limit funding to less than the ERISA minimum standard, since the OBRA '87 Full Funding Limitation was, after all, based on termination liabilities rather than going-concern liabilities.[46] Rolling back this provision for the purpose of providing plan sponsors with greater flexibility to fund their plans when business conditions are good may well be worth the cost in terms of lost tax revenues.

Notwithstanding differences in the samples for these three years, the results presented above are important not so much for what they amount to on the dates used in the study, as for the direction of change they reveal and for the very substantial sensitivity they have demonstrated relative to changes in market interest rates. For the insurance fund, this means that in addition to assuming major credit risks, substantial unhedged interest rate risk compounds the direct long-term threat to American taxpayers. This risk will persist regardless of the value of any unfunded liabilities at a particular moment and regardless of the current state of the economy.

Is this risk offset by the interest rate exposure associated with other federal programs? Clearly, the mismatch between the duration of pension assets and liabilities is opposite to that seen in the banking system as well as in other depository institutions guaranteed by the federal government. Some therefore might be tempted to argue that the ERISA pension termination insurance program produces a "gain from diversification." Yet any advantage from diversification must be examined in the context of all federal exposure to interest rate risk. Federal credit demands generally tend to run counter to those of other borrowers over the course of the business cycle. Income taxes grow more rapidly than the economy itself, assuming that tax rates remain unchanged, when economic activity expands. Conversely, federal borrowing grows during recessions, when tax revenues fall and spending on unemployment compensation and other income support programs increases. The interest rate risk associated with the current

ERISA termination insurance program consequently has a high positive correlation with major cyclical risks to the federal budget.[47] Moreover, the claim of any major gain from diversification is weakened as long as the programs in question suffer from a large measure of moral hazard and adverse selection. So, it would seem that a defense of ERISA pension insurance on grounds of diversification fails to hold up under close examination.

SUMMARY

The goal of this chapter was to mark pension assets and liabilities to market values using sample data for 1981, 1986, and 1987. At the beginning of the 1980s, the actual condition of private defined-benefit pension plans was considerably better than sponsors were reporting because interest rates had risen to unprecedented levels. However, this situation had reversed by the middle of the decade, in a pattern of change that extended to union and nonunion plans alike in both the manufacturing and service sectors.

Large divergences between the actual and reported condition of underfunded plans call into question actuarial and accounting practices that were in widespread use at the time. Confidence intervals for aggregate unfunded liabilities range from a low of between $16 billion and $51 billion in 1981 to a high of between $51 billion and $163 billion in 1986. An estimated 6.9 percent of all single-employer, defined-benefit plans were less than fully funded in 1981, while 17.3 percent of these plans were underfunded in 1986.

These results are consistent with the widely held belief that the condition of a typical defined-benefit plan will erode as interest rates decline. With respect to the government's termination insurance program operated by the PBGC, the findings strongly suggest that, in addition to major credit risks, substantial interest rate risk also represents a long-term threat to taxpayers. This risk will persist regardless of the value of unfunded liabilities at any particular moment and regardless of the current state of the economy.

Although the results presented in this chapter are highly relevant to the current debate about PBGC reforms, it is much more important for policymakers to focus on the credit quality of private pension promises and on the value of the ERISA termination insurance guarantee. At the root of the problem facing the PBGC are the perverse behavioral incentives created by the gap between the value of this insurance and the premiums the agency charges.

ENDNOTES

1. See William F. Marples, *Actuarial Aspects of Pension Security* (Homewood, IL: Richard D. Irwin, 1965), p. 64.

2. See Table 2–1 as well as U.S. Department of Labor, Pension and Welfare Benefits Administration, *Trends in Pensions 1992*, (Washington DC: U.S. Government Printing Office 1992) p. 597. By way of contrast, Table 2–2 reports total contributions to defined-contribution plans.

3. Form 5500 is filed annually by sponsors of qualified employee benefit plans. It is an interagency form required by the U.S. Internal Revenue Service, the U.S. Department of Labor, and the Pension Benefit Guaranty Corporation.

4. Detailed information concerning actuarial assumptions is not collected in machine-readable form for each of the 65,000 defined-benefit pension plans that are currently insured by the Pension Benefit Guaranty Corporation. Only sample data are available for the period 1981–87.

5. Throughout this chapter, the term *discount rate* refers to the rate used to calculate the present value of a future cash benefit payment. Actuaries sometimes refer to the same rate as the *interest rate,* and instructions for the Form 5500 state that the interest rate assumption should reflect expected investment returns. Although the Form 5500 interest and discount rates were identical during this period, they need not be the same in corporate financial reports to shareholders.

6. Table 2–3 reports both nominal and real asset levels for defined-benefit plans. Table 2–4 includes the same information for defined-contribution plans.

7. As interest rates rise, the present value of future benefit payments falls. At the same time, the value of pension assets is reduced but to a lesser extent, due to, among other factors, the tendency of a defined-benefit plan to hold precautionary cash balances.

8. In other words, the firm's cost of borrowing.

9. See Fischer Black, "Estimating Expected Return," *Financial Analysts Journal*, September–October 1993, pp. 36–39.

10. The Omnibus Budget Reconciliation Act of 1987 established a corridor of permissible interest rate assumptions and thereby reduced flexibility in this area. The corridor was narrowed slightly by the Retirement Protection Act of 1994.

11. The PBGC used a table derived from the Unisex Pension-1984 (UP-84) mortality table before the Retirement Protection Act of 1994 was signed into law.

12. The PBGC subsequently revised its method for setting the official interest rates to more closely reflect differences in mortality table assumptions.

13. See Alicia H. Munnell and Leah M. Cook, "Explaining the Postwar Pattern of Personal Saving," *New England Economic Review*, November–December 1991, pp. 17–28.

14. A defined-contribution plan resembles a tax-exempt savings account. It promises only the initial contributions plus subsequent investment returns. On the other hand, a defined-benefit plan makes regular benefit payments to retired workers based on their previous earnings and length of service. As stated earlier, there is no direct link between contributions made on behalf of workers and their retirement benefits.

15. An anonymous reviewer pointed out that, based on Tables 2–3 and 2–4, the ratio of average assets per participant for defined-benefit plans relative to defined-contribution plans only went down from 1.34 in 1981 to 1.31 in 1989. However, in order to assert that there was little change in assets required to meet pension needs (i.e., in those assets available from defined-pension plans relative to defined-contribution plans), it would be necessary to show that the age distributions of vested participants in these two systems also remained relatively stable. If anything, the proliferation of defined-contribution plans, together with demographic changes in the labor force during the 1980s, would have produced a younger participant age distribution for that type of plan. These changes suggest the possibility of a substantial improvement, in terms of assets per participant, among defined-contribution plans relative to defined-benefit plans when one considers participant age.

16. For example, see "Survey of Actuarial Assumptions and Funding," The Wyatt Company, Washington D.C., various years. Some of this increase may be due to the "corridor" for interest rate assumptions es-

tablished by the Omnibus Budget Reconciliation Act of 1987. The corridor tracks bond rates on a lagged basis; in April 1993 it ranged from 7.16 percent to 8.75 percent. For additional background, see Joseph Applebaum, "Trends in Actuarial Assumptions, Cost Methods, and Funded Status of Defined Benefit Pension Plans," in John A. Turner and Daniel J. Beller, eds., *Trends in Pensions 1992* (Washington, DC: U.S. Department of Labor, 1992), pp. 509–29.

17. See The Wyatt Company, "Survey," various years.

18. The benefits of collectively bargained plans typically are renegotiated approximately every three years or during each new round of collective bargaining. In effect, these plans become de facto final pay plans as a result of an entire series of amendments. However, the cost of future amendments cannot be prefunded under current IRS regulations. The combined effect of the collective bargaining process and these IRS regulations has been to weaken the condition of many plans which cover hourly workers.

19. The PBGC uses rates based on monthly surveys of private insurance companies active in the group annuity market.

20. In general, the PBGC termination liability includes all vested benefits up to the maximum guaranteed amount which were granted under provisions of the plan at least five years prior to the date of plan termination. The maximum benefit is indexed to rise with inflation at the same rate as social security. For 1993, it was set at $2,437.50 per month. The PBGC termination liability therefore may not be as large as the vested benefit obligation in cases where vested benefits exceed the maximum guaranteed amount or where benefits have been improved within the previous five years. On the other hand, the termination liability usually is somewhat smaller than the liability for vested benefits of an ongoing plan.

21. Plan sponsors may file Form 5500 based on a fiscal year or "plan year" of their choosing.

22. Investment performance was assumed to equal the quarterly measures published by Wilshire Associates, Inc., as part of the "Trust Universe Comparison Service."

23. See Appendix 1 for documentation for this "imputed flows" model.

24. A dedicated bond portfolio matches the cash flows from bond interest payments and from principal repayments with the benefit payments anticipated in connection with a specific group of liabilities (usually those attributable to retired lives). In connection with the Form 5500

pension data used here, the presence of dedicated portfolios was problematic. Sponsors were known to report dedicated assets at market value. At the same time, many of them used the higher discount rates, which were equal to the yield on the dedicated bonds for valuing the dedicated liabilities. However, the only interest rate assumption reported on Schedule B and on the official Department of Labor sample tapes was the lower one that applied to the remaining benefit liabilities. It therefore appeared that the liability value had been obtained by using the lower reported rate even though it actually was estimated by using the dedicated rate. Tabulations based on an unadjusted reading of Department of Labor universe and sample tapes can materially understate the value of plan liabilities for this reason.

25. For example, an unpublished study prepared at the PBGC simply adjusted reported liabilities to the PBGC immediate annuity rate. Based on this method, the agency produced estimates of $10.3 billion in unfunded liabilities in 1981, $20.7 billion in 1986, and $22.3 billion in 1987. See "Briefing on Risks, Trends, Forecasts, and Modelling to 1993 PBGC Working Group," March 15, 1993.

26. The Department of Labor database used in this analysis consisted of a stratified sample where selection probabilities were constant within each stratum but different across strata. For background on developing universe estimates from a stratified simple random sample, see Leslie Kish, *Survey Sampling* (New York: John Wiley & Sons, 1965), pp. 75–104; and William G. Cochran, *Sampling Techniques*, 3d ed. (New York: John Wiley & Sons, 1977), pp. 89–111.

27. Based on results of the sensitivity analysis discussed later, it seems plausible that approximately half of the difference in total unfunded liabilities reported for 1986 and 1987 was attributable to differences in these two samples.

28. A 95 percent confidence interval will span the distance of approximately two standard errors above and below the single point estimate.

29. This indicates that the observed deterioration according to this measure was statistically significant at the 5 percent level.

30. For a discussion of appropriate methods for estimating ratios, see Cochran, *Sampling Techniques,* pp. 150–88.

31. Such increases can become an important tacit feature of a company's retirement program, even though the cost-of-living adjustments remain voluntary on the part of the sponsor.

32. For a discussion of the coinsurance feature of federal pension insurance, see Richard A. Ippolito, *The Economics of Pension Insurance,* (Philadelphia: Pension Research Council of the Wharton School at the University of Pennsylvania, 1989), pp. 10, 21–4, 37, 183–84.

33. McNemar's test evaluates symmetry about the main diagonal of a two-way contingency table. See Alan Agresti, *Categorical Data Analysis* (New York: John Wiley & Sons, 1990), pp. 347–51.

34. Stratification was ignored in this part of the study because category sample sizes were too small to do otherwise.

35. The difference in the aggregate unfunded liability for 1986 between the base case and Scenario B suggests that perhaps half of the volatility detected in the universe estimates between 1986 and 1987 may be attributable to differences in the samples for those years.

36. See Ippolito, *The Economics of Pension Insurance,* p. 46.

37. See Lawrence J. White, *The S&L Debacle* (New York: Oxford University Press, 1991), pp. 86–7.

38. Financial Accounting Standard 87 requires some, but not complete, balance sheet recognition of these liabilities.

39. See Sylvester J. Schieber and John B. Shoven, "The Consequences of Population Aging on Private Pension Fund Saving and Asset Markets," September 1993.

40. With respect to pensions, the IRS plan audit program has contributed to the increase in interest rate assumptions discussed earlier. In addition, IRS regulations prohibit advance funding of reasonably anticipated benefit increases negotiated in connection with collectively bargained plans. As a result, these plans typically become underfunded over time. For additional background on incentive problems and regulatory failures plaguing these two programs, see White, *The S&L Debacle*; and Zvi Bodie, "The Pension Benefit Guaranty Corporation: Is the PBGC the FSLIC of the Nineties?" *Contingencies*, March–April 1992, pp. 34–38.

41. However, the universe estimates presented ealier do not suffer from this shortcoming.

42. The analysis of data from the one stratum covering plans with 1,000 or more participants yielded very similar results. In that case, the problem of unequal probabilities of selection was avoided.

43. The four sampling strata included plans with more than 100 participants. Four additional strata on the sample tapes cover smaller plans.

In these cases, Form 5500 Schedule B (containing actuarial data) is an optional submission. For this reason, nonresponse in this range was higher still and subject to potentially extreme bias. Plans with less than 100 participants therefore were not included in this study.

44. Of course, this assumption was made at the stratum level in that part of the study reflecting the sample design (i.e., the universe estimates of unfunded liabilities and the aggregate surplus). The same assumption was also made at the universe level in the unweighted categorical analysis.

45. See Jelke G. Bethlehem, "Reduction of Nonresponse Bias through Regression Estimation," *Journal of Official Statistics,* 1988, pp. 251–60; and Elizabeth T. Huang and Wayne A. Fuller, "Nonnegative Regression Estimation for Sample Survey Data," *Proceedings of the Social Statistics Section of the American Statistical Association,* 1978, pp. 300–303.

46. See Edwin C. Hustead, Toni S. Hustead, and Robert H. Selles, "OBRA 1987: The Impact of Limiting Contributions to Defined-Benefit Plans" (Washington, DC: Hay/Huggins Company, Inc., September 1989), p. iii.

47. For a discussion of federal borrowing activity over the course of the business cycle, see Paul Meek, *U.S. Monetary Policy and Financial Markets* (New York: Federal Reserve Bank of New York, 1982), pp.170–71.

PENSION ASSET FORECASTING ALGORITHMS

While it is true that Form 5500 calendar-year filers accounted for approximately 78 percent of private pension assets, the remaining noncalendar-year assets create a substantial inconsistency within the official flow of funds accounts compiled by the Federal Reserve Board. For this reason, the Flow of Funds Section at the Federal Reserve developed a deterministic model to adjust noncalendar-year asset data to a calendar-year basis. We used the same model in the context of this project to restate noncalendar-year asset values. This appendix documents its essential features.

The model utilizes beginning and ending Form 5500 balances for each asset category, together with the quarterly Trust Universe Comparison Service indexes of returns to pension assets compiled by Wilshire Associates, Inc. Altogether, 29 Form 5500 investment assets were included in the four broader categories for which end-of-calendar-year balances were estimated: equities, fixed income securities, cash equivalents, and other assets.

The arithmetic needed to arrive at the category-level estimates differs somewhat in the case of a *net inflow* from that needed in the case of a *net outflow*. The first step was to examine evidence of a flow or F_{Ri}. In the case of a net inflow, F_{Ri} represents the difference between the ending asset balance, as reported on Form 5500, and the expected ending balance (i.e., the beginning asset balance adjusted by the value of the Wilshire category-level performance measure for the full year). The algebraic expression is

$$F_{Ri} = E_i - [B_i \times (1 + I_{Ai})]$$

where F_{Ri} is the evidence of a flow, E_i is the ending balance, B_i is the beginning balance, and I_{Ai} is the annual performance measure, all for asset category i. Thus, in the case of a net inflow, F_{Ri} measures the residual evidence concerning the flow observable at the end of the year. That magnitude, of course, includes a return earned on the amount of the flow after the period during the year when the flow occurs. The second step of the algorithm, therefore, draws an inference about the amount that actually flowed into a particular asset category. It does so by using the appropriate Wilshire index to adjust for the estimated value of the return that followed the occurrence of the inflow. The *imputed flow* therefore can be interpreted as the net new money coming into an asset segment or, alternatively, the change in asset levels that is not explained by investment returns. Flows resulting from reallocation of these assets were assumed to occur once and instantaneously halfway through the fiscal year.

Algebraically,

$$F_i = \frac{F_{Ri}}{\left(1 + I_{Li}\right)}$$

where, again for asset category i, F_i is the imputed flow and I_{Li} is the performance measure for the last six months of the year. For a specific pension plan, the accuracy of the resulting estimate of imputed flows will depend on the extent to which investment experience of the plan conforms with the Wilshire performance measure as well as on the timing of reallocation across categories.

On the other hand, when there has been a net outflow, the model measures F_{Ri} with reference to the beginning of the year. In this case, F_{Ri} is defined as the difference between the Form 5500 beginning asset balance and the ending balance deflated by the value of the annual index. Consistent with the terms used above,

$$F_{Ri} = \frac{E_i}{\left(1 + I_{Ai}\right)}$$

Thus, F_{Ri} does not reflect the return that was earned prior to the time of an outflow. However, the same assumption that reallocation across categories occurs halfway through the plan year applies for

both net inflows and net outflows. In both cases, the FRB algorithms
assume that plan sponsors implement no deliberate choices to rede-
ploy assets across these four categories but not necessarily within
them during the first half of the year. For cases involving net outflows, the second part of the algorithm therefore imputes a return to
the realized flow during the first half of the year. Here,

$$F_i = F_{Ri} \times (1 + I_{Fi})$$

where, for asset category i, I_{Fi} is the performance measure for the
first six months of the year. This, of course, contrasts with the algorithm for the case of a net inflow where a return is estimated for the
amount of the imputed flow during the second half of the year. As a
final step, the algorithm computes an ending balance based on three
factors: the beginning balance, the imputed flow, and the returns
indicated by the performance measure.

Three Wilshire series for pension plan investment performance
(corresponding to equities, fixed income investments, and cash
equivalents) provided a basis for these estimates. However, it was
necessary to develop a blended index for use with a fourth category
consisting of investment company holdings,[48] real estate, insurance
contracts, and other investments. Although Wilshire produces an
index for a category it designates as *other assets,* its behavior does
not correspond well with that of the "other assets" reported on Form
5500. Therefore, a blended index was constructed by weighting only
three of the Wilshire performance measures (encompassing equities,
fixed income investments, and cash equivalents) according to the
asset allocation within each plan. For the first six months of a fiscal
year, that measure was

$$I_F = \left(\frac{1}{\sum_{i=1}^{3} B_i} \right) \sum_{i=1}^{3} R_{Fi} B_i$$

For the last six months of the fiscal year, the measure was

$$I_L = \left\{ \frac{1}{\sum_{i=1}^{3} \left[B_i \left(1 + R_{Fi} \right) + F_i \right]} \right\} \left\{ \sum_{i=1}^{3} R_{Li} \left[B_i \left(1 + R_{Fi} \right) + F_i \right] \right\}$$

Finally, for the entire year, the measure was

$$I_A = \left(\frac{1}{\sum_{i=1}^{3} B_i} \right) \sum_{i=1}^{3} R_{Ai} B_i$$

where for i,

    1 = Equities
    2 = Fixed income investments
    3 = Cash equivalents

and where I_F represents the index for the first six months, I_L represents the index for the last six months, and I_A represents the index for the entire fiscal year. B_i represents the balance for asset category i as of the beginning of the plan year, R_{Fi} represents the rate of return during the first six months of the fiscal year for asset category i, and R_{Li} represents the rate of return during the last six months of the fiscal year for asset category i. R_{Ai} is the rate of return during the entire fiscal year for asset category i. Finally, F_i represents the imputed flow for asset category i.

ADJUSTMENT OF REPORTED LIABILITIES

The calculating procedures used to adjust pension liabilities to a common standard were based on PBGC methods for estimating the value of guaranteed benefits under that agency's financial reporting system. The agency makes these estimates in cases where it cannot complete full audits of terminating underfunded plans before the close of its fiscal year.

First, the reported value of vested benefits attributed to active workers was increased to reflect accruals subsequent to the actuarial valuation date. The nature of the adjustment depended on the actuarial cost method originally used to value plan liabilities. For plans using the *accrued benefit* (i.e., unit credit) method, 80 percent of the "normal cost" (i.e., one year benefit accrual) for each year that had elapsed since the valuation date was added to the amount reported. For plans using the *aggregate* method, 7 percent of the reported value for "other vested benefits" (i.e., benefits not attributable to retirees or their survivors) was added in a similar manner. For all other plans, a prorated amount based on the full reported normal cost was simply added to other vested benefits.

By way of contrast, the five remaining liability adjustments were multiplicative in nature. Most significant among them, the discount rate assumptions were adjusted to the current PBGC interest rates as of the end of the calendar year in question. For liabilities attributable to retired lives, that adjustment was

$$A_I = .94^{(PBGC_i - PR)}$$

For other liabilities, the discount rate adjustment was

$$A_O = \frac{\left[A_I \left(1 + PR\right)^{15} \right]}{\left(PBGC_{K1} \right)^8 \left(PBCG_{K2} \right)^7}$$

where

> PR = Plan discount rate
> $PBGC_I$ = PBGC interest rate for immediate annuities
> $PBGC_{K1}$ = PBGC interest rate for the first deferral period
> $PBGC_{K2}$ = PBGC interest rate for the second deferral period

A second multiplicative adjustment reflects the difference between the plan assumption for expected retirement age and industry experience in the 1980s. That adjustment was

$$A_R = \left(\frac{ERF_1}{ERF_2} \right) \frac{\left[XRA_{\text{Plan}} - \left(AA / ä_{AA} \right) \right]}{\left[XRA_{PBGC} - \left(AA / ä_{AA} \right) \right]}$$

where

> AA = Liability-weighted attained age (56 for collectively bargained plans and 47 for other plans)
> XRA_{PBGC} = PBGC expected retirement age (59 for collectively bargained plans and 62 for all others)
> XRA_{Plan} = Expected retirement age reported for the plan
> ERF_1 = Early retirement factor for the plan at XRA_{PBGC}
> ERF_2 = Early retirement factor for the plan at XRA_{Plan}
> $ä_{AA}$ = Annuity factor for AA from the PBGC annuity tables using the $PBGC_I$

A third multiplicative adjustment reflects the passage of time between the actuarial valuation date (AVD) on which the Schedule B data were based and the end of the calendar year in question. For liabilities attributable to retired lives, that adjustment was

$$A_{TR} = .96^n$$

For all other liabilities, the adjustment was

$$A_T = PBGC_{K1}^n$$

where

n = Years between AVD and the end of the calendar year in question

A fourth multiplicative adjustment to the reported liability data standardized for differences in mortality table assumptions. It was derived from a model developed for the PBGC by actuaries at the firm of Milliman & Robertson. Use of appropriate mortality table adjustment factors is necessary because the PBGC interest rate sets accurately replicate prices in the private annuity market only when combined with the PBGC mortality table assumption (i.e., the Unisex Pension 1984 table with a one-year setforward). Differences in mortality table assumptions have been a topic of considerable interest to members of the actuarial profession.[49]

The treatment of dedicated bond portfolios, relative to the present values reported on Schedule B, made a final adjustment necessary. To summarize the problem, a common investment strategy in the 1980s was to fund the anticipated payouts of the retired-lives obligation with matched interest and principal repayments from a portfolio of "dedicated" bonds. To the extent that the issuer did not subsequently call the bonds, the strategy insulated the pension plan as well as its sponsor from interest rate risk unless the bonds were sold and the funds reallocated. "Reoptimization" was also a common practice during this period.

To see how this strategy could substantially reduce the value of reported plan liabilities and the associated funding requirements, consider the example offered by Christensen and Fabozzi.[50] A pension plan with $271,457,335 in payouts projected to current retirees uses an actuarial discount rate of 7 percent. Accordingly, the present value of that obligation amounts to $133,424,859. However, a yield of 11.12 percent could be obtained on investment quality bonds in August 1985. To match the expected payouts at that discount rate would have required an initial investment of only $100,358,089.

For the purpose of this study, dedications were problematic because it was common for sponsors simply to report the lower present value without raising the reported actuarial discount rate to reflect the yield on the portfolio. As a result, the unadjusted values for plans engaging in this practice frequently were understated by material amounts. Table 2–13 reports the proportion of plans, surveyed by Greenwich Associates, that engaged in dedications during the seven years covered by the DOL sample tapes. For half of proportions shown in the table, it was assumed that the sponsor marked the liabilities to market but failed to increase the reported actuarial discount rate. For each new increment of obligations that was matched with dedicated assets, the reported discount rate was then changed to reflect market rates at the end of the calendar year in question. Plans assumed to be engaging in this practice were identified as those with the most onerous burden for current retirees as measured by the reported ratio of retirees to active workers. The assumed discount rates are reported in Table 2–14.

APPENDIX ENDNOTES

48. This Form 5500 item includes mutual fund holdings and other assets subject to the Investment Company Act of 1940.

49. For example, see Rita Lawlor, "Effect of Different Mortality Tables on Accumulated Benefit Obligation," *Pension Section News*, September 1990, pp. 3–4.

50. See Peter E. Christensen and Frank J. Fabozzi, "Dedicated Bond Portfolios," in Frank J. Fabozzi and Irving M. Pollack, eds., *The Handbook of Fixed Income Securities*, 2d ed. (Homewood, IL: Dow Jones-Irwin, 1987), pp. 704–17.

3

THE DYNAMICS
OF DEFUNDING

One of the first steps that a company takes when it begins losing money is to stop contributing to its pension plans. As companies shrink and become mere shadows of their former selves, an entire panoply of endgame strategies is put to work to undermine the assets that provide security for retirement promises made to workers. These perfectly legal practices also allow companies to create hidden liabilities that won't be funded before they are transferred to the PBGC. The process of systematically eroding the pension plans, however, usually begins many years before companies actually go out of business.

Certainly it is true that firms face the ERISA minimum funding standard. But that standard has been notoriously ineffective in stanching the growth of unfunded pension liabilities. Sick companies can increase pension promises in lieu of providing workers with more wages and salaries in cash.[1] Special shutdown benefits and early retirements are also common in industries that represent the greatest risks to the insurance fund. Many of the pensions that are paid in these situations—because they start earlier, are often paid in lump sums, and provide higher benefits than assumed—turn out to be much more expensive than the actuaries previously estimated. In fact, total pension liabilities of terminating plans often grow by as much as 20 percent as a result of shutdowns; and, under current law, sponsors cannot fund these obligations in advance. Desperate companies can request waivers of minimum required contributions from the Internal Revenue Service. Sponsors can even use pension assets to cover business expenses, subject to interest charges and a modest penalty. As a result of all these strategies, unfunded liabilities often greatly exceed amounts reported only months before pension termination. Sometimes no assets at all are left in plans that were supposed to provide pensions for thousands of workers.[2]

Chapter 2 said little about how the condition of the defined-benefit system has changed since 1987. At least two government indicators strongly suggest that the situation has deteriorated since then. In 1988, the PBGC itself reported that the 50 companies with the largest unfunded liabilities were responsible for a combined shortfall of $13.5 billion. However, the latest version of the "Top 50" list, based on 1993 data, showed that this group accounted for unfunded guaranteed liabilities of almost $32.3 billion: an increase of more than 135 percent in just four years.[3] The agency also estimated that total unfunded liabilities attributable to its single-employer program almost tripled—after adjustments for inflation—from $27 billion to $71 billion during the same period. Have the long-term risks to the insurance fund actually risen by this much? And to what extent does this adverse trend reflect a deterioration in credit quality and corporate financial performance as opposed a decline in interest rates?

No sample Form 5500 data have been collected for periods after 1987.[4] Pension data released to shareholders (despite several attempts to strengthen financial reporting standards) can be grossly misleading.[5] Regular public reports to shareholders that comply with Financial Accounting Standard 87 lack information about actual contribution levels as well as accurate data on the termination liability. This chapter therefore aims to shed additional light on the recent condition of several very large defined-benefit plans. Recognizing that unfunded liabilities generally are thought to have grown, the chapter takes two approaches in addressing these questions. First, it examines over an extended horizon the changing profile of some of the most egregiously underfunded terminations that have confronted the PBGC. These cases include plans sponsored by LTV, a steelmaker that has now emerged from Chapter 11 bankruptcy protection, as well as plans sponsored by two airlines that failed to escape liquidation: Pan Am and Eastern.

Once the profile for major previous claims against the insurance fund has been established, attention will then shift to the status of currently ongoing pension plans in the airline, automotive, and steel industries. Since much of the risk to the PBGC is thought to be concentrated in the steel and automotive industries, this chapter also reviews a consistent time series of actual plan asset and liability values (i.e., on a termination basis), and contribution levels for substantial plans sponsored by the companies in these industries. In some cases, the time series cover periods as long as 18 years. The instrument for introducing a reasonable measure of consistency, not only across different plans and companies but also between different reporting periods, will be the PBGC's "Plan Asset Insufficiency" model. The PAI model adjusts liability data to account for differences in several actuarial assumptions, including the interest rate, mortality table, retirement age, and valuation date.

ACTUARIAL SOUNDNESS AND FINANCIAL SOLVENCY: TWO CONCEPTS

What does it mean for a pension plan to be actuarially sound when the assumptions used to calculate benefits extending into the distant future are based on past experience? Can the past provide a reliable guide for the main factors that determine pension costs: retirement age, employee turnover, disability, mortality patterns, and investment returns? Is it possible for a pension plan to be financially solvent without being actuarially sound? Or, conversely, can a plan be actuarially sound without being financially solvent? One usually thinks of pension plans in terms of whether they are both or whether they are neither. To understand these essential distinctions, consider the hypothetical balance sheet in Table 3–1. Table 3–1 represents an economic balance sheet in the sense that it includes the flows into and out of the pension plan both prior to the valuation date and subsequent to it.

This hypothetical pension plan is fully funded as of the valuation date with $152.5 million of assets currently in the plan and $150

TABLE 3-1

Pension Fund Economic Balance Sheet

Assets		
1.	Investment portfolio—market value	$150,000,000
2.	Cash	2,500,000
3.	Total assets in plan	$152,500,000
4.	Present value of contributions for future service—consistent with plan provisions and current actuarial assumptions	40,000,000
5.	Present value of future contributions to meet unfunded past service obligations and net experience losses	17,500,000
6.	Present value of contributions to be scheduled for future deficiencies in (4) and (5)	40,000,000
7.	Total economic assets	$250,000,000
Liabilities		
8.	Present value of benefits for current retirees	$50,000,000
9.	Present value of accrued benefits for active workers	70,000,000
10.	Previous obligations for past service credits and net experience losses	30,000,000
11.	Present value of benefits for future service	100,000,000
12.	Total going-concern liabilities	$250,000,000

million in accrued liabilities (i.e., the sum of Items 8, 9, and 10). However, the plan isn't actuarially sound, because an additional $100 million in liabilities will be incurred in the future, while only $57.5 million in contributions have been scheduled to cover them. The plan therefore faces a shortfall with a current value of $40 million (Item 6) unless scheduled contributions are increased. A central dilemma for pension funding in the United States hinges on the fact that the Internal Revenue Code permits only Items 8, 9, and 10 to be funded in advance. Nevertheless, the present value of benefits for future service (Item 11)—if the firm is a going concern—also represents a claim on the sponsor and its economic net worth.

To appreciate the weakness of the actuarial soundness concept, consider the testimony of William Fellers, a leading pension actuary, who appeared as a witness before the U.S. Senate Committee on Labor when ERISA was being drafted. According to Fellers, a pension plan sponsored by the Michigan Tool Company had been "actuarially sound" when it was terminated under circumstances that bore a striking similarity to the classic Studebaker case. Nevertheless, many newly unemployed workers lost their entire pension wealth as a result of that event. A heated exchange followed Fellers' testimony, with Senator Jacob Javits demanding a better explanation of the term *soundness*. The actuaries apparently expected future contributions to eliminate Michigan Tool's unfunded liability had the plan been continued.

The Senate Labor Committee no doubt would have reacted to Fellers' testimony more sympathetically if it had focused instead on the obvious lack of financial solvency of plans like Studebaker's and Michigan Tool's. After all, whether a defined-benefit pension plan is financially solvent depends on the resources available to the company standing behind it. Virtually every defined-benefit plan in the United States must rely on the sponsor to meet at least some of the going-concern liabilities because investments in the pension fund typically are not maintained at that level. For a pension plan to be solvent, the sponsor must be able to repay all of the obligations that the plan will eventually incur. A judgment concerning financial solvency therefore amounts to treating the pension plan and its sponsor as a combined entity. In other words, the hypothetical company with the hypothetical pension plan described in Table 3–1 must be able to show that it has at least the $57.5 million in unencumbered net worth to cover the currently planned contributions as well as an additional $40 million to fund the growth of the unfunded liability.[6]

In reality, the growth of the unfunded liability shown as Item 6 illustrates a simple truth about the frequently arcane complexities of pension finance: That the ultimate cost of any pension plan is independent of its actuarial assumptions. The notion of actuarial soundness therefore is unsatisfying, because it implies that the goal of funding policy—even when it aims to bring plan assets into balance with estimated liabilities—may turn out to be unrelated to the actual cost of future benefits. In fact, many sponsors that negotiate retirement benefits with labor unions deliberately seek to preserve a lack of actuarial soundness in the belief that inadequate funding reduces the ability of unions to extract additional benefit promises from the company. For this reason, one cannot determine whether the retirement promises of underfunded pension plans are empty without first considering the financial strength of the employer.

This distinction comes into sharper focus when we compare the approaches to pension funding taken in other countries. The Swedish system, for example, allows creditworthy employers to make promises without any advance funding. These pensions are financed by the terminal funding method whereby one contribution is made for each worker at the time that he or she retires. The employer then uses that contribution to purchase an annuity from an insurance company. The Swedish companies permitted to make retirement promises on this basis are carefully monitored to maintain solvency. However, no knowledgeable person would describe their pension plans as "actuarially sound" in any way that could reasonably be applied to the American context. Germany, Japan, and Finland also allow private employers to finance their retirement obligations with a "book reserve" that amounts to nothing more than an unsecured claim on the sponsor. By way of contrast, the investment portfolios of American-style defined-benefit plans allow the bankruptcy risk to be diversified based on equity and other claims against a potentially long list of companies, not just one particular sponsor.

In the United States, plans that are not actuarially sound more often than not start from a position that is less than fully funded. Their unfunded liabilities then usually increase. This doesn't necessarily imply that their condition is deteriorating or even that they are insolvent. In fact, unfunded liabilities can actually grow by billions of dollars (as the case of Chrysler demonstrated) while the ratio of pension investments to plan liabilities improves. Even though some companies like Chrysler have traveled the road to better financial health while taking on more unfunded pension debt, it has also been possible to:

set up an inadequate funding system in which the funded ratio goes up each year for a long period before turning down but in which the unfunded amount expressed in dollars keeps getting larger and larger. The curve of the funded ratio in such a case approaches a maximum point at less than 100 percent before turning downward.[7]

Before ERISA, firms were able to contribute only the entry age normal cost for newly accrued benefits, plus the interest on the unfunded liability, as a deliberate funding policy that was capable of producing exactly this result. Yet this was viewed as actuarially sound at the time and had the advantage of producing level contributions as a percentage of payroll. Even now, with the ERISA minimum funding standard that requires previous unfunded liabilities to be amortized, Bronson's scenario can still occur, because some plans pay out more in benefits than the sponsor is required to contribute in order to amortize the unfunded liability. Although difficult from a labor relations point of view, a sponsor can reduce benefit accruals as one way to restore both solvency and soundness when the financial condition of a pension plan deteriorates too much. Terminating the plan represents, of course, the ultimate step for reducing the liabilities in cases of insolvency. Both of these outcomes unfortunately involve substantial costs for workers. Those costs, of course, would be even greater if the firm liquidated.

To sum up, defined-benefit pension plans sponsored by dying companies have collapsed with large unfunded liabilities that previously were not reported, even though some of those same pension plans were characterized as actuarially sound years later. The four factors depicted in Figure 3–1 fuel this process of implosion, a process that can all but deplete plan assets. The slippery concept of actuarial soundness presumes either that the pension plan is fully funded on the basis of the accumulated-benefit obligation (ABO) or the guaranteed-benefit obligation (GBO) and will remain so; or, that the plan is on an orderly schedule to become fully funded. Financial solvency, on the other hand, is a very different standard. It presumes that the sponsor actually is capable of funding a measure like the projected benefit obligation (PBO), or perhaps even the indexed benefit obligation (IBO), regardless of the assets in the plan. An actuarially sound pension plan clearly can be financially insolvent, and vice

FIGURE 3-1

Death Spiral of a Flat-Benefit Plan

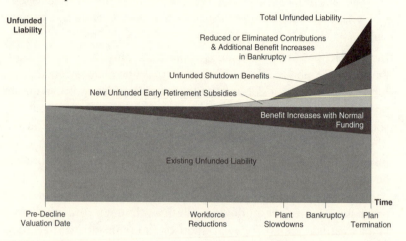

versa. The first of these two situations would represent a major concern for any guarantee fund standing behind plans required to fund their obligations in advance. As for the second, the more immediate policy issues involve the terms on which financially solid companies can borrow, using the pension system, and on whether those terms are conducive to a desirable allocation of credit throughout the economy.[8]

FUNDING OBJECTIVES

By the beginning of the 1980s, a literature had identified two factors that influence pension-funding behavior by corporations: a tax effect and an insurance effect.[9] According to the so-called tax-arbitrage theory advanced by Fischer Black and Irwin Tepper, the tax effect motivates plan sponsors to fund at the maximum permissible level in order to take advantage of the immediate tax deduction. Pension assets then should be fully invested in bonds because interest payments are taxed at a lower rate than stock dividends. The tax-arbitrage theory goes on to assert that the sponsor can maximize shareholder value by borrowing whatever is needed to make the maximum permissible contribution to the pension plan. After all, the interest payments on that debt are tax deductible.[10]

The insurance effect provides an incentive for companies to adopt exactly the opposite strategy, due to the terms of PBGC cover. According to this strategy, sponsors should contribute no more than the minimum requirement and then invest the entire portfolio in high-risk stocks. So while the tax effect leads to reduced risks for the PBGC, the insurance effect—a concept tantamount to moral hazard in this context—increases them. There is no middle ground between the two approaches. Consistent with these objectives, companies that usually earn positive returns have a strong incentive to make the maximum allowable contributions to their pension plans. During most of the 1980s relatively conservative actuarial assumptions were permitted so that they could make larger contributions. On the other hand, companies that operated in declining markets or consistently lost money for other reasons derived little or no benefit from the available tax deductions. Sponsors in this category therefore adopted more liberal actuarial assumptions and aimed to minimize contributions to their defined-benefit pension plans.

Why then do most defined-benefit plans invest in both stocks and bonds? Bicksler and Chen believe that the asymmetric impact of the U.S. tax code plays a major role. Firms expect to pay taxes when their income is positive, but they cannot be certain of using all available tax credits when losing money or going out of business. The insurance effect meanwhile is diluted by "deadweight loss" in the form of legal expenses for terminating an underfunded pension plan, as well as by higher wage demands in response to the probability that some retirement benefits will not be paid.[11] Still, Bodie et al., found evidence that underfunded pension plans held more equity on a proportional basis than fully funded plans, thereby lending support to the importance of the insurance effect.[12] This same conflict also can determine the funding decision.

Two legislative developments later in the 1980s had major effects on pension funding in practice. First, the Omnibus Budget Reconciliation Act of 1987 (OBRA '87) narrowed the gap between the ERISA minimum funding standard and the maximum funding limit.[13] OBRA '87 also made permissible funding levels that were far more volatile on a year-to-year basis. Second and less importantly, the Tax Reform Act of 1986 (TRA '86) reduced sponsors' flexibility to prepay contributions for future years. Previously, companies had been able to prepay these contributions without penalty. The tax deductions, however, could be used only when the contributions in question actually became due. TRA '86 imposed a 10 percent excise tax on the plan sponsor, who had to pay it on the excess every year until the contribution actually became due.[14] Furthermore, the OBRA '87 full funding limit prohibited contributions to plans with assets exceeding 150 percent of the termination liability. It stipulated that an excise tax of as much as 40 percent can be imposed on any underpayment of taxes that results from overstated pension liabilities. Employers can also face an excise tax of as much as 100 percent if minimum contributions are not made.[15] Plan sponsors naturally have a strong incentive to avoid both types of penalties.

In addition, sponsors enjoy far less ability to recover surplus pension assets than was the case until the mid-1980s. The Tax Reform Act of 1986 initially placed an excise tax of 10 percent on reversions. This was subsequently raised to 15 percent in 1988 and to 50 percent in 1990.[16] Short of an outright termination for reversion, then, sponsors can eliminate surplus pension assets, through a slower process of reducing contributions or skipping them altogether. This remaining option, however, is less than ideal for companies with surplus pension assets because they tend to attract hostile takeover bids. Incumbent management therefore wants flexibility to remove surplus assets quickly from the pension plans by way of terminations. For a company under seige, even today's high excise taxes would not stand in the way of this type of transaction. Yet the penalty imposed by the taxes remains onerous, so sponsors have become extremely reluctant to accumulate pension surpluses. According to several well-known actuaries, virtually all sponsors now are aiming to fund at no more than the minimum required level.

For its part, OBRA '87—and the Pension Protection Act that was incorporated into it—has been particularly ineffective in strengthening the minimum funding requirement. In fact, the Pension Protection Act was even used to relax the minimum funding standard applicable to many poorly funded plans. The U.S. General Accounting Office found that almost half of the underfunded plans in a randomly selected sample actually received no contributions at all due to offsetting credits in OBRA '87. Only a third of the underfunded plans in the sample were receiving additional contributions as a result of OBRA '87. Many of these plans experienced reductions in the additional funding due to the same offsetting credits.[17]

Anecdotal evidence also points to one additional funding target for sponsors that anticipate a Chapter 7 bankruptcy liquidation. Declining companies that sponsor pension plans for highly paid workers may have an incentive to fund the first three benefit categories established by the allocation rules in Section 4044 of ERISA. Section 4044 of ERISA directs the PBGC to "allocate" the assets in terminating pension plans according to the following priorities. First, all voluntary employee contributions are repaid. Second, all mandatory employee contributions are repaid. Third, all benefits of participants who have been in "pay status" (i.e., retired and receiving benefits from the plan) for three years before the termination are paid, with their benefit payments determined by provisions of the plan in effect during the five-year period ending on the termination date. Fourth, all other guaranteed benefits are paid.[18]

To see why a dying firm might aim for a funding level adequate to cover the first three benefit categories and no more, consider the hypothetical case of a pension plan for pilots sponsored by a liquidating airline. In this case, retired pilots receive pensions of $85,000 per year. However, the maximum pension guaranteed by the PBGC currently is about $30,000 per year. If the plan were so underfunded that no assets remained after paying benefits attributable to Categories 1 and 2, then no pilot would receive a pension greater than the PBGC maximum guaranteed benefit. Yet pilots who had been retired for three years or more would receive a full, unreduced pension of $85,000 per year if enough assets remained in the plan to cover Category 3 benefits upon termination. The PBGC would then assume the cost of all unfunded guaranteed benefits up to the maximum in effect upon termination for the remaining pilots (those retired less than three years and those not retired before the termination). Neither the airline nor its pilots have anything to gain under these allocation rules if assets remain in a terminating plan that exceed obligations attributable to Categories 1–3.

On the other hand, public utilities and other companies that set prices on the basis of cost together with a regulated return on investment still have an incentive to fund their defined-benefit pension plans up to the maximum allowable level. In addition, the Clinton Administration's pension bill may generate renewed interest in the maximum funding limit in unregulated lines of business.[19] Some companies may choose to fund at the highest permissible level out of concern about the prospect of paying substantially increased PBGC premiums. The Retirement Protection Act of 1994 removed the cap—previously set at $53 per participant—on the $9 annual charge for every $1,000 in unfunded liabilities. As noted earlier, OBRA '87 reduced the difference between the minimum and the maximum funding limits. One complicating factor in this situation is that companies report plan condition less favorably when using the interest rate assumptions required for PBGC premium calculations than they do when using assumptions connected to the ERISA funding limits. The larger penalty for becoming less than fully funded on a PBGC premium-determination basis therefore could motivate sponsors to accumulate a buffer. Unfortunately, the OBRA '87 maximum funding limit remains in effect. It will not afford much flexibility for maintaining such a cushion, for reasons we will discuss in Chapter 7.

To put these funding objectives into context: Any system that permits less than complete advance funding of private employer-sponsored pensions suffers from several weaknesses. This applies to those arrangements both here and abroad (e.g., in Finland, Japan, Germany, Sweden, and the United Kingdom) that use a wide spectrum of approaches, including outright pay-as-you-go financing, terminal funding, book reserves, and defined-benefit systems like our own that require some but not complete advance funding. These arrangements have been criticized for impairing the discipline that capital budgeting otherwise would impose within corporations.[20] In other words, capital is prevented from flowing to its most productive uses. Returns on pension assets—a substantial asset amounting to an unsecured claim on the sponsor—can't be maximized. As a general proposition, unfunded pension liabilities weaken control of invest-ment decisions, limit the choice of investments, inhibit the develop-ment of local capital markets, and help conceal management errors. They also encourage investment decisions that take inadequate ac-count of the default risk. This type of self-investment will produce better results only if capital markets are poorly developed relative to the internal processes within firms for allocating capital to invest-ment projects.

AIRLINES: SOURCE OF THE LARGEST PREVIOUS LOSSES FOR THE PBGC

To see how the systematic defunding of pension plans works in prac-tice, consider the airlines. Deregulation of the industry in 1978 rep-resented the defining moment for the carriers that serve America today; it caused tremendous upheaval in the industry, but it shaped these companies into a group that competes vigorously on the basis of price as well as service. The Civil Aeronautics Board (CAB) a U.S. government agency, had previously set fares and determined access to domestic intercity routes. For most carriers, the transition following the end of CAB regulation was difficult.

The old route structures were poorly suited to the new com-petitive environment. For example, Delta had been largely a North–South airline. It needed East–West routes as well as a pres-ence on the West Coast in order to become a national carrier. Before 1978, American had been concentrated in the Northeast and Mid-west. It believed that its main growth opportunities were in the Sun-belt. New route configurations, in turn, meant that existing aircraft fleets suddenly became inappropriate and needed to be replaced. The carriers also began the period with too much debt, because airlines didn't go out of business in the old regulated environment. Managers now needed to become entrepreneurial, adept at flexible pricing and at controlling costs. With CAB's old rate-making formula, cost in-creases had simply been passed on to consumers in the form of higher fares.[21]

Some of the airlines couldn't make these changes. Braniff went bankrupt in 1982: the first carrier to do so. Continental followed the next year.[22] In one of the ERISA termination insurance program's first major claims, the PBGC assumed a $58 million unfunded liability in connection with Braniff.

Almost immediately after deregulation, new carriers—such as New York Air and People Express—came into existence to tap a market segment that was extremely sensitive to price. The entry of these firms drove fares down substantially on the most heavily traveled routes. Elsewhere fares rose, or service to remote destinations was discontinued entirely. One study concluded that, on average, fares are now 22 percent lower than they would have been without deregulation. The traveling public saves $12.4 billion annually as a result. Deregulation clearly provides many benefits, more frequent flights and more online connections among them.[23] The airline industry has experienced dramatic growth in terms of passenger miles throughout the post-ERISA period. Yet there have been tradeoffs. Passengers are taking flights with higher load factors. Some trips require more connections and many also involve longer travel times.[24] Furthermore, ineffective pension funding standards allow the cost of some consumer benefits to be shifted to the PBGC.

In the late 1980s, the new post-deregulation entrants began to disappear as the industry consolidated. The list of older, more established carriers absorbed by mergers is substantial as well: Ozark, Western, PSA, Air California, Piedmont, Southern, North Central, and Hughes Airwest. Still, more airlines were operating in 1993 than existed just before deregulation. And competition is more intensive at the route level, even though the effective number of national competitors has fallen since the late 1980s. In fact, competition is now nearly as great as it has ever been—even after those consolidations and the liquidations of three other carriers (Eastern, Midway, and Pan Am).[25]

In terms of financial performance, only Southwest Airlines—an innovative, unionized carrier that does not sponsor a defined-benefit pension plan—has emerged as consistently profitable. Given the capital structure of most airlines, an operating margin of about 5 percent is required to provide investors with a "normal" 12 percent pretax return. Between 1974 (when ERISA was adopted) and the times when they were liquidated in bankruptcy in 1990 and 1991, Eastern never reached this level, and Pan Am achieved it in only one year: 1978. Nearly all carriers experienced substantial losses from 1990–93. The red ink during this period totaled nearly $13 billion. Yet deregulation cannot be blamed for the industry's disappointing financial performance. Profit margins under the old CAB fare schedules had been inadequate as well.[26] Today, several of the surviving carriers remain weak and could be vulnerable in the next recession, if not sooner. Among them are TWA, Continental, Northwest, and USAir.

Pan Am: The 13-Year Endgame

For its part, Pan Am was profitable only in two years between 1980 and 1991. The company also had trouble integrating the operations of National Airlines with its own following their merger in 1978. It then proceeded to go through the usual death spiral—in slow motion—by selling off its most valuable assets: the InterContinental Hotel chain, the company headquarters building, virtually all of its remaining equipment (which it leased back), the best planes and overseas routes, and the profitable Pan Am shuttle. Meanwhile, the IRS approved the company's request to skip the minimum required pension contributions in 6 out of the last 10 years before it liquidated. These waivers gave Pan Am an additional $200 million to stave off bankruptcy. The Department of Labor and the IRS even allowed the company to sell the leasehold for its terminal at New York's John F. Kennedy Airport to the pension plans.

Ordinarily, federal regulators would have prohibited this type of transaction. In this case, they not only made an exception but they structured the transaction in a way that provided a new and even more costly twist. The leasehold had been appraised at $170 million, but the pension plans purchased it to replace $104 million in back contributions. So, Pan Am's severely underfunded pension plans actually paid the company $66 million in cash. The leasehold then represented 29 percent of pension assets. The tenant was Pan Am itself: a poor credit risk, with $2.8 million in monthly rent.[27] These decisions resulted in higher costs for the PBGC insurance fund when the company liquidated four years later.[28]

The three Pan Am plans guaranteed by the PBGC were frozen (no additional benefits were accrued and no new participants could be added) at the end of 1983. Even with this freeze, however, the unfunded liabilities of these three plans rose from $798 million in 1984 to $994 million in 1989, an increase of almost 25 percent. Guaranteed benefits totaled $914 million when the company was finally liquidated. So, participants apparently lost $80 million in vested benefits that exceeded the maximum guaranteed, notwithstanding the ERISA allocation rules which in some cases allow for payments considerably above the maximum guaranteed amount.[29] Before the bankruptcy, Pan Am had missed a total of $364 million in contributions. The company had not even paid $2.6 million in PBGC insurance premiums. Of all these claims, only $53 million was secured. The collateral consisted of stock in the Pan Am shuttle, which had been pledged in return for a contribution waiver.

Eastern Airlines: Bankruptcy's Perverse Incentives for Creditors

The case of Eastern Airlines shows how unsecured creditors often become unwilling participants in high-risk strategies to gamble for redemption once a bankruptcy petition is filed. In many cases like the Eastern bankruptcy, companies have barely enough assets to cover the claims of secured creditors. A liquidation of the company therefore would leave several influential groups significantly worse off, including employees of the company, unsecured creditors, and shareholders.

One year before the demise of the airline, Eastern gave unsecured creditors a choice of three business plans. One plan would have given them 40 percent of the equity in the reorganized airline. Another plan would have combined Eastern with Continental Airlines (Eastern's ailing corporate affiliate). The third plan would have immediately liquidated Eastern. Liquidation would have left the unsecured creditors with nothing. As the unsecured creditors saw it, a plan that had only a remote chance of allowing the company to survive long enough to pay some interest on its previous debts was worth more than nothing at all. Both the unsecured creditors and the company itself faced a powerful incentive to gamble with other people's money. In these desperate situations, the condition of pension plans almost invariably worsens as time goes on.

New benefits continue to accrue. Cash flows out of the plans as pension benefits are paid, but the company—as long as it continues to operate in bankruptcy—makes no additional pension contributions. Under these circumstances, Eastern correctly anticipated that unsecured creditors would decide to keep the company alive for at least one more year.[30]

The Eastern case illustrates how unsecured creditors can have a motive to keep the company going even when there is no realistic prospect that the business can survive. Two months before Eastern was actually liquidated, the court-appointed trustee, Martin Shugrue, Jr., presented a business plan to the creditors committee showing the company on a steadily improving path for five years. On October 5, 1990, the PBGC terminated seven Eastern Airlines pension plans with unfunded liabilities of $752 million. At the time of the termination, it received $30 million from Eastern but expected no further recovery from the airline. One of Eastern's corporate affiliates, Continental Airlines, was also in bankruptcy with substantial assets available for distribution to unsecured creditors. Within two years, the PBGC settled its claims against Continental for the Eastern Airlines pension plans in exchange for cash, notes, and other securities valued at $115 to 130 million. The PBGC previously had filed claims for $183.2 million against Continental in connection with that carrier's own pension plans. The Continental pension plans were not terminated.

TWA and the Problem of Political Intervention
As the agent of the President and the U.S. Congress, the PBGC not only is subject to overwhelming political influence as general policies are formulated, but must also accede to the wishes of outside political figures as the terms of specific bankruptcy and composition proceedings are negotiated. A case in point was the December 1992 settlement with TWA and its owner, financier Carl Icahn. With the airline then under Chapter 11 bankruptcy protection and facing a $1 billion unfunded pension liability, the PBGC actually had threatened to use its legal authority to terminate the TWA pension plans. In that event, Icahn would have lost his entire equity position in the airline. The PBGC would then have pressed to collect on its claim for the

unfunded pensions from Icahn's other businesses, as well as from his personal assets.[31] At the time, *Forbes* magazine had estimated Icahn's net worth to be in the $650 million range.

After negotiations began between Icahn and the agency, high government officials outside the PBGC not only got involved in the negotiations but interjected themselves between the agency and Icahn. In the end, they released Icahn from further liability for the TWA plans in return for commitments to make contributions worth an estimated $150 million in current dollars (most of it in the distant future). The plans themselves were left in the hands of TWA, but benefits were frozen.[32] Those close to the negotiations believe that several hundred million dollars more could have been recovered for the pension plans without this intrusion on the part of individuals with no operational responsibility for the pension insurance program. After the deal was initialed, the same high government officials from outside the agency pressured the executive director to make a favorable recommendation to the agency's board of directors. As if those terms were not generous enough, the financially ailing carrier returned to the PBGC within two years seeking further concessions.[33] The floundering carrier sought Chapter 11 bankruptcy protection once again in June 1995.

The TWA case also illustrates one of the most serious threats facing the ERISA termination insurance program: the incentive for financially weak plan sponsors to increase guaranteed pension benefits as a substitute for cash compensation. This became apparent in early 1992, when TWA negotiated a new collective bargaining contract with the International Association of Machinists. The agreement called for a sizable increase in guaranteed pension benefits without any significant change in wages. At almost the same time, a similar pattern was occurring in negotiations between Continental Airlines—while it was under Chapter 11 bankruptcy protection—and its pilots' union.

The Pan Am, Eastern, and TWA cases, as well as the experience with other pension plans in the airline industry, illustrate important problems in the management of the ERISA pension guarantee. First, financially distressed companies face a powerful incentive to raise guaranteed benefit levels to substitute for cash compensation that they cannot afford to pay. This can provide additional time for inefficient companies to pursue high-risk strategies at the expense of more productive parts of the economy. Second, a freeze on benefits by itself is not capable of stopping the erosion of an underfunded pension plan. Even with a freeze, the plan remains vulnerable to the effects of interest rate risk, as well as other sources of deterioration. Third, no minimum funding requirement can protect the insurance fund from substantial losses if the government has the legal authority to grant waivers and other exceptions to those requirements, particularly when there is a political incentive to use it. Fourth, the bankruptcy process itself is replete with perverse incentives that can substantially increase unfunded pension liabilities. Fifth, political influence not only produced unstable and unnecessarily costly features in the design of this program, but it also adds to those costs as a result of meddling in operational decisions and negotiations with the sponsors of seriously underfunded pension plans. Finally, the PBGC would not be effectively protected given the availability of plan assets for other uses even if funding requirements were binding. These uses are currently subject to penalties and interest charges. Looking ahead, several claims against the PBGC, ranging upwards from a billion dollars, could occur within the next decade as a result of future liquidations in the airline industry. TWA, Continental, Northwest, and USAir all could become candidates for bankruptcy following strategic errors or an economic downturn.

THE CONTINUING DECLINE OF AMERICA'S MAJOR STEEL PRODUCERS

The steel industry has been a source of numerous and substantial claims against the PBGC. The steel industry plans that were permanently transferred to the insurance fund so far have not involved claims as large as those produced by the airline industry.[34] That may change. Unfunded liabilities at Bethlehem Steel and LTV have exceeded $2 billion for many years. Meanwhile, Armco has adhered to a corporate philosophy that emphasizes funding its pension plans by no more than the absolute minimum requirement since the pre-ERISA period. More recently, transition rules for the OBRA '87 minimum funding provisions included a special exemption for steel industry pension plans. As a result of this and other features, the new law did not compel steelmakers to improve the funding of their pension plans.[35]

Much of the continuing plight of major steel industry pension plans can be explained by an abrupt decline in domestic and worldwide demand for steel products starting in 1975. And strategic missteps by the major steelmakers, along with new domestic competition from highly efficient minimills also has created major turmoil, periodically calling into question the survival of some of the most venerable names in the industry. Costly early retirement provisions, lump sum payments, and persistent underfunding from the time that many of these pension plans were first set up, added to the PBGC's losses in a long list of cases. Compounding the problems facing the insurance fund were a failure by steelmakers to pay even the minimum contributions when legally due, extensive use of minimum funding waivers by the IRS, and regulation that was otherwise ineffective.

Steelmakers began the post-ERISA period facing a recession; but their prospects otherwise looked optimistic. Raw steel production had reached an all-time high of 150.8 million tons amid shortages in 1973. The industry then embarked on a belated but ambitious effort to modernize by replacing open hearth facilities with large basic oxygen furnaces. Following in the footsteps of Japanese and European steelmakers, American companies also began installing continuous casters for the first time. These new investments might have been successful if demand had continued to grow. Unfortunately, it did not. Raw steel production never returned to the level reached in 1973. During the economic recovery of the late 1970s, for instance, it averaged 130 million tons. Then it collapsed, abruptly falling to 74.6 million tons in 1982.[36] Just as with the airlines after deregulation, overly optimistic demand forecasts were a major factor contributing to the industry's poor financial performance.

Meanwhile, import penetration grew and exports fell. A strong dollar helped fuel this trend from 1981 to 1985. New and more efficient domestic competitors in the form of so-called minimills also took business away from the large integrated mills. As a result, the market for major American steel producers fell from 102 million tons per year in 1974 to just 58 million in 1985. This left the steel companies in an awkward position. To obtain protection from their foreign competitors, they needed strong political support from the communities where they operated. Keeping that support would be difficult if plants or major facilities within plants were closed. Many inefficient plants therefore remained open, and the results of their earlier investments in these facilities were poor. Yet the major producers were unable to abandon them in favor of smaller and more efficient electric furnace plants like those operated by the minimills. Their local political allies would not have tolerated it.[37]

Certainly, one barrier to exit in these cases involved special early retirements, among other "shutdown" benefits negotiated by the United Steelworkers' Union. During the mid-1980s, costs typically averaged $55,000 per early retiree. Although these retirement packages included group health and life insurance, the pension covered a $400 monthly supplement until the early retiree became eligible, at age 62, for social security. These early retirements also involved additional costs because the accrued benefits weren't reduced to reflect the younger retirement age. In the case of a steelworker who would have been eligible for a monthly benefit of $600 upon reaching the plan's normal retirement age of 65, the additional cost to the pension plan consisted of two elements: the $400 monthly supplement, and the incremental cost of providing an unreduced accrued benefit of, say, $500 per month, starting at a typical age of 55, relative to that of the slightly higher normal pension commencing 10 years later. Accepted actuarial and accounting practices did not require plan sponsors to reflect the probability of these occurrences beforehand in their financial reports. And the additional costs were not funded in advance—just like the benefit improvements periodically negotiated in collective bargaining.

Early retirements became a major priority for labor negotiators during this period as the industry faced an urgent need to reduce capacity. Aside from more formidable exit barriers, these arrangements imposed a higher level of fixed costs on major steelmakers. They also placed a floor under wage givebacks, reduced capacity utilization, and motivated steelmakers to refurbish some

underutilized plants instead of closing them. This combination resulted in a serious threat to the financial performance of every
major producer. These costly early retirement provisions kept open
plants that would otherwise have been closed and they inflicted substantial new costs on steel industry pension plans when plants did
close. The PBGC estimated that 50 percent of LTV's unfunded pension liability can be attributed to early retirements related to shutdowns. This proportion has also been high in other cases involving
steel companies.[38]

To assess the risk of pension losses from the steel industry, consider the following background concerning four major producers.

LTV: The PBGC's First Billion-Dollar Crisis

The formation of LTV Steel was originally conceived as this fabled
conglomerate's answer to the need to reduce costs and eliminate excess capacity at its flagging steel unit. As part of an ambitious merger
strategy, LTV combined 3 of the top 10 domestic steel producers:
Youngstown Sheet & Tube, Jones & Laughlin Steel, and Republic
Steel. Unfortunately, the success of subsequent efforts to reduce
costs fell far short of the level necessary for LTV to become viable.
The company could not negotiate satisfactory contracts either with
its suppliers or with the United Steelworkers' union. After severe
downsizing, the cost of retiree health care as well as LTV's required
pension contributions spiraled out of control, and the new combination failed on a spectacular scale. By mid-1986, the entire enterprise
was pushed into bankruptcy.

At the time of the bankruptcy, LTV Steel's four principal pension plans were underfunded by an estimated $2.5 billion. On aver-
age, funding remained in the plans to cover 35 percent of guaranteed
benefits. But the Republic Steel Pension Plan for Salaried Employees had all but collapsed; only $7,700 was left in the plan to cover al-
most $220 million in liabilities.[39] For the ERISA termination
insurance program, this situation was nothing less than traumatic. To
make matters worse, the crisis came on the heels of the Wheeling-
Pittsburgh bankruptcy, which had involved a $475 million unfunded
liability the previous year. Another fiasco was looming at Kaiser

Steel. Kaiser was liquidated the following year with unfunded pension promises of about $232 million.

Five years before LTV sought bankruptcy protection, the Republic Steel salaried plan held assets totalling $275 million. Then Republic Steel's four senior executives, with the concurrance of their board of directors as well as the enrolled actuary, decided to reduce the discount rate used to determine lump-sum payments. The result was highly favorable to those who were lucky enough to qualify for retirement before the plan was terminated.[40] But as sizable numbers of new early retirees became eligible for lump-sum payments, total erosion of the plan's funded position occurred in a relatively short period. By the beginning of 1986, the market value of assets in the plan had fallen to $60 million with 3,739 workers remaining. Some of these remaining workers were lucky enough to retire with inflated lump-sum payments before the PBGC terminated the plan that summer. The others were not nearly as fortunate.

LTV did not emerge from bankruptcy until June 1993, after spending more than six years in Chapter 11 bankruptcy protection. During the bankruptcy, the company took a partial contribution holiday and, as a result, unfunded liabilities rose to more than $3 billion. As part of the Chapter 11 reorganization, the company transferred approximately $1 billion in cash to the pension plans. In the future, however, the condition of the plans is expected to erode from that level, because contributions probably won't match the growth of new benefits.

Bethlehem Steel: A Case of Parlous Survival

Bethlehem Steel apparently had accumulated an unfunded liability of $2.4 billion by 1977 when the company employed 101,000 workers. Bethlehem's pension plan soon was subjected to new pressures due to huge cuts in the labor force and the resulting early retirements, despite temporary relief afforded by high interest rates during the early 1980s. The company's narrow escape from bankruptcy on the heels of actual Chapter 11 filings by two of its competitors (Wheeling-Pittsburgh and LTV) underscored the role of the minimum contribution requirement in determining the order of exit in the industry.[41]

Plant closings were numerous during this period. Despite subsequent fluctuations in the condition of the plan and heavy contributions in some years, the unfunded liability remained at approximately $2.4 billion 1992—the same level as in 1977. However, Bethlehem had reduced employment to less than 25,000 people by that point, and the company had granted no postretirement increases in pension benefits in 15 years. Looking to the future, steel industry analysts expect Bethlehem's Sparrow's Point facility in Baltimore to close. The next recession represents a major threat to the company's prospects; Bethlehem once again could find itself tottering on the brink of bankruptcy sometime during the next decade.

U.S. Steel: Using the Momentum

The mammoth U.S. Steel pension plan appears to have recovered from its underfunded status during the late 1970s. This improvement occurred despite a reduction in the size of U.S. Steel's workforce as dramatic as that experienced at Bethlehem. Many early retirements also accompanied the downsizing at U.S. Steel. Still, vested benefits were fully funded in every year after 1981 despite a complete lack of contributions from the company since 1985.

Inland Steel: Emerging Vulnerability

Inland Steel, too, ended the 1970s with an underfunded plan. The cumulative effect of substantial contributions during that period together with the higher interest rates that followed helped to put the plan on a fully funded basis from 1980 until 1991. However, Inland's pension plan appeared to be underfunded by $185 million at the end of 1992. One year later, the PBGC actually included Inland on its "Top 50" list with an unfunded pension liability of $384 million. Inland hadn't contributed to the plan since 1984, but its own financial health had weakened significantly in the meantime. At that point, Standard & Poor's no longer rated Inland as an investment-grade credit. As this book went to press, the PBGC released its Top 50 list for 1994. Inland was not included following a contribution from the company. The condition of the plan also improved as a result of a temporary increase in interest rates.

Future Prospects

To conclude, risks to the PBGC from major steel producers could, if anything, grow during the decade ahead. There is no realistic hope that sustained and significant progress will be made in reducing the unfunded pension liabilities that companies have accumulated apart from what temporarily may result from the ebb and flow of interest rates. To the extent that integrated steel producers attempt to raise prices in order to amortize previous unfunded liabilities, their remaining market share will become vulnerable to further incursions by the minimills. Looking ahead, McClouth, Gulf States Steel, and National Steel could all become candidates for Chapter 7 bankruptcy liquidation during the next 10 years. For their part, Armco, Bethlehem, Inland, Weirton, and Wheeling-Pittsburgh could face reorganizations—in Wheeling-Pittsburgh's case for the second time—in Chapter 11 bankruptcies.

PENSIONS AND FINANCIAL PERFORMANCE AT THE BIG THREE AUTOMAKERS

The auto industry certainly has not been immune from the problems that led to major claims against the PBGC. The Studebaker bankruptcy in 1962 is frequently cited as the case that originally inspired Congress to establish the ERISA termination insurance program. Much later, one of the starkest examples of rapid defunding during the post-ERISA period involved the Allis-Chalmers United Auto Workers' pension plan. When the plan was terminated in 1985, only $2.3 million in assets remained to pay $176 million in benefit obligations.[42] Five years earlier the funding ratio had been 60 percent. This almost total depletion of plan resources occurred despite the fact that the actuarial assumption for interest rates was slightly less than the average for all plans in 1985 (i.e., 7 percent compared with an average of 7.6 percent). The company also never requested a minimum funding waiver. The spectacular collapse of the Allis Chalmers plan resulted from frequent benefit improvements combined with the burden associated with a relatively old work force. Unfortunately, these cases were not rare exceptions.[43] Early in the 1980s, plan terminations in the auto industry involved unfunded liabilities of $74 million at the White Motor Company and $56 million at the White Farm Equipment Company.

The global auto industry has evolved to the point where it is now mature and cyclical, with little real growth in demand. Sales in the U.S. domestic market during the 1980s were consistent with this general picture and remain so even today. For America's Big Three automakers, the 1980s were a difficult period from the beginning. The economy was mired in recession and imports were gaining market share at a rapid pace. By 1980, Japanese car producers had achieved a 35 percent cost advantage relative to the Big Three—that was up from just 5 percent in 1975. Chrysler avoided bankruptcy only with the help of a massive government bailout. In fact, a $1 billion unfunded pension liability has been cited by Secretary of Labor Robert Reich as one of the principal motivations for that bailout.[44] The prospect of a bankruptcy at Chrysler represented a direct threat to the new PBGC insurance program. Meanwhile, Ford—while not quite as desperate as Chrysler—was losing large amounts of money before the introduction of its successful Taurus line during the mid-1980s.

For its part, GM seriously misgauged the Japanese competitive advantage. As a result, the company embarked on an ill-fated campaign under the direction of Roger Smith to introduce new automation. GM was motivated by two goals: to reduce costs by eliminating workers on the assembly line and to improve quality. Unfortunately, the technology was untested, and Smith's results were disastrous. GM went from being the industry's low-cost producer in 1980 to being its high-cost producer in 1983. The company became the decade's biggest loser of market share. Smith's fundamental premise was simply wrong: The Japanese competitive advantage did not result primarily from automation but from management techniques and effectiveness. Among the most important differences at the Japanese auto companies were organizational methods (e.g., Kanban); human relations (e.g., quality control circles); means of production (few job classifications, little hierarchy, no gulf between line workers and engineers or managers); and corporate culture (no executive lunch rooms and offices).[45]

The productivity gap with Japan has been closing. In 1990, GM employed 329,000 hourly paid workers in the United States. In 1995, it employed 250,000, who were paid at the rate of $42 per hour. By 1997, it may employ only 200,000 hourly paid workers in the United States. During the past four years, the company has taken charges for about $9.6 billion in restructuring costs. The writeoffs covered employee buyouts and unaccrued pension costs to the normal retirement date.[46] In 1992, manhours per vehicle ranged from 125 at GM to 64 at Ford and 66 at Chrysler. Vertical integration explains most of the difference in labor requirements for the Big Three. GM adds more value per car internally than Ford or Chrysler.

Automakers encounter a major problem when reducing verticle integration, because they must pay former employees for quite some time following a workforce reduction. Just as in the steel industry, labor has essentially become a fixed cost; contracts with the United Auto Workers Union contain strong provisions protecting income security. People laid off as a result of productivity improvements or simply following a sales decline receive benefits amounting to 95 percent of previous pay. The UAW showed foresight in negotiating these provisions for its members during the 1980s. However, the effects of the recession for the automakers were much more costly as a result. GM now has many opportunities to improve productivity, but it will be difficult for the company to realize any major financial gains from those improvements in the short term. The cost of early retirements for the many additional workers that GM no longer needs will impair the company's performance for years to come.

In other areas, America's Big Three have made considerable strides during the past several years. Chrysler has excelled with new products, and it has demonstrated the advantage of working cooperatively with a small group of suppliers in ways that resemble Japanese approaches. GM and Ford are expected to follow suit by reducing the number of their suppliers and relying more heavily on long-term contracts. The number of dealers in the United States with franchises from the Big Three will also decline, producing major savings for the companies with respect to marketing costs. The rate of new engine introduction by the Big Three is currently unprecedented. According to at least one influential analyst, the Japanese have no significant advantage in engines today. This follows a period particularly noteworthy for its lack of American innovation. Ford, for example, didn't introduce a new engine anywhere in the world during the 1980s. And, in North America, the Big Three have been regaining market share as a result of the weak dollar. GM's costs have been falling, and the company introduced new products for the 1995 model year that impressed the critics.[47]

To sum up, differences in management techniques and effectiveness explain the weak performance of the Big Three American auto producers compared with their Japanese counterparts starting in the early 1980s. However, the Japanese advantage in unit costs has diminished and will continue to do so for the foreseeable future. Of the Big Three, Chrysler currently has the best-received products. Ford has the strongest balance sheet, and GM could still become the quintessential turnaround. All of these companies are expected to survive for at least the next 25 to 30 years. The Big Three—particularly GM—learned a painful lesson during the 1980s: Technology is not necessarily the key to lean and competitive manufacturing. That key, rather, is a knowledge and understanding of production systems, along with a labor force organized and motivated to eradicate sources of waste. Having learned this lesson, the Big Three automakers must now prepare for a new set of challenges as the manufacturing paradigm of lean production is replaced by one of "agile production."[48]

General Motors: Dinosaur of the Pension Age?

GM's domestic pension shortfall certainly appeared to have gone up sharply—from about $1.43 billion at the end of 1988 to $18.6 billion at the end of 1992, according to Form 5500 data as adjusted by the "Plan Asset Insufficiency" model. At that point, the paper trail ended. The company refused to provide any subsequent Form 5500 data for this study, and more recent information wasn't available from other sources. Elsewhere, GM itself disclosed that the pension plan for the United Auto Workers was underfunded by $11.4 billion at the end of 1992 and by $18.3 billion a year later. Although the PAI model made substantial adjustments to the data that GM reported on the Form 5500 reports, the adjusted values are remarkably consistent with the representations the company made in connection with its "Prohibited Transaction Exemption Application" for its United Auto Workers pension plan.[49] General Motors maintains separate pension plans for white-collar and blue-collar workers in the United States. Company officials have indicated that the total unfunded liability for its operations in the United States approached $25 billion, due in part to further declines in interest rates and benefit increases negotiated in 1993 with the UAW.

That GM fell so far raises the question of whether its pension plans will ever regain a sound and stable financial footing again. Here the answer depends on the company and its employees. Recent signals about their intentions were not clear. The company proposed to close $6.1 billion of the gap by issuing Class E shares to the pension plan for its blue-collar workers.[50] As many expected, the U. S. Department of Labor approved that transaction in March 1995, and the risk to the PBGC will not diminish as long as these shares remain in the pension plan. Shares issued to pension plans by employers generally become worthless in the event of bankruptcy.[51] GM could also use the presence of Class E shares to reduce the minimum funding requirement in years when the company does poorly. A claim against the PBGC for the unfunded liabilities attributable to GM's pension plans would almost certainly precipitate a taxpayer bailout of major proportions.

Ford: A Quality Credit

Among the automakers, the most surprising pension data came from Ford: the company with the best credit rating among all the steel and auto firms. Despite never having appeared on the PBGC's "Top 50" list of sponsors with the most severely underfunded plans, Ford's United Auto Workers' plan was underfunded by some $2.26 billion at the end of 1991 and by $1.56 billion at the end of 1992. Furthermore, the vested-benefit security ratio remained relatively unchanged during this period after adjusting the data to a PBGC termination basis. According to the PAI model, Ford's UAW plan has been underfunded by at least $1 billion since 1980. Meanwhile, Ford's salaried plan is in surplus and that surplus has grown over time. As with the UAW plan, Ford has also maintained a relatively stable vested-benefit security ratio during the period considered in this study.

This situation demonstrates once again that official pension data can be quite misleading. The group that prepares the "Top 50" list at the PBGC relies on FAS 87 pension data provided to shareholders according to generally accepted accounting standards. The actuarial adjustments made by the PBGC's own PAI model, however, are not part of that exercise. As a result, the official termination liability frequently can exceed the estimates produced in connection with the "Top 50" list by more than 100 percent. Still, Ford has the best credit rating in the auto industry. It clearly has the resources to support its retirement obligations for the foreseeable future.

Chrysler: The Tentative Recovery

Despite the impression to the contrary given long ago by Secretary of Labor Robert Reich,[52] Chrysler started the 1980s with its three major U.S. pension plans underfunded to the tune of $2.45 billion. Assets in all of Chrysler's major pension plans covered only 32 percent of liabilities. By the end of 1991, the unfunded liability had risen to $3.73 billion before falling by about $500 million during the next 12 months. At that point, Chrysler's ratio of pension assets to vested benefits also had improved, but at only 62 percent it was still far from healthy.

The condition of Chrysler's UAW plan remained a source of concern until late 1994. Its funded ratio had risen from an appalling 22 percent in 1981 to just 42 percent 10 years later. Meanwhile, the unfunded liability increased from approximately $2 billion to $2.9 billion during the same period. Benefit payments exceeded the amortization schedule by about $940 billion.[53] However, Chrysler's sales and profits were booming in 1994. As a result, the company announced plans to contribute $2.5 billion to the pension plans, and the PBGC removed Chrysler from the "Top 50" list.

The Chrysler story clearly is one of defunding followed by re-funding. Does this mean that the company no longer represents a threat to the insurance fund? This much is clear: the United Auto Workers Union will continue to negotiate benefit increases for its members, as it has in the past. If Chrysler falls on hard times again, the same incentives to defund the pension plans will operate in the absence of significant reform in this area. Further reductions in Chrysler's labor force could also create new instability and reverse previous improvements in benefit security. The example of GM just cited demonstrates how a relatively healthy level of pension funding can erode to become a massive shortfall in only a few years.

The Automakers' Dilemma

To sum up, the largest unfunded private pension liabilities are found in the auto industry. Some of these obligations were incurred long before ERISA was enacted. Others became apparent more recently, after plant closings and relentless corporate downsizing. As a recent study by the World Bank noted, labor negotiations in the auto indus-try allocate the projected increase in labor costs among wages for young workers, the level of pension benefits granted to new retirees, and cost-of-living adjustments for older pensioners. However, the Big Three automakers can't automatically pass on the cost of amor-tizing previous unfunded pension liabilities to consumers. Any at-tempts to do so would drive their customers elsewhere, possibly to imports or to other domestic producers (i.e., "transplant" facilities set up in the United States by foreign automakers) not similarly bur-dened. Output and employment at the Big Three would decrease even further and the ratio of retirees to active workers would con-tinue to rise. For this reason, American automakers have chosen to shift the cost of protecting the real value of pensions to new workers in the form of lower starting wages. However, this tactic can work only in a depressed area with few alternative employment opportuni-ties or in a situation where industrywide or occupationwide collective bargaining impedes worker mobility in the direction of higher-wage firms. In competitive product and labor markets, signficantly underfunded defined-benefit plans are unlikely to raise the money to cover their pension promises over the longer run.[54]

CONCLUSION

ERISA left substantial control over the funding decision in the hands of companies that sponsor defined-benefit pension plans. Today, many opportunities remain available to those firms for making empty retirement promises to their employees and even to divert pension assets to nonpension uses. On the strength of the ERISA termination insurance guarantee, for example, companies can go on borrowing from their workers long after they have become insolvent. The true magnitude of the resulting pension obligations doesn't become apparent until companies go out of business and their pension plans have been terminated.

The presence of such large contingent claims on the PBGC—particularly from the auto industry—has been used to reinforce political incentives for providing costly assistance in the form of special tax breaks, loan guarantees, waivers of minimum pension-funding requirements, and individual company exemptions from ERISA investment standards. Without such assistance, unfunded pension liabilities do not appear viable in competitive product and labor markets when the size of the labor force declines significantly. Looking to the future, other industries could decline to the point of making major claims on the insurance fund. Tire and rubber companies, for example, already have accumulated large unfunded liabilities and industries that are now relatively healthy (e.g., computer manufacturing) may also become distressed in the years ahead.

Meanwhile, the official indicators of risk to the insurance fund are likely to reflect substantial volatility. The Financial Accounting Standards Board favors classification systems that are highly sensitive to changes in interest rates as well as corporate credit ratings. As the major rating agencies reevaluate companies with large unfunded pension liabilities, claims that the PBGC reports as probable or reasonably possible are likely to change by billions of dollars from year to year. But these shifts may not accurately reflect the level of risk to the insurance fund. That risk always has been large and it will remain so without effective reforms. At some point, much better models may be available to estimate systemwide risks to the PBGC. Chapter 4 examines prototypes for two such models.

SUMMARY

This chapter began by drawing the important distinction between the actuarial soundness of a defined-benefit pension plan and financial solvency. The tricky concept of actuarial soundness presumes only that a pension plan is fully funded—on the basis of the accumulated-benefit obligation (ABO) or the guaranteed-benefit obligation (GBO)—and will remain so or that the plan is on an orderly schedule to become fully funded. Financial solvency presumes that the sponsor is capable of funding projected-benefit obligation (PBO), or perhaps even the indexed-benefit obligation (IBO), regardless of the assets in the plan. A pension plan that is actuarially sound can be financially insolvent and vice versa. The former case should represent one of the most serious concerns for any guarantee fund standing behind plans that are required to fund their obligations in advance.

The chapter also discussed the three industries most frequently cited as the principal sources of risk to the insurance program: airlines, steel, and auto manufacturing. So far, terminations involving the largest unfunded liabilities have occurred in the airline industry. Today, four carriers remain in financially weakened condition. An economic downturn combined with strategic mistakes on the part of any one of these carriers could produce additional claims on the PBGC involving upwards of a billion dollars. However, much larger unfunded pension promises can be found elsewhere.

Major integrated steel producers in the United States continue to see their markets erode, primarily as a result of competition from highly efficient minimills. In many cases, the integrated producers entered the post-ERISA period with substantial unfunded pension liabilities. These shortfalls have remained large and could grow in the future as a result of additional plant shutdowns. Meanwhile, the financial health of major steelmakers has weakened. Looking ahead to the next recession, some of the smaller integrated producers could liquidate in bankruptcy. The existence of some major names in the industry meanwhile could become tenuous. As a result, the PBGC will almost certainly be facing substantial claims from the steel industry within the next decade or so.

The auto industry so far has accumulated the largest unfunded liabilities. Starting in the early 1980s, each of the Big Three companies substantially increased its pension shortfall. One motivation for these decisions has been a desire by the automakers to avail themselves of cheap credit in the form of unsecured pension promises to their employees. Yet, this is an industry that faces highly cyclical swings in sales and earnings. Chrysler's credit rating periodically has been downgraded to weak levels, while the once unassailable blue chip standing of General Motors and Ford sometimes has slid as well. Over the long term, the safety and soundness of any defined-benefit pension plans sponsored by a single company closely approximate the credit quality of its sponsor.

ENDNOTES

1. Benefit increases are subject to a five-year phase-in requirement before the termination insurance guarantee becomes completely effective. The increases become guaranteed at the rate of 20 percent each year during that period.

2. See U.S. General Accounting Office, "Pension Plans: Hidden Liabilities Increase Claims against Government Insurance Program" (Washington, DC: U.S. General Accounting Office, December 1992), p. 18.

3. In addition, the same group of firms also was responsible for $6.4 billion in unfunded pension promises that were not guaranteed by the agency in 1992. The PBGC's "Top 50" list is based on FAS 87 pension data from annual reports released to shareholders. Unfunded liabilities attributable to the Top 50 decreased in 1994 for the temporary and potentially misleading reasons noted in Chapter 1.

4. As this book went to press, universe tapes existed for 1988–91. Unfortunately, these tapes did not include the detailed actuarial information necessary to permit the adjustments we made in Chapter 2. Such detail should be available on subsequent universe tapes, albeit with a 30-month lag following the end of the calendar year in question.

5. For example, large unfunded liabilities can appear on corporate balance sheets like those of GM, which also reflect foreign operations. Of course, these benefits are not insured by the PBGC.

6. The term *net worth* here refers to the net present value of future cash flows from a company's capital investments.

7. Dorrance C. Bronson, *Concepts of Actuarial Soundness in Pension Plans* (Homewood, IL: Richard D. Irwin, 1957), p. 97.

8. Of course, another major policy concern involves plans that are neither financially solvent nor actuarially sound.

9. For a summary of this literature, see Thomas E. Copeland and J. Fred Weston, *Financial Theory and Corporate Policy,* 3d ed. (Reading, MA: Addison-Wesley, 1988), pp. 648–54.

10. See Fischer Black, "The Tax Consequences of Long-Run Pension Policy," *Journal of Finance,* July–August 1980, pp. 21–28; and Irwin Tepper, "Taxation and Corporate Pension Policy," *Journal of Finance,* March 1981, pp. 1–13.

11. See J. Bicksler and A. Chen, "The Integration of Insurance and Taxes in Corporate Pension Strategy," *Journal of Finance,* July 1985, pp. 943–55.

12. See Zvi Bodie, Jay O. Light, Randall Morck, and Robert A. Taggart, "Corporate Pension Policy: An Empirical Investigation," *Financial Analysts Journal,* September–October 1985, pp. 10–16.

13. For a detailed discussion of the OBRA '87 provisions concerning minimum funding, see Michael A. Archer, "Minimum Funding Requirements," in Martin Wald and David E. Kenty, eds., *ERISA: A Comprehensive Guide* (New York: John Wiley & Sons, 1991), pp. 119–51.

14. See Internal Revenue Code (IRC) § 4972.

15. Pension plans subject to amortization charges for past service costs, or net experience losses, must establish an account (known as the *funding standard account*) that compares actual contributions with the minimum requirement. Any deficit in the funding standard account is known as the *accumulated funding deficiency.* The accumulated funding deficiency, in turn, is subject to the excise tax penalty for underfunding.

16. Although the 50 percent excise tax rate can be reduced to 20 percent if proceeds of the reversion are used for "participant purposes," this still represents a significant deterrent in most cases, because the corporate income tax also applies.

17. See Joseph F. Delfico, "Private Pensions—Most Underfunded Plan Sponsors Are Not Making Additional Contributions," testimony before the Subcommittee on Oversight, Committee on Ways and Means, U.S. House of Representatives, GAO/T-HRD-93-16, April 20, 1993, U.S. General Accounting Office, Washington, DC.

18. Two additional benefit categories are not relevant to terminations that involve losses to the PBGC. Those are: all other vested benefits (i.e., remaining benefits that exceed the maximum guaranteed amount or recently improved benefits that have not been completely phased in); and all other benefits (i.e., those that have accrued but are not vested).

19. The Retirement Protection Act of 1994 was adopted, according to some observers, because it raised $1.3 billion in PBGC premiums and other taxes related to pensions. These revenues were needed under congressional budget procedures to offset tariffs lost as a result of the new General Agreement on Tariffs and Trade.

20. For example, see Ronald Weichert, "Pensionskassen starken den Kapitalmarkt," *Sparkasse* 105, Jahrgang (November 1988), pp. 506–09.

21. See Michael W. Derchin, "Understanding Airline Industry Basics," in *The Transportation Industry—Airlines, Trucking, and Railroads* (Charlottesville, VA: Association for Investment Management Research, 1992), pp. 15–20.

22. Continental emerged from its first Chapter 11 bankruptcy in August 1986 and then filed a second time for Chapter 11 protection from creditors in December 1990.

23. Other countries have come to appreciate the benefits for consumers demonstrated by America's experience with deregulation. Australia, Canada, and Japan subsequently deregulated their own airline fares, and the European Community plans to follow suit in 1997.

24. See Steven A. Morrison and Clifford Winston, *The Evolution of the Airline Industry* (Washington, DC: The Brookings Institution, 1995), pp. 25–26.

25. Despite intense competition in the industry, the carriers have found ways of establishing horizontal control of specific geographic markets. The large scale requirement on routes connected to any carrier's major hub certainly can represent a formidable barrier to entry. Frequent flier

programs and computer reservation systems owned by individual airlines also serve to impede competition. See Morrison and Winston, *The Evolution of the Airline Industry,* pp. 49–61.

26. Ibid., pp. 30–31.

27. Thomas G. Donlan, *Don't Count on It* (New York: Simon & Schuster, 1994), pp. 29–31.

28. The World Port leasehold that was sold to the pension plans was then resold by the PBGC to Delta Airlines for $124 million after Pan Am liquidated.

29. The Section 4044 provisions of ERISA that allocate the assets of terminating pension plans according to the priorities described earlier in this chapter can be particularly important for airline pilots and other highly paid workers who have been retired for more than three years when their pension plans terminate. However, other participants are not so fortunate. In one study, the U.S. General Accounting Office found that participants in 31 terminated pension plans lost 11.6 percent in promised benefits. See Joseph F. Delfico, testimony before the Subcommittee on Oversight, Committee on Ways and Means, U.S. House of Representatives, GAO/T-HRD-92-58, September 24, 1992, Washington, DC, U.S. General Accounting Office.

30. See Linda Sandler, "Eastern Air Makes Risk Investing an Understatement," *The Wall Street Journal,* December 6, 1990, sec. C, pp. 1–2; and Bridget O'Brien, "Eastern Air Business Proposal Retreats from Pledges to Pay Debts in Full Cash," *The Wall Street Journal,* January 26, 1990, sec. A, p. 3.

31. Icahn's personal net worth was exposed to the prospective PBGC claims because the entrepreneur owned more than 80 percent of TWA.

32. James P. Miller, "Pension Agency and Icahn Reach Accord on TWA," *The Wall Street Journal,* December 8, 1992, sec. A, pp. 3, 5.

33. See Patricia B. Limbacher, "PBGC Deal Key to Keeping TWA Operating: Airline Asks Agency to Swap Debt for Equity," *Pensions & Investments,* October 17, 1994, p. 1.

34. In early 1987, the PBGC restored three LTV pension plans that had been terminated during the previous year. Unfunded liabilities attributable to those plans were estimated at $2.4 billion.

35. The Pension Protection Act of 1987, which was part of OBRA '87, required sponsors of underfunded defined-benefit pension plans to calculate an additional contribution amount. However, the additional

contribution amount was reduced by a feature of the PPA requirement known as the *offset*. A design flaw in the offset made the reduction too large for many underfunded plans. The U.S. General Accounting Office estimated that the offset eliminated the additional contribution for 60 percent of the underfunded pension plans in its sample and substantially reduced the additional contribution for another 30 percent of the underfunded plans. See "Private Pensions: Funding Rule Change Needed to Reduce PBGC's Multibillion Dollar Exposure," GAO/HEHS-95-5, October 1994, Washington, DC, U.S. General Accounting Office, pp. 3–4.

36. Donald F. Barnett and Robert W. Crandall, *Up from the Ashes: The Rise of the Steel Minimill in the United States* (Washington, DC: The Brookings Institution, 1986), p. 37.

37. Ibid., p. 47. Nevertheless, the major integrated producers managed to reduce raw steelmaking capacity from 150 million tons to about 110 million tons between 1977 to 1985.

38. See Richard A. Ippolito, *The Economics of Pension Insurance* (Philadelphia: Pension Research Council of theWharton School at the University of Pennsylvania, 1989), p. 235.

39. The "three-year solvency rule" contained in the Retirement Protection Act of 1994 was intended to prevent cases of almost total defunding such as this.

40. See Donlan, *Don't Count on It,* pp. 1–3.

41. The minimum funding requirement played a role in determining when companies would file for bankruptcy protection. Complete as well as partial plant closings were typical after such filings.

42. See Ippolito, *The Economics of Pension Insurance,* pp. 39, 114.

43. Ibid., p. 115. At least 34 other plans have been terminated with funding ratios of less than 20 percent.

44. Estimates based on the PBGC's "PAI" model suggest that Chrysler's unfunded pension liability really was about $2.45 billion based on plan termination assumptions. If that termination had been accompanied by a liquidation of Chrysler itself, the unfunded liability probably would have been even higher. For the earlier estimate by Reich, see Robert B. Reich and John D. Donahue, *New Deals: The Chrysler Revival and the American System.* (New York: Times Books, 1985), p. 174.

45. Melvyn A. Fuss and Leonard Waverman, *Costs and Productivity in Automotive Production* (Cambridge: Cambridge University Press, 1992), p. 231.

46. For example, if a worker who is expected to retire at 62 retires at 55 the company must accrue, at the time of early retirement, the pension costs that would have been accrued during the next seven years.

47. See Maryann N. Keller, "The Basics of the U.S. Automobile Industry," in *Industry Analysis: The Automotive Industry* (Charlottesville, VA: Association for Investment Management Research, 1994), p. 10.

48. See James C. Rucker, "Competitive Factors in a Manufacturing Setting," in *Industry Analysis: The Automotive Industry* (Charlottesville, VA: Association for Investment Management Research, 1994), p. 60.

49. See Steven J. Sacher, Evan Miller, and Francis S. Jaworski, "Prohibited Transaction Exemption Application of General Motors Corporation to Permit the General Motors Hourly Rate Employees Pension Plan to Acquire and Hold Class E Stock," paper submitted to the U.S. Department of Labor, June 9, 1994, p. 2.

50. GM Class E shares pay dividends from the earnings of Electronic Data Systems (EDS): a wholly owned GM subsidiary. However, the Class E shares actually represent an equity claim on GM itself. As this book went to press, GM was requesting approval from the IRS to sever its link to EDS. A divestiture—should it proceed—would be structured as a tax-free exchange of the EDS capital stock for all outstanding Class E shares.

51. See James H. Smalhout, "Labor's Wrong Call on GM Pensions," *The Wall Street Journal,* March 14, 1995, sec. A, p. 14.

52. See Reich and Donahue, *New Deals,* p. 174.

53. The amortization schedule includes charges for past service liabilities and net experience losses, together with interest on both of these items. To the extent that benefit payments exceed the amortization schedule, assets will flow out of the pension plan faster than liabilities are extinguished, as long as all other factors remain constant. This situation may produce erosion in the plan's benefit security ratio. Interest rate changes and investment returns that differ from plan assumptions can work to offset or accelerate this process.

54. See The World Bank, *Averting the Old Age Crisis* (Washington, DC: The International Bank for Reconstruction and Development, 1994), p. 189.

4

MEASURING
INSURANCE VALUES

$\mathbf{A}$ remarkable feature of public discussion about the problems facing the PBGC has been the failure to pay adequate attention to the substantial gap between the value of the insurance and premiums charged by the agency. Nor has this factor been reflected in the series of "reform" measures proposed to address increasing unfunded liabilities since ERISA was enacted. In fact, most of these proposals have perversely widened this gap in the very cases that present the most immediate threats to the insurance fund. This mismatch represents the central structural defect in the design of the program. The purpose of this chapter is to examine the earlier literature in this area, and to provide additional benchmarks for estimating insurance values.

By emphasizing more stringent minimum funding requirements without effectively restricting both the growth of unfunded pension liabilities and the ability of portfolio managers to make risky investments, the perennial "reform" proposals put before Congress have created new risks for the PBGC and jeopardized substantial numbers of jobs. Almost every administration since the enactment of ERISA has attempted to raise the minimum funding requirement without addressing these other needs. Although several previous reforms also adjusted premiums to reflect some measure of risk, the adjustments were only slight, and any effect on moral hazard has yet to become apparent. All these efforts were misguided, as they ignored the economic principles concerning the value of financial guarantees that have been developed in the pension and financial literature for almost a generation.

How can additional pension contribution requirements create new risks for the PBGC and thereby increase insurance values? On close inspection, the intuitive answer is clear, but only as it applies to those cases that involve seriously underfunded pension plans sponsored by financially weak companies. To understand the principle at work, consider the case of an employer with a net worth of $20 million and an unfunded pension liability of $100 million. If a new funding standard were adopted that required the company to reduce the unfunded pension liability by $10 million, what would happen?

First, half of the company's net worth would be eliminated, putting the firm that much closer to liquidation. The pension fund's portfolio managers would thus have an even greater incentive to adopt high-risk investment strategies in an attempt to help the firm gamble for redemption. If the risky investments appreciated, the company might receive a new lease on life, since the investment gains could be used to reduce funding requirements in the future. If there were losses, the PBGC would eventually be left to absorb the additional shortfall. The company meanwhile could go on making more empty promises to its workers until it actually closed its doors and went out of business. In all likelihood, those obligations would eventually be paid by the insurance fund as well.

Accepted principles of corporate finance therefore argue for investment restrictions on seriously underfunded pension plans sponsored by financially shaky companies. To limit risks facing the insurance fund, pension portfolios should be "immunized" against the effects of interest rate changes. This can be achieved by purchasing investment grade bonds whenever investment losses or new benefit obligations eliminate surplus funding.[1] Sound practice would also prevent sponsors in this category from promising workers additional benefits that aren't immediately funded and secured by similarly immunized bond investments. These policy prescriptions flow from the option-pricing literature that now represents a cornerstone of modern corporate finance.

THE PREVIOUS LITERATURE

Several academic and government-organized studies have attempted to value PBGC insurance by using adaptations of the Black–Scholes option pricing model. Some of the more theoretical among them have modeled the value of the insurance, assuming that the date at which the underfunded pension plans will be terminated is nonrandom.[2] As two analysts have recently noted, this is a convenient assumption because it permits the insurance to be valued as a standard (European) put option.[3] However, claims arising from underfunded pension plans occur when the sponsor is suffering from severe financial distress and, under current policy, usually result from a liquidation in bankruptcy. Virtually without exception, the date of this event was highly uncertain when the insurance first was provided and will remain so at most subsequent dates prior to any termination.

One study that avoided this lack of realism was conducted by Alan J.Marcus.[4] He made the first attempt to link the value of the guarantee to both the financial condition of the sponsor and the funded condition of the pension plan. However, the Marcus formula suffered from a different shortcoming. It assumed that the PBGC would recover surplus funds from the termination of an overfunded plan if the sponsor liquidated. In reality, the PBGC has no legal claim against overfunded plans regardless of the size of any unfunded pension liabilities attributable to the same sponsor.[5] The Marcus model therefore can produce the implausible result of a negative value for PBGC insurance. In other cases involving positive insurance values, the Marcus model systematically understates the value of PBGC insurance, since the agency could receive surplus pension assets from overfunded plans.[6]

The Marcus study also failed to shed the necessary light on this subject due to the choice of data. Specifically, Marcus used estimates of plan liabilities reported under Financial Accounting Standard (FAS) 36. Although FAS 36 has been superseded by FAS 87, accounting problems remain serious in view of the PBGC's 1992 estimate of a $7.7 billion shortfall at Chrysler.[7] At that time, the company was reporting a $3.4 billion unfunded liability to shareholders. Another problem with these studies results from well-known limitations of the Black-Scholes model itself.[8]

For their part, Pennacchi & Lewis (P&L) offered a measure of the "gross subsidy" that the Federal government provides to individual pension plans.[9] They overcame the modeling deficiencies of the Marcus study by valuing the PBGC's liability as a contingent put option[10] instead of a contingent forward contract. Aggregate values ranging from $60 billion to $90 billion for PBGC insurance based on the P&L studies were then reported in the federal budget. Only a year earlier, the Office of Management and the Budget had estimated this range to be $25 billion to $40 billion.[11] In a more recent paper, P&L extended their model to reflect the value of future PBGC premiums. They concluded that PBGC insurance represents about 11.66 percent of the value of accrued benefits for overfunded plans and about 35.94 percent for underfunded plans.[12] They also estimated that eliminating the $53 cap on the variable-rate premium would produce only a slight reduction in insurance values. Nevertheless, exactly this proposal emerged as a central feature of the Retirement Protection Act of 1994. Authors of that legislation estimated that eliminating the variable-rate premium cap would increase revenues by $1.094 billion over five years. Despite such a limited effect, however, OMB reduced its estimate for the value of PBGC insurance to between $20 billion and $40 billion in the subsequent budget document.[13]

Meanwhile, the PBGC has embarked on an effort of its own to produce a simulation model known as the Pension Insurance Management System (PIMS). This model is designed to forecast claims experience over a wide range of economic scenarios and also to simulate the effects of specific pension plan design (e.g., flat-benefit plans compared to final salary plans) in its forecasts. PIMS was originally intended to complement the OMB studies. However, it will produce a measure that is considerably less than total insurance value because it fails to model indirect and opportunity costs related to the insurance program.

Bodie and Merton[14] used Merton's original model to show how a risk-based premium would vary with the extent of immunization and the funding ratio.[15] In the case of no immunization and full funding, they estimated that the annual premium should be 8 percent of guaranteed benefits. With half the liabilities immunized, the premium for this plan should be 4 percent of guaranteed benefits. With complete immunization, there would be no premium. A pension plan with assets that exceeded guaranteed benefits by 20 percent would need to immunize 70 percent of those benefits before the insurance premium fell to zero. The same study also evaluated risk-based premiums as a function of the term of the guarantee and the funding ratio. According to Bodie and Merton, a pension plan that was 20 percent overfunded and made no use of immunization would need to pay a premium of 18 percent of guaranteed benefits if the contract covered a 10-year period.

Hsieh, Chen, and Ferris used an option pricing model with an uncertain exercise price to derive PBGC insurance values for a sample of 176 individual firms.[16] These authors assumed that the PBGC insurance contract has a term of one year. However, a failure to pay PBGC premiums has never resulted in cancellation of coverage. In fact, claims for unpaid PBGC premiums are quite common in bankruptcy cases. Modeling the PBGC insurance contract based on a one-year term therefore has the effect of greatly understating insurance values. Despite this shortcoming, Hsieh, Chen, and Ferris concluded that the value of insurance coverage received by 22 underfunded sponsors significantly exceeded PBGC premiums as of 1989. The 154 firms remaining in their sample also received more insurance coverage than their premiums reflected. However, these researchers concluded that the difference was not statistically significant in these cases.

This chapter brings two additional perspectives to bear on these efforts. The first approach, outlined by Brealey and Myers, recognizes that the value of a financial guarantee can also be estimated by a yield-spread analysis. This method recognizes that a financial guarantee is nothing more than a credit upgrade or the difference between two present values.[17] With respect to pension liabilities guaranteed by the federal government, the value of that upgrade would translate into a quantity that economists refer to as the *delta* (i.e., the projected cash benefits discounted at the "risk-free" cost of funds minus the smaller value of those obligations discounted by using a risk premium appropriate for the sponsor).[18]

This approach has produced reliable estimates of the value of deposit insurance.[19] It also can be implemented with Form 5500 pension data to estimate the value of PBGC insurance.

The second approach involves the concept of *shadow pricing*. Shadow pricing is commonly used in cost–benefit studies involving goods or services provided by government entities. However, no premium study in connection with PBGC insurance has made use of this technique. The essence of shadow pricing is to reflect the opportunity cost of a program or project. Market prices for similar goods or services are frequently used as benchmarks because they provide an objective, impersonal guide to valuing benefits and costs. Resources that would be utilized elsewhere in the economy are priced according to values suggested by their alternative uses. Prices that are set by regulation or by the legislative branch may also be adjusted to reflect the value of the good or harm that government may impose on producers and users of the good or service in question. Spillover effects on other parties usually are included in these calculations as well.[20] Consistent with these principles, one can estimate the shadow price of PBGC insurance based on anticipated losses from unfunded pension liabilities as well as the capital and operating costs that private financial guarantors would incur by providing essentially the same insurance coverage. The sample Form 5500 pension data from Chapter 2 can also provide a basis for shadow pricing.

YIELD-SPREAD ANALYSIS

Extending the statistical analysis begun in Chapter 2, we initially used three stratified random samples of pension plan data covering the years 1981, 1986, and 1987 to value PBGC insurance consistent with contemporaneous yield spreads. As a first step, we linked pension data to credit ratings of individual plan sponsors provided by Standard & Poor's. S&P credit ratings were found to correspond with 681 pension plans in the 1981 sample. For the 1986 dataset, there were 858 of these matches, and a total of 1,124 of these matches in the larger 1987 sample. Table 4–1 begins by reporting universe estimates of insurance values based on the yield spread for these three years. Table 4–2 reports the assumed borrowing costs

TABLE 4-1

Summary Estimates

	1981	1986	1987
Value of guarantee (yield-spread method)	$29.9 billion ($4.2 billion)[1]	$103.3 billion ($12.6 billion)	$66.3 billion ($6.6 billion)
Value of guarantee (shadow price)	$38.6 billion ($4.9 billion)	$110.2 billion ($12.6 billion)	$83.3 billion ($7.0 billion)
Pre-enhancement benefit value	$294.5 billion ($53.6 billion)	$620.4 billion ($102.9 billion)	$496.4 billion ($49.4 billion)
Guaranteed benefits[2]	$333.1 billion ($58.2 billion)	$730.6 billion ($114.1 billion)	$579.7 billion ($54.7 billion)
Credit enhancement[3]	11.6%	15.1%	14.4%
Shadow premium	$5.9 billion ($869 million)	$14.7 billion ($1.9 billion)	$11.8 billion ($1.1 billion)
Guarantee/participant	$1,199 ($143)	$3,581 ($326)	$2,820 ($216)
Shadow premium/ participant	$183 ($26)	$477 ($50)	$400 ($36)

[1] Numbers in parentheses denote standard errors.

[2] Represents sum of pre-enhancement benefit value and the shadow value of the PBGC guarantee.

[3] Value of the guarantee expressed as a percent of guaranteed benefits.

used for computing the valuations. A technical appendix at the end of this chapter explains the statistical methods and actuarial adjustments in more detail.

The estimates at the beginning of Table 4–1, which were based on yield spreads for the value of the guarantee, tend to exceed those in previous work, with the exception of the latest studies by Pennachi and Lewis. The P&L studies use more recent FAS 87 pension data. Yet, the estimates developed here are a noteworthy result, because the aggregate value of benefit obligations generally was thought to increase with the passage of time, inflation, and renegotiation of collective bargaining agreements.

Estimated guarantee values ranging from $29.9 billion in 1981 to $103.3 billion in 1986 are consistent with this impression. Moreover, the standard errors reported in the table reveal that there were significant differences (i.e., at the .05 level) between the aggregate

T A B L E 4–2

Cost of Borrowing

	Maturity		
Credit Rating	5 Years	10 Years	30 Years
December 31, 1981			
Risk-free[1]	14.15	13.96	13.64
AAA[1]	14.42[2]	14.75	15.00
AA[1]	14.75[2]	15.13	15.38
A[1]	15.20[3]	15.63	16.00
BBB[1]	16.52[2]	17.00	17.25[7]
BB	17.55[6]	17.55[8]	18.22[4]
B+	18.18[6]	18.18[8]	18.83[4]
B	18.48[6]	18.48[8]	19.13[4]
B–	19.90[6]	19.90[8]	20.52[4]
CCC	28.00[6]	28.00[5]	28.45[4]
December 31, 1986			
Risk-free[1]	6.82	7.23	7.49
AAA[1]	7.04[2]	7.63	8.70
AA[1]	7.25	8.00	8.90
A[1]	7.45[3]	8.25	9.25
BBB[1]	7.90[2]	8.75	9.65
BB	10.70[6]	10.70[8]	11.51[4]
B+	11.41[6]	11.41[8]	12.21[4]
B	11.94[6]	11.94[8]	12.72[4]
B–	13.04[6]	13.04[8]	13.80[4]
CCC	13.86[6]	13.86[7]	14.62[4]

insurance values reported for each of these three years.[21] To the extent that lower interest rates are responsible for the increase in insurance values, these results suggest the need for caution when using option pricing models to estimate the value of pension insurance. An option pricing model assumes that, all other things being equal, the relationship between the value of the insurance and interest rates is direct. In other words, higher interest rates will produce higher insurance values, and vice versa. However, this assumption ignores a very important detail related to the nature of the insured pension

T A B L E 4-2

(continued)

Credit Rating	Maturity		
	5 Years	10 Years	30 Years
December 31, 1987			
Risk-free[1]	8.39	8.86	8.99
AAA[1]	8.77[2]	9.30	9.70
AA[1]	8.90	9.45	9.90
A[1]	9.05[3]	9.65	10.20
BBB[1]	9.35[2]	10.00	10.70
BB	11.61[6]	11.61[8]	12.40[4]
B+	12.39[6]	12.39[8]	13.17[4]
B	13.78[6]	13.78[8]	14.53[4]
B–	14.76[6]	14.76[8]	15.49[4]
CCC	15.49[6]	15.49[7]	16.20[4]

[1]Source: Salomon Brothers bond series unless otherwise indicated.

[2]Interpolated or extrapolated based on neighboring values.

[3]Index value provided by CS-First Boston.

[4]Estimated using the regression model $y = 1.03 + .98 \cdot x + \varepsilon$, where x equals the 10-year rate.

[5]Imputed using the B– rate and the spread for January 1991.

[6]Five-year rates assumed to approximate 10-year rates below the investment grades.

[7]Smoothed using the five-month median rate.

[8]Culled from unpublished monthly bond series.

obligation. Specifically, the value of the benefit obligation itself has an inverse relationship to interest rates, and this effect appears to have dominated the estimated values of the ERISA guarantee. In option trading parlance, this is tantamount to changing the "strike price" at which the option can be exercised.[22]

Interest Rates and the Structure of Insurance Risk

Lending involves many sources of risk. As a practical matter, most observers consider the risk-free interest rate to be the yield on U.S. Treasury securities.[23] However, a substantial literature has developed over the years that evaluates a variety of factors explaining the differentials between U.S. Treasury securities and other debt instruments. Among the factors that have contributed to these spreads are credit risk or the pure risk of default, interest rate risk, market liquidity risk, industry or sector risk, and call or early redemption risk. Bank reserve requirements have also played a role, as has the exemption of interest on Treasury securities from state and local taxation. Finally, the fact that almost all U.S. Treasury bonds issued before 1971 (i.e., "flower bonds") were redeemable at par for estate tax purposes also contributed to lower yields on those securities. The interest-rate sets reported in Table 4–2 reflect many of these factors. The course that they took over the business cycle created wide fluctuations in the government's exposure to losses from the PBGC and, hence, the value of ERISA termination insurance.

At the end of 1981, the rates in Table 4–2 were approaching all-time highs. The previous economic expansion had created unprecedented inflationary pressures, and the Federal Reserve moved aggressively to restrict the growth of money and credit. As a result, short-term Treasury rates rose above long-term rates. This inverted yield curve is apparent from the differences among the 5-year, 10-year, and 30-year bonds shown in the table. However, the effort to combat inflation, which actually began late in 1979, also helped to produce a recession. Interest rate spreads between different credit-quality sectors in late 1981 therefore approached all-time highs as well.

Ordinarily, the yield curve would invert at the peak of the business cycle when demand for credit and money from the economy itself tends to push up short-term rates relative to the cost of long-term funding. As Table 4–1 suggests, high rates of interest seem to reduce the value of PBGC insurance. This is consistent with economic intuition. When the economy is performing well and experiencing robust growth, the imminent threat of default on unfunded pension liabilities is reduced. Two opposing forces therefore were inducing major effects on insurance valuations at the end of 1981: the high and unprecedented level of interest rates that reduced insurance values, and heightened investor concern about the risk of default that made PBGC cover more valuable.[24] Despite the extremely fragile state of the economy, the level of interest rates—and not the wider yield spreads—seems to have dominated insurance values at that point.

By the end of 1986 and 1987, both interest rates and yield spreads had fallen considerably. Investor preferences for the un-matched liquidity of Treasury issues had changed with the improved state of the economy and lower inflation. With more importance attached to liquidity during the extended recession of the early 1980s, this motivation contributed to increased risk premiums in chaotic, depressed credit markets. In turn, these same risk premiums would be reduced during the more prosperous times that followed. Less concern about liquidity and default risk also fueled the expansion of the junk bond market starting in the middle of the decade. Just as was the case in 1981, the level of interest rates itself appears to have exerted a much more powerful influence on insurance values in 1986 and 1987 than the yield spreads considered by themselves. Figure 4–1 depicts the course of 30-year U.S. Treasury borrowing rates as well as yield spreads for the period beginning in 1974 when the PBGC was first set up.

One concern about relying on unadjusted yield spreads to esti-mate the value of PBGC insurance involves the presence of call risk relative to the bonds included in the various indexes used to con-struct Table 4–2. As Richard Bookstaber points out, a callable bond will never be worth as much as a similar noncallable bond, since there is always the possibility of interest rates dropping to the point that the call will be exercised. Following the redemption, the in-vestor could only reinvest the principal in another bond of equiva-lent credit quality in return for a lower yield.[25]

A potential problem for the yield-spread analysis conducted here therefore involved potentially higher yields on the corporate bond indexes than would be the case if those indexes had been com-piled using "option-adjusted spreads."[26] However, the argument in favor of adjusting the reported index values for this reason is less than compelling. In support of this view, Crabbe examined the call provisions of 3,999 bonds sold in U.S. markets by U.S. corporations between 1977 and 1990. His results suggested that for the 1983–88 period, corporations were able to include call options without having to pay a significant premium.[27] Another study found that sponsors with lower credit ratings—and more substantial yield spreads—were more likely to issue callable bonds.[28] In view of these two studies,

FIGURE 4-1

Interest Rates and Yield Spreads: 1977–1994

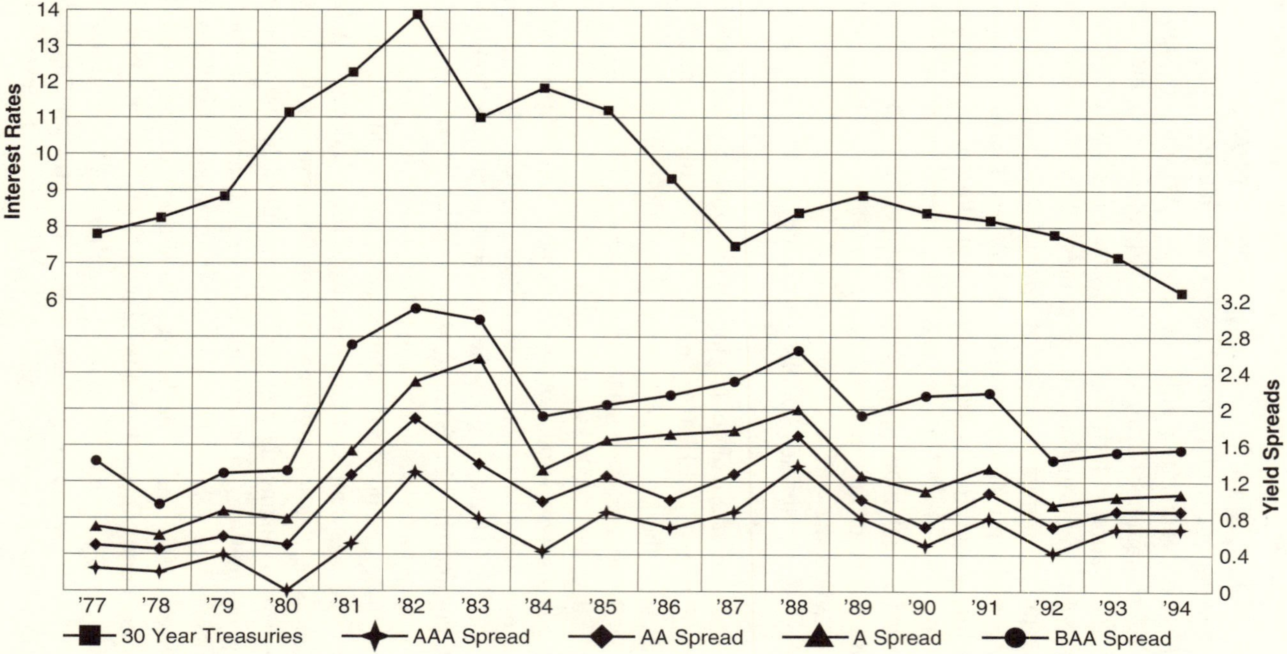

Source: Moody's Investors Service, Inc.

150

there seemed little reason to engage in a complicated adjustment of yield indexes if the call options were not being fully priced during this period and if the slight value that had been detected in previous studies was more directly applicable to cases involving sizable yield spreads.

Another question related to yield-spread data is whether historical indexes should be adjusted to account for the lower interest rates on government bonds due to their tax advantages. By way of a response, it is reasonably clear from the literature that the exemption from state and local income taxes of interest on risk-free U.S. Treasury securities has resulted in lower yields on those securities at the short end of the maturity range (i.e., on three-month and six-month bills).[29] However, the evidence of this effect on yield spreads between Treasuries with longer maturities and corporate bonds is less than convincing.

Consider this question in qualitative terms. The different tax treatment would not affect yield spreads if the marginal buyers of risky bonds (e.g., pension funds and private foundations) are not taxed or are unable to pass through the tax advantage of the Treasury exclusion. Even in municipal bond markets, where the evidence is incontrovertible that the exemption from federal tax affects spreads, neither investors on one side nor bond issuers on the other are consistently able to capture the entire yield spread. Instead, yields tend to fall between two extremes: those nearly equivalent to comparable Treasury securities that allow investors to capture the full advantage; and those reflecting the comparable Treasury rate less the highest federal tax rate that allow issuers to reap the full benefit of the federal tax exemption.

In 1991, maximum personal income taxes ranged from no tax at all in Washington State to 14 percent in Connecticut.[30] For states with taxes, the average rate was 7.3 percent. If even a 7.3 percent rate of state tax was fully reflected in the yield spread, the U.S. Treasury rates reported in Table 4–2 would have been approximately 7.9 percent higher.[31] The implied five-year, risk-free rate therefore would have been 15.26 percent in 1981, 7.36 percent in 1986, and 9.05 percent in 1987. The effect of recalibrating the risk-free rate to reflect even this level of state tax would have implied that U.S. Treasury securities should yield approximately the same returns as single-A rated corporate bonds. The effects for other maturities would have been similarly implausible. It therefore seems unlikely that more than a minor fraction of the state tax rate, if any, could have been reflected in the yield spread. For this reason, significant upward adjustment of the risk-free rate set was not indicated.

Elements of Insurance Value

To investigate factors that determine the value of the guarantee, we developed a model that explains the variation of insurance value per participant across different pension plans and time periods. The modeling effort utilized a weighted least-squares regression framework in conjunction with backward elimination, to reduce a large initial number of independent variables one by one until each variable that remained was significant at the 5 percent level. The last variable eliminated in this process was the intercept term. As in the previous regression, each plan was treated as a cluster to account for intraplan correlation in insurance values in cases where the same pension plan appeared in datasets for more than one year. The following regression model used all of the computed insurance values from 1981, 1986, and 1987:

$$\text{INSURANCE} = b_1 \text{BENEFITS} + b_2 \text{INTEREST} + b_3 \text{SPREAD} + b_4 \text{RATING} + b_5 \text{TIME} + \varepsilon$$

Here are definitions and a brief discussion of these variables.

INSURANCE : The difference in the present value of vested-benefit payments discounted using the risk-free rate set, and the present value of the same benefits discounted using the rate set corresponding with the sponsor's credit rating divided by the number of participants in the pension plan.

BENEFITS: The present value of vested-benefit payments discounted using the risk-free rate set divided by the number of participants in the pension plan.

INTEREST: The absolute level of interest rates as measured by the yields on five-year U.S. Treasury notes.

SPREAD: The yield spread in basis points between the sponsor's five-year borrowing cost and INTEREST immediately above. This variable reflects cyclical changes in credit risk.

RATING: The S&P credit ratings mapped onto an ordinal scale ranging from one for the AAA rating to 18 for CCC ratings and below. This variable provides a measure of default risk.

TIME : An ordinal categorical variable corresponding to the valuation date. For the 1981 data, that valuation date was December 31, 1981, and TIME was set to equal zero. For the 1986 data, TIME equaled five; and for the 1987 dataset, time equaled six.

Table 4–3 reports the regression results. The parameter estimates call into question previous expectations concerning the growth of liabilities in the defined-benefit pension system. They also provide a cautionary tale about the application of the standard textbook version of the option pricing model when valuing guarantees of this sort. One of the most striking results concerns the estimated decline in PBGC insurance values with respect to TIME. The PBGC projects that its total insured liabilities grow at approximately 4 percent annually, due both to projected future accruals and

TABLE 4–3

Insurance Value Regression Results

Independent Variables	Coefficient	Standard Error	t-Statistic	P-Value
BENEFITS	.1375	.0168	8.1852	.0000
INTEREST[1]	−1.4041	.2061	−6.8127	.0000
SPREAD	5.6879	1.627	3.4960	.0005
RATING[1]	182.15	48.93	3.7231	.0002
TIME	−195.54	56.71	−3.4478	.0006

Sample size: 2,663 observations.

F-statistic: 294.74 approximately distributed as $F(5,1505)$.

[1]Per basis point.

to benefit improvements that are granted as part of regular collective bargaining as well as for other reasons.[32] However, this result should be interpreted with caution. The sample size increased in both 1986 and 1987. The inverse relationship between TIME and guarantee values could reflect changes in the sample composition rather than any clear trend in the direction of lower benefit and insurance values on a plan-by-plan basis. On the other hand, this result could also accurately reflect either the reduction in benefit formulas that often accompanied the introduction of 401(K) plans after 1983, or the well-documented decline of American labor unions.

Another result that might not be consistent with expectations concerns the negative sign of the INTEREST variable. The standard textbook discussion of option pricing models assumes that the value of the contract is a positive function of the rate of return.[33] Although this can be appropriate for a call option, it clearly does not apply in the case of a long-term guarantee of pension liabilities that amounts to a put option instead. A related issue involves the effect of interest rate changes on the present value of benefit obligations. That effect is to move the price at which the sponsor can exercise its put option from the PBGC; it also was reflected in the universe estimates for the value of the guarantee presented previously. With reference to future studies that estimate PBGC insurance values using option pricing models, this feature strongly argues in favor of approaches that model the strike price as a random variable.

The remaining variables—BENEFITS, SPREAD, and RATING—behaved in a manner consistent with expectations. The parameter estimate for BENEFITS suggests that, on average, 14 cents of insurance will be provided for every dollar in additional benefits. The model seems to be most sensitive to changes in SPREAD. Still, the reason why the effect of INTEREST dominated during this period is readily apparent. The risk-free interest rate declined by 733 basis points between 1981 and 1986, while the spread between that rate and the BBB rate narrowed by only 129 basis points. Finally, the effect of RATING indicates that for every downgrade by one rating

level, participants on average received $182 in additional PBGC in-
surance protection.

The categorical variables examined in Chapter 2 (i.e., unionization, sector, and retiree burden) did not have a statistically significant influence in the context of the above regression. It seems
plausible that their impact on the guarantee is captured by those
variables included in the model. To identify the relationship between the categorical variables and insurance values, separate *t*-
tests were conducted on these variables for each year. Table 4–4
reports the results. Unionization never had a significant *t*-statistic,
even at the 10 percent level. The hypothesis that there was no difference between collectively bargained pension plans and other plans
therefore cannot be rejected. Economic sector (i.e., manufacturing
versus services) was statistically significant in 1986 and 1987. Finally, retiree burden alone was statistically significant in all three
periods. However, much of the information that it contained apparently was reflected in variables that were ultimately included in the
regression model above. After all, a continuous variable representing the ratio of retirees to total participants was not significant in
that model. Still, these results do not preclude the possibility of statistically significant interaction effects or nesting among these three
categorical variables (i.e., unionization, sector, and retiree burden).

T A B L E 4–4

The Effects of Unionization, Sector,[1] and Retiree Burden[2]

	1981		1986		1987	
	t-Statistic	*P*-Value[3]	*t*-Statistic	*P*-Value	*t*-Statistic	*P*-Value
Unionization	−.775	.438	−.529	.597	−1.586	.113
Sector	.817	.414	3.418	.001	2.243	.025
Retiree burden	2.696	.007	4.943	.000	2.218	.027

[1]Distinguishes between manufacturing and services.

[2]A dichotomous variable indicating whether a plan is in the highest quartile with respect to the ratio of retirees to total
participants.

[3]These are two-sided *P*-values.

For example, differences still might exist between unionized and nonunionized plans in the manufacturing industries.

How Much Do Pension Assets Matter?

To some, these estimates for the value of PBGC insurance may seem overstated because the extent of the credit upgrade does not explicitly reflect the presence of pension assets. The S&P implied senior credit ratings used above correspond with those that apply to unsecured corporate bonds issued by plan sponsors. Unlike deposit insurance, which is invoked by the conditional probability of insolvency on the part of a depository institution, pension insurance involves a joint conditional probability encompassing two events: liquidation of the sponsor, and the existence of an unfunded pension liability. The discounting method for valuing the guarantee used here, however, does not explicitly model these two events. One possible modification to the unadjusted yield spreads would increase the S&P implied senior credit rating for the sponsor by one full letter grade to reflect the presence of pension assets. Alternatively, the funded portion of the pension liability could be treated as secured debt and the unfunded portion as senior unsecured debt issued by the sponsor. In a third modification, the average funded ratio—37.5 percent—for terminating plans trusteed by the PBGC could be treated as risk-free debt.[34] The remaining 62.5 percent of each pension plan's liabilities would then be assigned S&P's implied senior rating for the sponsor in question.

Would any of these changes be appropriate? One argument against these approaches is that rating agencies don't materially upgrade secured obligations when they are backed by a portfolio of unrated securities. There is no upgrade whatsoever for investment-grade bonds and only a one-third letter grade improvement for speculative issues (e.g., a BB credit becomes BB+).[35] No indication of the credit quality of most fixed-income investments held by pension plans is available on the U.S. Department of Labor sample tapes. So, it is difficult to justify assigning pension assets a credit rating any higher than the above standard would suggest. Another problem is that the commercial rating agencies would not apply an upgrade on a dollar-for-dollar basis relative to the funded benefits. Both Moody's and

S&P have published overcollateralization tables in connection with structured financings. An upgrade to the AAA level involves overcollateralization ratios of as much as 220 percent for CCC-rated corporate bonds and 290 percent for common stock.[36] Parenthetically, an AAA-rated financial guarantee, although extremely strong, is still weaker than the risk-free position of debt backed by the U.S. Treasury. Even these high overcollateralization ratios therefore might not be high enough to offset the full value of PBGC insurance.

Furthermore, it seems doubtful that unfunded pension obligations deserve to be treated as senior corporate obligations consistent with the last two modified approaches to a yield-spread analysis mentioned above. Although the frequency of default may be similar, recovery rates appear to be much worse. Since the PBGC was established in 1975, it has, on average, recovered just 11.5 percent of unfunded pension liabilities from plan sponsors. The PBGC also reports that it has received $3.014 billion in pension assets and recovered $626 million from employers of terminated underfunded pension plans since it began operations in 1975. These figures compare with $8.014 billion in guaranteed-benefit obligations, implying an overall recovery rate relative to all guaranteed obligations of about 45 percent.[37] This rate corresponds much more closely with the mean loss function of 56.5 percent for senior unsecured debt estimated by Altman and Eberhart.[38]

The original approach using simple yield spreads also seems to be supported in part by a report from S&P. The report concludes that, over the long term, the credit quality of corporate defined-benefit plans approximates that of their sponsors.[39] S&P analysts found it doubtful that any overfunded pension plan sponsored by a company experiencing financial distress over an extended period would remain overfunded. Another drawback with the third modification to the yield spreads is that it treats risky debt as risk-free debt. Not all pension plans terminate with a funded ratio of 37.5 percent. In fact, several have terminated with essentially no assets at all. One of these was a large plan (i.e., the Republic Steel Retirement Plan for Salaried Employees).

To conclude, standards used by the well-known credit-rating agencies provide considerable support for the approach to valuing

PBGC insurance based on simple, unadjusted yield spreads. However, no method is perfect. Limitations of both the available pension data and the existing valuation models leave far too many questions unanswered to assert such a claim. Uncertainty like this is quite common when costs and benefits must be estimated in connection with public programs and projects. In most cases, it is simply impossible to know the exact value of the goods or services that the government provides. Still, reasonable approximations are feasible despite the limitations. It usually is helpful to consider results based on a variety of methods supported in the economic and financial literature.[40] Shadow pricing represents another alternative that is worthy of consideration in the context of the ERISA termination insurance program. This method explicitly takes account of the presence of pension assets.

SHADOW PRICING

After reporting universe estimates for PBGC insurance values based on the yield-spread analysis, Table 4–1 summarizes the shadow pricing results for 1981, 1986, and 1987. Estimates for the value of the guarantee based on shadow prices range from a low of $38.6 billion in 1981 to a high of $110 billion in 1986. Although the shadow-price values are consistently higher than the yield-spread estimates for each of these three years, none of the differences was statistically significant at the 5 percent level. The fact that both sets of estimates fell within such a relatively narrow range represents one of the more striking results of this study. Based on shadow pricing,[41] credit enhancement in the form of PBGC insurance ranged from approximately 11.6 percent of the value of guaranteed liabilities in 1981 to 15.1 percent in 1986.

What explains the consistently higher shadow-price estimates (even if they involve only modest differences) relative to the initial yield-spread analysis? Shadow prices for PBGC insurance included three basic elements. First, anticipated claims against the insurance fund were modeled as a Markov process involving published one-year transition probabilities across the different credit ratings and ultimately into default.[42] The reported pension liabilities were treated as immediate or deferred annuities, depending on whether they were attributable to retired lives or to active workers. The scheduled annuity payments were then discounted for the time value of money and mortality. The difference between the present value of these annuities and their expected value as reduced by projected defaults—net of the 45% recovery rate experienced by the PBGC—represented the present value of expected claims against the insurance fund.

Second, insurance company operating costs were assumed to be consistent with recent experience for the private financial guarantee industry in the United States. Industry analysts report that these costs have averaged 0.3 percent of the par value for the insurance.[43] Par value represents one measure of the insurance carrier's risk exposure. As we will discuss in Chapter 8, the par value of a pension insurance contract, based on an appropriate adjustment for portfolio risk, amounts to the difference between guaranteed liabilities and the assets in the pension plan. For the typical pension plan, the market value of pension assets would require a reduction of approximately 25 percent to arrive at a risk-free equivalent.

Finally, the shadow-price estimates included capital costs. Insurance carriers are required to maintain capital reserves of no less than 6 percent of par value for private financial guarantee contracts. Before 1987, the industry used an after-tax hurdle rate of 20 percent for equity capital. The rate then fell to 15 percent, where it has since remained. This factor, in conjunction with the yield on high-grade municipal bonds, determined the industry's net cost of reserve capital. Companies purchased these investments—with yields approximating the after-tax equivalent available from AAA-rated corporate bonds—and held them to meet capital adequacy standards established both by state insurance commissioners and by the major credit rating agencies.

Shadow-price estimates for the value of the insurance therefore reflected: the effect of default by plan sponsors before any guaranteed benefits had been paid in full, the present value of insurance company operating costs during the same period, and the capital costs necessary to comply with insurance company solvency standards. Perhaps the most likely factor resulting in differences between the two sets of estimates was the treatment of vested obligations attributable to active workers. Two features—subsequent benefit accruals and the time

value of money[44]—cause these benefits to grow until the expected retirement age. This expansion of liability values was not, however,
modeled in the yield-spread analysis. On the other hand, default rates
worked to reduce the expected value of these liabilities with the passage of time.[45]

    The implied premiums reported in Table 4–1 provide new in-
sights concerning the extent of mispricing of PBGC insurance. Total
implied premiums ranged from a low of $5.9 billion in 1981 to a
high of $14.7 billion in 1986.[46] In terms of an average premium per
participant, this translates into a range of approximately $183 per
year in 1981 to about $477 per year in 1986. Table 4–5 reports actual

T A B L E 4–5

PBGC Premium Revenue

9/74–6/75	$ 21,870,000[1]
7/75–9/76	29,664,000
1977	25,062,000
1978	47,417,000
1979	69,685,000
1980	71,171,000
1981	74,952,000
1982	79,639,000
1983	81,522,000
1984	80,488,000
1985	81,736,000
1986	201,433,000
1987	267,576,000
1988	464,448,000
1989	603,200,000
1990	659,400,000
1991	741,000,000
1992	876,000,000
1993	890,000,000
1994	955,000,000

Source: PBGC annual reports.

[1]Includes some premiums received by the Multi-Employer Fund. Figures for subsequent years cover the Single
Employer Fund only.

premium revenues to the PBGC's Single Employer Program since 1974. During the period covered by these estimates, the agency collected between $75 million in 1981 and $268 million in 1987. From 1981 to 1985, the annual PBGC premium was set by law at $2.60 per participant. In 1986, it was raised to $8.50 per participant. Since the end of 1987, this flat-rate premium has been increased twice, and a variable-rate supplement has been added.

These shadow prices do not suggest that private defined-benefit pension obligations can be secured only by imposing costs of this magnitude on the economy. Nor do they imply that the PBGC or any private insurance carrier that might assume its work should actually charge insurance premiums in this range. Subsequent chapters will examine methods that have been used successfully elsewhere to secure long-term pension obligations for much less. Much of the excessive cost of PBGC coverage results from the indefinite term of its insurance contract and its lack of effective intervention rights in cases of deteriorating credit quality. The requirement that it insure the pension promises of all tax-qualified sponsors regardless of their financial health also results in higher costs.

CREDIT QUALITY AND INSURANCE VALUES

Table 4–6 reports insurance and benefit values by credit rating. For the very strongest credits with AAA ratings, PBGC insurance represented in 1981 approximately 3.6 percent of the total value of guaranteed benefits. For the very weakest credits with CCC ratings or below, it represented as much as 90.6 percent of the total value of pension promises. Key differences between these results and previous studies should be noted. In particular, the Marcus study reported negative values for the insurance in cases of seemingly well-funded plans sponsored by companies with stock trading in fairly stable ranges. Pennachi and Lewis subsequently estimated that PBGC insurance represented approximately 35 percent of benefit value for underfunded plans.

Another benchmark reported in Table 4–6 is the value of the guarantee per participant. In the most recent year covered by the

T A B L E 4-6

Estimated Insurance and Benefit Values by Credit Quality

Credit Rating		1981	1986	1987
AAA	Guarantee value/participant	$ 547	$ 2,794	$1,604
	Pre-enhancement benefits value/participant	14,804	21,478	22,144
	Risk-free benefits/participant	15,351	24,272	23,748
	Credit enhancement	3.6%	8.7%	6.8%
AA	Guarantee value/participant	$ 545	$ 2,245	$ 1,326
	Pre-enhancement benefits value/participant	9,285	27,819	24,332
	Risk-free benefits/participant	9,830	30,064	25,658
	Credit enhancement	5.5%	7.5%	5.2%
A	Guarantee value/participant	$ 816	$ 2,164	$ 1,630
	Pre-enhancement benefits value/participant	8,400	15,343	14,002
	Risk-free benefits/participant	9,216	17,507	15,632
	Credit enhancement	8.9%	12.6%	10.4%
BBB	Guarantee value/participant	$ 1,708	$ 3,743	$ 3,297
	Pre-enhancement benefits value/participant	6,191	18,952	14,608
	Risk-free benefits/participant	7,899	22,695	17,905
	Credit enhancement	21.6%	16.5%	18.4%
BB	Guarantee value/participant	$ 2,945	$ 5,813	$ 5,278
	Pre-enhancement benefits value/participant	3,805	12,471	16,327
	Risk-free benefits/participant	6,750	18,284	21,605
	Credit enhancement	43.6%	31.8%	24.4%
B	Guarantee value/participant	$ 6,318	$12,915	$ 7,198
	Pre-enhancement benefits value/participant	6,545	13,896	8,100
	Risk-free benefits/participant	12,863	26,811	15,298
	Credit enhancement	50.9%	48.2%	47.1%
CCC and below	Guarantee value/participant	$ 8,941	$12,896	$15,371
	Pre-enhancement benefits value/participant	4,309	1,340	2,051
	Risk-free benefits/participant	13,250	14,236	17,422
	Credit enhancement	67.5%	90.6%	88.2%

DOL sample data, this measure ranged from approximately $1,600 per participant for AAA sponsors to more than 10 times that amount for the weakest sponsor groups.[47] Table 4–7 reports the implied premiums by credit rating. Ninety-five percent confidence intervals for each of the single point estimates suggest lower bound premiums of approximately $63 per participant in 1987 for AAA-rated firms and a higher bound premium of $4,890 per year for sponsors rated CCC or weaker.[48] Implied premiums increased by statistically significant amounts (i.e., at the 5 percent level) during the period for the three credit-quality groups, which included companies with ratings of AA down to those with ratings of BBB (i.e., credits just above the investment grade threshold).[49]

With respect to overall shifts in credit quality, American nonfinancial corporations had annual decreases in book-value equity of

TABLE 4–7

Implied PBGC Premiums by Credit Quality[1]

Credit Rating	1981	1986	1987
AAA	$ 62	$ 195	$ 109
	(18)[2]	(78)	(23)
AA	79	243	152
	(15)	(54)	(17)
A	118	245	191
	(15)	(31)	(17)
BBB	249	469	414
	(24)	(65)	(29)
BB	450	904	758
	(72)	(167)	(143)
B	1,121	2,173	1,323
	(253)	(349)	(275)
CCC and below	1,608	1,982	2,840
	(93)	(346)	(1,025)

[1]Average annual premium per participant.

[2]Numbers in parentheses denote standard errors.

about $75 billion during the 1984–1988 period. This was accompanied by rising levels of new debt taken on during the many corporate restructurings completed at this time. When financial leverage increased sharply, credit ratings were lowered. For every upgrade by the rating agencies, there were 1.75 downgrades.[50] The effect of this trend was evaluated in terms of the three samples of pension data used here.

To determine the effect of the erosion in credit quality across samples, we conducted a regression test of the difference in average credit ratings relative to the datasets for each year. Three dummy variables indicated the year of the data point in question. Then, sample-weighted least squares estimated the following regression.

$$\text{RATING} = \alpha + b_1\text{DUMMY86} + b_2\text{DUMMY87} + \varepsilon$$

As reported in Table 4–8, the t-statistics for both coefficients (as computed with PC Carp) indicate that the differences were significant at the 1 percent level.[51] The hypothesis that credit quality was as high in 1986 and 1987 as it was in 1981 therefore can be rejected. The F-test for this model represents a test of the hypothesis that the average credit rating for these three years was the same. Since the F-value of 7.49 is significant at the .005 level, this hypothesis also can be rejected. To conclude, the direction of change in credit quality was clearly negative.[52]

T A B L E 4–8

A Regression Test for Differences in Credit Rating

Dependent Variable: Credit Rating

Independent Variables	Coefficient	Standard Error	t-Statistic	P-Value
INTERCEPT	7.5050	.2865	26.1972	.0000
DUMMY86	1.5965	.4125	3.8700	.0001
DUMMY87	1.0825	.4298	2.5183	.0118

Sample size: 2,663 observations.

F-statistic: 7.4939 approximately distributed as $F(2,1505)$.

CONCLUSION

The regression coefficients reported in this study lend support to the assertion that previous efforts to reform the ERISA pension insurance program have been misguided in ways that have increased the risks to taxpayers. The variables—BENEFITS, SPREAD, and RATING—each had a strong influence on the value of the guarantee. If anything, attempts to apply more stringent minimum funding requirements have the effect of eroding corporate credit ratings for financially weak companies with seriously underfunded pension plans, thereby increasing the differential (as measured by SPREAD) between their borrowing costs and the risk-free interest rate. At the same time, other estimates reported here suggest that as much as 90 percent of each additional dollar in benefits could consist of PBGC backup insurance for the weakest corporate sponsors. Without restraining the ability of companies with below-investment-grade credit ratings to expand pension promises to workers, proposals that have principally emphasized additional funding therefore create a powerful incentive for those companies to increase pension debt on the strength of federal support.

Estimates developed here for the total value of PBGC insurance are higher—in some cases substantially so—than those produced in previous studies. On the other hand, there is some reason to think that time may be working, at a very slow pace, to reduce some of the risk to the insurance fund. Certainly, one noteworthy aspect of the data used to construct these estimates is the substantial amount of time that has elapsed since the end of the period that they cover. Unfortunately, no comparable sample of detailed liability data has been drawn for any subsequent period. Another positive factor is the relatively thin yield spreads at the moment.

Two final tables compare PBGC insurance with private insurance using the same datasets. Table 4–9 reports insurance values per participant as estimated using the shadow pricing model. Note that private insurance has no value in the case of triple-A rated credits because the guarrantor would not be any stronger financially than the plan-sponsor combination. The reported values in Table 4–9 are highest in 1986 when interest rates and yield spreads (50 percent of

T A B L E 4-9

Estimated Insurance Values by Source of Guarantee[1]

Sponsor's Credit Rating	Source of Guarantee	1981	1986	1987
AAA	PBGC	$ 645	$1,376	$1,305
		(141)[2]	(488)	(321)
	Private[3]	0	0	0
		—	—	—
AA	PBGC	584	2,660	1,692
		(90)	(347)	(178)
	Private	207	854	396
		(33)	(109)	(42)
A	PBGC	758	1,988	1,278
		(114)	(209)	(119)
	Private	435	948	522
		(69)	(102)	(49)
BBB	PBGC	1,183	3,056	1,971
		(115)	(426)	(176)
	Private	883	1,990	1,971
		(85)	(308)	(102)

[1]Per participant.
[2]Numbers in parentheses denote standard errors.
[3]Source of the private guarantee is assumed to be an AAA-rated insurance company.

the yield spread was one factor in the shadow-pricing estimates) also were highest. Table 4–10 reports economic annual premiums that correspond with the insurance values reported just above. Private coverage is less costly for every cell in each of these three years and the difference is statistically significant at the five percent level in all cases except for the triple-B rated credits in 1986.

The estimates based on yield spreads cover only current vested benefits as of the respective valuation dates. They ignore both projected future accruals and benefit improvements that are granted as part of regular collective bargaining or occasionally for other reasons. In drawing any inferences relative to the value of PBGC insurance today, the totals for insured liabilities should reflect changes in the value of benefit promises attributable to subsequent salary

T A B L E 4-10

Estimated Economic Insurance Premiums: by Source of Guarantee[1]

Sponsor's Credit Rating	Source of Guarantee	1981	1986	1987
AAA	PBGC	$14	$ 26	$42
		(3)[2]	(9)	(9)
	Private[3]	0	0	0
		—	—	—
AA	PBGC	20	63	63
		(3)	(9)	(7)
	Private[4]	2	25	11
		(1)	(10)	(4)
A	PBGC	34	54	47
		(6)	(6)	(5)
	Private[4]	24	33	19
		(4)	(4)	(2)
BBB	PBGC	65	122	78
		(6)	(27)	(7)
	Private[4]	55	93	45
		(5)	(21)	(4)

[1]Annually per participant.

[2]Numbers in parentheses denote standard errors.

[3]Source of private guarantee is assumed to be an AAA-rated insurance company.

[4]Represents 50 percent of the yield spread on risk-free benefits as well as insurance company reserve requirements and net cost of capital.

increases, job tenure, and the amortization of benefits for current retirees. If the PBGC is correct and new benefit promises resulted in additional growth of plan liabilities at approximately 4 percent annually,[53] the value of the insurance could be considerably higher than the levels that this yield-spread analysis suggests. Another striking and negative factor has been the subsequent decline in interest rates that have almost certainly had major effects on the value of guarantee since 1987.

More generally, one important caveat concerning the methods discussed in this chapter should affect our perception of this problem. Contingent-claims analysis, whether we implement it using an option-pricing model or based on the yield spread, does not consider the effects of moral hazard. Insofar as moral hazard is known to result from poorly priced insurance, we can reasonably assume that estimates based on the application of these methods will still understate the true value of the insurance. Moral hazard could affect the frequency of corporate defaults as well as the recovery rates relative to PBGC bankruptcy claims. The shadow-pricing estimates reported here would also be highly sensitive to changes in these two factors. Finally, one should not assume that the value of this insurance accrues entirely to pension plan participants. Depending on the structure of competition in specific industries, some of this value may be captured by shareholders, management, and even consumers.

SUMMARY

This chapter introduced the important concept of insurance value. Insurance value is a notion quite distinct from both the actuarial measures of the funded condition of a pension plan discussed in Chapter 2 and the concept of financial solvency developed in Chapter 3. The same Form 5500 sample pension data analyzed in Chapter 2 were used here to estimate the value of PBGC insurance by two alternative methods: one based on contemporaneous yield spreads, and the other involving shadow prices. The estimates for total PBGC insurance value exceed those produced in previous studies. However, PBGC premiums clearly fell significantly short of levels implied by accepted commercial pricing methods. Revenues of approximately 2 percent of guaranteed liabilities would have been necessary, on average, to offset the shadow price of PBGC insurance. Much of the excessive cost of PBGC insurance results from the indefinite term of its insurance contract, the lack of effective intervention rights in cases of deteriorating credit quality. The requirement that pension promises of all tax-qualified sponsors be guaranteed regardless of their financial health also results in higher costs.

A regression analysis for the period 1981–87 identified the principal determinants of PBGC insurance values as these: the absolute level of interest rates, yield spreads, the value of risk-free benefits, credit rating, and time. Depending on the year and the sponsor's credit rating, PBGC insurance represented between 3.6 percent and 90.6 percent of promised benefits. Another important result was the extreme sensitivity of PBGC insurance values to contemporaneous interest rates. This result suggests that interest rate-induced movement in the exercise price at which unfunded pension liabilities can be put to the PBGC should be modeled explicitly in future studies.

One result that was not consistent with expectations was the relatively small but statistically significant decrease in insurance values attributable to time. However, readers should interpret this finding with caution due to the differences in the samples across years covered in the study.

ENDNOTES

1. Immunization would match the cash flows from the bond investments with those resulting from the pension obligations. Alternatively, their *durations* could be matched. With respect to credit ratings, a BBB represents the lowest investment quality grade. A BBB rating indicates adequate capacity to pay interest and repay the principal of the debt in question. However, adverse economic conditions or otherwise changing market developments are more likely to weaken that capacity than would be the case for higher-rated debt. Lower-rated debt in the BB, B, CCC, and CC categories is considered speculative with respect to capacity to pay interest and repay principal in accordance with the terms of the obligation. The suitability standard for bond investments made by pension plans would also need to reflect the risk of downgrading. Protection against this possibility can depend on appropriate terms in the indenture agreement for each bond. See *Standard & Poor's Debt Ratings: S&P's Corporate Finance Criteria* (New York: Standard & Poor's Corp., 1991), p. 7.

2. For example, see Robert C. Merton, "An Analytical Derivation of the Cost of Deposit Insurance and Loan Guarantees: An Application of Modern Option Pricing Theory," *Journal of Banking and Finance* 1 (1977), pp. 3–11.

3. See George G. Pennacchi and Christopher M. Lewis, "The Value of Pension Benefit Guaranty Corporation Insurance." Paper prepared for the Conference on "Federal Credit Allocation: Theory, Evidence, and History," October 18–19, 1993, sponsored by the Federal Reserve Bank of Cleveland and the *Journal of Money, Credit and Banking.*

4. Alan J. Marcus, "Corporate Pension Policy and the Value of PBGC Insurance," in *Issues in Pension Economics,* Zvi Bodie, John B. Shoven, and David A. Wise, eds. (Chicago: University of Chicago Press, 1987), pp. 49–79; and "Spinoff Terminations and the Value of Pension Insurance," *Journal of Finance,* July 1985, pp. 926–91.

5. For example, several relatively small pension plans sponsored by the LTV Corporation were overfunded despite the fact that four major plans covering steel industry employees had accumulated unfunded liabilities of $2.4 billion. When LTV declared bankruptcy in 1986, three of the underfunded plans were terminated, only to be reestablished several months later. However, assets of the overfunded plans could not be used to reduce the shortfall attributable to the other plans.

6. The gross subsidy represents the present value of the PBGC's exposure to future unfunded liabilities. It ignores premium revenues. See Pennacchi and Lewis, "The Value of PBCG Insurance," p. 3.

7. Under FAS 87, Chrysler reported an unfunded pension liability of $3.6 billion in its 1990 Annual Report, but it subsequently released an estimate of $4.4 billion to the Securities and Exchange Commission.

8. It is generally acknowledged that the Black-Scholes model is not reliable for the valuation of options that are deeply in the money or deeply out of the money. The sponsor of a seriously underfunded pension plan, in effect, holds a put option that is deeply in the money. For example, see J. MacBeth and L. Merville, "An Empirical Examination of the Black-Scholes Call Option Pricing Model," *Journal of Finance,* December 1979, pp. 1173–86.

9. The gross subsidy represents the present value of the PBGC's exposure to future unfunded liabilities. It ignores premium revenues. See Pennacchi and Lewis, "The Value of PBGC Insurance," p. 3.

10. The value of this put option was modeled as a function of four variables: the value of the sponsoring firm's assets, the value of the sponsoring firm's liabilities, the pension plan's assets, and the pension plan's accrued vested liabilities.

11. Office of Management and the Budget, *The Budget of the United States Government 1995: Analytical Perspectives* (Washington, DC: U.S. Government Printing Office, 1994), p. 134.

12. See Pennacchi and Lewis, "The Value of PBGC Insurance," p. 16.

13. See Office of Management and the Budget, *The Budget of the United States Government 1996: Analytical Perspectives* (Washington, DC: U.S. Government Printing Office, 1995), p. 122.

14. Zvi Bodie and Robert C. Merton, "Pension Benefit Guarantees in the United States: A Functional Analysis," in *The Future of Pensions in the United States,* Ray Schmitt, ed. (Philadelphia: The Pension Research Council of the Wharton School of the University of Pennsylvania, 1993), pp. 194–234.

15. See Merton, "An Analytical Derivation."

16. See Su-Jane Hsieh, Andrew H. Chen, and Kenneth R. Ferris, "The Valuation of PBGC Insurance Premiums Using an Option Pricing Model," *Journal of Financial and Qualitative Analysis,* 29, no. 1 (March 1994), pp. 89–99.

17. See Richard Brealey and Stewart Myers, *The Principles of Corporate Finance,* 2d ed. (New York: McGraw-Hill, 1984), pp. 485–6.

18. For another source supporting this approach, see John Karekeu and Neil Wallace, "Federal Credit Programs and Desired Investment," in *Issues in Federal Debt Management* (Boston: Federal Reserve Bank of Boston, 1973), pp. 223–24.

19. See U.S. Securities and Exchange Commission, "Estimating the Value of Federal Deposit Insurance," March 29, 1991, p. 12.

20. See E. J. Mishan, *Cost-Benefit Analysis* (London: George Allen & Unwin, 1975), pp. 81–97.

21. According to a widely accepted statistical rule of thumb, the hypothesis can be rejected that there was no difference between aggregate insurance values for any two years (i.e., at the .05 level) if the single-point estimates for those years are separated by more than 1.5 times the sum of the standard errors.

22. The value of an option consists of two elements: the *intrinsic value* and the *time value.* The intrinsic value represents the value of the option if exercised at the present time or the difference between the current market price and the strike price. The time value represents the additional value in holding the option because the intrinsic value may appreciate subsequently. In turn, the time value depends on the value of the underlying security, the level of interest rates, and the time until the option expires. The relationship between time value and each of these variables is direct. It increases as the variable increases and decreases as the variable decreases.

23. For example, see James C. Van Horne, *Financial Market Rates and Flows* (Englewood Cliffs, NJ: Prentice Hall, 1990), p. 171.

24. Typical investors judge default risk based on credit ratings assigned by major agencies like Moody's and Standard & Poor's. For a discussion

of default risk based on Moody's ratings, see Jerome S. Fons, "Default Rates and the Term Structure of Credit Risk," *Financial Analysts Journal,* September–October 1994, pp. 25–32.

25. Richard Bookstaber, "The Valuation and Exposure Management of Bonds with Imbedded Options," in Frank J. Fabozzi and Irving M. Pollack, eds., *The Handbook of Fixed Income Securities* (Homewood, IL: Dow Jones-Irwin, 1987), p. 858.

26. For a discussion of option-adjusted spreads and their use, see Tom Windas, *An Introduction to Option-Adjusted Spread Analysis* (Princeton, NJ: Bloomberg Magazine, 1993).

27. Crabbe estimated that for the period 1983–88 callable industrial bonds sold at a yield discount of 3.65 basis points relative to noncallable bonds. See Lee Crabbe, "Callable Corporate Bonds: A Vanishing Breed," in *Finance and Economics Discussion Series 155* (Washington, DC: Federal Reserve Board, March 1991), p. 18.

28. See A. Barnea, R. Haugen, and L. Senbet, "A Rationale for Debt Maturity Structure and Call Provisions in the Agency Theoretic Framework," *Journal of Finance* 5 (1980), pp. 1223–34.

29. For example, see Alan K. Severn and William J. Stewart, "The Corporate–Treasury Yield Spread and State Taxes," *Journal of Economic and Business* 44 (1992); and Frank J. Fabozzi and Thom B. Thurston, "State Taxes and Reserve Requirements as Major Determinants of Yield Spreads among Money Market Instruments," *Journal of Financial and Quantitative Analysis* 21, no. 4 (December 1986), pp. 161–66; or Timothy Q. Cook and Thomas A. Lawler, "The Behavior of the Spread between Treasury Bill Rates and Private Money Market Rates since 1978," *Economic Review of the Federal Reserve Bank of Richmond* 69, no. 6 (November–December 1983), pp. 3–15.

30. These results come from the first in a series of annual surveys concerning state personal income tax rates. See *The Bond Buyer 1992 Yearbook* (New York: Thompson Financial Information, Inc. 1992), pp. 68–72.

31. The necessary increase can be estimated algebraically where x is the market yield and y is the market yield adjusted for the full 7.3 percent tax effect:

$$x = y - .073 \times y \quad \text{or} \quad x = .927 \times y$$

Now, this implies that:

$$y = 1.0787 \times x$$

32. See Pennachi and Lewis, "The Value of PBGC Insurance" (revised January 1994), p. 8.

33. See Thomas E. Copeland and J. Fred Weston, *Financial Theory and Corporate Policy* 3d ed. (Reading, MA: Addison-Wesley, 1988), p. 245.

34. See Pension Benefit Guaranty Corporation, *1993 Annual Report,* p. 20.

35. See Alan Backman, et al., "November 1990 Structured Finance Special Report: Corporate-Debt-Backed Securities Update" (New York: Moody's Investors Service, 1990), p. 2.

36. See "Structured Preferred Stock," *Standard & Poor's CreditReview* 26 (October 1992), pp. 46–48; and "Moody's Investors Service Overcollateralization Tables & Guidelines," January 1993.

37. Disposition losses may reduce this further. See the PBGC, *1993 Annual Report.*

38. See Edward I. Altman and Allan C. Eberhart, "Do Seniority Provisions Protect Bondholders' Investments?" *Journal of Portfolio Management,* Summer 1994, pp. 67–75.

39. However, one caveat applies. The S&P report focused on nonbenefit obligations of these pension plans. See Scott Sprinzen, "Assessing Corporate Pension Funds' Credit Quality," *Standard & Poor's CreditWeek Reprint,* October 11, 1993, pp. 1–3.

40. See Edward M. Gramlich, *Benefit-Cost Analysis of Government Programs* (Englewood Cliffs, NJ: Prentice Hall, 1981), pp. 77–8.

41. These liability values were adjusted to a PBGC termination basis by the same methods used in Chapter 2.

42. Cumulative default rates for any future year can be obtained by multiplying the one-year transition matrix by itself once for each year during the intervening period. For average one-year transition rates covering the period 1981–93, see "1993 Corporate Default, Rating Transition Study Results," *Standard & Poor's Credit Review,* May 2, 1994, p. 6.

43. See Fitch Investors Service, "Bond Insurers Dance the Limbo," August 15, 1994, p. 7.

44. The value of a given dollar of pension benefits grows by the interest rate until the worker retires.

45. Retirement ages were assumed to be 59 for union members and 62 for other pension plan participants. Liability-weighted ages for the two groups were assumed to be 56 and 47 respectively. Meanwhile, the liability-weighted age for benefits attributable to retired lives was assumed to be 67.

46. For retired lives, premiums were modeled as a declining annuity based on a constant percentage of expected benefit payments. For active lives, the value of the insurance was amortized over the deferral period.

47. These results represent estimated group averages. Guarantee values per participant could be quite different for individual pension plans within each group.

48. The commonly used 95 percent confidence interval extends by a distance of two standard errors above and below the respective single point estimate.

49. Again, a widely used statistical rule of thumb indicates that the difference between two single-point estimates is significant at the 5 percent level if it exceeds 1.5 times the sum of their standard errors.

50. See James C. Van Horne, *Financial Market Rates and Flows,* pp. 192–93.

51. PC Carp was developed to conduct statistical analyses of sample survey data. See Wayne Fuller et al., *PC Carp* (Ames, IA: Iowa State University Statistical Laboratory, 1986).

52. Weaker S&P credit ratings correspond with higher numeric values for the RATING variable. Therefore, the positive coefficients indicate a decline in credit quality.

53. See Pennachi and Lewis, "The Value of PBGC Insurance" (revised January 1994), p. 8.

STATISTICAL METHODS AND RELATED ACTUARIAL ADJUSTMENTS

The U.S. Department of Labor initially prepared the sample tapes by stratifying the population of pension plans for a given year according to the number of participants in each plan. The entire population of pension plans formed eight different subpopulations or strata. Then, simple random samples of pension plans were scientifically drawn within each stratum. The selection probabilities were constant within each stratum but different across strata.

Numerous errors and omissions on the DOL computer tapes reduced the number of plans included in the original sample to a smaller number that could be processed to yield a standardized vested-benefit security ratio (VBSR).[54] This problem of "nonresponse" was particularly severe among the four sampling strata that covered plans with 100 or fewer participants. In these cases, the Form 5500 Schedule B containing the actuarial data related to plan liabilities is not a required submission. The estimates produced here, like those in Chapter 2, therefore are based on data from the four remaining sampling strata that included plans with more than 100 participants. Approximately 95 percent of all participants in single-employer, defined-benefit plans are covered by plans in these strata. This study treated sampled plans for which VBSRs could be computed as a simple random sample of the original plan population within each stratum. As a result, every sampled plan in a stratum represented the same number of plans in the population.

The subsample of plans for which credit ratings also could be established tended to have larger participant counts and higher VBSRs than the original sample of plans that were processed to yield VBSRs. To compensate for the missing plans, each subsampled plan in a stratum was assigned its own sampling weight. Essentially, a sampling weight is the number of plans in the population that a subsampled plan represents. The weights were calibrated using a squared distance measure.[55] This ensured two things: that the number of participants represented by subsampled plans equaled the number represented by sampled plans; and that the average VBSRs according to the number of participants in the subsampled plans equaled the average VBSR per participant for all sampled plans. Bethlehem[56] shows how a weighting scheme of this sort can be used to reduce the potential for bias that, in this case, might otherwise have been caused by the absence of credit ratings for all plans.

All statistical analyses were conducted using PC Carp.[57] Most of the analyses employed the weights described above. However, each weight was multiplied by the number of participants in the corresponding plan for those analyses conducted on a per participant basis. The standard errors computed by PC Carp do not reflect any potential reduction in variance resulting from the calibration of the weights. As a result, the statistical tests may be slightly conservative. The standard errors of regression coefficients in multiyear analyses may also be slightly conservative because the impact of stratification on variance had to be ignored in order to apply PC Carp successfully across survey years.

To arrive at an estimate of the value of the guarantee based on the yield spread for each pension plan in the sample, similar liability-side adjustments were made here relative to those used in Chapters 2 and 3. In particular, a multiplicative adjustment was made to reflect the date of the actuarial valuation and to standardize for the effect of the passage of time. An additive adjustment was made to reflect benefit accruals, if any, between the time of the actuarial valuation and the end of the calendar year in question. The probable use of dedicated bond portfolios was identified, and their effect on benefit values reported on Form 5500 Schedule B was removed. A multiplicative adjustment was also included to reflect a common early retirement age. However, the annuity factors used in this chapter to compute the adjustment for retirement age assumptions were not taken from the PBGC tables because, in some cases, the applicable borrowing costs from Table 4–2 exceeded the range of interest rates covered in the official PBGC tables. The annuity factor therefore was calculated[58] as part of the computer program that estimated the effect of the yield spread for each plan. Finally, interest rate assumptions themselves were changed to reflect the risk-free rate set and, in a second part of the computer program, the rate set that corresponded with the sponsor's credit rating.

APPENDIX ENDNOTES

54. The vested-benefit security ratio consists of the ratio of plan assets to liabilities after both assets and liabilities were adjusted to a common basis in Chapter 2.

55. See J.C. Deville and C.E. Särndal, "Calibration Estimators in Survey Sampling," *Journal of the American Statistical Association* 87 (1992), p. 377.

56. See Jelke G. Bethlehem, "Reduction of Nonresponse Bias through Regression Estimation," Journal of Official Statistics, 1998, pp. 251–60.

57. See Fuller, *PC Carp.*

58. For the algorithms used to compute annuities due, see Chester W. Jordan, Jr., *Life Contingencies* (Chicago: Society of Actuaries, 1975), pp. 3–42.

5

COMPARATIVE BENEFIT
SECURITY SYSTEMS

The problem of securing private pension promises from the risk of underfunding and plan termination is neither new nor unique to the United States. One termination insurance system—Finland's—suddenly collapsed after precautionary reserves had been built up methodically for 28 years, thereby demonstrating that the specter of a financial debacle involving the PBGC cannot be dismissed as idle speculation. When considered as alternative approaches for resolving the PBGC's problems, the systems that perform similar functions abroad can provide many important lessons. For their part, experts in other countries have also spent substantial time studying termination insurance programs set up elsewhere. Table 5–1 presents summary comparisons of benefit levels in nine countries and Table 5–2 reports the distribution of guaranteed benefits across the labor force in those same systems. Figures 5–1 and 5–2 on pages 192–4 graphically depict much of this data.

The United Kingdom's Secretary of State for Social Security convened that country's Pension Law Review Committee (i.e., the Goode Committee, chaired by Professor Roy Goode of Oxford University) in 1992, to examine the rights of pension fund participants and the accountability of fund officials. This initiative followed the discovery that over $600 million was missing from retirement funds

(Text Continues on p. 193)

TABLE 5-1

Comparative Benefit Data: Explanatory Notes

Benefit	Amount	Methods and Sources
		Finland
		OECD Purchasing Power Parity Rate: FMK 6.49 = US$1.00 (1992)
Social minimum retirement income	$4,584	Represents the basic flat-rate national pension of Fmk 437 monthly plus the maximum "Basic Amount Addition" or "Support Pension" of Fmk 2,042 monthly. The Basic Amount Addition varies by location and is integrated with other retirement income. Only retirees with very small employment pensions qualify for the maximum. More than half of all Finnish retirees receive some Basic Amount Addition. Source: *IBIS Briefing Service*, March 1993, p. 11.
Average national old-age pension	$2,382	Includes the basic flat-rate national pension from above and the average Basic Amount Addition. Source: *Statistical Yearbook of Pensioners in Finland: 1993* (Helsinki, Finland: The Central Pension Security Institute), p. 72.
Maximum national old-age pension	$4,584	This is the same as the social minimum. Source: *IBIS Briefing Service*.
Average private pension	$6,213	This represents the average for the mandatory employment pension system. Source: Statistical Yearbook of Pensioners in Finland: 1993, p. 76.
Maximum guaranteed private pension	$120,185	Estimate provided by researchers at the Central Pension Security Institute based on the assumed maximum earnings for Finland.
		Germany (The Western Lander)
		OECD Purchasing Power Parity Rate: DM 2.11 = US$1.00 (1992)
Social minimum retirement income	$4,926	Represents an average based on total Sozialhilfe benefits of DM 43,933,000,000 paid to 4,227,000 recipients in 1993. Source: *Statistisches Jahrbuch 1993*. Wiesbaden, Germany: Statistisches Bundesampt, pp. 493–495.

Average national old-age pension	$6,865	Average monthly payment of DM 1,207.12 from durchschnittlicher Rentenzahlbetrag. Estimate provided by the staff of the Verband Duetscher Rentenversicherungsträger.
Maximum national old-age pension	$17,712	Source: *Rente berechnenleicht gemacht 1993/1994* (Frankfurt/Main, Germany: Verband Deutscher Rentenversicherungsträger) p. 12.
Average private pension	$2,275	Source: Peter Ahrend, Wolfgang Förster, and Norbert Walkiewicz, *Die betriebliche Altersversorgung in Bayern* (Munich, Germany: Bayerisches Staatministerium für Arbeit und Sozialordung, 1991), p. 102.
Maximum guaranteed private pension	$122,844	Three times the national pension contribution ceiling of DM 86,400 annually in 1993. This amount is scheduled to be reduced to 1.5 times the national pension contribution ceiling as of 1999.

Japan
OECD Purchasing Power Parity Rate: ¥190 = US$1.00 (1992)

Social minimum retirement income	$3,881	The flat-rate pension of ¥737,304 per year on April 1, 1993 to a retiree at age 65 with 40 years of contributions or credits. The National Basic Pension pays lower amounts to all residents based on prior contributions. Source: *IBIS Briefing Service*, March 1993, p. 19.
Average national old-age pension	$9,855	Represents the average mandatory national old-age pension of ¥1,872,492. Source: *Annual Business Report of Employees' Pension Funds*, March 1993.
Maximum national old-age pension	About $20,000	This measure is based on adjusted career average bands of earnings and months of coverage. Source: The Pension Fund Association of Japan.
Average private pension	$2,956	The average annual supplementary component benefits paid by Employees' Pension Funds of ¥561,725. Source: Ibid.
Maximum guaranteed private pension	$4,836	The guarantee secures supplementary benefits up to 30% of contracted-out national old-age pension benefits provided by Employees' Pension Funds. The guarantee fund is currently processing its first claim.

(continued)

TABLE 5-1

(continued)

Benefit	Amount	Methods and Sources
		The Netherlands
		OECD Purchasing Power Parity Rate: Dfl 2.18 = US$1.00 (1992)
Social minimum retirement income	$8,329	Represents the flat-rate national old-age pension from the AOW program for a single resident as of January 1, 1993.
Average national old-age pension	$8,329	All residents qualify for flat-rate AOW pensions upon reaching the age of 65 with 50 years of paid or credited contributions.
Maximum national old-age pension	$8,329	Same as above.
Average private pension	$3,743	Calculated as total company and industrywide pensions paid of Dfl 5,103,000,000 divided by the total retirees of 625,440. Source: *Financiële gegevens pensioenfondsen 1991* (Apeldoorn, The Netherlands: The Verzekeringskamer), pp. 6, 12.
Maximum guaranteed private pension	N/A	The Netherlands relies on stringent funding standards instead of a backup guarantee system.
		The Province of Ontario
		OECD Purchasing Power Parity Rate: C$1.28 = US$1.00 (1992)
Social minimum retirement income	$7,898	Represents the flat-rate pension from Old-Age Security of C$4,548 plus the maximum Guaranteed Income Supplement to a single person of C$5,404. Source: *IBIS Briefing Service*, January 1993, p. 8.
Average national old-age pension	$7,250	Based on averages for Ontario residents of the annual Old-Age Security pension of C$4,479 plus the annual retirement pension from the Canada Pension Plan of C$4,656. Source: Statistics Canada, *Statistical Bulletin: Canada Pension Plan: Old Age Security*, January 1993, pp. 11, 35, 36.

Item	Value	Details
Maximum national old-age pension	$9,965	Includes a maximum Old-Age Security pension of C$4,548 and a maximum Canada Pension Plan benefit of C$8,008 as of January 1993. Source: *IBIS Briefing Service*, January 1993, pp. 8, 30.
Average private pension	$6,717	As of January 1, 1992. Source: Statistics Canada, *Pension Plans in Canada*, 1993, p. 54.
Maximum guaranteed private pension	$9,524	Source: William M. Mercer, Ltd.

Sweden
OECD Purchasing Power Parity Rate: SKr 10 = US$1.00 (1992)

Item	Value	Details
Social minimum retirement income	$5,094	Represents the full flat-rate AFP pension of SKr 32,364 for a single person in 1993 plus the maximum supplement of SKr 18,542 paid to retirees with little or no earnings-related pension income. Source: *IBIS Briefing Service*, February 1993, p. 20; and *Social Insurance Statistics: Facts 1993* (Stockholm, Sweden: Riksförsäkringsverket), p. 60.
Average national old-age pension	$8,985	Includes estimated average AFP pension for 1993 of SKr 31,190 plus the estimated average ATP pension of SKr 58,664. Source: Ibid., p. 51.
Maximum national old-age pension	$16,384	Consists of the full flat AFP pension of SEK 32, 364 from above plus the maximum ATP pension of SEK 131,477. Source: *IBIS Briefing Service*.
Average private pension	$1,726	Reflects the weighted average for blue-collar STP pensions combined with white-collar ITP and ITP-k pensions. Some 324,500 blue-collar retirees received an average of SKr 11,955 in 1993 while 285,000 white-collar retirees received an average of SKr 23,239 according to the FPG/AMFK Pensionsgaranti organization.
Maximum guaranteed private pension	$44,310	The maximum ITP pension of SKr 417,100 for 1993 plus the estimated maximum ITP-k pension of SKr 26,000.

(continued)

TABLE 5-1

(continued)

Benefit	Amount	Methods and Sources
		Switzerland
		OECD Purchasing Power Parity Rate: SF 2.21 = US$1.00 (1992)
Social minimum retirement income	$5,104	Represents the flat-rate national old age pension of SF 8,347 for 1993 plus the minimum earnings-related national old-age pension for a worker with a full career. Source: *IBIS Profile: Switzerland*, June 1993, p. 3.
Average national old-age pension	$7,048	Consists of total AHV benefit payments in 1992 of SF 20,863,000,000 divided by 1,306,000 retirees in pay status. Source: The Swiss Embassy.
Maximum national old-age pension	$10,208	The flat-rate benefit plus the maximum earnings-related AHV pension in 1993. Source: *IBIS Briefing Service*.
Average private pension	$7,626	The average mandatory LPP pension plus voluntary pensions to both public and private-sector retirees in 1990. Calculated as total benefit payments of SF 9 billion divided by 534,000 retirees. Source: *La prévoyance professionelle en Suisse: Statistique des caisses de pensions 1990* (Bern: Office fédéral de la statistique), pp. 20, 29.
Maximum guaranteed pension	$2,170	Author's estimate reflecting the maximum LPP pension payable to a male employee retiring at age 65 in 1993 based on contributions from 1985, and 4% accumulated interest. A full career starting in 1993 would produce a maximum of SF 48,805.
		The United Kingdom
		OECD Purchasing Power Parity Rate: £0.629 = US$1.00 (1992)
Social minimum retirement income	$5,068	Consists of £44/week of Income Support plus £17.30/week for the Pension Supplement. Data provided by the U.K. Department of Social Security.
Average national old-age pension	$5,806	The flat-rate national old-age pension plus the average for the State Earnings-Related Pension Scheme as of 9/30/93. Data provided by the U.K. Government Actuary's Department.

(continued)

184

Maximum national old-age pension	$12,016	The sum of the maximum flat-rate national old-age pension £ 2,917 for 1993 plus the estimated Graduated Pension of £ 335 plus the maximum SERPS benefit of £ 4,306 reported as the maximum guaranteed private pension below.
Average private pension	$3,696	Author's estimate of average benefit payments in excess of the Guaranteed Minimum Pension. Total pensions paid to former employees in 1991 of estimated £ 8.3 billion initially divided by 3 million retirees in pay status. Then, adjusted to remove assumed average GMP (i.e., assumed average for contracted-out SERPS benefits) of £ 522 for the 84.6% of the private labor force with those benefits. No guarantee applies to this benefit measure for workers retiring before the year 2000. Source: *Occupational Pension Schemes 1991: Ninth Survey by the Government Actuary* (London: HMSO), Tables 3.1, 4.4.
Maximum guaranteed private pension	$6,846	Represents the maximum SERPS benefit. Note that this amount was included in the Maximum National Private Pension above. SERPS benefits generally exceed the Guaranteed Minimum Pension for a contracted-out plan.

The United States

Social minimum retirement income	$5,208	Reflects the 1993 benefit for the Supplemental Security Income progam. Source: Social Security Administration, *Social Security Handbook*, 11th ed. (Washington, DC: U.S. Government Printing Office 1993), pp. 356-7 and 392-4.
Average national old-age pension	$7,831	Includes payments for early and delayed retirement but excludes supplements for spouses and dependents. Source: *Social Security Bulletin*, Fall 1993, Table 5.B2, p. 114.
Maximum national old-age pension	$13,546	Benefit reflects maximum taxable wages after a 35-year career and retiring at age 65 in 1993. Source: *Social Security Bulletin: Annual Statistical Supplement 1993*, Table 2.A28, p. 58.
Average private pension	$6,303	Estimate for 1989. Source: Daniel J. Beller and David D. McCarthy, "Private Pension Benefits," in *Trends in Pensions 1992* (Washington, DC: U.S. Government Printing Office), p. 247.
Maximum guaranteed private pension	$29,250	Represents the 1993 maximum benefit as reported by the Pension Benefit Guaranty Corporation.

(Table 5-1 concluded)

TABLE 5-2

Benefit Security and the Labor Force: Explanatory Notes

Group	Total Workers	Methods and Sources
		Finland
Total labor force	2,559,000	Average for 1991. Source: *Labor Force Statistics, 1971-1991* (Paris, France: The Organization for Economic Cooperation & Development), Table II.
Workers with national pension coverage	2,559,000	All workers covered by national pensions.
Private-sector workers	N/A	N/A
Workers with private pension coverage	1,690,000	Data provided by Finland's Central Pension Security Institute.
Workers with private defined-benefit pension coverage	1,690,000	The 1,690,000 workers counted above all are covered by defined-benefit plans.
Workers with guaranteed private pension benefits	198,000	Includes 63,000 workers covered by pension funds and 135,000 workers covered by pension foundations using credit insurance.
		Germany (The Western Lander)
Total labor force	30,678,000	Source: *Labor Force Statistics, 1971–1991.*
Workers with national pension coverage	30,678,000	All workers covered by national pensions.

Private-sector workers	19,212,000	Data provided by the German Embassy.
Workers with private coverage	8,800,000	Author's estimate based on 1990 survey data provided by Statistisches Pension Bundesampt. Some 7,690,975 workers had pension coverage of 16,698,270 in the survey.
Workers with private defined-benefit pension coverage	N/A	The vast majority of private pension plans in Germany provide defined benefits.
Workers with guaranteed private pension benefits	4,191,550	Source: *Versicherungsverein auf Gegenseitigkeit 1993* (Koln, Germany: Pensions-Sicherungs-Verein), p. 9.

Japan

Total labor force	65,050,000	Source: *Labor Force Statistics, 1971–1991.*
Workers with national pension coverage	68,350,000	Includes total labor force, spouses of salaried workers and low-income, part time workers not included in the total labor force. Source: Management & Coordination Agency, Statistics Department, *Annual Research Report of the Labor Force.*
Private-sector workers	48,030,000	Data as of March 1992. Does not include the self-employed. Source: Ibid.
Workers with private pension coverage	22,080,000	Number of participants as of March 1993 covered by Employees' Pension Funds (11,700,000) and Tax-Qualified Pension Funds (10,380,000). Most other workers are covered by a book reserve plan or an unfunded severance pay plan providing lump-sum benefits. Source: *IBIS Briefing Service*, March 1993, p. 16.
Workers with private defined-benefit pension coverage	22,080,000	Source: Ibid.
Workers with guaranteed private pension benefits	11,700,000	Represents total participants, as of March 31, 1993, in Employees' Pension Funds covered by the Pension Fund Association guarantee. Source: Ibid.

(continued)

Group	Total Workers	Methods and Sources
		The Netherlands
Total labor force	7,011,000	Source: *Labor Force Statistics, 1971–1991.*
Workers with national pension coverage	7,011,000	All residents of the Netherlands are covered by the national AOW pension program.
Private-sector workers	N/A	N/A
Workers with private pension coverage	2,942,000	Includes workers covered by an industrywide pension plan or a company pension plan. Source: *Financiële gegevens pensioenfondsen 1991* (Apeldoorn, The Netherlands: The Verzekeringskamer), p. 22.
Workers with private defined-benefit pension coverage	N/A	N/A
Workers with guaranteed private pension benefits	N/A	The Netherlands relies on stringent funding standards instead of a backup guarantee system.
		The Province of Ontario
Total labor force	5,276,000	Statistics Canada tabulations.
Workers with national pension coverage	5,276,000	All workers covered by national pensions.
Private-sector workers	4,220,000	Statistics Canada tabulations.
Workers with private pension coverage	1,299,000	Data as of the end of 1991 from Statistics Canada.

Workers with private defined-benefit pension coverage	1,053,000	Same as above.
Workers with guaranteed private pension benefits	1,053,000	The Province of Ontario guarantees vested and nonvested benefits—up to a maximum amount—in all tax-qualified private defined-benefit pension plans sponsored by single companies.

Sweden

Total labor force	4,430,000	Source: *Labor Force Statistic, 1971–1991.*
Workers with national pension coverage	4,430,000	All workers covered by national pensions.
Private-sector workers	2,968,000	Source: *Facts About the Swedish Economy 1993* (Stockholm, Sweden: The Swedish Employers' Confederation), p. 14.
Workers with private pension coverage	1,600,000	Source: The FPG/AMFK Pensionsgaranti organization.
Workers with private defined-benefit pension coverage	N/A	The vast majority of private pension plans in Sweden provide defined benefits.
Workers with guaranteed private pension benefits	627,000	Author's estimate. FPG credit insurance protects some 235,000 white-collar workers from a total of 600,000 in the ITP pension system. STP pensions for the remaining 392,000 blue-collar workers are assumed to be protected by AMFK credit insurance. STP pensions cover approximately 1,000,000 workers.

Switzerland

Total labor force	3,602,000	Source: *Labor Force Statistic, 1971–1991.*
Workers with national pension coverage	3,602,000	All Swiss workers are covered by the AHV national pension program.

(continued)

TABLE 5-2

(continued)

Group	Total Workers	Methods and Sources
		Switzerland
Private-sector workers	N/A	N/A
Workers with private pension coverage	2,600,000	Workers over the age of 25 and earning more than the minimum coordinated earnings level. This estimate was provided by researchers at the University of St. Gallen.
Workers with private defined-benefit pension coverage	N/A	The Swiss pension guarantee fund covers both defined benefit plans and defined contribution plans up to a mandatory level.
Workers with guaranteed private pension benefits	2,600,000	All Swiss workers with mandatory LPP pensions are protected by the guarantee fund.
		The United Kingdom
Total labor force	28,264,000	Source: *Labor Force Statistics, 1971–1991.*
Workers with national pension coverage	19,900,000	This estimate does not cover the unemployed, members of the civil service or the military. Data provided by the U.K. Department of Social Security.
Private-sector workers	16,700,000	Omitted 5.86 million public sector workers with occupational pensions considered private. Source: *Occupational Pension Schemes 1991: Ninth Survey by the Government Actuary* (London, The United Kingdom: HMSO).
Workers with private pension coverage	6,480,000	In addition, 4,255,000 public sector workers also have private pension coverage. Source: Ibid.

Workers with private defined-benefit pension coverage	5,580,000	Includes private sector workers covered by both contracted-in and contracted-out SERPS benefits. The additional 4,255,000 public sector workers cited immediately above can be assumed to be covered by contracted-out defined benefit plans. Source: Ibid.
Workers with guaranteed private pension benefits	5,040,000	Represents total private sector workers in contracted-out defined benefit plans as reported in the same survey by the Government Actuary cited above. In addition, 4,255,000 public sector workers were in contracted-out defined-benefit plans.
United States		
Total labor force	126,867,000	Source: Labor Force Statistics, 1971–1991.
Workers with national pension coverage	110,500,000	Represents number of workers covered by Social Security in 1991. Source: Social Security Bulletin: Annual Statistical Supplement, 1992, Table 3.B1, p. 121.
Private-sector workers	94,772,000	Calculated from data in Employment and Earnings, January 1991; and U.S. Department of Labor, Private Pension Plan Bulletin: Abstract of 1990 Form 5500 Annual Reports 2 (Summer 1993), Table A2, p. 6.
Workers with private pension coverage	42,439,000	Source: Private Pension Plan Bulletin.
Workers with private defined-benefit pension coverage	26,323,000	Workers listed as covered by a defined-benefit plan as well as workers listed as covered by both a defined-benefit plan and a defined-contribution plan. Source: Ibid.
Workers with guaranteed private pension benefits	21,416,000	Number of workers with vested or partially vested benefits, plus separated participants with a vested right to benefits. Includes some double counting for workers with vested benefits from more than one employer. Source: Ibid.

(Table 5-2 concluded)

191

FIGURE 5-1

Annual Benefits Guaranteed by Nine Countries Compared with Social Security and Private Pensions

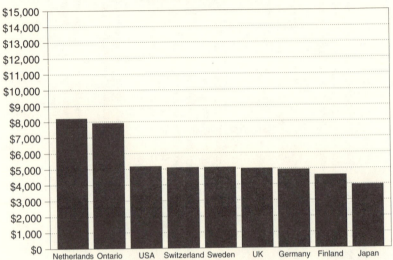

Social Minimum Benefits

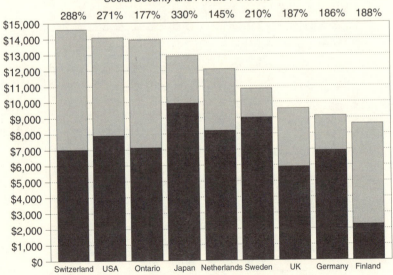

Combined Average Annual Retirement Income: Social Security and Private Pensions

FIGURE 5-1 (continued)

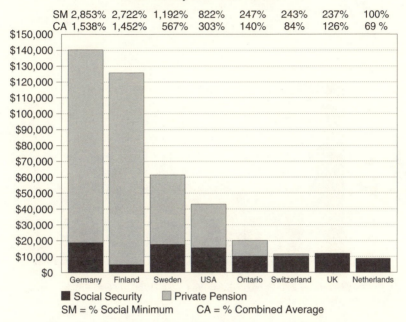

Combined Maximum Annual Guaranteed Benefits:
Social Security and Private Pensions

	SM 2,853%	2,722%	1,192%	822%	247%	243%	237%	100%
	CA 1,538%	1,452%	567%	303%	140%	84%	126%	69 %

Germany Finland Sweden USA Ontario Switzerland UK Netherlands

■ Social Security   ▨ Private Pension
SM = % Social Minimum   CA = % Combined Average

controlled by the late Robert Maxwell. The shortfall initially affected some 32,000 people, although voluntary settlements from investment houses and other institutions that benefited from the Maxwell embezzlement eventually will make them whole. In its final report, the Pension Law Review Committee recommended that a guarantee fund be created to protect plan participants from losses only in cases of fraud.[1] Before issuing its findings, members of the Committee traveled to the United States and Canada among other countries to evaluate guarantee systems already in operation.

Several years earlier, Japan's Ministry of Health and Welfare had set up its Study Commission on Corporate Pensions which, in turn, was strongly influenced by features of guarantee systems found abroad. That initiative was motivated by the effects of 16 plan terminations that occurred after the Employees' Pension Fund system was set up there in 1966. Japanese commentators believe that the Govern-

FIGURE 5-2

Benefit Security and the Labor Force

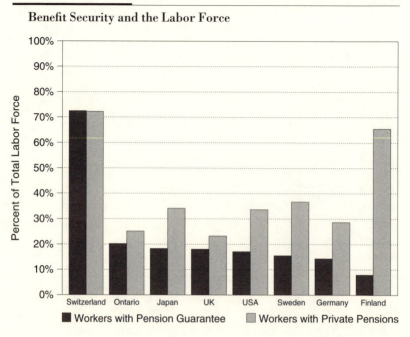

ment previously had not sufficiently understood the need for a guarantee system.[2] The study eventually led to legislation in 1988 that established a guarantee fund for securing basic retirement benefits.

    Apart from seeking insight to guide efforts aimed at reforming the PBGC, there are other reasons for examining pension guarantee systems from around the world. For one, the subsidies embedded in these arrangements have intruded on trading relationships between major industrial powers. In at least one case, Canadian steel producers publicly raised concerns that their counterparts in the United States benefited unfairly from a host of special government concessions, the most conspicuous among them being pension termination insurance provided by the PBGC.[3] At present, nine countries in addition to the United States are known to provide backup guarantee arrangements that secure private pension benefits: Austria,[4] Canada, Chile, Finland, Germany, Japan, Sweden, Switzerland, and the United Kingdom. In most of these cases, the role of the federal government in providing guarantees is much more circumscribed than in the United States. At one extreme, Canada has avoided any federal involvement.[5] However, the Province of Ontario there operates a system that closely resembles the PBGC.

The Japanese government even mandated a program that excludes an entire category of plans representing significant termination risks. Excluded plans cover about half of all Japanese workers participating in private pension plans. Meanwhile, the German system covering the Western lander (i.e., states making up what was formerly known as West Germany) excludes workers under the age of 35 with less than 10 years of service. For its part, Sweden offers one of the most helpful examples. The insurance offered by the FPG/AMFK organization stands out as a case that has successfully addressed the two classic insurance problems of adverse selection and moral hazard. Our tour of the world's pension guarantee systems will also demonstrate that the manner in which retirement obligations are secured can have profound effects on the savings behavior of households and corporations as well as on the development of local capital markets. The case of the Netherlands is useful to consider before we focus on the collective pension guarantee funds in these other countries.

THE NETHERLANDS

Holland effectively met the need to provide more secure pension benefits without resorting to the use of a collective termination insurance system.[6] The historical background there is remarkably similar to the pre-ERISA experience in the United States. However, the Dutch confronted this problem 30 years before it became a major concern in the United States. During the 1930s, the bankruptcy of a large Dutch shipping company, *Koninklijke Hollandsche Lloyd* (Royal Dutch Lloyd), reduced the pensions and pension claims of more than 1,000 employees and former workers to virtually nothing, because pension assets had been loaned to the employer. The company had been floundering since the period immediately following World War I, and one of the few sources of credit available to it was the employees' pension plan. This became one of the earliest known examples of the dangers of party-in-interest investment.

The disruption of normal commercial life during World War II prevented the Dutch Government from addressing this problem until Parliament adopted the 1952 Act on Employees' Pensions (*Pensioen-en Spaarfondsenwet*). The goal of the legislation was to sever the link between the financial situation of the employer and the credit quality of the pension promise.[7] The 1952 Act assigned responsibility for the supervision of Dutch occupational pension plans to the *Verzekeringskamer* (the Insurance Supervisory Board). The *Verzekeringskamer* originally was organized in 1923 as an agency within the Dutch government's Treasury Department.[8] Since 1952, no Dutch pension plan has been terminated without sufficient assets. However, many years ago there was one case of a minor shortfall, relative to some of the required reserves, that was attributed to the "65-X" actuarial cost method. That particular method backloads charges for pension benefits onto the later years of the career. A move is now afoot to prohibit use of the 65-X method. More recently, another pension fund became troubled when the sponsor experienced financial difficulty. Plan participants in that case were made whole as a result of financial assistance from an insurance company. These outcomes represent a huge improvement since the Royal Dutch Lloyd case and compare favorably with distributions following terminations involving the PBGC in the United States.

The 1952 Act relies on five protective principles to insulate private pension funds in the Netherlands from the business risks facing plan sponsors. First, organizations entirely separate from the employer assume operational responsibility for the pension plans. For example, companies may join a multiemployer pension plan that is active in their trade or industry. Alternatively, companies may purchase annuity contracts on behalf of their employees from life insurance carriers or make special payments to them so that they may purchase annuity contracts for themselves. Finally, an employer may set up a legally separate foundation to manage a pension plan for its workers. Employers cannot determine the pension plan investment policies or funding requirements in any of these cases. In practice, these plans are operated by insurance companies or pension trusts.

The second line of protection in the 1952 Act restricts investments by company pension plans in the employer organization to no more than 5 percent of total assets. This is a general rule. If the plan holds assets that exceed all required reserves by an additional 5 percent, that amount also may be placed in party-in-interest investments of any sort (e.g., stocks, bonds, or mortgages). Under current policy, party-in-interest investments therefore will never exceed 10 percent of total plan assets and in most cases will be considerably less.

Under current policy, accrued benefits must be fully funded, with the value of that obligation calculated using a conservative discount rate of four percent. The current policy also requires that plans with stock or real estate investments maintain volatility reserves. The volatility reserve consists of 30 percent, on average, of the value of these assets. Volatility reserves are not required in cases where stock and real estate fund less than 20 percent of accrued benefits. At the other extreme, a pension plan with all accrued benefits funded by stock or real estate investments would be required to set up and subsequently to aim for a volatility reserve of 100 percent of accrued benefits. The Verzekeringskamer has shown significant flexibility if poor investment performance erodes the volatility reserve substantially below this level. In such cases, the plan would be expected to restore the required reserves over a reasonable period.

The Verzekeringskamer's approach for setting the level of additional reserves represents a sophisticated effort to protect pension promises both from the relative risk of alternative portfolio allocations and, importantly, from the risk of insolvency on the part of the employer. Current policy also requires pension plans to set aside additional reserves for providing postretirement inflation protection. The combination of conservative actuarial assumptions, the premium reserve, and these additional reserves has produced funding levels that are among the highest in the world. For this reason, the prevailing opinion at the Verzekeringskamer and throughout the local financial community is that a collective guarantee fund simply is not needed.

The emphasis on aggressive funding in Holland represents a polar opposite relative to the approach taken just a short distance away, in Germany. Companies operating in Germany are permitted to make retirement promises to workers without any prior funding at all. This financing method involves nothing more than creating a "book reserve" on the company's balance sheet to reflect the value of accrued benefits. Two reasons have been offered to explain this difference between these close and economically integrated neighbors. First, the structure of local capital markets varies considerably. The Amsterdam stock exchange has played an important role in Dutch commercial life for centuries and has been substantial relative to the banking sector throughout the period following World War II. In Germany, the role of equity financing has not been nearly as important during most of the post–World War II period. The country relied on a system of universal banking in which the large commercial banks owned controlling positions in Germany's major industrial companies.[9] Lack of access to a large and efficient equity market motivated German employers to search for ways to use retirement saving in their own businesses. Apart from those in precarious financial condition, Dutch employers never faced the same need.

Dutch pension specialists also attribute this difference to a strong pro-saving ethic in Holland, combined with the relative strength of organized labor there. After experiencing hyperinflation during the 1920s, German suspicions of organized saving schemes were understandable later when most company pension plans were set up. German workers were acutely concerned about the purchasing power of their benefit payments later in life. A more abstract and paternalistic commitment was what mattered for them. Dutch workers had more confidence in the local currency and wanted to see what they considered to be their money working for them by earning returns in the pension plans.

In the Netherlands, a third line of protection against employer insolvency risk involves annual independent audits of all pension plans and life insurance companies by certified public accountants and actuaries. These institutions also must report their financial data to the Verzekeringskamer on an annual basis. Every 10 years, the Verzekeringskamer must conduct its own audit of the pension plan. Based on these audits, the Verzekeringskamer provides advice concerning the management of the pension plan; that advice is considered binding in practice. As a further precau-tion, the Versekeringskamer conducts additional discussions with these institutions at more frequent intervals. The Dutch response to supervision of this sort stands in sharp contrast to reactions typically observed in the United States. Employee representatives are legally entitled to make up half of the board membership of individual pension plans in the Netherlands.

The Dutch don't consider pensions to be a gratuity but instead view them as an important part of compensation that belongs entirely to the workers once contributions have been made. In the absence of a PBGC-type guarantee fund, worker representatives therefore have a strong incentive to stay informed and to work closely with the Verzekeringskamer to make sure that the plan is sound. The staff of the Verzekeringskamer identified approximately 25 pension plans of a total of 1,126 to be in some way deficient during the 12-month period preceding June 1994. In each of these cases, the Verzekeringskamer gave the same advice: more contributions needed to be raised from participating employers. The plans obtained those without delay, and the conditions therefore became acceptable. Systematic defunding of a pension plan of the sort described in Chapter 3 is unheard of in the Netherlands.

One reason why the supervision of private pension plans has been so successful in the Netherlands is that the Verzekeringskamer retains some very potent weapons even when the regulations authorizing it to impose sanctions are not specific. The Verzekeringskamer can issue disapproving comments to the board of the pension fund as well as to the employer and employee organizations. The threat of public censure serves as a highly effective incentive for pension fund officials to take remedial action when requested to do so. Pension plan investments are managed mostly by banks, investment houses, and insurance companies. Adverse publicity released by the Verzekeringskamer would be devastating to any financial intermediary. This also represents a sharp contrast to the situation in the United States. Companies included on the PBGC's "Top 50" list are not nearly as threatened by adverse publicity because they serve different markets (e.g., steel), where customers do not insist on the same high standards of creditworthiness and financial integrity, in order to continue doing business. Moral suasion has worked for the Dutch in this area because the authorities use it to modify the behavior of the financial intermediaries. By their very nature, financial institutions are much more vulnerable to adverse reputational effects. Manufacturing companies simply are not as sensitive to bad publicity.

Despite all of these precautions, private Dutch pension plans are permitted to create unfunded liabilities in rare cases involving newly established pension plans. A fourth line of protection against employer insolvency in Dutch pension law therefore secures any unfunded liabilities of a new company or new multiemployer pension plans. These obligations must either be reinsured privately or transferred to a life insurance company, which then acts as the direct insurer. The Verzekeringskamer must approve of the manner in which these liabilities are funded.

The final line of protection set up in the 1952 Act prohibits both employers and employees from withdrawing pension capital. The intent here is to protect the worker against his or her own greed or shortsightedness as well as from designs on the use of those funds by employers and others. Although aspects of the 1952 Act may seem rigid, the Ministry of Social Affairs in rare cases can make exceptions when a strict application of the law would be injurious.

The example of Holland demonstrates that pension promises can be secured effectively without the use of a collective termination insurance fund. In fact, private pensions in Holland are among the most secure in the world when considered not only in terms of insolvency risk but also in terms of protection against postretirement inflation. Both employer and employee groups have compelling incentives to cooperate with the Verzekeringskamer. Meanwhile, a strong pro-saving ethic and the robust state of local capital markets add to the resilience of the private pension system in Holland. Despite this generally impressive example, the countries discussed below subsequently chose to set up collective guarantee funds in response to their particular needs and circumstances.

ONTARIO

Canada's pension guarantee system differs from all others insofar as the the federal government did not mandate it and does not administer it. For constitutional reasons, a political subdivision chose to assume this function instead. Of Canada's 10 provinces, only Ontario has adopted such a program; thus, this discussion is limited to the system operating in Ontario.

The motivation for establishing Ontario's Pension Benefit Guaranty Fund (PBGF) in 1980 was quite similar to the reasons that led to creation of the PBGC six years earlier in the United States. As in the United States, the benefits of single-employer, collectively bargained pension plans in Canada typically are renegotiated every three years or so, producing increases roughly at the rate of inflation. In Canada, the cost of those benefit increases is amortized over the subsequent 15-year period. Concern that successive layers of amortization payments eventually would become too onerous for many financially shaky sponsors led to the call for this back-up guarantee. When these employers are forced to liquidate, workers in those situations are faced not only with the prospect of losing their jobs but also with the loss of unfunded pension benefits.

The Ontario legislation, known as Section 85 of the Pension Benefits Act of 1987, retroactively guaranteed all benefits granted after the Province's Pensions Benefits Act of 1965. Critics of the new system, including the Canadian economist James Pesando, argued that windfall redistributive effects on an otherwise competitive labor market would accompany retroactive insurance of past service credits. The critics preferred an alternative approach for this reason; they also cited the difficulty of determining economic insurance premiums. They pointed out that improved disclosure of worker benefits in case of plan termination or improved disclosure in conjunction with tighter funding requirements avoided many of the problems involved with public termination insurance. If termination insurance were mandated, Pesando argued that it should be purchased from private insurers.[10]

Pesando also pointed out that, if workers were sufficiently risk averse that they wanted no exposure to unfunded pension promises, they could take action to avoid them. Workers could negotiate a larger fraction of their total compensation in the form of wages and then use the additional cash to set up their own Registered Retirement Savings Plans (i.e., defined-contribution plans).[11] Smaller firms in Canada, where the risk of plan termination was perceived to be very high, almost invariably offered money purchase plans anyway. Similar to ERISA termination insurance, Ontario's system freezes benefits in nominal terms as of the termination date. The inflation risk to plan members in these cases therefore is virtually equivalent to investment risk for fixed-income portfolios. Given that money purchase plans are not entirely invested in fixed-income instruments, members of money purchase plans can be less exposed to investment risk than members of defined-benefit plans.[12]

Despite these arguments, Ontario's PBGF became operational in 1983. The legislation gave it a lien on employer assets to the extent that the fund was required to make payments to plan members. Initially, premiums were set at 0.2 percent of any unfunded liability; an additional annual charge of C$1 per member was soon added. However, policymakers recognized that the reported condition of a plan was a highly imperfect measure of the risks to the insurance fund. The alternative was to require a test actuarial valuation solely for the purpose of determining the PBGF premium. This was rejected as impractical. The PBGF guarantees most accrued benefits with some exceptions. The liabilities of plans less than three years old are not insured, nor are any benefit improvements that were adopted within three years of a plan termination date. Multiemployer plans are excluded from the system altogether, and the maximum guaranteed benefit is C$1,000 per month. Unlike the maximum benefit guaranteed by the PBGC in the United States, Ontario's maximum guaranteed benefit has not been indexed or increased since the PBGF was set up in 1980.

By the end of 1990, the PBGF had collected C$11.4 million in premiums and experienced C$11.6 million in claims. Then, disaster struck. The farm equipment producer Massey-Ferguson declared itself bankrupt with an unfunded pension liability of C$29 million. The fund proceeded to borrow from the provincial government with interest costs absorbing all of the premium income. As of 1993, the insurance fund was in deficit by C$22 million, following a recovery of C$2.5 million in the Massey-Ferguson case.

Ontario implemented a new premium structure in December 1992 in response to this situation. It extended the C$1 annual premium per member to beneficiaries. In addition, a sliding scale was adopted for the risk-adjusted component. For plans that are under-funded on a termination basis, the risk-adjusted charge increased to 0.5 percent of those unfunded liabilities representing up to 10 percent of total liabilities. For additional unfunded liabilities representing up to 20 percent of total liabilities, the annual charge rose to 1 percent, and for unfunded liabilities beyond that level the charge increased to 1.5 percent. However, Ontario's new premiums remain much lower than those charged by the one system that has introduced market pricing—Finland.

In March 1993, the PBGF faced 37 potential claims as a result of the liquidation of 31 Ontario corporations. The potential liability attributable to these bankruptcies was approximately C$27 million. The PBGF also acknowledged in its annual report for that year that it could face an additional claim of C$250 million if the restructuring of the Algoma Steel company is not successful and the company becomes insolvent. A claim of this size would precipitate another financial crisis for the PBGF.

Notwithstanding its deficit, Pesando's criticisms, and the other problems that also plague America's PBGC, Ontario's system has three important advantages relative to the ERISA termination insurance concept. First, the maximum guaranteed benefit is much lower. It amounts to slightly more than one-third of the maximum guaranteed amount in the United States. The distribution of coinsurance throughout the labor force therefore is likely to be much more consistent. Hence, better-paid senior workers have a greater stake in the survival of the firm. Second, the system is smaller. It covers only 1.7 million participants in approximately 9,500 plans. The cost of any termination therefore will be spread over a much smaller base. As a result, sponsors have much greater motivation to press the authorities for effective solvency regulation, particularly with respect to the very largest plans, in the form of credit surveillance as well as timely intervention in seriously deteriorating cases.

Finally, participants are likely to have less confidence in a provincial guarantee. After all, Canada is a country that periodically threatens to break up. Significant uncertainty therefore surrounds the question of whether a federal government would even exist to bail out Ontario should PBGF losses grow to proportions unmanageable at the provincial level. As a result, workers are likely to be more skeptical of false pension promises that could be paid only at the expense of the insurance fund. Sponsors in poor and declining financial health probably will be less able to abuse the system by expanding retirement benefits as a substitute for cash compensation.

CHILE

In 1981, Chile adopted sweeping reform of its social security system by what has been described as firing "a shot heard around the entire social security world."[13] Chile had been the first Latin American country to set up a national system of old-age income support. Working in close collaboration with the International Labor Office, the Chileans had modeled their original program on the social welfare systems of major European countries as they existed during the early part of this century. The average Chilean today is strongly attached to the idea of social security, as a result of the country's long experience with the program. Three pension-related guarantees from the State were instrumental in gaining wide public acceptance for the new system.

The same social democratic views that inspired post–World War II growth of retirement systems in the United States and other Western democracies exerted influence in Chile. The welfare state was supposed to assure egalitarian treatment. The role of government—as seen by William Beveridge and his influential followers—was to minister to the population's "states of need." In return, public officials were granted new powers at the expense of individual freedom.

Reality increasingly diverged from social democratic ideals. Political patronage ruined the old system, which became highly fragmented. Three large systems—for manual workers, salaried employees, and civil servants—eventually emerged, along with another 50 or so smaller ones. Benefits varied greatly across these different arrangements; the result was an affront to the core value of equality.

Very low total benefit payments during the early years of the old system were followed by rising costs and mounting deficits. High inflation also reduced the value of many trust fund investments to virtually nothing during the years leading up to reform. The government was tapping general revenues to make 28 percent of all benefit payments by 1980. That share would have risen even higher without reform.

Politicians used the old system to buy votes from key groups in Chile. Extraction of social security concessions (e.g., premature retirement, cheap credit, and privileged inflation adjustments) became one of the most important goals of politics. Some groups could retire with nearly full benefits after just 25 years of work. A succession of governments spent more than 20 years telling the people that social security was in a state of crisis. The public completely lost confidence as a result.

Then came Salvador Allende's left-wing experiment with socialism during the 1970s. Most large- and medium-sized companies were nationalized. Hyperinflation and a foreign exchange crisis followed. A military *junta* led by Augusto Pinochet toppled Allende in 1974. Chile then reversed course. A handful of economic reformers working inside the government successfully promoted growth-oriented policies, and strong political undercurrents began pushing for the return to democracy that occurred in 1989.

According to Dr. José Piñera, Minister of Labor in the Pinochet regime and chief architect of the 1981 social security reforms, the reformers designed the guarantees to be "radical in approach, conservative in execution."[14] Chile's new social security system gives each contributor explicit property rights and freedom of choice to protect against bad management.[15] The reforms emphasized independence for workers and the importance of market forces. Equality was not a central goal. Chile's new system was designed to protect workers from political risk. After subsidizing a bankrupt system that promised far more than it could deliver, most Chileans believe that they are better off with a closer link between contributions and benefits.

The new system requires most working people in Chile to contribute 10 percent of earnings to individual retirement accounts.[16] Those not covered include members of the armed forces, the self-employed, and workers choosing to remain in the old system at the time of the reforms. The intent was to create a private, defined-contribution system capable of replacing about 70 percent of final salary after a full career.[17] Upon retirement, the worker chooses between phased withdrawals from the account or the purchase of an annuity from an insurance company. Retirees also can elect some combination of these two.

Contributions are deposited only with approved financial intermediaries known as *Administradoras de Fondos de Pensiones* (administrators of pension funds, or AFPs). As of December 1994, 21 AFPs covered almost 2.9 million contributors under close government supervision. AFPs also provide mandatory survivors and disability insurance for an additional 2 percent to 3 percent of covered income.[18] Chile has a limit of one AFP account per worker and one pension fund per AFP. But workers can switch AFPs anytime. In 1981, workers were given a choice of joining the new system or remaining in the old one. Today, 93 percent of the eligible workers participate in the new system. Account balances have grown to $22 billion (half of the GDP), and the real rate of return has averaged 14 percent.

The Government of Chile plays a major role in the new system by providing several pension guarantees. The 1981 law guarantees a significant minimum pension for any worker with 20 years of contributions.[19] The Government also guarantees 100 percent of the value of an annuity up to the minimum pension and 75 percent of the value of an annuity above that level to protect retired workers against the risk of insurance company insolvency. So far, there has been one insurance company bankruptcy covered by this guarantee. Failure of that carrier involved no loss to the government.

In addition, the government guarantees a minimum real rate of return that will be at least 2 percent below the average real return for all AFPs during the period in question, or 50 percent of that average, whichever is less.[20] Chile requires all AFPs to maintain capital reserves, known as the *encaje*, of 1 percent of assets under management, to secure any difference between actual performance and this guaranteed minimum. The government would invoke the guarantee only if the AFP's *encaje* is not sufficient to top up any inadequate returns. However, this appears to be an extremely unlikely event. The

1981 legislation restricts portfolio choices considerably, thereby limiting performance differences across AFPs. Furthermore, the AFPs are scrutinized by government authorities on a daily basis to ensure that investment practices conform with prescribed standards. So far, funds from an AFP's *encaje* have been tapped only once to bring portfolio returns up to the statutory minimum. In that one case, the gap between the minimum and actual performance was so slight that government funds were unnecessary.

Dr. José Piñera, the Minister of Labor during the Pinochet regime, favored these guarantees in order to eliminate resistance to the reforms, to reduce anxieties, and to make the new system more acceptable to the general public. A diverse group of Chileans working with the AFP system considers guarantees of some sort to be inevitable whenever a government mandates individual contributions. The guarantees in Chile reflect a social philosophy that aims to assure every citizen a decent standard of living in old age, but also a strong preference to rely on market forces for determining outcomes above that level.

Piñera expected from the start that the minimum guaranteed pension would involve fiscal outlays by the government. The reformers considered such spending as preferable to a highly redistributive, pay-as-you-go "first pillar" that is common to national retirement systems elsewhere. They made no attempt to estimate the cost of this guarantee before the reforms were adopted. However, Piñera designed the relative rate-of-return guarantee as well as the guarantee of life annuities based on the belief that they should never involve fiscal outlays by the State. A discussion of Chile's three guarantees follows.

The Minimum Guaranteed Pension

For participants in Chile's new social security system with 20 years of credited contributions, the State guarantees a minimum pension that amounted to 75 percent of the minimum wage and 25 percent of the average wage at the end of 1994.[21] Approximately 13,000 people currently receive the minimum,[22] but this number is expected to rise after the new social security system has been operating for more than 20 years. On the other hand, unexpectedly high returns achieved by the AFPs until now will reduce the need for minimum pensions among the first cohorts that otherwise would qualify for it.

The government finances minimum pensions on a current basis using general revenues. Many observers therefore view the minimum pension guarantee as a close substitute for the redistributive component of social security that is financed on a pay-as-you-go basis in most developed countries. This aspect of the system's design reflects one of the central objectives of the 1981 reforms: to target direct public spending for social security on the poor. The Chilean government also provides means-tested income support to the elderly in the form of an "assistance pension." Little if any substitution effect appears to exist between these two programs due to the very sizable gap between the two and the means-tested feature of the assistance pension. The normal retirement age in Chile is 65 for men and 60 for women. Women have a longer life expectancy and they are more likely to use the minimum pension for this reason.

The minimum pension can be invoked under two circumstances. First, a retiree may take down the entire balance in his or her AFP account under the phased-withdrawal option. The amount of each withdrawal can correspond to the minimum pension even though the balance in the account might not be enough to purchase a life annuity for the same stream of payments. When the participant's account balance is exhausted, the State simply begins making regular payments to the person in question. Alternatively, the minimum pension guarantee can be invoked if the minimum pension is increased in real terms to exceed the annuity that a retiree receives from an insurance company.[23] The cost of the minimum pension guarantee is highly sensitive to rates of return achieved by the AFPs, the timing of contributions, changes in the level of real wages, changes in the minimum wage, and changes in the level of the minimum pension itself.

Since the 1981 reforms, several studies have attempted to estimate the cost of this guarantee. Wagner projected that the annual cost to the government would amount to US$7.3 million in a long-term steady state. This translates into a present value of US$183 million. He modeled the guarantee in a deterministic framework.[24] At about the same time, Chile's Treasury Department developed a simulation model that showed more than 40 percent of the labor force qualified for assistance under the minimum pension guarantee at some point.[25] Subsequently, Zurita implemented an option-pricing model to simulate the value of the guarantee.[26] He was careful to qualify his results by stating that they should be treated more as an illustration of a suitable method than as a set of precise estimates. Still, the model estimated a present value of US$950 million, or about 3 percent of GDP in 1992. The results of these studies therefore are inconclusive, and weaknesses in the available data have prevented more authoritative work from being carried out before now.

Chile's minimum pension guarantee has raised several concerns related to moral hazard. First, the level of the minimum pension may be such that it reduces or eliminates the incentive for relatively low-paid workers to contribute during the early years of their careers when the time value of money is greatest. By working in the informal sector initially, participants at the bottom of the wage scale increase the probability that the guarantee will be invoked.[27] Another moral hazard arises from payment choices available to retirees with account balances equal to or slightly above the price of a life annuity for the minimum pension. By choosing the phased-withdrawal alternative, this group receives longevity insurance from the government at no charge.

Evasion also emerged as a conspicuous issue particularly among domestic workers employed in households. A lower minimum wage applies to this group, and they are likely to receive part of their income in the form of in-kind compensation (e.g., free room and board). In 1991, approximately 100,000 household workers were contributing to the new social security system. Then, a related indemnization fund was set up to provide unemployment benefits. The incentive for workers to participate is strong. Contributions are set at 4.11 percent of covered wages and they are linked to participation in the new social security system. Now, 350,000 domestic workers are contributing to AFP accounts, the increase largely resulting from this change. Altogether, some 450,000 people are employed as domestic workers in Chile.

The incentive to game the system by contributing for no more than 20 years figures among the most serious concerns about Chile's minimum pension guarantee. One alternative to the current arrange-ment would set an accrual rate per year of service in order to provide an incentive for contributing over a full career. The accrual rate might be based on the minimum wage or the average wage.

Early retirement provisions have created additional risks for the State in relation to the minimum guaranteed pension. Two condi-tions currently apply to workers when seeking to retire early: the AFP account balance must be adequate to purchase an annuity worth at least 110 percent of the minimum pension; and the annuity must pay at least 70 percent of the worker's average salary during the last 10 years. Authorities are currently studying the possibility of raising the required annuity purchase to 140 percent of the minimum pen-sion. In addition, the insurance companies could be required to in-crease their reserves for life annuities, thereby raising the cost of early retirement.

Finally, the question of adequacy is always a major factor in discussions about minimum pensions. Chile's minimum pension amounts to about 25 percent of the average wage, and it is consid-ered relatively low by those familiar with retirement systems around the globe. A minimum pension of 35 percent to 40 percent of the av-erage wage would be more consistent with international standards. Pressure therefore is expected for increases in the minimum pension during the years ahead. In an early sign of this trend, the widow's pension soon will be raised by 20 to 30 percent. These pensions had ranged between 60 and 75 percent of the general minimum pension.

The Relative Rate-of-Return Guarantee

Chile adopted the *relative rate-of-return guarantee* because there was no well-developed system in place to regulate the AFPs in 1981. This guarantee is more widely known as the *minimum rate-of-return guarantee*. Economic reformers in the government considered the alternative of requiring a 4 percent minimum rate of return but re-jected it on grounds that it would shift risk in ways that ultimately would prove unfair. The authorities wanted to provide incentives for AFPs to maintain rigorous standards in their investment policies and account management practices. They also set out to create a market-based mechanism to limit fees that fund managers could impose on the retirement accounts.[28] For the designers of the system, the only circumstance that could justify government intervention in response to inadequate AFP performance was an economic depression. They intended for that intervention to take place in the context of the minimum pension guarantee described just above. The relative rate-of-return guarantee has never been invoked, although, as mentioned, an AFP once tapped the *encaje* to bring pension fund returns up to the statutory minimum.

The three largest AFPs managed almost 53 percent of systemwide account balances at the end of 1994. The relative rate-of-return guarantee, together with the requirement that returns exceeding the industry average by 2 percent be placed in a special reserve, provide an incentive for smaller AFPs to monitor the portfolios of their larger competitors. In response, they have replicated those portfolios or adopted investment allocations that are just slightly riskier. Has this guarantee, combined with the volatility of Chile's emerging capital markets, created major risks for the government despite the intent of the system's designers?

The incentive to conform seemed to increase market volatility when only a short list of securities were eligible for AFP investment. Another effect was the apparent misallocation of retirement savings in Chile's capital-scarce economy. Qualified securities that attracted funds from the largest AFPs drew in virtually all of these institutions. Valuations quickly became excessive relative to alternative investments or so the argument goes. However, more investments qualify now. Chile also recently allowed the AFPs to diversify internationally in response to this concern. AFPs were permitted to place 3 percent of their portfolios in foreign equities and 6 percent of their portfolios in overseas investments of all types.[29] Virtually no one expects real AFP investment returns to continue averaging 14 percent annually with the greater diversification permitted today. This and other factors have created the expectation that real returns instead will fall to between 6 and 8 percent over the long term.

Of the three guarantees discussed here, dissatisfaction is greatest with the relative rate-of-return guarantee, as it does not permit portfolios to adjust to the preferences of individual social security participants. Their needs and circumstances can be very different.

Some AFP managers openly favor abolishing the guarantee for this reason. They believe that fund managers would be motivated to act in the interests of social security participants as a result of the requirement that each AFP's capital reserve—the *encaje*—be invested entirely in the AFP portfolio. The owners of the AFP therefore are exposed to the same risks as the affiliated workers who maintain accounts at the institution. For its part, the SAFP is considering two alternative approaches. One possible reform would adjust the required relative rate of return to reflect the level of risk in each AFP portfolio. Another possibility would be to set up a small number of different classes of AFP funds. Each of these classes would have its own relative rate-of-return requirement. SAFP staff members indicated that the motivation for these changes would not be to permit greater risk taking; on the contrary, the primary purpose would be to allow older social security participants to invest in less risky portfolios.

Certainly one of the original justifications for adopting this guarantee has weakened and may no longer apply. As the SAFP gained experience regulating the system, the use of the relative rate of return as a mechanism to limit what fees fund managers could extract from retirement accounts might have become unnecessary. However, other observers in Chile are skeptical that any change will be made in this guarantee. The political leadership still needs the assurance that investment outcomes will fall within a relatively narrow and socially acceptable range. Otherwise, popular support for Chile's approach to social security finance would simply unravel. At the moment, the demand for variety in the investment choices available to individual social security participants is quite low.

The Guarantee for Life Annuities
The architects of Chile's 1981 social security reforms, and others closely involved with the insurance industry there, believe that this guarantee is unlikely to result in fiscal outlays by the State. It therefore is not a candidate for reform in the foreseeable future. The gap between annuity values against which the insurance carriers are required to maintain reserves and the maximum amounts guaranteed by the government explains the widespread confidence.

If a worker chooses to purchase a life annuity upon retirement, the State guarantees the minimum pension plus 75 percent of the difference between the annuity and the minimum pension, up to 45 *unidades de fomento* (UF).[30] However, the insurance carrier is required to maintain technical reserves against the full value of the annuity. Losses by the insurance carrier therefore would need to be very substantial before the guarantee would be invoked. In the one case where a life insurance company was closed by the authorities, the annuities were transferred to other carriers without any losses to retirees or to the government. The liquidated company even had a positive net worth. It simply was not able to meet the reserve requirement. So, its charter was revoked, and the owners were reimbursed for the residual net worth.

Still, the life insurance companies in Chile must confront the classic insurance problem of adverse selection with no perfect instrument available to control it. Life insurance companies ordinarily cover a healthier pool of retirees who choose life annuities because they expect to live longer than the average. However, some of the cost attributable to this aspect of the annuity market could be avoided. Adverse selection risk could be substantially reduced if all workers were required to use a portion of their account balance to purchase an annuity upon retirement. That portion could correspond with the cost of the minimum pension.[31]

Life insurance companies are also required, in effect, to provide insurance against interest rate risk, and this protection is reflected in annuity prices. However, the phased-withdrawal option for retirees in Chile aggravates the problem for life insurance carriers operating there, because similar protection against interest rate risk isn't provided to retirees choosing the phased-withdrawal alternative. Interest rate risk is less of a concern for people with shorter life expectancy.[32] This provides an added incentive for the most profitable group of potential annuity purchasers to choose the phased-withdrawal option. The only tool available to the life insurance companies for controlling this problem is the use of conservative mortality tables. That tool, although imperfect, has certainly been adequate until now.

For the State, the risk of fiscal outlay pursuant to this guarantee always remains if capital requirements might be reduced for the insurance carriers at some unknown point in the future. Similarly, if surveillance and enforcement are relaxed, present expectations that Chile's guarantee of these life annuities will be cost free would also need revision.

Conclusion

The new social security system in Chile has earned substantial credibility both at home and abroad. Even so, Chilean authorities are not completely satisfied with the guarantees from the State as they stand at the moment. Change, if it comes at all, will be gradual, in order not to erode the high level of public confidence that has been achieved since 1981.

The World Bank estimates that 30 countries will restructure their retirement systems during the years just ahead. Chile's approach to pension reform already has been adapted by Argentina, Colombia, and Peru, to fit their own particular circumstances. Apart from addressing the financial problems of the old system and its social inequities, Chile's AFP system yielded an important by-product that has been indispensable to its economic development strategy: growing sophistication and depth of the local capital markets. For these reasons, several other countries in Latin America and Eastern Europe are considering the Chilean model as well. Guarantees from the State may not be as essential to address anxieties about reform in many of these situations. Simpler and fiscally safer guarantees will also be more appropriate for countries where prospects for the fiscal balance are not as favorable. Officials planning to restructure social security systems elsewhere should note that Chile was able to run a substantial budget surplus during the years leading up to the 1981 reforms.

FINLAND

The case of Finland serves as a cautionary example for students of benefit security arrangements linked to many types of pension systems. Until the end of 1993, Finland's Central Pension Security Institute (CPSI) provided specialized credit insurance to employers, allowing them to obtain loans from their pension funds or the financial institutions that manage them.[33] This concept originated as a product of the uniquely Finnish approach to lending that requires all loans to be collateralized. Corporate balance sheets—often with just 10 percent equity—tend to be much more highly leveraged in Finland than elsewhere. The creation of pension-related credit insurance there allowed employers, in effect, to borrow from workers and then to use pension capital in their own businesses while meeting the requirements for collateral security. The CPSI's credit insurance operations began in 1962 and ran smoothly for almost 30 years. However, substantial losses started accumulating in 1989, causing the system to collapse four years later. The CPSI then privatized its credit insurance operations at the beginning of 1994. A joint stock company known as Garantia was set up to provide pension-linked credit insurance on commercial terms.

Pension benefits in Finland were financed almost entirely on a pay-as-you-go basis at the outset. However, significant advance funding now is being made to cover obligations to future retirees. In Finland, full funding of annual pension premiums (i.e., contributions to cover both the pay-as-you-go and prefunded obligations) is mandatory, and credit insurance is required when borrowing occurs against plan assets. The basic pension contribution is currently 20.6 percent of total compensation, with the worker paying 3 percent and employers paying the remainder. However, adjustments can be made to the basic premium based on the age distribution of the workforce when a company's total employment exceeds 50. In these cases, pension premiums can account for between 13.1 and 29.5 percent of payroll. Pension coverage is mandatory for all of Finland's 1,350,000 workers.

These mandatory employer-provided pensions supplement national old-age retirement benefits. Mandatory occupational benefits are standardized and set by law, but otherwise the system is decentralized. Employers may arrange to provide workers with pension benefits through one of seven Government-approved pension insurance carriers or through a pension foundation created for the company itself or by participating in a pension fund that covers several companies usually in the same industry. Finland's legislation concerning mandatory private pensions took effect in 1962, at the same time that CPSI credit insurance became operational. The central goal of that law was to provide a benefit of 60 percent of final covered earnings after a 40-year career.[34] This level of earnings replacement is based on coordination with Finland's social security benefits.[35] Employers contribute an additional 4.2 to 5.7 percent of payroll to cover national social security pensions and employees contribute another 2.05 percent.

Employer groups initially favored setting up mandatory private pensions as a means of avoiding an expanded state system. Finland's capital markets were relatively undeveloped at that time. Although many in Finland now believe that the so-called TEL loans[36] and related pension "reborrowing" are no longer needed as a source of corporate finance, there is no sign that they will be abolished, even in the wake of the recent credit insurance debacle.

The collapse of CPSI's program represented a fiasco of major proportions in the context of Finland's economy. The CPSI's accumulated credit insurance exposure amounts to Fmk 37 billion. In the event that future credit insurance premiums won't cover losses from this amount, CPSI has the authority to collect any remaining shortfall directly from future pension contributions. Ignore for a moment the effect of shifting costs across age groups by means of future credit insurance premiums. Current estimates suggest that between Fmk 3 billion and Fmk 4 billion will need to be raised directly from pension contributions. These direct levies alone amount to at least $500 per worker in a system with approximately 1.4 million workers who will absorb the losses. After adjusting for the size of the labor force, this means of financing previous CPSI credit insurance losses would translate into a bailout of $50 billion in the context of the American economy.

As one founder of the new Garantia organization, CPSI received 48 percent of Garantia's shareholder equity. The remainder of the stock was distributed among Finland's pension insurance companies, its single-employer pension foundations, the multiemployer pension foundations, and the labor market associations representing workers as well as employers. Garantia was capitalized with Fmk 250 million of owner's equity. The formation of Garantia combined with the newly acquired right allowing all credit insurers in Finland to deny insurance to poor credits could place new pressure on the economy as financially weak employers are forced to reduce the scale of their operations and in some cases even to liquidate.

Those involved with CPSI credit insurance attribute its woes largely to the severe downturn in economic activity there starting in 1989. Certainly it is true that the Finnish economy has experienced a very severe adjustment following disruption of trading relationships with the former Soviet Union and a secular decline in the shipbuilding industry. Finland's exports had been sold in generally robust markets during the 1980s, but those markets became extremely weak during the early 1990s as Europe and North America both slipped into recession. Prices of forestry products experienced a particularly severe decline in world markets. The effects of these developments more nearly resembled those of a depression than a recession. Unemployment rose to 20 percent, and—for the first time in a generation—the country's political leadership allowed large companies that became troubled to go bankrupt. Social attitudes toward business failure underwent a sea change. Bankruptcy previously had been considered something shameful. Then, it suddenly became accepted and even routine. Claims against the CPSI rose from Fmk 25 million in 1988 to more than Fmk 1 billion both in 1992 and 1993.

But responsibility for CPSI's losses can't be assigned to the condition of Finland's economy alone. To understand the array of forces that contributed to the collapse of Finland's pension-linked credit insurance, consider the following background concerning the country's pension and financial systems. Political influence over Finland's retirement system has been strong. For example, farmers receive pensions from Finland's Government but make contributions covering only 20 percent of the cost necessary to finance them. The benefits are funded from the country's general tax revenues instead. All other private workers in Finland are required to contribute to their retirement plans.

Political forces also influence the terms on which pension borrowing occurs. Evidence that pension-related borrowing—TEL loans—can occur on "soft" terms is provided by the fact that the interest rate on pension-linked borrowing—known as the TEL rate—is set by Finland's Parliament. In practice, the Parliament ratifies a

TEL rate negotiated by labor market organizations representing Finland's trade unions and employer groups. Companies and unions apply pressure to keep the TEL rate low. So, the TEL rate can differ by large amounts from the market rates charged by the country's banks. This can lead to the classic problem of disintermediation seen previously among America's banks and savings and loan institutions before the Federal Reserve Board's Regulation Q was rescinded.[37] In the American context, disintermediation was the tendency for funds to be withdrawn from a depository institution when market interest rates exceed the rate paid on the deposits.

Predicting possible effects of the specific form of disintermediation apparent in Finland requires information about the relevant interest rate elasticities. Nevertheless, it was clear that disintermediation was motivating Finland's employers to repay TEL loans and other pension reborrowing during the first half of 1994. As of May 1994, the TEL rate was 6.5 percent and Garantia's credit insurance premium ranged from 1.5 to 4 percent. Thus, companies would have paid between 8 and 10.5 percent for pension-linked credit. Meanwhile, commercial bank lending rates ranged from 7.5 to 8 percent. Not surprisingly, Garantia had not written any new credit insurance coverage between the time that it began operations in January 1994 and May of that year.[38] On the other hand, the bank rate stood at 15 percent one year earlier. A substantial subsidy is therefore available at times, due to TEL lending.

Be that as it may, the opportunity for corporate borrowers to disintermediate relative to the banking system or the pension-linked credit insurance had been curtailed slightly at the end of 1993. Companies subsequently were not permitted to liquidate a TEL loan and then to use pension-linked credit insurance system later to borrow against the same pension commitments. Still, employers now can reborrow against new accruals or pension obligations that previously had not been used to obtain a TEL loan. So, disintermediation should continue to influence the flow of funds in Finland's capital markets during the foreseeable future. In the American context, periods of disintermediation were associated with low earnings on the part of the financial institutions in question.[39] It also seems reasonable to expect that Garantia's own financial performance will be adversely affected from time to time as a result of this factor.

Commercial banks in Finland as well as other financial intermediaries also provide credit insurance to cover pension-related borrowing by employers. The credit insurance is priced on a case-by-case, risk-related basis. While credit insurers were required to offer a guarantee to any employer requesting one before the end of 1993, the premium could be made prohibitively expensive to borrowers who were not creditworthy. Starting in 1994, credit insurers received the right to deny coverage. The maximum guaranteed amount covers 70 percent of the employer's annual pension contribution, and the credit insurance premium averaged 0.3 percent of the credit insurance liability in 1988.[40] Finland's non-life insurance companies reinsure almost 7 percent of the CPSI's credit insurance portfolio, with reinsurance required for all risks exceeding FMK 35 million. Garantia plans to continue the practice of using reinsurance cover.

As the country's capital markets matured, this source of financing for Finland's corporations became increasingly controversial. At one point in the late 1970s, the Ministry of Finance even recommended that it be abolished. An official working group came to the conclusion that this reborrowing produced a misallocation of funds, since loans were made at below-market rates and, with the guarantee, lenders failed to consider the relative merits of competing loans.[41] Not surprisingly, the insurance companies managing the pension funds, among others, disputed these findings, with particularly strong opposition coming from groups that represented small business and rural interests. Nevertheless, Finland adopted new legislation in 1989 that extended CPSI insurance to two additional groups of pension plans: the Local Government Pensions Institution, and the Seamen's Pensions Funds. Early critics of reborrowing now believe they have been proved right following the subsequent fiasco.

CPSI never had the same intervention powers that have served Sweden's FPG/AMFK system so well. In deteriorating situations, the only alternatives available to the CPSI were to request more collateral from the employer and to increase the credit insurance premiums. CPSI did not have the authority to require financially shaky companies to eliminate their pension borrowing over a period of five years, as was the case in Sweden. Had the CPSI been given this right, sources in Finland believe that the political influence of the country's largest employers would have made the use of such powers unlikely. Today, even in the wake of the recent debacle, the practical ability of Garantia and other institutions providing credit insurance to intervene in financially deteriorating situations has not changed appreciably.

Before the end of 1993, the Finnish system represented a mixed model in the sense that credit insurance was available from both the CPSI (a quasi-governmental agency) and private sources. By 1992, CPSI guaranteed FMK 37 billion in TEL loans and pension-linked reborrowing. For their part, Finland's five largest banks provided credit insurance for FMK 82.4 billion of this type of debt. The banks were better informed than CPSI about the commercial prospects of these borrowers. They therefore were faster to demand whatever collateral the companies could provide in deteriorating situations, to secure not only pension-related debt but conventional loans as well. Still, Finland's banks incurred major losses during the recent economic turmoil. Before 1989, the supply of credit had been excessive as capital flowed into the country from abroad. Banks aggressively sought out new borrowers in what became known as a *bubble* economy. When the pace of economic activity slowed down, delinquent loans became so common that the Ministry of Finance drew on general tax revenues to rescue many banks. As for the country's savings banks, they were consolidated and closed.

Before the crisis, employers had the option of obtaining coverage directly from the CPSI if they so chose, and this arrangement remained financially stable for a very long time.[42] In the early 1980s, the CPSI estimated the reserves necessary for its insurance operations to withstand a depression scenario as severe as the experience of the 1930s. As a result, the CPSI subsequently retained half of all premium revenue to accumulate precautionary reserves, while spending approximately 40 percent of premiums to settle current claims and the remaining 10 percent for administrative expenses. Between 1982 and 1990, the CPSI paid slightly more than FMK 530 million in connection with insurance claims resulting from 450 bankruptcies. The year 1990 itself had been unusually bad, with claims of FMK 199 million. By the end of 1990, the precautionary reserve still remained large enough to cover 10 years of normal claims experience, or about FMK 500 million.[43] Still, those reserves could have been as high as FMK 3 billion within constraints imposed by Finland's tax law. Yet, even reserves at this extremely conservative level—implying an exposure-to-reserve ratio of 10—would not have been enough in 1991 to avert the collapse that followed.

The experience of Finland provides many lessons with implications for the United States. First, risk-related premiums will not necessarily lead to a better allocation of insurance if they fail to reflect the value of the guarantee. Second, according the bankruptcy claims of insurance providers first priority can represent an inadequate remedy if companies are indirectly subsidized through pension insurance arrangements and allowed to continue operating with no positive net worth. Third, reliable accounting and financial reporting systems are essential for alerting managers and policymakers to the existence of a problem. Fourth, pension insurance systems used to promote other goals (e.g., supporting small business, regional interests, or larger companies individually) can lead to a serious misallocation of resources. According to officials at Garantia, the CPSI lacked the flexibility to conduct "efficient" insurance operations because, as a government agency, it had been conceived by people without substantial experience in insurance management. Sweden's system operated by the FPG/AMFK companies does not suffer from this drawback.

Fifth, building reserves to protect against a depression scenario may still be inadequate if the guarantor is not strong enough to withstand that type of shock from the outset. By the end of 1990 when the CPSI's loss reserves reached their peak level, they covered only 1.5 percent of the agency's credit insurance exposure. Sound practice suggests the need for reserves at least in the 4 to 5 percent range, combined with close monitoring of insured credits.[44]

Sixth, unstable pension insurance systems can operate for many years while giving the appearance of safety and soundness before suddenly collapsing. CPSI officials have reported that it usually was much too late when the agency finally recognized the need for remedial action such as demanding additional collateral or raising credit insurance premiums. By way of contrast, Finland's banks were better informed and therefore more able to limit their losses in deteriorating situations. Be that as it may, banks in Finland also experienced devastating losses, notwithstanding their relatively favorable position with respect to the CPSI.

One final lesson from Finland involves the comparative ease with which this type of credit insurance could be obtained from the CPSI relative to the competing bank guarantees. There is a widespread recognition that weaker employers received more favorable terms from the CPSI before 1991, and that subsequently, credit insurance was virtually unavailable to them from banks. A mixed model that pits subsidized government insurance against coverage sold by private carriers can be a recipe for trouble.

To conclude, sources in Finland attribute the collapse of the country's pension-linked credit insurance system to extremely adverse conditions in the local economy. Yet, conditions were almost as bad in neighboring Sweden, and a similar debacle did not occur there. These polar opposites underscore the importance of not predicating the design of a backup guarantee system on the assumption of economic stability. Geopolitical change is inevitable; it periodically spells profound adjustment in most countries throughout the world. Any viable pension guarantee must be able to withstand the stresses that will result.

In 1993, Finland made a significant attempt to restructure its troubled pension-linked system of credit insurance. CPSI has abolished its program of quasi-government credit insurance. For the first time, credit insurance now can be denied to companies that are not sufficiently creditworthy. Garantia has increased staff resources—relative to the previous situation at CPSI—assigned to evaluate credit risk. However, room for improvement still remains. The pricing of pension-related debt is negotiated between employers and unions as part of a process that clearly favors borrowers. This feature of the TEL loan system appears capable of imposing significant distortions on Finland's capital markets akin to those once observed in the United States when Regulation Q imposed interest rate ceilings on savings deposits. Disintermediation in response to interest rate differentials between TEL loans and competing sources of credit could produce substantial volatility in the financial performance of Garantia: the new private credit insurance carrier. Garantia's viability may also depend on whether the company can obtain the type of intervention powers available to the FPG/AMFK in Sweden and develop the practical ability to use them. The outlook here is not encouraging. Large corporate interests in Finland show no sign—at least, not yet—of acceding to such a request.

GERMANY

At almost the same time that the United States adopted ERISA, Germany set up a system for securing pension benefits very different than the one that emerged in the United States. When the German Government took the initial steps to set up a guarantee fund in 1974, the German Employers' Association promptly joined with the Federation of German Industries and the Federation of German Life Insurance Companies to form a separate mutual insurance association known as the *Pensions-Sicherungs-Verein* (PSVaG) or the *Pension Guarantee Association*. Shortly thereafter, Germany's parliament designated the PSVaG as the sole carrier of mandatory pension termination insurance.

The PSVaG premium is not risk related but is payable at a uniform rate based on the system's total pension liabilities as well as the total claims for the year in question. Under the German system, premium rates have been low, averaging less than 0.16 percent of the contribution basis. The PSVaG contribution basis in most cases consists of the employer's book reserve for pensions as calculated for tax purposes. It therefore represents one measure of the total pension obligation.[45] According to one study, book reserves account for about 58 percent of total funds accumulated for pension benefits, while support funds account for about 9 percent.[46] The total PSVaG contribution basis consisted of these two sources. As of 1992, it stood at DM 275 billion, or about $130 billion based on the OECD purchasing power parity exchange rate for that year.

The German book reserve system completely integrates the pension plan into the sponsor's corporate financial structure. German

employers using this method—as well as those in Sweden and Finland—report a liability on their balance sheets to represent the pension obligation. Companies receive tax deductions at the time that
pension benefits accrue. Without the reserve (or another tax-privi-
leged facility having the same effect), employers in Germany could
not claim the tax deductions until they actually paid the benefits. The
main tax advantage associated with book reserve financing, therefore,
is deferral.[47]

Meanwhile, German workers also receive a tax deferral. They
are not subject to personal income tax on benefit accruals when the
employer, in effect, funds those benefits by creating book reserves
against its own retained earnings. Personal income taxes don't fall
due until the time that the benefits are paid. When American, British,
or Dutch companies make contributions to their funded pension
plans, taxes are similarly deferred. The essential difference between
book reserve financing and a funded pension plan is that the assets
are invested inside the sponsoring company and not in a diversified
portfolio of claims on other firms. As long as pension liabilities are
not shrinking, the book reserve system can represent an inexpensive
source of new funds for German employers.

A debate occasionally has erupted in Germany concerning the
reliance on book reserve financing. The criticism heard there could
also apply to a range of approaches both in the United States and
elsewhere that permit less than complete advance funding of private
employer-sponsored pensions. These include outright pay-as-you-
go financing, terminal funding, book reserves (e.g., in Finland, Germany, Japan, and Sweden), and defined-benefit systems that require
some but not complete advance funding. German critics assert that
these approaches weaken the discipline that capital budgeting
within corporations otherwise would impose.[48] In other words, capital is prevented from flowing to its most productive uses. Returns
on pension assets—the only asset in some cases being an unfunded
benefit claim on the sponsor—can't be maximized. As a general
proposition, the critics argue that unfunded pension liabilities limit
control of investment decisions, reduce the choice of investments,
inhibit the development of local capital markets, and help conceal

management errors. Unfunded pension liabilities also encourage investment decisions that take inadequate account of the default risk.

However, even the critics acknowledge some possible advantages of using pension capital internally within the firm. Managers and directors of the company, when compared with outside investors, have a much better understanding of the investment opportunities available to it. Keeping pension capital inside the firm therefore might lead to a better allocation of resources than would otherwise occur. Within the German system of universal banking, bankers also have information that would be considered privileged and confidential in a more market-oriented setting.[49] Whether outside capital markets or managerial processes within the firm can better allocate the flow of funds to new investments may very much depend on the structure of the local financial system. Since World War II, relatively undeveloped capital markets in Germany clearly provided one incentive for employers to finance their investment needs and retirement plans internally.

In the German PSVaG system, the insured event is insolvency of the employer. This contrasts with the original termination insurance concept of ERISA and with the credit insurance systems of Sweden and Finland. With the exception of the mammoth AEG-Telefunken rescue operation,[50] and similar composition proceedings in 1993 involving the Klöckner and Saarstahl steel companies, most PSVaG claims involve smaller employers. The insolvency insurance system therefore produces extensive cross subsidies, with small business benefiting at some expense to larger enterprise. Stronger German companies do not seem to object to this arrangement because they regard it as a small price to pay for continued access to this source of internal financing. However, large multinational companies have expressed disappointment concerning the PSVaG premium structure following large claims against the system.[51]

Book reserve financing is attractive for capital-intensive firms when other long-term borrowing costs exceed the book reserve rate and they have investment opportunities that can produce returns above that level. The interest cost for book reserve pension capital was set at 6 percent as of December 1981, and it has remained at that level until now. Even though the contribution basis (i.e., the size of the book reserve) exceeded DM 10 million for only 7 percent of all sponsors covered by PSVaG insurance, those same companies accounted for about 85 percent of the insurance fund's total exposure.[52] This therefore seems to be a case in which the incentives created by federal tax subsidies are more compelling than those set up by cross subsidies within the insurance system. Another study found that these tax incentives may offset the effects of adverse selection: a process by which large and financially stronger companies otherwise would abandon book reserve financing in response to PSVaG premiums that favor riskier firms.[53]

Prior to the formation of the PSVaG in 1974, pension benefits were treated as general wage claims in bankruptcy, some of which were not recovered by former workers. Germany's book reserve system therefore forced workers to assume significant risks in the absence of prior funding of a separate trust and significant portfolio diversification. The German system of insolvency insurance was conceived as a way of retaining the public support necessary to preserve the use of book reserve funding. For their part, labor organizations were not actively involved in developing the PSVaG concept. They saw their role in industrial relations primarily as one of negotiating higher wages. With respect to pensions, German labor groups—even as late as the 1970s—had favored expansion of national retirement programs to perform the function currently assigned to the private system.[54] Their position with respect to the PSVaG proposal was one of indifference. They expected that the concept would fail and that a substantially enhanced role for national old-age pension programs inevitably would come next. In the meantime, the unions had no objection to the experiment. Some German pension specialists believe that book reserve financing would not be permitted today without a backup guarantee of the sort provided by the PSVaG. The political environment simply would not have tolerated a significant loss of pension benefits in the many bankruptcies that followed.

In 1994, PSVaG insolvency insurance covered some 7.2 million participants and 38,179 corporate sponsors. Employees at these firms who had not met the minimum vesting requirement (those under 35 years of age and who had not completed 10 years of service) were not protected by PSVaG cover. Between 1974 and 1994, the system assumed claims from 5,107 corporate insolvencies involving 497,078 plan participants. They totaled approximately DM 8.4 billion. When an employer goes into receivership or liquidates, the PSVaG purchases single-premium annuity contracts from a consortium of almost every German insurance company to cover all benefits owed to present and former workers as well as to their survivors. These insurance companies therefore are exposed only to the actuarial risks associated with the annuities sold to the PSVaG. PSVaG policyholders (i.e., participating employers) mutually assume the credit risk and pretermination interest rate risk associated with this arrangement. In 1994, the maximum guaranteed benefit was set at DM22,800 per month but the average monthly benefit provided by plans terminated with the assistance of PSVaG funds was only DM189. However, new legislation will reduce the maximum by 50 percent effective on January 1, 1999.

A striking feature of the PSVaG system is its essentially private nature. When pressed to characterize the PSVaG in terms of the degree of government involvement, German pension specialists described it as completely private. In fact, demand for greater benefit security might have produced a government program to provide the insurance had it not been for the initiative of the German Employers' Association and the private life insurance industry. However, the PSVaG is subject to supervision from the Federal Supervisory Office for Insurance Companies. If that agency withdraws its permission for the PSVaG to continue its operations, or if continuation should become impossible for some other reason, the assets and liabilities of the PSVaG would be transferred to the *Deutsche Ausgleichsbank* (Federal Bank for Compensation Payments). Both of these events are considered extremely unlikely by the German pension community.[55]

Another interesting aspect of the PSVaG concept is its pay-as-you-go approach to financing. At the beginning of each year, the initial premium is based on estimated losses during the subsequent 12 months. This estimate is then divided by the contribution basis (i.e., insured pension liabilities) to arrive at a contribution rate. Before the PSVaG closes its books at the end of a year, it can assess employers for additional amounts if claims exceed the original estimate. On the other hand, the PSVaG frequently returns surplus funds to employers when claims fall short of initial premiums. The PSVaG's claims experience has been somewhat volatile both in 1982 and 1993—the period of the AEG rescue as well as the Klöckner and Saarstahl bankruptcies—with annual insurance costs fluctuating in those years as a result. PSVaG officials are quick to point out that these fluctuations would have been much greater in the absence of cash reserves that are used to smooth the occasional costs of large claims.

However, PSVaG loss reserves are not substantial enough to cover a series of extraordinary losses that might occur in a 1930s-type depression. As of December 1994, the PSVaG had accumulated loss reserves of DM 273.5 million, approximately 0.09 percent of the total contribution basis. Is this amount adequate? German pension specialists believe that it is. If the German economy were to suffer to that extent, employers almost certainly would reduce retirement benefits as well as wages.[56] The PSVaG's exposure to losses in such a scenario therefore may be more limited than it would appear from a reading of the current financial data. The new legislation that takes effect on January 1, 1999, also grants the PSVaG the right to return unsettled pension liabilities to employers that make a financial recovery. Still, other observers remain concerned that pay-as-you-go financing of PSVaG operations may not be adequate to cope with large-scale bankruptcy and workout situations.

To what extent does the PSVaG suffer from the effects of moral hazard? The previous one-year phase-in period for insurance coverage relative to benefit improvements will be extended to two years starting at the beginning of 1999. While this period seems considerably less stringent than the five-year period imposed by ERISA in the United States, PSVaG officials believe that they are adequately equipped to deal with strategic behavior in advance of corporate liquidation. German law apparently gives them the authority to withdraw insurance cover if benefit commitments are changed by troubled firms to exceed levels prevailing elsewhere.

In the future, attempts to achieve greater integration within the European Community (EC) could produce pressures to expand PSVaG coverage. Some of the foremost challenges to PSVaG insolvency insurance today result from the need to harmonize aspects of German law and regulation concerning corporate pension plans in general and insolvency insurance in particular with that in the rest of the EC. In the broadest terms, the EC's main concern is with promoting the free movement of people, goods, services, and capital within its boundaries. The EC's long-term goal for corporate pension plans is to create the conditions whereby cross-border participation is possible. The EC Commission therefore aims to enable consolidation of the retirement plans sponsored by all affiliates of single companies throughout the EC countries. However, the diverging tax treatment of both pension benefits and contributions within the EC has complicated this effort greatly.

The EC Commission believes that vesting practices in Germany represent a significant impediment to the free movement of labor. The German requirement for 10 years of company service and pension coverage or 12 years of service and three years of pension coverage exceeds the EC average. The effect of reducing the vesting requirements would add liabilities to the existing PSVaG contribution basis because only vested benefits are now covered by the insolvency insurance. In addition, the level of systemwide insolvency risk would rise, as relaxed vesting requirements would extend PSVaG coverage to newer companies. In Germany, like many other countries, the probability of bankruptcy is highest during the first 10 years of a new company's life.

However, German observers believe that no standardization of insolvency insurance within the EC would be feasible given the vast differences in pension-funding mechanisms and the framework of labor law. PSVaG insurance currently does not secure retirement annuities purchased directly from German life insurance companies. Providing that the members have an irrevocable right to the benefits and there is no loan to the employer from the insurance company, the investment practices of these firms now are subject to stringent regulation imposed by the German Insurance Supervision Law. However, the recent EC insurance directive could relax these standards, thereby reducing the safety of many additional retirement obligations. Higher levels of risk then might produce a call for an additional backup guarantee from the PSVaG. At least one German commentator has expressed the concern that pressures resulting from European integration potentially could undermine the PSVaG's financial viability.[57] These concerns have been allayed for the time being because the EC has not made further progress with its draft Pension Fund Directive.

JAPAN

In 1989, the Japanese government set up a termination insurance program that contrasts sharply with the systems in other industrialized countries. The system is privately administered by the Pension Fund Association of Japan (PFA) but, as is customary in that country, it is subject to strong informal influence from the government. The chief executive officer of the PFA is a retired senior civil servant from the Ministry of Health and Welfare.

As of fiscal year 1994, the system insured 1,842 "employees' pension funds" covering approximately 12 million workers.[58] However, a company must employ at least 500 people to establish a single-employer pension plan, or several companies collectively must employ at least 3,000 people in order for them to set up a multiplan. The original motivation for creating the employees' pension fund system in 1966 was to provide retirees with 60 percent of pre-retirement income when combined with benefits paid by public retirement programs. Smaller firms can set up "tax-qualified" plans for their workers, but these plans are not covered by the termination insurance program. As of 1992, Japanese companies had established 92,083 tax qualified plans covering another 10.4 million workers.[59] In Japan, it is also legal for employers to offer completely unfunded or book reserve pension plans.[60] These arrangements are not covered by the guarantee fund.

In late 1988, the Study Commission on Corporate Pensions sent a mission to the United States to consider aspects of the PBGC system in light of Japanese requirements. The group's conclusions were as follows:

- The new Japanese insurance system should promote sound financial health of pension funds and have the capability of designing and implementing preventive measures. Shortly after the group returned, the full committee recommended the introduction of a new liability measure known as the *termination obligation reserve* (TOR). The group also endorsed the proposed practice of making annual comparisons between pension fund assets and the TOR in order to encourage remedial action where needed.

- The insurance premium should be simple and fair. The full committee subsequently decided to set per capita premiums based on the number of participants in individual pension plans. A seven-level classification system was established to stratify pension plans according to size. The annual insurance premiums vary across these seven groupings; however, they have been kept low without exception. In 1992, premiums ranged from just 90 yen per participant for plans with less than 3,000 participants to 60 yen for plans with 30,000 participants or more.

- Insurance costs and standards should not impose onerous burdens on newly established plans.

- Both the level of the guarantee and the insurable events should be carefully defined. Here, the committee determined that the maximum guaranteed benefit should not exceed 130 percent of the "substitutional component."[61] However, the committee was less precise concerning the definition of the insurable event. It recommended only that the terminating fund be in great difficulty and that a termination review committee should make the decision as to whether the guarantee could be invoked. These conditions were subsequently determined to include bankruptcy of the sponsor, severe deterioration of the sponsor's financial performance or that of its industry, and conditions under which continuation of the pension plan becomes extremely difficult for other reasons.

During the year ending on March 31, 1988, 1,857 tax-qualified plans were terminated, representing 2.6 percent of the tax-qualified plans operating at the beginning of that year.[62] The guarantee did not apply in any of these cases. Subsequently, one employees' pension fund was terminated in 1990; it had assets sufficient to cover all guaranteed benefits. Based on the record until recently, many believed that the Japanese government had created a system that was largely insulated from the risk of major termination losses. In fact, one observer of this situation even suggested that the Japanese system was designed so that it never would be required to pay a single claim.

This optimism no longer seems justified. Japan's Minister for Health and Welfare authorized the termination of the Nihon Bosekigyo Employees' Pension Fund (Nitibo) in November 1994. Nitibo was a relatively old pension fund established in 1968 for companies in the textile industry. At one time, the plan covered 28,700 participants. That number later fell with the fortunes of Japan's spinning industry; only 2,200 participants remained in the plan when the Minister for Health and Welfare terminated it. Poor investment performance (resulting, in part, from the decline in Japan's stock market) added to Nitibo's problems. After April 1993, it attempted to raise contributions by so much that plan sponsors could no longer support the burden. The Pension Fund Association has yet to process the Nitibo case, but it could make a claim on the fund of as much as ¥2.5 billion, thereby reducing program assets to approximately ¥3.5 billion. This prospect suggests that loss reserves are far from adequate.[63] It also underscores the need to address several additional problems.

Many other Japanese pension plans are not fully funded. According to the PFA, 28.9 percent of all employees' pension funds are underfunded on a book value basis, and 56 percent of those plans are underfunded on a market value basis.[64] However, most companies that sponsor employees' pension funds remain strong financially, and guaranteed benefits do not approach total liabilities in most cases. Total liabilities of the typical employees' pension plan include the substitutional component (used to replace a portion of social security benefits) of which 130 percent is guaranteed, as well as a supplemental component, which varies across firms and even plans within individual firms. The PFA guarantee therefore covers both the substitutional component as well as the supplementary component up to a maximum capped at 30 percent of the substitutional component. The Government would assume any obligations for substitutional component benefits if the PFA were unable to pay them.

Against this backdrop, claims against the guarantee fund may grow during the period immediately ahead. Investment returns have fallen short of prior assumptions for several years now. Actuarial estimates of liability values have risen following the adoption of more conservative mortality assumptions in November 1994. Insurance companies are likely to reduce the interest rates guaranteed on pension fund investments to levels far below the discount rate used for actuarial valuations. Meanwhile, economic stagnation in Japan has limited the ability of plan sponsors to increase pension contributions to the necessary levels.

The quality of financial data reported by employees' pension plans also leaves much to be desired. Plan assets are officially reported using book values, but the actual condition of these pension plans is determined by current market values for both assets and liabilities.[65] In addition, the Japanese continue to examine the question of whether the current maximum guaranteed benefit is adequate and how it should relate to premiums charged by the insurance fund. Definition of the insurable event also needs refinement. For example, the posttermination liability of plan sponsors that subsequently make a financial recovery has become a concern for the PFA. Essentially, this is an untried system because the guarantee fund has not yet processed its first insufficient termination (i.e., Nitibo). Procedures for terminating and auditing plans as well as for invoking the guarantee apparently need further development. And the Pension Fund Association is reviewing the extent to which managers and directors of a fund should be held responsible for losses resulting from their decisions.

Finally, the Japanese seem very concerned about the need to implement concrete preventive measures to guard against the possibility that plans will terminate without sufficient assets. A new corporate pension law, perhaps modeled on ERISA, could facilitate many of these changes. Japan currently lacks a single governing pension law; but an advisory panel to the President of the Pension

Fund Association has formally recommended that such a law be proposed to the Diet (Japan's legislature).[66] On the other hand, the explicit link between the guarantee and universal benefit security levels provided by Japan's national old-age pensions represents an important strength of the PFA pension guarantee program.

SWEDEN

From the American point of view, probably the most instructive system of securing retirement benefits in existence today is found in Sweden. Established in 1960, the Swedish system provides workers with benefits that are guaranteed by a credit insurance arrangement while allowing employers to retain the use of pension saving for meeting the capital needs of their own businesses. In effect, all Swedish employers provide full funding for each year's pension accruals.

Should the employer choose not to retain the pension capital in its business, that company may purchase an annuity for salaried employees directly from a life insurance company known as the *Försäkringsbolaget SPP* (i.e., SPP). The cost of providing benefits through the SPP is identical to the ultimate cost when using the credit insurance facilities. On average, that cost amounts to 6 percent of payroll for salaried employees. By purchasing credit insurance, the average employer receives access to approximately SKr 10,000 (i.e., $1,300) of additional credit annually for each salaried employee. Use of credit insurance is tantamount to creating a book reserve for future retirement obligations on the employer's balance sheet.

The credit insurance is linked only to the third level of Sweden's retirement income security system. Parenthetically, the first level of that system today consists of a small basic pension provided to every Swede. It is known as the *AFP pension*. Even housewives who never work outside the home receive this benefit. The second level—known as the *ATP pension*—consists of a state pension based on earnings. The goal of the first two levels is to replace 65 percent of final salary. However, these two levels are seriously underfunded and benefits will be reduced in most cases as a result. In June 1994, the Swedish Parliament made a decision in principle to eliminate the

AFP program and to amend the ATP program in ways that will reduce the replacement rate. New minimum guaranteed pensions will be set up by the year 2000, and restructured ATP benefits will be based on lifetime earnings by then. One reason that the current system is more expensive is that benefits are based on the highest 15 years of earnings during an assumed career of 30 years. The goal of the third and final level of Sweden's retirement income system (i.e., the private one) currently is to replace an additional 10 percent of final salary. Future collective bargaining may lead to changes in this replacement goal.

Separate insurance companies exist to guarantee the ITP pensions of salaried employees (i.e., the Pension Guarantee Mutual Insurance Company, or FPG) and the STP pensions for blue-collar workers (i.e., the Labor Market Insurances Mutual Credit Insurance Company, or AMFK). A common administrative organization operates both of these entities. In both cases, only creditworthy employers are allowed to participate. In the context of the FPG system, a third entity known as the Pension Registration Institute (PRI)[67] records the pension promises made by each employer, calculates the value of these obligations on a standard basis, and serves as an intermediary that receives the employer contributions and eventually makes the benefit payments to retirees.[68]

There are two unusual and, for a mobile labor force, attractive features of the private pension system in Sweden: immediate vesting[69] and complete portability.[70] This portability exists within the centralized systems that serve salaried employees (i.e., ITP pensions)[71] and blue-collar workers (i.e., STP pensions) respectively. Figure 5–3 depicts the relationships between the groups and organizations that are party to Sweden's FPG system.

The ITP pension system for white-collar workers was set up in 1960 to replace many of the "pension foundations" sponsored by various Swedish employers. These pension foundations in some ways resembled single-employer, defined-benefit plans in the United States before ERISA was enacted in 1974. They received contributions from the sponsor to pay promised benefits, but funding levels varied greatly. The ITP system was established at the instigation of employers in order to preempt pressure from labor groups to expand

FIGURE 5-3

The Three Faces of Sweden's FPG Guarantee System:
A Sophisticated Example of Pension-Linked Credit Insurance

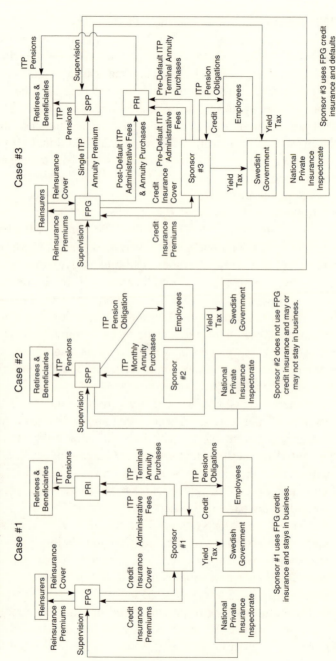

the state-sponsored AFP and ATP retirement programs. The originator of the idea had been employed at the Swedish Confederation of Employers (SAF). The motivation for the ITP concept was to allow private companies to create book reserves so that pension capital could be used internally within a firm.[72] Sweden's economy was booming then but the regulatory situation had produced a shortage of bank loans. Equity capital was not abundant either. The banks were not assigned a role in this arrangement for another reason: labor market organizations (i.e., the Swedish Employers' Confederation and the white-collar PTK) were hoping to create an independent source of capital. In addition, the business community wanted to ward off further domination of the Swedish economy by the state— at the time a debate was raging about the merits of nationalizing basic industry—or, alternatively, by insurance companies over which organized labor groups would have significant control.

The blue-collar STP pension system, established in 1973, is not financed with book reserves. Instead, employers pay the STP premiums to the AMF pension organization.[73] They are then permitted to receive 15-year "STP loans" subject to the approval of the AMFK credit insurance company. The effect of borrowing in this way is similar to creating a book reserve (i.e., pension capital can be used within the firm), but STP loans more closely resemble bank loans in many other respects. Book reserves were not permitted because the blue-collar collective bargaining organization (the LO) wanted to include past service credits in the plan. These credits allowed workers who were older at the time that the system was set up to receive pensions sooner.

Both the FPG and the AMFK are organized as mutual insurance companies. In 1993, 2,435 companies held policies in FPG while 997 participated in the AMFK system. These arrangements clearly are viewed as nongovernmental. At the beginning of 1994, the FPG's total exposure amounted to SKr 71 billion, but the exposure of the AMFK was much less at SKr 5.1 billion. However, transformation of several state-owned authorities (e.g., the post pffice, telephone company, and electric utilities) into limited companies[74] soon will raise the FPG's exposure probably by another SKr 5 billion. At the moment, liabilities insured by the FPG cover pension obligations to an estimated 50,000 Swedish retirees and 240,000 salaried workers. Annual premiums are uniform for all policyholders. In 1995, the FPG charged 0.3 percent of insured liabilities and the AMFK charged 0.4 percent.[75] Both the FPG and AMFK intend to maintain net worth at the point where "consolidating capital" represents 8 percent of insurance exposure.[76] The maximum contract period is three years. In keeping with global trends favoring deregulation and promoting competition, the FPG no longer has a formal monopoly position in its segment of the credit insurance market. However, other companies seem unlikely to enter this market in the foreseeable future.

Pension-related credit insurance is available only to financially solid companies or those able to provide adequate collateral. Six credit analysts are currently employed to evaluate companies applying to the FPG or AMFK for first-time coverage. This group also monitors the existing book of business on an ongoing basis. Each analyst typically performs one initial credit evaluation per week and follows 580 companies that are among the system's approximately 3,500 policyholders. The initial credit evaluation might take four to five hours. The FPG/AMFK responds in four ways to initial requests for coverage: insurance can simply be provided to financially strong companies; insurance can be offered to slightly riskier companies contingent on the assignment of collateral; insurance can be offered to corporate subsidiaries contingent on the provision of a surety bond from a financially healthy parent or affiliate; or insurance can be offered if the company provides a backup credit guarantee from a commercial bank. This last alternative is tantamount to a rejection.

Swedish companies must complete annual financial reports within six months of the end of each fiscal year. In routine cases, the credit analysts monitor the condition of policyholders by spending 15 minutes reading these annual reports and examining four or five of the most salient financial indicators.[77] FPG/AMFK officials attribute much of their system's success to effective use of basic credit analysis from the outset. They believe that reliance on statistically based approaches to forecast claims experience in Finland and elsewhere is not justified, particularly in view of changing business conditions. In fact, they attribute the 1993 collapse of pension-related credit insurance in Finland to a preference for using model-based approaches instead of sound credit judgment.

If the condition of a participating company deteriorates, the FPG can step in to limit the growth of pension liabilities or to demand collateral. One of the most common times to demand collateral is when the insurance contract is considered for renewal. In more dire circumstances, the FPG can require that the entire liability be phased out during a period of five years through the purchase of SPP annuities.[78] The FPG therefore commits itself to remain involved with the policyholder for a period as long as eight years. The insurance contract itself runs for three years, and the conversion period when policyholders must replace FPG-insured pension debt with SPP annuities might run for another five years. If an employer actually winds up its business operations or engages in transactions that undermine the value of the company or impair the value of any collateral, then the FPG has the authority to intervene by immediately demanding that the employer purchase pension annuities from the SPP to cover all liabilities guaranteed by the FPG.[79] This has the effect of terminating the pension plan and, in many cases, also can result in liquidation of the sponsoring company.

Of course, these standards frequently prevent small companies from using the credit insurance system. Even within the group of creditworthy employers, risks are highly concentrated. The 20 largest companies in Sweden account for 50 percent of the FPG's total insurance exposure. So far, the FPG has not faced a claim from any one of these companies. For the most part, they are diversified and export-oriented, with shares traded on the public stock exchanges. Only three of Sweden's 30 largest companies have not joined the FPG system. FPG officials attribute this situation to a combination of factors. Secured pension debt is generally attractive to Swedish companies due to tax incentives and competitive borrowing costs. The two companies that have refrained from using FPG insurance are large, capital-intensive concerns with relatively small numbers of employees (e.g., an electric power company). FPG-guaranteed credit available to them would not be significant relative to their total needs. They also may be concerned about the potential for cost shifting within the FPG system. Some evidence of adverse selection therefore is apparent in a very restricted number of cases.

During the past 30 years, retirement obligations covered by the FPG and AMFK grew at remarkably stable rates despite vastly different economic conditions facing the country. In the 1960s, the Swedish economy grew rapidly. The 1970s produced two oil crises and several recessions. During the 1980s, financial markets were deregulated and foreign exchange controls were abolished. By 1994, the country had been in a recession for more than two years. Unemployment stood at 15 percent and was expected to go even higher. Gross domestic product (GDP) had declined to a level not seen since mid-1987, and the government was running a huge budget deficit of 13 percent of GDP, or SKr 180 billion.

The credit insurance system responded to the recent economic turmoil by changes in three principal areas. First, the insurance premium was increased from 0.3 percent of pension liabilities to 0.4 percent at the beginning of 1993. In addition, the mutual liability was raised from 1 to 2 percent, effective in September of that year. Finally, the terms of credit insurance became more stringent. Before 1993, the FPG could demand that a liability be terminated over a period of 10 years. That was reduced to five years. Within this framework, the policy for providing credit insurance became much tighter. With growing frequency, the FPG requested that companies reduce pension-related borrowings and that additional assets be pledged as collateral. The FPG also shifted staff resources to permit more thorough credit analysis and surveillance of those companies that continue to use guaranteed borrowings.

These precautions helped reduce the net cost for claims from 0.32 percent of insurance exposure in 1992 to 0.24 percent in 1993 and to 0.01 percent in 1994. In addition, large Swedish export companies have been doing extremely well recently. Since the devaluation in November 1992, the Swedish krona has been floating and becoming successively weaker. Capital investment by those large exporters, and many of their suppliers, has reduced employment; and they are using their improved cashflow to reduce pension liabilities guaranteed by the FPG. However, demand in the domestic economy has yet to recover to previous levels. These factors have combined to push the FPG's capital position to 8 percent of its insurance exposure. The company has begun discussions with its policyholders about the possibility of distributing surplus capital funds that may accumulate in the future.

An American financial guarantee company is among a group of companies that currently provides reinsurance cover to the FPG and the AMFK. In 1992, the cost of reinsurance amounted to 9 percent of premium income for the FPG and 19 percent of premium income for the AMFK. In order to protect both companies from extremely adverse claims experience, this reinsurance has been structured as an excess-of-loss treaty arrangement. In 1993, FPG's reinsurance provided stop-loss protection against 55 percent of that year's accumulated claims ranging from SKr 350 million to SKr 1,875 million. Similar reinsurance cover applied to 50 percent of AMFK's claims ranging from SKr 60 million to SKr 240 million. FPG's reinsurers have never paid a claim since 1973 when this backup protection was first used. However, AMFK first began using reinsurance some time later in the 1970s. AMFK's reinsurers paid claims in 1981 and 1992.[80] AMFK's reinsurers paid SKr 11 million in claims-related expenses in 1992. Those same AMFK reinsurers received premium income of SKr 3 million during the same period. The management of both organizations expects negative trends affecting Swedish credit markets and the credit insurance system in particular to have an adverse effect on the ability of these companies to obtain reinsurance in 1994 and possibly beyond.

The Swedish system also differs from its counterpart in the United States insofar as it has been able to recover an impressive proportion of its bankruptcy and other claims. In fact, the FPG has been able to recover an average of 45 percent of the face value of those claims during the past five years.[81] FPG claims in bankruptcy are accorded special priority only for a small portion of total pension commitments. Of course, that proportion can be higher when the insured borrowings have been collateralized. However, the most important source of these high recoveries has been surety bonds that the FPG requires from parent companies and former parent companies before extending credit insurance to a corporate subsidiary.

To summarize, the Swedish credit insurance system provides a stark contrast with America's ERISA termination insurance program in several important areas. First, the FPG/AMFK administrative organization plays a continuing and effective role as a manager of insolvency risk. Initial credit evaluation when companies first apply for FPG or AMFK insurance, as well as subsequent monitoring and the use of intervention rights, all have contributed to this system's success. Second, most pension obligations are standardized and estimated by an independent organization (i.e., the Pension Registration Institute). Private retirement benefits in Sweden are negotiated on a nationwide basis by employer and employee group representatives. This arrangement is a product of traditionally strong roles for labor market organizations representing both workers and management in collective bargaining. Dollar for dollar, these retirement obligations involve identical funding requirements across firms and industries. A single authority, the Pension Registration Institute, also estimates and reports their value. Although Swedes who have worked closely with the FPG system believe that this standardization has many advantages, they also believe that commercial pension insurance of the sort provided by FPG/AMFK could be viable with heterogeneous retirement claims.

Third, the Swedish system differs from the American system in that only a single flat-rate premium is charged for the credit insurance based on the amount of the insured liability. There is no adjustment to individual premiums based on some measure of risk to the insurance fund, nor is it directly linked to the number of participants covered by the pension plan. Finally, the Swedish system makes sophisticated use of reinsurance as well as cross guarantees among controlled groups of companies. In sum, employers and workers in pension plans guaranteed by the FPG/AMFK systems must bear the costs of the agreements that they reach among themselves. Both the FPG and the AMFK are organized as mutual insurance companies in which the losses are shared among the policyholders. This situation is quite different from arrangements found in North America where a third-party—the taxpayer—ultimately is exposed to the risk of loss. As a model for reform in the United States, the major drawback of Sweden's pension guarantee system is its monopolistic structure.

Still, there clearly is much to consider here for students of the American pension insurance system.

SWITZERLAND

Central features of the Swiss pension guarantee fund challenge a common presumption in the United States that there is nothing to guarantee in the context of a defined-contribution system. The Swiss guarantee fund provides participants in mandatory defined-benefit plans as well as mandatory defined-contribution plans with the assurance that they will receive benefit entitlements defined by Swiss law. Although Chile also has set up a system to protect defined-contribution participants against the risk of default, no other OECD[82] country apart from Switzerland operates a pension insurance system for defined-contribution plans. The Swiss guarantee fund insures pension obligations up to a maximum specified in that country's Law of Old-Age, Survivors and Disability Pension Plans (LPP). The LPP law took effect in 1985.

The growing complexity of Swiss pension law and generally increasing costs have recently caused many sponsors to convert defined-benefit plans into defined-contribution plans. Slightly less than half of all participants in Swiss pension plans are now covered by defined-benefit plans. For its part, the guarantee fund provides insurance only for fixed monetary amounts that are uniform across all plan types.[83] Accordingly, the Swiss backup guarantee is based on a concept more closely akin to a defined contribution than to a defined benefit.

Swiss pension specialists frequently cite the metaphor of a three-pillar house to explain the country's retirement system. The retirement benefits provided by the national old-age, survivor and disability program—known as the AHV and IV (for disability) systems—represent the first pillar. These benefits are relatively austere by European standards but comparable to those provided by Social Security in the United States. This first pillar of Switzerland's retirement system is financed on a pay-as-you-go basis. It therefore faces severe financing problems after the year 2010 as a result of the post-World War II baby boom generation and the larger number of retirements that will begin at about that time. Nevertheless, approximately one-third of Switzerland's voters—the socialists—favor an expansion of these first-pillar benefits accompanied by a curtailment in the role of second- and third-pillar retirement savings. Swiss voters rejected a proposal along these lines in June 1995.

The system's second pillar consists of mandatory occupational pensions provided by 3,457 publicly registered plans, extramandatory supplemental benefits provided by the same plans, and 10,232 unregistered private pension plans that are not part of the mandatory system and that are not covered by the guarantee fund. The pension funds take the legal form of foundations that are entirely separate and distinct from the sponsors. Relative to the situation in the United States, the Swiss private pension system clearly delivers a superior level of benefits, as noted by the combined averages in Figure 5–1 and the coverage rates in Figure 5–2. Most employees working in Switzerland are covered by these arrangements. Many others will be covered after spending more than three months in a job[84] or reaching the age of 25.[85] Benefits are transferable among all employers and minimal benefit standards apply across all plans and plan types.[86] A new law went into effect at the beginning of 1995 that extended immediate vesting and portability to all benefits and pension foundations. Another new law promotes investment in residential property using funds that employees are permitted to withdraw from second-pillar pension plans.

"Shadow accounts" are maintained for every participant between the ages of 25 and 65 in these mandatory plans as proof of the accumulated balance of legal retirement credits. These shadow accounts are maintained within the framework of a *defined-credit plan* that must correspond with any mandatory plan. One of the most important effects of the LPP law was to establish these defined-credit plans as the core of the mandatory pension system in Switzerland. The legal retirement credits include a legally required rate of interest of 4 percent. Employers must provide at least half of the required contributions; workers pay the remainder. The average contribution rate weighted to reflect the age-distribution of participants in all mandatory plans amounts to 14 percent of covered earnings. In 1995, the effect of coordination with the first pillar of social security was to limit the contribution and credit schedule to earnings above SF 23,280. Mandatory credits are not made on annual earnings below SF 23,280 because income in that range is covered by the AHV component of Switzerland's social security system.

The guarantee fund insures all mandatory benefits (i.e., old age, survivors, and disability benefits) promised by second-pillar occupational plans. In Switzerland, the credit levels for second-pillar retirement funds are determined by age, gender, and salary levels in the range that is coordinated with the AHV program. Seven percent of coordinated earnings is credited on behalf of workers between the ages of 25 and 34. The credit rate increases to 10 percent for workers between 35 and 44. It rises again to 15 percent between 45 and 54. Finally, 18 percent of coordinated earnings is credited on behalf of workers between 55 and 65.[87]

Switzerland's LPP law does not require mandatory credits on earnings above the maximum level coordinated with the AHV program (i.e., SF 69,830 in 1995) because the Swiss consider that to be the range in which pre-retirement income should be replaced with personal savings or supplemental corporate plans not presently covered by the guarantee fund. Therefore, the maximum coordinated earnings was SF 46,560 in 1995. Today, approximately one-third of the labor force is covered by plans that substantially exceed the country's legally required minimum contribution rate. However, the guarantee fund insures benefits that, combined with the first-pillar AHV pension, are intended to replace 60 percent of final salary up to the legal maximum. AHV benefits are adjusted every year to reflect changes in a mixed formula based on wages and the cost of living. Switzerland has formalized its replacement goal for retirement income to the extent of including them as provisions to its federal constitution. That goal assumes 40 years of credited service.

The Swiss intentionally reserved a role for individual responsibility as part of their retirement system in recognition of a cultural tradition that emphasizes moderation and economic restraint. As the third pillar of the metaphorical retirement income house, use of individual saving and insurance is encouraged under the Swiss tax system. Contributions to individual retirement savings accounts are tax deductible up to a maximum of about SF 5,600 per year in the formal sector. The maximum for self-employed workers is SF 27,936 per year.

The Swiss pension system operating today represents the product of a lengthy evolution that began in the 19th century. In fact, the plan for teachers in Bern was set up 175 years ago.[88] However, the first-pillar national old-age benefit system—the AHV—was introduced in Switzerland later than in most other industrialized countries. That did not occur until 1948. By the time that the LPP law was drafted in the mid-1980s, Swiss employers had established additional, voluntary private pension plans for about two-thirds of the country's labor force.[89] Then, a broad cross section of political groups pressed for universal coverage as well as for the creation of a guarantee fund to insure minimal benefits. The guarantee system protects against insolvency on the part of the pension fund. This usually implies insolvency of the foundation or a bankruptcy liquidation of the employer as well. It covers every mandatory pension plan enrolled in the public register up to the legally defined earnings level, and it was designed to back up a considerable variety of plan designs. However, the insurance applies only to credits that occurred after the LPP system was adopted in 1985.

Switzerland's federal congress initially attempted to create a guarantee fund by public law that would have been linked to the reserve fund for the first-pillar AHV program. Employer groups opposed the proposal. Legislators then struck a compromise in the LPP law that gave Swiss trade unions and employer groups a right to set up a private foundation as a joint venture chartered to guarantee mandatory old age, disability, and survivors benefits. The joint venture never came into being, as these constituencies were unable to reach the necessary agreement among themselves. The executive branch of the Swiss federal government therefore established a public foundation. This foundation appointed the Bern office of the accounting and consulting firm ATAG Ernst & Young to carry out the work of the guarantee fund. The Zurich office of Schweizerische Treuhandgesellschaft Coopers & Lybrand was also appointed as auditor of the guarantee fund.

Would the Swiss government ever become involved if the guarantee fund were faced with massive losses? Swiss pension specialists with a detailed knowledge of this system don't think so. The initial response to increased losses would be to increase premiums. Since the system is mandatory, no adverse selection problem would result unless the increase became so great that companies began to shift employment outside the country.[90] In the event that losses during a particularly bad year could not be covered immediately by its capital stock of about SF 300 million, accumulated loss reserves, and reasonable premiums, the guarantee fund would rely on bank loans to tide it over. Before now, bank borrowing has not been needed. The cost of the average claim, however, seems bound to grow somewhat as the LPP system matures and workers, on average, accumulate larger balances of guaranteed benefits.

No direct link therefore exists between the exposure of the guarantee fund and premiums charged for the arrangement. The method of financing represents nothing more than a levy on wages. It was chosen because of its administrative simplicity. If anything, the Swiss believe that they initially set premiums far too high—at 0.2 percent of coordinated earnings (i.e., earnings between SF 23,280 and SF 69,840 in 1995).[91] Guarantee fund premiums therefore were reduced to 0.04 percent of coordinated earnings in 1990.

Of the 3.4 million participants in Swiss pension plans, 1,132,019 were covered by 1,187 strictly defined-benefit plans, according to survey data published by the Federal Statistical Office. Another 1,219,525 participants were covered by 5,136 defined-contribution plans, and 52,304 were covered by 550 discretionary pension plans. In a typical split plan arrangement for the highly paid, all employees would be covered by a basic defined-benefit plan up to the top level of the salary range that is coordinated with social security. Above that, pre-retirement earnings are replaced by supplemental pensions involving one or more defined-benefit plans and/or defined-contribution plans. Finally, 1,119,514 participants were covered by an additional 94 plans of unknown variety.[92]

Some employers choose not to establish a separate pension fund or to join one that is organized collectively by a bank or an insurance company. These companies are required to affiliate with the *suppletory institution* that is managed by six Swiss insurance companies. The LPP law that established the guarantee fund also set up the suppletory institution. The employer together with its employees must remit the required minimum contributions to this institution. Insofar as many of the weakest companies provide the LPP minimum benefits (i.e., credits) by affiliating with the suppletory institution, it initially absorbs many of the losses that otherwise would accrue directly to the guarantee fund. However, the guarantee fund compensates the suppletory institution for its administrative costs and casualty losses. The question of whether the operations of the suppletory institution reduce the costs that the guarantee fund otherwise would incur is currently under review. When a company affiliated with the suppletory institution falls behind in its payments, the suppletory institution promptly takes steps to collect the payments that are in arrears. This can have the effect of precipitating a liquidation of the company. Relative to the PBGC in the United States, the work of the guarantee fund also is circumscribed by law because officials of the bankruptcy courts handle much of the litigation work and also purchase annuities to replace lost benefits. The only role of the guarantee fund in such terminations is to remit payment for shortfalls to the official bankruptcy receiver.

Switzerland's backup guarantee program also provides for unique and substantial cross subsidies when the average legally required credit rate to a particular plan exceeds 14 percent of coordinated earnings for all active participants. This feature of the Swiss system was adopted as part of a quid pro quo between companies with an older average workforce age and companies with a younger average workforce age.[93] Given the cross subsidies due to unfavorable age structure, the Swiss pension termination insurance system does not rest on a purely defined-contribution basis but instead takes on some of the characteristics of a defined-benefit approach in which benefits bear no direct relationship to initial contributions.[94] The subsidies due to unfavorable age structure unfortunately are not well suited for promoting employment and job mobility among older workers.[95] This explicit system of cross subsidies in Switzerland has been expensive, the subsidies greatly exceeding payments to cover plan termination costs in most years. As a result, those familiar with the arrangement think that the subsidies could be abolished by 1997.[96] However, the recession in Europe recently fueled opposition to a move in that direction. The future of the subsidies therefore is unclear. As a quid pro quo for abolishing the cross subsidies, a reduction in the maximum credit rate from 18 percent to 15 percent for employees between the ages of 55 and 64 might be considered.

Swiss observers predict that the insolvency insurance not only will survive but will be extended to cover pre-1985 obligations. Significant support also has developed to extend the guarantee to cover most benefits that aren't mandatory as well. Rising losses from insolvencies reinforce the impression that the Swiss may increase premiums for their pension benefit guarantee fund. During the past few years, underfunding has increased noticeably. A new interest rate corridor of 3.5 percent to 4.5 percent mandated by the 1995 vesting and portability law contributed to this deterioration. In addition, sponsors borrowed from the plans and delayed contribution payments. Recent economic difficulties are thought to lie at the root of this behavior despite the fact that such practices generally are frowned upon. Still, such borrowing is legal within limits in Switzerland, and reporting requirements concerning late contributions have been strengthened.

A third, but temporary, function for the guarantee fund that has recently become significant involves making up for any funding gaps when plans terminate at the time of corporate divestitures. The guarantee fund has been assigned this responsibility for a period of five years. If assets in a plan are not sufficient to cover guaranteed benefits owed to participants in the business units being spun off or closed, then the guarantee fund pays the difference relative to guaranteed benefits for the group of participants involved in the divestiture, but not for the other participants remaining in the plan. The guarantee fund makes payments in these situations even though the pension plan itself remains ongoing for workers employed by business units not divested by the company.

Most of the terminations so far have involved plans with fewer than 10 participants. The largest claim against the guarantee fund was for SF 3.5 million, in connection with the bankruptcy liquidation of OMAG AG of St. Gallen. The bankruptcy claims of the insurance fund now are accorded second priority in a ranking system with five levels. However, a law that took effect at the beginning of

1996 consolidates these groupings into three levels and since then, the guarantee fund's claims have been among those receiving the highest priority. Nevertheless, premiums are expected to rise somewhat from the current level of 0.04 percent of coordinated salaries in the wake of Switzerland's recent and lengthy recession. Risks to the insurance fund also will grow with the passage of time, as more guaranteed benefits accumulate in the mandatory second-pillar plans. Benefit accruals in these plans were guaranteed starting in 1985.

The Swiss pension insurance system clearly has several defects. Foremost among them is moral hazard. A classic pension put is created when employers are permitted to borrow from their retirement funds or when they postpone contribution payments. Those familiar with the history of this arrangement also report that many companies reduced contributions to the legal minimum immediately following the 1985 LPP pension legislation.

However, one area where moral hazard has been less apparent than in many other systems is investment policy. Many Swiss pension fund managers have taken a conservative approach to asset allocation, preferring lower levels of risk and accepting the resulting lower returns. Although cultural factors appear to contribute to this behavior, the principal explanation involves the fixed and legally required interest that must be paid on the mandatory pension credits combined with the contribution levels. There also is no doubt in Switzerland—unlike in the United States—concerning ownership of pension assets. Surplus assets belong to the workers. So, there has been little reason for Swiss pension fund managers to favor risky portfolios in the hope of achieving high returns.

Risky investment policies may become more of a concern for the guarantee fund in the future. Swiss pension fund managers are becoming increasingly sensitive to comparisons that show their performance lagging far behind that of their counterparts elsewhere. In addition, the guarantee could be extended to benefits that correspond with income above the coordinated salary range. This would produce a one-time reduction in the "free capital" of Swiss pension plans. Until now, the plans' own free capital has been sufficient to cover all losses attributable to derivative transactions.

Another shortcoming of the Swiss guarantee system is the uneven use of coinsurance resulting from losses of nonguaranteed benefits. A significant level of coinsurance is always desirable to limit the effects of moral hazard. The Swiss model exposes older workers to greater losses of benefits that exceed the mandatory LPP levels while failing to protect younger workers against some of the effects of post-termination inflation. These two sources of potential loss can be inequitable in opposite directions, thereby producing a more level burden of coinsurance across the age distribution of the labor force. However, sustained changes with respect to wage levels or the returns to pension assets conceivably could create problems even within this system.

The central lesson from studying the Swiss guarantee program is that explicit cross subsidies by way of a pension insurance fund is an experiment that has been tried and found wanting. However, the Swiss are not willing to compromise another aspect of their pension insurance system: the guarantee that participants in mandatory second-pillar retirement plans at least will receive the legally required minimum benefits regardless of plan type. Swiss observers complain that the guarantee program is unnecessarily complicated and involves too much paper work.[97] Despite this view, most still seem satisfied with the overall result. The fact that the guarantee applies to the legally required benefits for every Swiss worker probably assures sufficiently broad support for this system to survive for quite some time.

Broader problems facing the Swiss retirement system include the need to finance indexation of old-age benefits and demographic pressures on the first-pillar AHV system after the year 2010. The Swiss case serves as a useful benchmark for indicating the necessary level of saving to prepare for a decent retirement under these conditions. The Swiss have determined that between the ages of 25 and 65, they should save an average of 12.5 percent of earnings in excess of those to be replaced by the first pillar of social security in order to replace 60 percent of final salary.[98] The first two pillars of the Swiss system deliver the highest combined benefits, on average, of those covered in Figure 5–1. Average second-pillar benefits also can be expected to grow as the LPP system matures. In addition, one-third of all Swiss companies currently are thought to make contributions substantially in excess of this required minimum. Whether this level of saving is enough will depend critically on investment returns, worker longevity, the relationship between future salary increases and interest rates, and a host of other factors specific to individual cases. However, an average mandatory saving rate of 12.5 percent of coordinated earnings seems like an eminently reasonable target.

THE UNITED KINGDOM

The United Kingdom has a developed system of discretionary pension guarantees that differs from the other models examined here insofar as it has been repeatedly (although not frequently) used, even though the government has no legal obligation to make up for any unfunded pension commitments. This implicit guarantee is inextricably linked to the national old-age retirement system in that country. To understand the guarantee and why the government acts on a belief that it has an obligation to make whole the participants in private pension plans, consider the following background.

The national old-age pension system is organized into two different programs. The first consists of a basic pension that is not linked to earnings, but instead, the full amount is paid after 39 years of contributions for women and 44 years for men.[99] The maximum basic pension for a single person in 1994–95 was £57.60 per week, or $4,472 per year in U.S. dollars. The second aspect of the national old-age system is linked to a worker's earnings and is known as the State Earnings-Related Pension Scheme (SERPS).[100] Employers may contract out of SERPS under certain conditions. Defined-benefit pension plans that are used to substitute for SERPS must provide an earnings-related pension that equals or exceeds the guaranteed minimum pension (GMP). SERPS benefits are generally higher than the GMP and, upon retirement, the GMP is deducted from the worker's SERPS entitlement.

The GMP is a statutory obligation. However, unfunded liabilities relative to GMP benefits have remained after private companies went bankrupt. The British government has discretion concerning whether to collect additional premiums from liquidating companies necessary to fund the GMP. The informal guarantee from the British government therefore secures the GMP. When private companies liquidate, the GMP benefits are maintained by transferring the corresponding assets or whatever lesser amount remains in the plan to the State system. If a private pension plan involving contracted-out SERPS benefits does not have sufficient assets to cover the GMP obligations, the shortfall is treated in practice as a loan that the British Government gradually amortizes.

The Robert Maxwell scandal created a need for the government to examine security issues related to benefits that exceed the GMP. Readers outside the United Kingdom may be surprised to learn that the money lost in the Maxwell scandal did not disappear directly from the pension plans sponsored by Maxwell's companies. Instead, it disappeared as a result of transactions involving two Maxwell-controlled entities that did business under the names of Bishopsgate Investment Trust and Bishopsgate Investment Management (BIM).[101] BIM had been authorized to serve as a pension fund investment manager under the Financial Services Act of 1986.

Maxwell borrowed money on many occasions for his private companies from his public companies. Maxwell also used pension money from Maxwell Communications and from the Mirror Newspapers—both companies that he controlled—to buy large positions in his public companies as well as in other companies that he was targeting in takeover bids. If the value of his public companies went down, he needed to find some way of shoring them up. Otherwise, he would have been called for more collateral, and his financial empire already was highly leveraged.[102]

Against this background, consider the effect of a pending regulation in 1989 that capped self-investment (i.e., party-in-interest investment) at 5 percent of pension plan assets. In the name of various Maxwell pension plans, BIM was holding 46 million shares in Maxwell Communications. The new regulation required that this position be reduced to just 4 million shares. In an elaborate fraud, BIM frantically began selling the excess shares and then buying them back at artificially high prices; BIM itself was setting these prices. But the deception couldn't be sustained. Half of the shares that BIM dealt in apparently didn't exist. Maxwell's suicide soon followed. The Maxwell scandal provides yet another example of the risks involved with party-in-interest investment. Liquidating that position can result in a precipitous decline in share prices whenever a pension plan holds a large equity position in the sponsor. This situation vividly illustrates the value of the pension put we discussed in Chapter 4.

The British government subsequently formed an independent committee—the Pension Law Review Committee (PLRC) under the direction of Professor Roy Goode, a professor of law at Oxford University—to study the resulting problem.[102] The PLRC specifically did not want to create a complete guarantee fund like that of the United States, the Province of Ontario, and elsewhere. According to one member of the Committee, a consensus emerged that the guarantee-fund concept was unfair.[103] If one plan were to have an unfortunate investment experience, the rationale for imposing the resulting costs on other pension plans could not be justified to the satisfaction of the PLRC. PLRC members came to the conclusion that every pension plan in the country was exposed to the same investment risks and opportunities. To create a guarantee fund would merely invite abuse of the arrangement due to excessive risk taking clearly apparent in the context of several financial guarantee systems elsewhere. A general concern also developed that any collective insurance fund inevitably would become subject to strong political influence. If political figures were to define the terms of the insurance contract, the risks would never be reflected in the insurance premiums or the rights of the insurance carriers to minimize their losses in deteriorating situations.

For its part, the British government was not seeking an active role in the development of any guarantee fund concept or the subsequent administration of any insurance arrangement that might be created. Since private pension coverage in the United Kingdom is not mandatory, the government did not consider this to be a legitimate function for the public sector to perform. Members of the PLRC thought that the government role should be limited to "providing a policeman." However, there was serious doubt that the government would agree to do so. PLRC members were concerned that if anything went wrong after more regulatory responsibility had been assumed, the government would become obligated for the expense of bailing out private pension plans. For this reason, the PLRC proposed a private "compensation fund" to cover losses due to fraud and theft only. The arrangement would be operated as a mutual backup insurance cover without reserves or any other significant capitalization. The British government subsequently concurred with that recommendation[105] and the necessary legislation was enacted in July 1995. However, workers retiring before the year 2000 will not be covered.

To summarize, the United Kingdom has established an interesting and instructive division of labor between markets and government regulation in the provision of private pension benefits. Private employers in the United Kingdom are not required to sponsor pension plans. This central fact has worked to circumscribe the government's role as regulator, subsidizer, and guarantor of these arrangements. However, the government has set forth some highly specific standards for determining that pension promises, once made, will be kept. For example, vesting and portability standards are much more favorable to mobile workers there than they are in the United States. In the United Kingdom, workers who leave a job after two or more years of credited service are entitled to the accrued benefits. Those benefits subsequently are increased by 5 percent each year until the worker reaches retirement age or by the rate of increase of the retail price index, should that be less. Alternatively, the worker may receive a transfer of the cash equivalent of his or her accrued benefit rights for payment to another pension plan or to a personal pension scheme. A general preference in the United Kingdom for lower accrual rates combined with much greater portability and inflation protection thus is reflected in government regulation of private pensions there.

CONCLUSION

This survey of benefit security systems outside the United States leads to the following conclusions:

Unsecured or inadequately collateralized pension fund investment in the employer's own businesses can have disastrous consequences for workers, taxpayers, and retirees. This was demonstrated by a 1935 bankruptcy in the Netherlands and more recently in Finland.

Perfectly adequate security for private pension benefits can be achieved in the absence of a collective guarantee fund, as the case in Holland demonstrates. Labor groups in that country do not consider the stringent funding standards to be hostile to their interests. On the contrary, those groups have been supportive of the standards and efforts to enforce them.

If a decision is made to establish a collective guarantee fund, that fund can be operated as a viable private insurance business. The pension guarantee concept developed in Sweden has successfully withstood major economic stress in recent years. Effective risk evaluation procedures and subsequent intervention powers in financially deteriorating cases were essential for maintaining the solvency of the insurance fund. However, even the Swedish approach is not free from transfers and cross subsidies that can produce a suboptimal allocation of savings and investment in the economy.

Substantial costs can result from political intrusion into the operations of a financial guarantor and from using collective guarantee funds to "cultivate constituencies." This applies to setting actuarial assumptions and the interest rates charged for pension borrowing; pricing the insurance itself; efforts to obtain sufficient collateral; and other attempts to protect the interests of a guarantee fund in financially deteriorating situations.

One approach to reform allows different treatment for previous guaranteed obligations relative to those that arise after the restructuring of whatever arrangements exist to secure pension benefits. Of necessity, Finland adopted this approach following massive losses there.

With respect to benefit comparisons among industrialized countries, the combined average retirement income in the United States exceeds that in seven of the eight other OECD countries studied here both in absolute terms and as a percentage of the social minimum, as reported on Figure 5–1. With respect to the social minimum for retirement income, the countries fall into two groups. Canada and the Netherlands provide relatively high minimums of

$7,898 and $8,329 per year, respectively. The United States falls at the high end of the less generous group, where the minimum ranged from $3,881 to $5,208 in 1993.

The combined maximum guaranteed benefits—including social security as well as pensions guaranteed by the PBGC—are also relatively high by international standards. At $42,796 per year, they amounted to 822 percent of the social minimum and 316 percent of the combined average discussed immediately above. In both absolute and relative terms, the combined maximum in only three countries—Germany, Finland, and Sweden—exceeds that in the United States. These are the three countries with guarantee systems that secure book reserve financing or the practical equivalent of a book reserve.[106]

The share of the total labor force with guaranteed private pension benefits also is smallest in these same three countries with book-reserve financing systems: Germany, Finland, and Sweden. Of the remaining countries and the Province of Ontario, the United States provides the smallest share of the total labor force with guaranteed private pensions, as noted on Figure 5–2.

ENDNOTES

1. When corporate bankruptcies in the United Kingdom do not involve fraud, employees already have considerable protection against pension losses. To qualify for tax approval, pension plans must be established as irrevocable trusts. Plan assets therefore have been alienated from the employer and can't be reached by the receiver or liquidator before benefit obligations have been met. In addition, the U.K. Department of Employment is required to pay some of the contributions that were due from the employer but not previously paid. Finally, legal impediments exist that often result in the use of any surplus funds to improve benefits instead of returning them to the employer or its estate. See J. Cunliffe, "The Guarantee of Pension Rights in Case of Bankruptcy of the Employer," in Leo Mok, ed., *International Handbook on Pensions Law & Similar Employee Benefits* (London, UK: Graham & Trotman, 1989), pp. 178–83; and "British Pension Law: Goode in Parts," *The Economist,* October 2, 1993, p. 84.

2. See Akira Suzuki, "Payment Guarantee Program in Japan Seen from the Pension Fund's Perspective." Paper presented at the 9th International Meeting of Insolvency Insurers, Tokyo, Japan, October 1993.

3. Other arrangements that provoked Canadian criticism at that point included low-interest bonds, cut-rate power deals, and local tax deferment programs. See Peter Scolieri, "Canada Set to Retaliate vs. US Steel: Anti-Dumping Petitions in Pre-Clearance Stage," *American Metal Market,* July 9, 1992, p. 1.

4. The Austrian Government operates a program known as the *Insolvenzausfallgeld-Fond* or the IAG (i.e., the Insolvency Compensation Fund). The IAG has been accumulating substantial losses since 1992 and they became particularly severe in 1995. The fund secures pensions for less than 200,000 workers. For a detailed description of this arrangement, see Helmut Kapl, "Safeguards in Austrian Old-Age Pension Systems," Paper presented at the 10th International Meeting of Insolvency Insurers, Cologne, Germany, September 1995.

5. With the exception of applicable tax provisions, pension issues are regulated by the provincial governments in Canada.

6. See Leo Mok and Philip Van Huizen, "The Legal Framework of Dutch Pension Plans Including the Guaranty of Private Pension Plans," in Leo Mok, ed., *International Handbook on Pensions Law & Similar Employee Benefits,* p. 199.

7. The private pension benefits are offered voluntarily by employers in the Netherlands and they complement the old-age pensions provided by the social security system. The national pension consists of uniform flat-rate payments. In 1993, those payments consisted of Dfl 18,157.80 for a single person and Dfl 12,572.34 for each married person. Payment amounts are adjusted automatically when Holland's minimum wage index changes over a period of six consecutive months. To support this system, workers contribute 14 percent of earnings up to a maximum of Dfl 74,646 per year.

8. The Verzekeringskamer was privatized in August 1992, becoming an independent legal trust chartered to perform supervisory functions of occupational pension plans and insurance companies operating in the Netherlands. Its employees are no longer civil servants. However, the Dutch Ministry of Finance appoints the Verzekeringskamer's own Board of Supervisors. The organization also has a separate pension advisory board consisting of representatives from employer and employee organizations.

9. German industrial companies recently have been attempting to place large equity issues with nonbank investors.

10. See James E. Pesando, "Investment Risk, Bankruptcy Risk, and Pension Reform in Canada," *The Journal of Finance* XXXVII, no. 3 (June 1982), pp. 741–49.

11. Registered Retirement Savings Plans are tax-deferred savings accounts available to individuals and groups in Canada. They are similar to Keogh Plans and some Individual Retirement Accounts in the United States.

12. Pesando, "Investment Risk," pp. 745–48.

13. Robert J. Myers, "Chile's Social Security Reform, After Ten Years," *Benefits Quarterly,* Third Quarter 1992, p. 41.

14. The author is indebted to José Piñera for this comment.

15. For a detailed discussion of Chile's social security system, see Superintendence of Pension Fund Administrators, *The Chilean Pension System,* 1995.

16. There were substantial credits, *bonos de reconocimiento* (recognition bonds), offered to encourage individuals to transfer voluntarily to the new system. See Peter Diamond and Salvador Valdés-Prieto, "Social Security Reforms," in Barry P. Bosworth, Rudiger Dornbusch, and Raúl Labán, *The Chilean Economy: Policy Lessons and Challenges* (Washington, DC: The Brookings Institution, 1994), pp. 257–320.

17. A replacement rate this high combined with contributions of only 10 percent of earnings would assume higher real rates of return, a longer period spent in the labor force, and/or higher mortality rates than would be typical in a more developed country. See Dimitri Vittas and Augusto Iglesias, "The Rationale and Performance of Personal Pension Plans in Chile," Policy Research Working Paper #WPS867 (Washington, DC: The World Bank, February 1992), p. 4.

18. These additional costs include commission fees charged by AFPs for managing the personal retirement accounts. AFPs are required by regulation to limit their exposure to disability and survivor insurance losses by negotiating a reinsurance treaty with a Chilean life insurance company. The State would promptly liquidate an AFP in the event of catastrophic survivor and disability claims that could not be covered by the reinsurance treaty and the AFP's own capital reserves. This gives rise to a fourth guarantee insofar as the

government would absorb unfunded claims remaining after liquidation of the AFP.

19. In June 1992, the minimum pension was 25.2 percent of Chile's average taxable income after contributions for that month. See Diamond and Valdés-Prieto, "Social Security Reforms," p. 262.

20. Returns are compared monthly, based on 12-month moving averages. In a variation of the Chilean approach, Colombia recently adopted a minimum rate-of-return guarantee that is linked to a market index.

21. Chile's minimum wage amounted to $150 per month for most workers. A lower minimum was set at $110 per month for domestics employed in households.

22. All of these people apparently had credited service under Chile's old social security system.

23. Annuities in Chile are indexed to reflect inflation.

24. Gert Wagner, "La Seguridad social y el programa de pensión mínima garantizada," *Estudios de Economía,* June 1991, pp. 35–91.

25. Mario Marcel Cullel and Alberto Arenas de Mesa, "Proyecciones del gasto previsional 1991–2038: Garantia estatal en pensiones minimas del sistema de AFP," June 1993, p. 5 (attachments).

26. Salvador Zurita, "Minimum Pension Insurance in the Chilean Pension System," *Revista de Análisis Económico,* June 1994, pp. 105–26.

27. Participation in social security is optional for workers in the informal sector as well as for certain professionals.

28. Any returns that exceed the industry average by 2 percent must be placed in a special reserve account. This discourages risk taking substantially in excess of the industry average.

29. The *Superintendencia de Administradoras de Fondos de Pensiones* (SAFP) monitors the investments of each AFP on a daily basis.

30. The value of the UF is linked to changes in the consumer price index and is adjusted daily. UFs are used extensively in Chile for indexing financial contracts. As of 6/16/95, one UF was worth 11,873.27 pesos, or US$31.83.

31. Barry Bosworth, Rudiger Dornbusch, and James Poterba, "Public Policies to Support Saving and Investment in Mexico," (undated), p. 32.

32. However, this may not affect people close to the minimum pension. The guarantee of a minimum pension provides an incentive to choose

phased withdrawal, because the government in effect provides longevity insurance at no cost to retirees close to the minimum.

33. The CPSI is a quasi-governmental agency that reports to the Ministry for Health and Social Affairs. Among other responsibilities, it administers a pooling arrangement among Finland's mandatory private pension plans to pay current retirement benefits. Credit insurance operations accounted for 10 percent of the organization's total staff.

34. Many of Finland's workers do not work for 40 years. In those cases, salary replacement is generally less than 60 percent.

35. For all of Finland's workers, incremental rights to social security benefits decrease with the accumulation of pension wealth in the private system. Additional voluntary pension arrangements are sometimes provided for salaried employees and special groups such as workers born before 1936 who otherwise would not be able to qualify for full pensions due to changes in Finland's pension laws. Voluntary plans can also be used to provide selected groups of workers with the same level of benefits after only 30 years of service.

36. These loans are in general referred to as *TEL loans* because the largest pension system for private workers is known as the TEL system.

37. The Federal Reserve Board's Regulation Q placed a ceiling on interest rates paid by member banks on savings deposits.

38. Garantia gradually began to write new business during the second half of 1994.

39. For a summary of the destabilizing effects of disintermediation in the U.S. economy, see Edward F. McKelvey, "Interest Rate Ceilings and Disintermediation," Staff Economic Studies Paper #99 (Washington, DC: Board of Governors of the Federal Reserve System, April 1978).

40. See Esko Prokkola, "Survey of Insolvency Insurance Operations: 1987–89," Paper presented at the 7th International Meeting of Insolvency Insurers, Stockholm, Sweden 1989, p. 3.

41. In late 1992, the interest rates charged in these loans was 9.5 percent, that is, between 4 and 5 percent below current market rates.

42. See Esko Prokkola, "Can We Learn Something from the Experience of the Credit Insurance Business of the Central Pension Security Institute?" Paper presented at the Ninth International Meeting of Insolvency Insurers, Tokyo, Japan, October 1993.

43. This implied an exposure-to-reserve ratio of 65. By way of contrast, Sweden's FPG/AMFK was much better capitalized.

44. As noted in Chapters 4 and 8, insurance companies in the United States are required to maintain capital reserves of 6 percent relative to this type of risk exposure.

45. In addition to retirement plans financed by unfunded book reserves, PSVaG insurance covers asset-backed book reserve plans as well as *Unterstutzungskasse,* usually known in English as *support funds.* German sources indicate that a better translation for this term would be *welfare fund.* A support fund is a separate legal entity but employees do not have a legal claim against it for benefits. Instead, they have a legal claim against the employer should support fund assets not be sufficient to pay all promised benefits. PSVaG insurance also covers direct insurance contracts that employers use as collateral. On the other hand, PSVaG insurance does not secure other deferred annuities purchased directly from insurance companies or those provided by *Pensionskasse* or *pension funds.* The German pension funds are quite different from the arrangements referred to by that same term in the United States. Large German employers operate pension funds as captive insurance companies subject to federal insurance regulation and supervision. None of these institutions has failed during the post–World War II period.

46. See Peter Ahrend, "Pension Financial Security in Germany," Paper presented at the Pension Research Council Conference on "Securing Employer-Based Pensions: An International Perspective," at the Wharton School of the University of Pennsylvania, May 5–6, 1994, p. 12.

47. Additional but less important tax advantages include relief from the property tax.

48. For a concise summary of the criticisms of book-reserve financing, see Ronald Weichert, "Pensionskassen stärken den Kapitalmarkt," *Sparkasse,* November 1988, pp. 506–9.

49. The German system of universal banking has limited the development of the local capital markets. In universal banking, the major commercial banks hold controlling equity positions in Germany's largest private companies. The importance of the stock market therefore is greatly reduced. Recently, industrial companies in Germany have sought to place large equity issues with nonbank investors.

50. In 1982 composition proceedings, the PSVaG voluntarily assumed 60 percent of AEG's pension liabilities, thereby contributing in a major way to the company's survival.

51. The Ford Motor Company was required to pay $6 million to the PSVaG at the time of the AEG restructuring.

52. See Jurgen Paulsdorff, "Insolvency Insurance in the Federal Republic of Germany, Survey of Operations: 1990–1993," Paper presented at the 9th International Meeting of Insolvency Insurers, Tokyo, Japan, 1993, p. 22.

53. Although German observers do not view the problem of adverse selection in terms this stark, see James E. Pesando, "The Government's Role in Insuring Pensions," p. 18. Paper presented at the Pension Research Council Conference, "Securing Employer-Based Pensions: An International Perspective," at the Wharton School of the University of Pennsylvania, May 5–6, 1994.

54. This view later changed. German labor unions later came to accept a role for private pensions but these benefits only recently have become significant issues in collective bargaining.

55. Ahrend, "Pension Financial Security in Germany," p. 26.

56. The author is indebted to Dr. Klaus Heubeck for bringing this to his attention.

57. See Herbert Giese, "The Influence of the Integration of the European Community on Corporate Pension Plans and on Insolvency Insurance Policy," Paper presented at the 9th International Meeting of Insolvency Insurers, Tokyo, Japan, October 1993.

58. The Japanese Employees' Pension Fund replaces a portion of social security and may provide additional benefits.

59. See Nobuyasu Asaka, "Payment Guarantee Program Operation in Japan," Paper presented at the 8th International Meeting of Insolvency Insurers, Åbo, Finland, August 1991.

60. Employers are permitted to take tax deductions for 40 percent of the book reserve.

61. The substitutional component paid by a Japanese employees' pension fund replaces benefits that otherwise would be received as a national old-age pension. In the United States, these benefits would correspond with the old-age benefits provided by Social Security.

62. Robert L. Clark, *Retirement Systems in Japan* (Philadelphia, PA: University of Pennsylvania Press, 1991), p. 88.

63. Naoyuki Tsuru, "Summary of Operations of the Pension Benefit Guarantee Program (Fiscal 1993 to the 1st half of fiscal 1995)," Sep-

tember 1995. Paper presented at the 10th International Meeting of Insolvency Insurers. Colgne, Germany.

64. See Naoyuki Tsuru, "Investigative Report on the Funding Level of the Employees' Pension Fund," Paper presented at the 9th International Meeting of Insolvency Insurers. Tokyo, Japan, October 1993.

65. A source at the Life Insurance Association of Japan has pointed out that actual benefit payments are recorded using current market values if the pension plan is part of the trust bank system. However, accounting for the assets, liabilities, and benefit payments is based on book values in the life insurance system.

66. See Yasukazu Yoshizawa, "Proposal for New Management System of Employees' Pension Fund (Summary of the Report by the Technical Research Team for the Working Group No. 2 of the Committee on Actuarial Matters of Corporate Pension Funds)," Paper presented at the 10th International Meeting of Insolvency Insurers, Cologne, Germany, September 1995, p. 6.

67. The Pension Registration Institute performs actuarial valuations for ITP pensions only. PRI is owned by two labor market organizations: the SAF (Swedish Employers' Confederation), and the PTK (Federation of Salaried Employees in Industry and Services).

68. The discount rate used to value ITP pension obligations is 4 percent. Although this may seem low compared to rates used in the United States, it actually is not conservative in view of the indexation feature of ITP pensions. For a real interest rate, it is high. However, Swedes familiar with the ITP system do not expect the system to collapse. The white-collar PTK labor market organization sets aside 1 percent of member salaries as a reserve to finance future inflation-based benefit increases and—if that is not enough—those increases could be reduced.

69. Immediate vesting in Sweden has been cited as one reason contributing to credit insurance premiums that are somewhat higher than the insurance premiums charged by Germany's PSVaG. Germany requires that workers have 10 years of service and reach the age of 35 before vesting.

70. Portability was considered to be highly desirable when the ITP system was set up. The Swedish economy was in the throes of major structural change during one of the country's most prosperous periods. Labor markets were tight. There was a general consensus that vesting requirements should not impede labor mobility so that

workers could move without penalty from declining firms to more productive jobs in other sectors of the economy.

71. FPG also guarantees pension obligations exceeding ITP levels to white-collar workers. Many of these benefits are similar to those promised to highly paid executives in the United States in connection with "top hat" plans that are not tax deferred. This type of obligation represents a minor share of FPG's business. Meanwhile, ITP pensions for white-collar workers also are secured by an additional guarantee provided by the ITP system itself. This guarantee covers benefits that otherwise would be lost if employers fail to pay contributions when due. Claims against this program usually cover the ITP premiums during the last two or three months before liquidation of the employer.

72. For a general discussion of book reserve systems, see the earlier description of Germany's PSVaG insolvency insurance.

73. The AMF Pension organization is owned jointly by the Swedish Employers' Confederation (the SAF) and the blue-collar collective bargaining organization (the LO).

74. In Sweden, limited companies issue stock, all of which may be publicly or privately held. All shares of the public authorities currently slated for restructuring will be owned by the state without additional reform.

75. STP loans are priced at 40 basis points above the government bond rate. The strongest Swedish companies are able to borrow at approximately 100 basis points above government rates. This is exactly the yield spread implied by the combined cost of the STP loans and the AMFK premium. A cross subsidy therefore exists within the AMFK system in favor of companies that are not among the very strongest. The strongest Swedish companies nevertheless are motivated to participate in the system by tax incentives.

76. Consolidating capital includes equity, untaxed reserves, and surplus values on assets.

77. The most important indicators are the debt-to-equity ratio, turnover, profit after financing costs, equity, and other reserves.

78. Before 1993, the FPG could require that the entire liability be eliminated over a period no less than 10 years. The five-year conversion period now in effect places the FPG in a much stronger negotiating position in deteriorating situations. Of course, the FPG must trade off the risk of continued coverage against the loss of premiums whenever policyholders liquidate book reserves.

79. Also, when a corporate subsidiary with FPG-insured pension debt is sold or otherwise divested, the FPG may retain the surety bond from the previous owner or demand a new one from the purchaser.

80. Although reinsurance generally has worked well for the FPG and the AMFK, officials at Germany's PSVaG organization have declined to use it apparently out of concern that capacity might not be adequate for their needs in the context of a much larger economy.

81. According to the sources at the PBGC, net realized value of recoveries have not exceeded 5 percent of the agency's bankruptcy claims in recent years. However, the agency officially reported recoveries of $312 million from employers and losses of $2.4 billion from terminating plans from 1988 to 1993. This implies a recovery rate of about 11.5 percent. See Pension Benefit Guaranty Corporation, *1993 Annual Report,* p. 20.

82. The Organization for Economic Cooperation and Development consists of 24 industrialized countries.

83. These amounts represent the legally required minimum retirement credits set by the LPP pension law.

84. Among the 3.8 million workers who contributed to the AHV national old-age pension system in 1991, 2.6 million (almost 68 percent) were covered by the mandatory second-pillar plans. Those not covered included the self-employed, the unemployed, workers under the age of 25, workers employed for less than three months, and workers earning less than SF 23,280 per year as of 1995. This earnings limit is indexed.

85. Coverage begins at the age of 18 for the disability and survivors' benefits mandated by the LPP law.

86. Ralph Segalman, *The Swiss Way of Welfare: Lessons for the Western World* (New York: Praeger, 1986), pp. 75–76.

87. Under Swiss law, participants are entitled to receive benefits amounting to the total credits made on their behalf plus annual interest of 4 percent on the LOB amount. The *LOB amount* is a uniform percentage of salary that applies to every Swiss worker and increases with age but at different rates for men and women. Only the principal plus the 4 percent minimum interest is guaranteed.

88. The Canton of Bern guarantees these benefits.

89. According to one source, before 1985 40 percent of the labor force would receive adequate replacement of pre-retirement earnings or

roughly the objective of the combined first and second pillars today. Another 40 percent also were covered by a private, employer-provided plan but would receive less than the minimum required benefits today. Finally, 20 percent of the labor force were not covered at all by a private pension plan. See Daniel Durr, *Wesen und Aufgaben des Sicherheitsfonds gemaess BVG.* Unpublished dissertation at the Höher Betriebs und Wirtschafts Schule, Bern, Switzerland (1987), p. 6.

90. Swiss pension specialists point out that a shift of employment outside the country would be unlikely even in extreme circumstances. The legal maximum for the guarantee fund premium is 0.3 percent of coordinated salary.

91. This band is adjusted for inflation every year as noted above.

92. For the most recent data from 1992, see Statistique officielle de la Suisse, *Statistiques des caisses de pension 1992, no. 13, Sécurité sociale et assurances* (Bern: Office fédéral de la statistique Suisse, 1994), pp. 142–43.

93. New companies with younger workers have higher failure rates than older companies with older workers. As a result of these higher default rates and relatively early vesting requirements, new companies originally were expected to place disproportionate burdens on the insolvency insurance aspect of the new system. The purpose of the subsidies for unfavorable age structure therefore was to offset the effect of insolvency insurance transfers by reducing the burden that the LPP pension law otherwise would have imposed on companies with an older average age for the labor force.

94. As manifested in the Swiss constitution and the resulting shadow accounts maintained in the corresponding defined-credit plan.

95. This has been confirmed by research commissioned by the Swiss Government. For example, see Frohmuth Gerheuser, "Die Wirkungen der beruflichen Versorge auf den Arbeitsmarkt," 1991.

96. During the Summer of 1994, a government commission began to study a long list of possible reform initiatives related to the guarantee fund. Extending guarantees—possibly involving alternative sources of private insurance cover—to nonmandatory benefits provided by some second-pillar plans represented a priority interest. Use of reinsurance by the existing guarantee fund was also considered. For one study conducted by outside advisors, see Jacob van Dam and Hans

Schmid, "Insolvenzversicherung in der beruflichen Vorsorge" (Bern: Bundesamt für Sozialversicherung, December 1994).

97. In 1993, ATAG Ernst & Young personnel spent 9,500 hours on business related to the guarantee fund.

98. This replacement rate assumes 40 years of saving and covers income only up to the maximum earnings coordinated with the federal old-age social security program. Insofar as the LPP law was passed in 1985, many Swiss workers retiring before 2025 may not be able to achieve this level of replacement despite a special transfer of supplementary benefits intended to bring them closer to the new constitutional replacement rate.

99. Contribution credits are given for periods of extended illness and other special circumstances. See *A Guide to Retirement Pensions,* Leaflet NP47 (London, UK: Department of Social Security, 1990), pp. 10–11.

100. Pesando, "The Government's Role in Insuring Pensions," p. 13.

101. For a discussion of relationships among Maxwell's companies, see Tom Bower, *Maxwell the Outsider* (New York: Viking Penguin, 1992).

102. Maxwell's financial empire had come under severe pressure as a result of his acquisition of the Macmillan publishing company in the United States. Some believed that Maxwell had overpaid by about $1 billion for Macmillan. See p. 426.

103. See the Pension Law Review Committee, *Pension Law Reform: The Report of the Pension Law Review Committee,* vols. 1 and 2 (London, UK: HMSO, 1993).

104. That member was Stuart C. James.

105. See the Secretary of State for Social Security, *Security, Equality, Choice: The Future of Pensions,* vol. 1(London: HMSO, June 1994), p. 34.

106. The combined maximum guaranteed benefit in the United States also would exceed that in Japan. However, Japan's Pension Guarantee Program is not paying benefits and, at the moment, it is processing its first claim.

6

THE ETHICS OF PENSION INSURANCE

Despite the large and undesirable incentive effects of ERISA termination insurance, there has been little progress in reforming the Pension Benefit Guarantee Corporation. This outcome results, in part, from a tendency by public officials to ignore the very real conflicts produced by ethical contradictions in our retirement system. The prevailing view on Capitol Hill until recently has been limited to creating a moral imperative that requires taxpayers and other third parties to keep the pension promises made by employers of sometimes doubtful creditworthiness and credibility. In fact, this ethical priority has dominated virtually every other consideration. What market failure or other shortcoming could justify such an approach, and how strong is that justification?

Violation of promises is undesirable for any retirement system. Yet, most long-service workers absorbed huge pension losses when their employers liquidated and went out of business before ERISA. These workers often had firm-specific skills they could not transfer readily to another employer. Most of their net worth—present and future—therefore depended on the survival of just one company, and this was a risk that could not be diversified. The authors of ERISA therefore believed that one of the most important functions incumbent on government was to protect average citizens from excesses like promise breaking in these situations. Has ERISA successfully performed this function? And on a broader level, did this legislation create another set of victims with compelling grievances of their own? Finally, was this government intervention forged so awkwardly that private markets subsequently performed even less well from an ethical point of view?

Tiresome and seemingly pedestrian financial concerns about this particular program's costs and its long-term solvency can seem so unimportant that high government officials sometimes scarcely consider them. Yet, the ERISA termination insurance commitment also involves opportunity costs. When government provides benefits for one group, it has fewer resources available to meet other needs. Where should this priority rank, compared with the alternatives? ERISA pension termination insurance puts government in the business of fulfilling private contractual obligations to relatively well-off groups at levels far above the socially agreed safety net. As noted in Chapter 1, the maximum guaranteed retirement income, consisting of social security and private pension benefits guaranteed by the PBGC, represented 822 percent of the $5,208 social minimum provided by the Supplemental Security Income (SSI) program. Can a government responsibility to honor private pension promises at this level and higher be justified?[1] Or should the same resources be used instead to raise the SSI safety net or some other means-tested program?

Ethics involves determining standards for making choices like these, not ignoring the resulting costs. With respect to the ERISA termination insurance program, ethics and financial analysis are inextricably intertwined. A judgment about whether society in general has an obligation to the participants in defined-benefit pension plans lies at the core of this problem. If so, what are the limits of that obligation? It is a fallacy to think that an ethical basis exists for promising government benefits to one group if at the same time one ignores potentially destructive consequences for others who are vulnerable to the effects of misdirected or ill-framed policies. Creating new risks for taxpayers and future generations also involves significant ethical concerns.

Some of the most publicized shortcomings in private retirement systems both here and abroad have come to light as a result of blatant ethical lapses. In one recent example, Robert Maxwell's misappropriation of $600 million in pension assets resulted in the British government's undertaking to identify an array of legal reforms aimed at improving benefit security in that country. Some observers in the United Kingdom believe that the thrust of this initiative was tragically misguided. Workers and retirees in the Maxwell case will be made whole following the effective use of moral suasion and voluntary settlements by the investment houses and financial institutions that benefited in some way from this rare case of chicanery. Still, the principal thrust of proposed legal reforms in the United Kingdom has been determined by the particulars of this one case. Should fraud represent the main focal point of ethical and legal concern in the pension arena? The Maxwell incident certainly has the potential to make it so for years to come in the United Kingdom.

Without adequate attention to the ethical underpinnings of many aspects of our retirement system, public policy concerning pensions will inevitably sink into a deep morass of problems. Predictably enough, pension policies in the United States have been criticized—often legitimately—for a lack of consistency and fairness. The following examples serve to indicate the moral confusion that has plagued our approach to the ERISA termination insurance guarantee.

FOUR REVEALING CASES

Pension Losers

Consider the case of the so-called Pension Losers Bill. ERISA guaranteed the benefits only of plans that were terminated after it was signed into law. The Pension Losers Bill would require the Pension Benefit Guaranty Corporation to provide benefits to about 40,000 workers and their surviving spouses who otherwise would have received pensions from underfunded plans terminated before 1974. Many of these workers subsequently received no benefits at all as a result of the termination of their pension plans. Others received reduced benefits. Compare their situation with the outcome after

ERISA was adopted. Some 27,000 participants in 266 underfunded pension plans that were terminated by the PBGC between 1974 and 1978 qualified for guaranteed benefits after paying annual insurance premiums of just $1. What was the justification for the seemingly arbitrary difference in treatment of these two groups?

On the one hand, PBGC insurance itself is difficult to justify on the basis of equity or need. These concerns represent the motivating forces for U.S. universal pension programs: Social Security, and Supplemental Security Income (SSI). The maximum benefit guaranteed by the PBGC was set at $29,950 for 1993. Social Security payments raised the combined maximum to $42,796.[2] Less than 17 percent of American workers, however, are vested in private defined-benefit pension plans, and these workers are highly paid relative to the rest of the labor force. Private defined-benefit pension plans represent deferred compensation for this group, as well as one form of personal saving. Even if it can be shown that the rest of society somehow should stand behind these promises, can America extend coverage to the Pension Losers without embarking on an untenable course that would attempt to correct past injustices retroactively and without limit?

The Executive Life Insurance Collapse
Other groups have bitterly complained that they were cheated when their overfunded pension plans were terminated so that employers could recover surplus funds. The procedure was perfectly legal and simple enough. The sponsor was required only to publicize the pending termination and notify the PBGC that it would purchase annuities from a private insurance company. The PBGC applied no standards of financial soundness to the insurance companies that sold these annuities and, after annuities were purchased, the agency no longer guaranteed benefits. Not surprisingly, defaults followed. In one case, 84,000 participants suffered immediate benefit reductions of 30 percent when the Executive Life Insurance Company failed.[3] As a result of this case, there has been recurring pressure to extend PBGC coverage to retirement annuities sold by private insurance companies. The Executive Life debacle as well as the Pension Losers situation provide case studies in what some have called creeping guaranteeism.

Initially, the government provides subsidized insurance to a diffuse set of interest groups. Demands soon follow to extend the subsidy to a growing number of other constituencies.

So far the PBGC has been able to resist these pressures because—just as in the Maxwell case in the United Kingdom—moral suasion made whole many of those who lost some of their retirement income.[4] Millionaires and corporations that benefited when Executive Life annuities were purchased to substitute for PBGC-guaranteed pension promises have found this situation extremely embarrassing. Several have stepped forward and voluntarily purchased additional annuities to make up for the retirement income that was lost as a result of the default. Most, but unfortunately not all, of those affected will be made whole as a result of the Executive Life rehabilitation plan negotiated by California's Insurance Commissioner. Should taxpayers in any of America's 50 states accept responsibility for ineffective regulation in this situation? If so, in which state? Would it be appropriate to extend PBGC coverage to retirement annuities sold by private insurance companies?

Or should the companies and businessmen who have already stepped forward be informally but effectively encouraged to make the remaining participants whole? In effect, such a choice would impose punitive damages on companies and their owners beyond those necessary to cover pensions lost by their own workers. Be that as it may, moral suasion still represents one of the mildest approaches to enforcement. It can be criticized for a basic inability to deter criminals and others who are truly bent on abusing the system. In fact, the abusive personality might well favor an emphasis on moral suasion for exactly this reason.

The Pitfalls of Early Retirement

In Pueblo, Colorado, 275 retirees not only were confronted with an immediate cut in benefits of up to $400 per month, but the PBGC actually told them to reimburse the agency for 10 early retirement supplements. They received those supplements before the agency terminated a plan sponsored by the CF&I Steel Company with a $220 million unfunded liability. It is difficult to believe that these workers would have accepted the company's early retirement offer less than a year before the termination had they fully understood the risks involved. Yet, any reasonable theory of fair contracts and bargaining would require that all parties understand the terms of the agreement.

When the PBGC terminates pension plans, some retirees often find that their benefits are reduced. The public tends to perceive these reductions as promise breaking. If in fact they are that, where do these ethically tainted reductions rank in the hierarchy of culpability? Did employers actively work to deceive the workers? Or did they simply fail to inform the workers about risks to their subsequent income? Even when disclosure occurs, do employers—particularly those in poor financial health—have a duty to emphasize such risks when offering early retirement? What is the obligation on the part of labor unions to inform their members about these risks? And, to what extent should workers themselves be responsible for obtaining this information?

The principle that workers and retirees themselves are responsible for obtaining the relevant information (much of which is not always included in plan documents) today has become enshrined in American case law. Yet, it is virtually impossible to predict all the conceivable circumstances that can impinge on the retirement decision. Some legal experts therefore believe that employers should be required to assume new disclosure responsibilities. Others, meanwhile, have argued for withdrawing PBGC insurance coverage from shutdown benefits and early retirement benefits. After all, these benefits cannot be funded in advance under current tax law and in many ways they are more akin to a severance benefit than to a retirement benefit.

The Bethlehem Steel Case

Major ethical concerns impinge on regulatory approaches to dealing with seriously underfunded plans when the sponsor remains in business. For example, Bethlehem Steel had accumulated an unfunded pension liability of $2.4 billion by 1978 when it employed more than 100,000 workers. Seventeen years later, Bethlehem was producing approximately the same amount of steel each year with a labor force of just 24,000. As of the beginning of 1994, Bethlehem's unfunded pension liability remained at approximately $2.4 billion. To what extent should the company be required to close this funding gap? The burden for previous underfunding now approaches $100,000 per worker!

This represents one of the most important problems facing the PBGC because cases like Bethlehem Steel are so common. Any company that starts with a sizable unfunded liability and then downsizes will face a similar burden. If the government will not or should not make today's workers pay a price this high for a windfall received by their predecessors, how should the cost of funding these shortfalls be distributed? Certainly contracts among contemporaries will allow for redress among the relevant parties if unforeseen inequities arise. One dilemma facing any intergenerational system, however, is that mechanisms to renegotiate burdens and benefits cannot include all of the parties to the arrangement. Some of them may no longer be living while others may not yet be born.[5]

As a result of episodes like these, appeals to moral sensibilities are frequently used to justify specific approaches concerning pension issues. Three scholars recently observed that many appeals of this sort concerning national policies can be

> facile, simplistic, judgmental, and ill considered. Emphasis on values is often used in what might charitably be called a protean way, its meaning shifting in every use. Value-based arguments are sometimes presented as if some great eclipse has cut the less favored off from moral sunlight.[6]

Meanwhile, a literature addressing ethical questions related to unfunded pension liabilities has begun to emerge.[7]

This chapter aims to contribute to the ongoing debate in this area by examining the ethical precepts available to assist policymakers as they arbitrate competing pension claims. Although the perspective of policymakers represents a logical point of departure for any interested observer, the existing literature has focused instead on the ethical values of two parochial interests: unions working with their presumed proxy in the form of the PBGC, and management. On the one hand, labor has been portrayed as having a moral imperative to recover lost benefits that were earned by workers and therefore owed to them. In cases involving Continental Can, International Harvester, and LTV, it was alleged—perhaps overzealously—that such payments were denied by means of deception and illegality. On the other hand, corporations can claim that social welfare actually will improve if economic efficiency can be enhanced by the unpleasant business of firing workers and thereby reducing pension costs. According to this approach, the public good will be served by companies pursuing their private interests. The search for loopholes in the law to make this possible therefore has been viewed as entirely legitimate.

Unfortunately, any public contest of morality that is limited just to these perspectives will overlook some of the most fundamental ethical questions involved with the design or restructuring of pension guarantees. Among those questions are the following:

- What is a fair rate of saving to impose on any generation of workers?
- Should current and future workers be responsible for the effects of inadequate pension funding that occurred previously?
- What is the moral position of taxpayers relative to previous unfunded pension liabilities as well as to those that now are accumulating?
- Do current policymakers have an obligation to protect future workers and taxpayers? If so, from what?
- Is the ERISA termination insurance concept a moral one and does the PBGC promote or retard the interests of economic justice?
- Do workers now and in the future have an obligation to support and preserve the ERISA termination insurance concept?
- Should the future value of costs and benefits attributable to the program be discounted when making policy choices?

While considering these questions one should recognize that in good times—at least during the second half of this century—governments often have failed to resist the temptation of creating entitlements that cannot be sustained. When conditions later deteriorate, these same governments will either subsidize the resulting systems from general revenues or undermine the insurance function by allowing inflation to erode the real value of benefits. In this context, policy makers should critically examine different concepts of economic justice to determine whether they yield a workable framework for approaching the distributional tradeoffs involved with pension insurance. The essential ethical questions are interrelated. The most seminal among them suggest answers to others and point to a structure of priorities for sorting out competing claims in this area.

ETHICAL VALUES IN PRIVATE PENSIONS

What are the ethical values that have shaped and continue to reshape our system of private pensions? One of the most challenging aspects of these institutions, which represent products of the Western democratic process, is that they are characterized more often than not by an array of perfectly reasonable and broad, sometimes even comprehensive, moral doctrines that can be quite incompatible. The central problem facing people responsible for the evolution, development, regulation, and management of these institutions therefore is to formulate approaches that are consistent with a plurality of these beliefs.[8] Certainly an overriding value, one that subsumes most others, should be that a financially sound private pension system can provide enormous advantages for the American economy—its workers and retirees as well as the firms and governments that depend on the efficiency of its capital markets. Within this framework, the following pension-related values and concerns are among those that somehow must accommodate each other as part of this process:

- *The rights of participants and promise keeping:* Do defined-benefit plans as well as the policies that regulate them deliver what workers have a right to expect from these plans? Is it realistic to promote defined-benefit plans when this type of pension depends upon a very high standard of commitment and promise-keeping sustained over long periods of time?

- *Fair treatment:* Do differences in treatment across groups of participants call into question the fairness of individual pension plans or the PBGC insurance program?

- *The rights of nonparticipants:* Does public policy unfairly favor participants in defined-benefit plans over those in defined-contribution plans? Is the level of public assistance provided to participants in these arrangements appropriate compared to levels of retirement income provided by Social Security and SSI? Are the needs of the least advantaged being adequately addressed in the context of all these arrangements?

- *The limits of autonomy:* Do younger workers need to be protected from shortsightedness—in particular, their tendency to discount the need for prudent saving for the future? If so, are pension fund managers or government policymakers in a position to impose saving policies for the long-range good of workers? Haven't corporate pension fund managers and government officials themselves often failed to act prudently with respect to the long-term future?

- *Equity over the life-course:* Do practices such as vesting and backloading of benefit accruals provide equitable treatment to workers regardless of age?

- *Sustainability:* Are America's private pension systems sufficiently stable and sound so that future generations can depend on them?

- *Distributing the burden of past mistakes:* How should the cost of correcting past mistakes and failures in pension policies be distributed? What should be done when it is not possible to assign costs to groups who were responsible or who benefited in the past?

- *Promoting opportunity:* Will overly stringent regulation and excessive public scrutiny have a chilling effect on creative and innovative business decisions?

- *Conflict of interest:* Does secrecy, involving either the operation of the plans themselves or the PBGC insurance program, create opportunities for abuse in this area?

- *Truth telling:* What level of disclosure and truth telling should be required from pension managers of defined-benefit plans? What considerations should limit the degree of disclosure to their participants or to the public?

Temptations to Do the Wrong Thing

Many moral principles—like promise keeping, fair treatment of comparable groups of people, and truth telling—are accepted prima facie without much debate. Unfortunately, applying even these values to pension policy is not a simple matter. In the first place, which moral claim should take priority when these principles clash? Second, it may not be possible to apply those principles in a practical setting even if there is general agreement on the ethical principles. Some compromise or tradeoff may be necessary. But in the field of pension policy, and public insurance of private pension obligations in particular, there have been repeated instances where prima facie moral principles were violated. Those in positions of responsibility often failed to live up to clear and evident standards. The very structure or design of these systems often creates temptations to do the wrong thing, with disastrous results for the vulnerable: pensioners, taxpayers, and future generations. Some recurrent temptations to violate moral principles include the following:

- Making false pension promises to workers with the knowledge that the resources needed to keep them will not be there.
- Shifting costs to consumers, future taxpayers, and other groups unable to protect themselves through our imperfect political processes.
- Disregard by both unions and management of the pension interests of unorganized groups of workers.
- Intervention in regulatory decisions by members of Congress to promote constituent interests, as in the S&L scandal.
- Failure of government regulators to collect financial information necessary to determine the actual condition of federally insured pension plans.

Other perverse incentives facing plan sponsors and reinforced by poorly designed federal insurance can also be considered ethical problems. Among those discussed in previous chapters were:

- Underfunding of pension plans in the face of low corporate profitability.

- Underreporting of liabilities, distortion or outright falsification of accounting and actuarial information, also in response to low corporate profitability.

- Excessive risk taking with pension investments to make up for inadequate pension contributions.

Allocating Benefits: Objectives and Values

To sustain widespread support as well as to avoid potentially endless legal and other disputes, the ethics of any system of retirement guarantees should represent a rational reconstruction of generally accepted moral intuition in the country. Ethicists often cite three overriding ethical goals in relation to a broad range of problems: welfare, justice, and freedom of choice. Of these, the first two seem reasonably applicable to public retirement programs. Although welfare can be defined in different ways, particularly when it comes to planning for some subjective concept of future well-being, it encompasses all the elements of satisfaction that individuals value, including the confidence or peace of mind that retirement income will be received in the future (i.e., old-age security).

With respect to the similarly complex topic of justice, the principal concern to emerge in the context of most Western-style social security systems has been to meet the basic retirement income needs of the elderly despite an earnings-related component. The Supplemental Security Income Program (SSI) can be seen as a public attempt to provide for those who earned too little earlier in life or those whose earnings record was too sporadic to qualify for social security. The approach has been essentially paternalistic and egalitarian, assigning responsibility to the state for looking after those citizens who are unable to plan properly for their own needs during the final stages of life. The general public, as a result, has come to regard the retirement benefits provided by Social Security and SSI as a basic welfare right in modern society. In effect, these are America's universal pension programs.

For the United States, the prima facie ethical principles that determined the design and operation of private retirement programs are quite distinct from those that most heavily influenced the essential features of social security. One reason is that private pensions cover a relatively well-paid minority within the labor force. Workers have no abstract right to a private pension on the basis of equity or need in the same sense that they have a right to the social minimum for retirement income as defined under the SSI program. Private pensions represent deferred compensation and one form of personal saving. These arrangements place greater emphasis on deserved reward as well as on the proportionality between resources committed to retirement plans and the benefits that are subsequently received.

Public guarantees of private pension promises therefore must be justified on grounds other than social equity. Should people be left to fend for themselves when preserving property rights that exceed the social minimum? Is government support for claims at some higher level in the public interest? Certainly systems like the one currently operating in the Netherlands that rely on stringent funding standards and enforcement have no need for a backup guarantee. However, if the public is willing to tolerate lax regulation such as that prevailing in the United States, an obligation could exist for government to stand behind some portion of the pension promise.

Furthermore, the presence of a large and relatively prosperous middle class generally serves as a stabilizing influence for any country. Society therefore might be better off if great numbers of average people participate in private pension plans with the confidence that their retirement savings are reasonably secure. Indeed, the $60 billion in annual tax subsidies (i.e., foregone revenues that would otherwise be collected by the U.S. Treasury) represents evidence of an intent that private retirement plans contribute to society's general welfare and adhere to overall principles of fairness in distributing the country's resources.[9] With or without lax regulation, most would agree that government—after promoting these arrangements—has an obligation to provide a stable framework for operating them. In a system of lax regulation, central problems for policymakers become setting an appropriate ceiling on the obligation of third parties (e.g., taxpayers) to keep these promises, and deciding when promises are transparently frivolous and need not be kept.

More generally, values such as promise keeping and truth telling emerge as central to private retirement systems in America. These principles have come to form a minimal basis for regulating the private pension system at large. Although such core values enjoy strong support among most of the population, they still present policymakers with vexing problems in view of the contradictions that often arise in their application. The significance of the first fiduciary value, promise keeping, has repeatedly become manifest in situations when retirees were confronted with immediate benefit reductions following a plan termination (e.g., CF&I Steel) or the insolvency of an insurance company (e.g., Executive Life). Although the effects of these reductions have been most conspicuous in the case of retirees, the fact that accrued nonvested benefits must become vested when a well-funded pension plan is terminated suggests that promise keeping is a fiduciary value extending to the treatment of all plan participants.

The second fiduciary value, truth telling, implies that the details of plan documents should be easy for participants to understand and that workers should be provided with a clear impression of the resources needed to pay for an adequate retirement. Workers also should thoroughly understand the specific risks and limits of the pensions that are promised. In recent years, employers have made substantial efforts to ensure that plan documentation is understandable. However, adequate awareness of retirement savings needs has not yet become apparent. A typical worker today needs to contribute 15 percent of salary over a career of 35 years to a tax-deferred plan of some sort in order to prepare for a financially secure retirement. Unfortunately, a common contribution rate among private employers is only 5 percent, and most universities seem to be setting aside just 10 percent of payroll for retirement saving.[10]

Still another core value is autonomy or choice. This concept signifies a widely shared preference for relying on private markets and consumer decision making. The personal circumstances of different workers will vary, and so, as a result, will their retirement savings needs. Autonomy therefore suggests that workers should voluntarily make the decisions about participating in private pension plans and about the level of contributions. The development of so-called cafeteria plans, which give individual workers the freedom to select the various elements that make up their total benefit compensation, reflects this principle.

A complex set of relationships and tradeoffs between promise keeping, disclosure, and autonomy has emerged in the pension field. Promise keeping and autonomy come into conflict when an employee leaves a firm that provides a defined-benefit pension plan as a result of the quit losses discussed in Chapter 1. In effect, the quit loss occurs when part of the pension promise is withdrawn. For their part, employers are anxious to recover their investment in training workers and don't want employees to leave the firm before this happens. On the other hand, many workers employed in declining industries must go elsewhere anyway. In most of these cases, employers provide little or no training for many years. The quit losses that these workers experience can be wholly out of proportion to the employer's investment in training. Meanwhile, the relationship between disclosure and consumer choice in the context of many defined-contribution plans is very different from what one finds in the typical defined-benefit plan. Far more extensive and frequent disclosure becomes necessary when individual participants have the right to make investment choices.

Risks and Promises

The essence of the defined-benefit concept entails a far higher standard of promise keeping than applies in the context of a defined-contribution plan. Truth telling and disclosure are another matter. Companies often need to keep their business plans confidential. A plant shutdown or corporate liquidation therefore may come as a surprise to some workers. Thus, an ethical basis can exist for some entity to provide workers with backup security for defined-benefit pensions when the sponsor goes out of business and the plan terminates without enough assets. Consider the analogy of informed consent in medicine. If a patient gives informed consent to a procedure involving certain risks, the patient cannot subsequently claim compensation for harm that the doctor never promised to avoid in the first place. On the other hand, the doctor would be liable, morally and legally, if he or she did not disclose the risks associated with the procedure, and the harm occurred. In effect, the patient's consent was not "informed."

But if a defined-benefit plan terminates with an unfunded liability, who should bear the responsibility for making whole the participating workers and retirees? A similar problem occurs in the context of liability law. When an accident occurs and it is impossible to assign clear responsibility, or if the party at fault cannot pay or disappears, taxpayers do not become the payer of last resort. The resulting state of affairs is unfortunate and unfair to the individual harmed. However, public policy has assigned no responsibility to the state.

Why then do people seem to think that government has a responsibility to make good on unfunded pension liabilities? The burden of proof should be on those who assert that there is any obligation. Certainly workers can be provided with secure pensions in the absence of a government insurance program. Systems in other countries have demonstrated this fact. However, one certainly could argue that the government has some responsibility, after promoting the use of defined-benefit plans for many years with tax incentives and legal decisions.[11] Defective regulation also could be cited as the reason for insufficiently funded plan terminations. Dereliction of duty on the part of public authorities could imply taxpayer responsibility for lost pension benefits, just as cities must pay compensation for damage caused by potholes.

But is there any reason to think that society should or can eliminate every form of risk, and that when bad things happen the government is at fault? This position has not been taken in other areas that resemble the problem of inadequately funded pensions. For example, federal tax exemptions are used to promote municipal bond offerings. Taxpayers, however, have no obligation to cover investor losses in those cases—as in the Washington Public Power System (WPPS) fiasco—when the borrower defaults. WPPS had issued tax-exempt bonds.

Those who favor the current pension insurance program often argue that taxpayers are not responsible for the PBGC's losses. They point out that the insurance fund is structured as a collective arrangement among defined-benefit plans. That community alone, so the argument goes, is responsible for financing the unfunded liabilities transferred to the agency. This sleight of hand overlooks the political reality that major losses to federal insurance programs—like the now defunct Federal Savings & Loan Insurance Corporation—will be financed from general revenues. Of course, such a dire outcome need not occur in the context of the pension insurance program if the PBGC were restructured and put on a sound financial footing. Unfortunately, policymakers have yet to take significant steps in this direction.

Why is the moral response to the problem of lost pension benefits different from the observed responses to other types of risk such as flood and hurricane damage and deposit insurance? Government insurance also covers risks in these areas. The ERISA termination insurance program has come to be treated, at least by members of Congress, as a transfer program. Yet, flood and hurricane insurance are certainly not widely regarded as transfer programs. In fact, the flood insurance program is voluntary. Government flood and hurricane insurance are justified primarily on the grounds of some market failure.

Age is one factor that could explain the support for pension guarantees when other risks go uninsured or have become insured for altogether different reasons. Pension wealth represents many people's life savings. Furthermore, most participants have only one pension and they have no other opportunity to recover if it's completely lost in old age. After a government begins promoting the use of specific forms of saving for this group and regulating them, the calls for a public insurance program often follow. Tax-exempt bonds, on the other hand, are suitable only for very high-income individuals of any age. Investors holding Washington Public Power Systems bonds certainly were not impoverished by the WPPS default; however, they were much wealthier than the typical participant in a defined-benefit pension plan.

If age does explain the existence of ERISA termination insurance, why does the government protect an engineer working for

General Motors, who is covered by a defined-benefit plan, and not a reporter working for *The Wall Street Journal,* who is covered by a defined-contribution plan?[12] Furthermore, why doesn't the government insure the balances in Individual Retirement Accounts or Keogh plans if age is the determining factor? One reason might be that the pension system was very different 20 years ago when American political leaders conceived the ERISA termination insurance program. In 1975, about 40 percent of the private labor force was covered by at least one defined-benefit plan. By 1990, that share had fallen to just 28 percent.

A new set of ethical views concerning intergenerational burden sharing also gained wide acceptance since the mid-1970s. As the dangers from future overpopulation and pollution became more widely recognized, the problem of justice over time began to develop into a recognized field of inquiry within ethics and political philosophy. Leading economists, meanwhile, had been assuming that economic growth could remain at levels experienced during the 1960s. Most of them also believed that productivity increases would continue apace. These optimistic views no longer dominate.

A recent study by the World Bank observed that the OECD countries now face a dilemma of major proportions as a result of aging populations and stagnating productivity. Old-age income security programs have paid out large pensions over the past three decades of prosperity. Poverty declined faster among the old than among the young. However, payroll taxes will rise by several percentage points within the next few decades to support universal public programs like Social Security. At the same time, benefits will be cut. Intensified intergenerational conflict therefore looms between retirees and workers. The OECD countries now must face the challenge of introducing reforms that are in the long-run public interest. Those reforms may involve taking expected benefits away from some groups in the short run.[13]

To help with decisions concerning who should gain and who should lose benefits as major retirement systems are restructured, a theory that adequately addresses the problem of justice over time and across generations has yet to emerge from the literature.

Nevertheless, agreement has developed concerning the following points:

1. No present generation has the right to enrich itself at the expense of future generations.

2. The institutions that are passed on to future generations should be solvent and sustainable. This leads to a renewed emphasis on the role of stewardship.

On the other hand, there is no agreement about the future performance of economic variables that will determine pension outcomes. Honest differences can exist concerning what prudent judgment is and what represents an adequate level of reserves to protect against future contingencies. Unfortunately, parochial interest seems to have determined the outlook in a great many cases. In addition, there has often been a strong relationship between political perspectives, empirical interpretations, and ethical judgments among those in positions to influence retirement policies.

Justice between Generations

Defined-benefit plans in the United States raise some serious issues of intergenerational equity under present conditions. Further declines in coverage as well as benefit levels appear likely. Even the most optimistic scenarios, involving a strong revival of the manufacturing sector along with continuing favorable performance in the stock market, would leave many defined-benefit plans in weak financial condition.[14] With respect to collectively bargained plans, Kryvicky has examined the problem using a series of 50-year simulations.[15] The simulations showed that for plans set up in the 1950s, the initial past service liabilities, together with subsequent benefit increases and early retirements, typically produced a situation in which the benchmark plan was not sufficiently funded. In fact, the shortfall for this type of plan was so serious that even obligations to then-current retirees were not completely funded 30 years after a 25 percent decline in the labor force. In addition, the advance funding ratio (i.e., the ratio of assets to liabilities after covering obligations to current retirees) continually declines as a result of the process set in motion by the initial underfunded position and the subsequent work-force reductions. The plan therefore becomes increasingly insolvent each year. These arrangements impose rising costs on successive cohorts of workers, or so it would seem, even as their own benefit security is persistently eroded.

The prospects for different cohorts, of course, ought not be considered in the context of these defined-benefit systems alone. Unlike previous generations, workers reaching adulthood anytime after 1970 face the prospect of giving up a third or more of lifetime earnings to a politically engineered redistribution process over which they exercise minimal control. Most of these funds will be transferred to people of some other age. Meanwhile, those bearing the tax burden are expected to assume a very considerable risk that when they become elderly dependents themselves, the distributive rules may change—and not in their favor.[16]

Dependency burdens in the major industrial countries have doubled between 1900 and 1980, and they are expected to grow another 50 percent between 1980 and 2030. Welfare states, once youth-centered, have refashioned themselves into mechanisms benefiting their elderly populations ahead of all others. This factor, combined with the increasing cost of health care, leaves the state in a position where it will simply be unable to deliver to younger workers the advantages their older fellow citizens once enjoyed. The essence of major welfare activities has become a redistribution of resources between generations rather than between rich and poor as commonly assumed. Generation may even become a factor as important as social class for determining lifetime consumption opportunities. For the moment, however, members of the large post-World War II baby boom cohort have little trouble supporting generous benefits for the elderly because the dependency ratio is still relatively low.[17]

In addition to the cohort equity problem, there is also an age-group equity problem. This stems from the uneven distribution of coinsurance exposure described in Chapter 1. Coinsurance of termination losses imposes potentially huge sacrifices on younger workers whenever the PBGC, even with a massive federal guarantee, takes over a defined-benefit plan. The practice of "backloading," which charges more of the cost of a given dollar in benefits to the later years in a worker's career, can exacerbate this problem. Back-loading, in effect, pays workers a huge premium for seniority.

Many have argued that older workers (those at least in their 50s) should receive a greater measure of protection in these situations because they will have fewer opportunities to reach the point of vesting in some other pension plan. A 30-year-old and a 50-year-old face very different life chances. It makes sense to give the older worker a greater measure of security according to this view. In fact, the authors of ERISA were not concerned about people who spent a dozen years in one job before moving to another for exactly this reason.[18] One weakness in this approach is that any pension loss imposed on the 30-year-old worker is just as irretrievable because that worker will never be 30 again. Imposing a pension loss on that person guarantees that the opportunity for the value of any pension wealth to compound and accumulate for 35 years before the normal retirement age of 65 never will exist again. The time value of money over such a long period can be very great. Fairness across age groups requires that the design of defined-benefit pension plans recognize the fact that younger workers also face losses that they cannot later recover.

One could analyze vesting and backloading[19] issues by adopting something like Daniels's *normative life course*. This, in effect, involves making decisions about optimal consumption-saving choices over a lifetime—and also about the equity claims of workers of different ages—from behind the "veil of ignorance" concerning one's own age.[20] An important problem here, as in more general discussions of generational equity, concerns the need to distinguish between the roles of age-group equity and intercohort equity. Inequality among age-groups presents relatively little problem for a stable retirement system insofar as everyone can be assumed to have the same likelihood of living through each of the stages of life. But note that this assumption fails in systematic ways for certain groups of the population. Men have substantially lower life expectancy than women, minorities have lower life expectancy than whites, and so on. The normative life course therefore will not generate completely fair results, and the problem of fairness across generations can become serious when historical circumstances fluctuate widely.

Still, the results of Daniels's analysis are robust enough to give us good reason to accept a high degree of inequality among burdens and benefits distributed to different age-groups. Daniels's and Rawls's analyses lead to the conclusion that it is "fair" for young people to pay, year after year, much higher health insurance premiums than they are on average likely to benefit from. The reverse condition will obtain for the very old. From a lifespan perspective, this changing and unequal distribution of burdens and benefits can, in principle, be fair, as long as the system remains stable.

Those conditions do not hold for cohort equity because one cohort will never become another in contrast with real individuals who, over a lifetime, take on membership in different age groups. Furthermore, there is no "normative" view of the course of history in the way that there is of the life course. The life course in 2020 no doubt will continue to be one in which old people are more likely to be sick and one in which they will be subject to greater risks as a result. As for changing jobs, it is a point of great significance that the old more likely will be risk averse than the young.

To sum up, vesting and backloading practices that favor older workers can be consistent with widely accepted notions of age-group and intercohort equity only as long as conditions affecting coverage and benefit levels remain relatively stable. Assuring that stability is one way of preserving the original standard of equity and of making sure that people will continue to cooperate in the context of these arrangements. Unfortunately, well-documented trends, involving the long-term solvency of defined-benefit plans as well as demographic shifts in the population, call into question whether that stability is present in the American retirement system today. Under these conditions, limitations on the ability of employers and labor union representatives to increase benefit levels based on "past service" may be necessary in many cases to assure equitable retirement outcomes both for younger plan participants and for future workers. Certainly, the need to know who gets what and when, as well as who pays for the benefits and when, represents a prerequisite for determining whether any pension plan (or the backup insurance system standing behind it) satisfies a reasonable standard of intercohort fairness.[21]

RENEGOTIATING THE
DEFINED-BENEFIT CONTRACT

Any review of the ethical issues specific to the ERISA pension guarantee should examine both the essence of the defined-benefit promise itself and the question of whether the public interest is served by subsidizing and encouraging this particular form of retirement saving. Changes in the structure of the American labor market impinge directly on these assessments. For example, women's participation in the workforce has risen dramatically during the last two decades. Yet, even today, defined-benefit plans are poorly designed to meet the needs of most working women as a result of their discontinuous employment records, linked primarily to childbearing. Like most intermittent workers, women tend to have difficulty accumulating credit for significant retirement income due to the quit losses discussed in Chapter 1.

In addition, job creation has shifted to sectors of the economy where defined-benefit plans are less common and where rates of pension coverage are generally much lower. Consequently, there is a reduced likelihood that workers will even be offered another pension following a job change. These factors suggest that, far from serving as a vehicle for providing workers with deferred compensation and a safe form of personal saving, the traditional defined-benefit pension plan with its transfers and cross subsidies among participants instead creates groups of winners and groups of losers within the labor force. Not surprisingly, this situation discourages prudent behavior and sound retirement planning on the part of workers. In particular, it discourages long-term thinking. Yet, there is little evidence that the original designers of most defined-benefit pension plans fully understood the future social consequences of these features. For a more mobile labor force, the ability of the present defined-beneft concept to provide levels of retirement income commensurate with the opportunity cost of foregone consumption seems to have declined with the passage of time. As a result, the legitimacy of allowing companies to use defined-benefit pension plans as a tool to manage the workforce becomes more and more questionable.

Beyond allowing workers to accumulate claims for retirement income, there are two other policy objectives used to justify federal support for private pensions: to promote national savings, and to raise productivity. Unfortunately, the record of defined-benefit pension plans in both of these areas leaves something to be desired. As Table 2.1 indicates, contributions to defined-benefit pension plans declined by more than 50 percent between 1982 and 1990[22]—from $46 billion to $23 billion—even though the number of participants in these plans remained approximately the same.[23] Economists have cited strong stock market performance as the principal reason for this outcome. Even though the decline in contributions had a sizable adverse effect on national savings,[24] benefit payments tripled during the same period from $22 billion to $66 billion.[25]

Moreover, the rate of productivity growth for the U.S. economy has been disappointingly low, averaging only 1.12 percent annually from 1973 to 1993. The recent performance of these economic variables—both the rate of national saving and productivity growth—raises significant doubt about the effectiveness of costly public incentives to promote the use of defined-benefit plans. Ignoring for a moment all of the direct, indirect, and opportunity costs associated with providing ERISA termination insurance, the U.S. Treasury gives up $60 billion in revenues each year as a result of the tax incentives it provides to encourage the use of private pension plans. Defined-benefit pension plans cause at least a third of this loss, in part, because pension contributions are tax-deductible and returns earned on pension assets are not taxed.

Turning to the employer's point of view, the ability to impose the quit losses associated with defined-benefit plans can be desirable both as a means of ensuring that the company's investment in worker training is recovered and as a means of discouraging "shirking."[26] However, employers are wary of imposing such losses due to the adverse effects on their reputations. When firing or laying off workers because their productivity has declined, employers therefore use severance payments to compensate for lost wages and pension benefits. Such payments represent a mechanism for avoiding damage to the company's good name in the eyes of current and prospective employees. If the severance payment is less than the difference between the worker's wages and his or her value to the firm (i.e., the marginal product), both parties will be better off as a result of the payment. Unfortunately, problems in calibrating sufficient severance pay can mean that portability losses associated with defined-benefit plans will interfere with otherwise desirable redeployment of human resources.[27]

Backloading also has major labor market effects. Even though ERISA limits this practice somewhat, it is still permitted and can greatly increase the cost of employing older workers. This aspect of America's retirement system is working at cross purposes with the established policy of raising the retirement age in the context of Social Security and other public retirement programs. When Congress amended the Social Security Act in 1983 to avoid imminent bankruptcy of the system, it gradually raised the normal retirement age from 65 to 67 starting with individuals born in 1938. Congress also introduced incentives to encourage older workers to work longer—even after the normal retirement age. Conversely, private defined-benefit plans have been used to encourage older workers to leave the labor force at younger and younger ages.

Looking ahead to the time when members of the massive post–World War II baby boom generation retires, the pattern already set by Social Security probably will prevail. At that point, private employers will need to keep many older workers on the job longer as one way of dealing with the projected shortage of skilled labor. The widespread early retirements, to which many of today's older workers can look forward, will become increasingly rare after 2010. This situation suggests the need for a two-sided approach for the continuing evolution of the private pension system. One aspect of this approach would deal with the residual elements of the old industrial system and its defined-benefit plans. The other would focus on the postindustrial sector, consisting primarily of services and small businesses that rely to a much greater extent on part-time, intermittent, and mobile workers. Here, portable retirement balances will dominate.

To summarize, the utilitarian arguments many have used to justify public support for the private defined-benefit plans do not appear strong. Defined-benefit plans have been designed and managed in ways that are either not fully supportive of designated public purposes or contrary to them. Maximum labor market efficiency and national economic output require some mobility in the labor force so that workers can be placed in their most productive jobs. Although quit losses in some cases can serve to deter unproductive job changes and to discourage shirking by workers, the defined-benefit mechanism does not appear to be very well-suited for producing efficient levels of labor mobility in a dynamically changing economy.

THE HIDDEN COST OF PENSION SECURITY

As government programs go, the PBGC is not one that ought to command unqualified ethical admiration for a very simple reason: It is a program designed to provide benefits for a relatively small and well-to-do proportion of the working population and an even smaller proportion of the total population. Far from reducing inequality among the elderly, the program accentuates the inequities of America's pension system because it guarantees benefits that go substantially beyond those provided to retirees in general, not to mention those publicly provided under either Social Security or SSI. Furthermore, a substantial share of this program's real benefits does not go to threatened elderly pensioners but instead to financially irresponsible corporations and other funding intermediaries who reap vast rewards, courtesy of the taxpayers.

In trying to assess the ethical status of the PBGC program from a utilitarian point of view, one would do well to consider the matter from the perspective of *rule utilitarianism.* Rule utilitarianism, in effect, would ask the question: Does the insurance rule tend, overall, to produce greater benefits? Consider, by way of analogy, whether the government should provide public insurance coverage for mountain climbing. The effect of instituting such a rule would be to benefit those impoverished mountain climbers who have accidents and need emergency rescue, followed by health care and income support while they are unable to work, and so on. The package would represent a substantial benefit for those who fall off mountains, assuming of course that they survive to receive it. But, at the same time, the existence of "mountain-climbing insurance" might attract newcomers to the sport who would assume a free ride while undertaking a dangerous hobby.

Just for this reason, some national parks have adopted a different rule: namely, charging mountain climbers for the cost of rescuing them. Failing to impose this burden (the cost of rescue) would create a hidden subsidy. However, a paternalistic or even an authoritarian stance (e.g., prohibiting mountain climbing because, on balance, it is thought to be harmful) need not be adopted in order to provide greater benefits to society as a whole. Instead, the real cost or burden can simply be assigned to those who would benefit from the insurance cover, leaving prospective climbers then to make their own decisions.

The mountain climbing example is not wholly fictitious. Something similar seems to occur, for instance, with the federal flood insurance program. The existence of such insurance, combined with other interventions by the U.S. Army Corps of Engineers, has made it possible for Americans to live in dangerous flood zones. This is a classic case of moral hazard. Only recently, as a result of disastrous midwestern floods, have policymakers seriously considered eliminating this kind of insurance subsidy. The point is not simply that building and insuring houses in flood zones is likely to impose large costs on society by means of a government insurance program. It is that the existence of the insurance subsidy induces others to adopt costly and unsafe practices, with the outcome likely to be harmful even to the inhabitants themselves.

Something similar seems to be occurring with defined-benefit pension plans. The risk of irresponsible fiduciary behavior has risen enormously with the increasing instability of the economy. However, defined-benefit plans, like flood insurance, give participants in the plan a sense of security. For some, that feeling may be justified as long as the public subsidy continues and their pension plans don't terminate. Others will suffer painful dislocation as their underfunded pension plans collapse, even with federal insurance. The temptations created by the insurance make those unfortunate outcomes even more likely than otherwise.

CONCLUSION

Several conclusions flow from this application of ethical principles to the nation's current system of private pension plans as well as to government policies that were imposed as a result of previous failures.

First, a financially sound private pension system can have enormous value for the U.S. economy and American workers generally. However, private defined-benefit plans are not well-suited to meet the needs of today's mobile workforce. At another stage in our history, these plans were set up to encourage workers to do the right thing: to be loyal to their employers, and to discourage shirking. Today, this same form of retirement saving frequently serves to penalize and discourage desirable redeployment of labor in the economy.

Second, defined-benefit plans in practice have repeatedly violated fundamental and widely shared moral principles of promise keeping, truth telling, and prudent safeguarding of assets held in trust for workers and retirees.

Third, the nature of the defined-benefit concept itself creates a temptation to violate moral principles. It is difficult, if not impossible, for many private companies to live up to the required high standard of promise keeping in a world of risk. The effects of these temptations are particularly apparent in a rapidly changing economy.

Fourth, the public response to private pension vulnerability has been an understandable attempt to correct for the losses resulting from failed promises in the past. Yet, that public response has entailed deep moral contradictions of its own. In any reasonably organized system of retirement saving, a guarantee for voluntary private pension plans would not rise to the level of a government responsibility.

Fifth, public pension insurance has brought about a situation where other groups are put at risk. The needs of future generations of workers, pensioners, and taxpayers often have been neglected.

Finally, there has been a failure to acknowledge facts readily available to the regulators and policymakers who are in a position to take corrective action. This problem is disturbingly reminiscent of the savings and loan scandal. Too many groups have developed a vested interest in the status quo: members of Congress, corporate pension fund managers, labor unions, and consultants to the pension community. Their influence often provides those in positions of authority with a powerful incentive to deny the existence of a problem. In view of the magnitude of the risk to vulnerable groups both now and in the future, there is no acceptable alternative but to face the evidence, including the moral contradictions of past efforts.

SUMMARY

The structure and design of the ERISA termination insurance system, together with the private defined-benefit pension plans that it backs up, create temptations to do the wrong thing with potentially disastrous results for those who are vulnerable: retirees, taxpayers, workers, and future generations. Without adequate attention to its ethical foundations, government policy concerning pension insurance inevitably will sink into a deep morass of problems. Such problems have become manifest in many cases, including the Pension Losers Bill, the default by the Executive Life Insurance Company, benefit reductions as well as PBGC attempts to recover nonguaranteed benefits paid to early retirees, and efforts to compel groups of today's workers to repay unfunded pension liabilities from a previous generation.

An ethically viable system of pension guarantees somehow must accommodate a variety of values and concerns that are not always compatible. Among them are paternalism, promise keeping, truth telling, avoidance of conflict of interest, fair treatment and respect for the rights of pension plan participants, respect for the rights of nonparticipants, equity over the lifecourse, and sustainability. The values of promise keeping and truth telling emerge as central to private retirement systems. Autonomy, or freedom of choice, also plays a major role. Meanwhile, quite different moral standards have dominated the design and operation of public retirement systems such as Social Security and the Supplemental Security Income (SSI) program.

As future dangers from overpopulation and pollution became widely recognized, the problem of justice over time developed into a recognized field of inquiry within ethics and political philosophy.

Private defined-benefit pension plans, as they presently exist in the United States, raise some serious questions of intergenerational equity. Society has made a judgment that these arrangements should not be mandatory. Workers therefore have no abstract right to a private pension on the basis of equity or need in the same sense that they have a right to the social minimum for retirement income as defined under Social Security or the SSI program. At this point, further declines in private pension coverage as well as benefit levels appear likely. Costs meanwhile are being shifted in the direction of those who are less likely to receive retirement income from these arrangements. The ERISA termination insurance program represents one mechanism available to facilitate this cost shifting.

When it can be determined that government has an obligation to guarantee retirement benefits, the problem for policymakers becomes identifying the best way to carry out this obligation and setting appropriate limits on what is promised. Certainly the strongest precepts that flow from the idea of justice argue in favor of protecting the social minimum. Yet, there may be grounds for government to guarantee benefits beyond this level, particularly when official policy has promoted the use of private pension plans and then subjected them to lax or defective forms of regulation. Under those circumstances, relatively well-off segments of society compete for scarce public services, and fewer resources remain to meet more urgent needs.

ENDNOTES

1. As noted in Chapter 3, the ERISA allocation rules sometimes require the PBGC to make payments above even the maximum guaranteed level for certain categories of benefits.

2. See Figure 1–3.

3. Some but not all of these participants were later made whole by the companies that benefited from the earlier reversions. See Thomas G. Donlan, *Don't Count on It* (New York: Simon & Schuster, 1994), pp. 87–88.

4. Retired High Court Judge Sir Peter Webster is finalizing a confidential effort to collect £400 million for the Maxwell pension funds without the need for Court action. A London solicitor, Mr. Stuart C. James,

who served on the British government's Pension Law Review Committee, reports that if that goal is reached, it is unlikely that anybody else will know who has contributed what and why. However, it would be technically possible to advance claims of £700 million in an actual Court case. So, the prospective defendants have a clear incentive to contribute something voluntarily rather than run the risk of a Court case involving a lot more. According to Mr. James, some £200 million of the £400 million sought is likely to come from "well wishers" who have no reason to feel guilty but who profited in the past from doing business with the Maxwell companies and feel that, under the circumstances, some of those profits ought to go to pension plan members. Another £100 million will come from those who just want to avoid the bad publicity of being involved in a Court case and are quite happy to make a contribution from a moral viewpoint. The remaining £100 million will come from those who have been put under some pressure, with threats of "bad publicity, legal action, or worse." Mr. James suspects that the last £10 million will be extracted as a result of "threats of a very dire nature." Those threats might be directed against banks as part of an effort to recover shares owned by the Maxwell pension plans. Shares owned by the Maxwell pension plans had been fraudulently conveyed to banks—it is alleged—as collateral for loans to the Robert Maxwell Group.

5. See Peter Laslett and James S. Fishkin, "Introduction: Processional Justice," *Justice between Age Groups and Generations* (New Haven: Yale University Press, 1992), p. 2.

6. Henry J. Aaron, Thomas E. Mann, and Timothy Taylor, *Values and Public Policy* (Washington, DC: The Brookings Institution, 1993), p. 3.

7. See Gordon L. Clark, *Pensions and Corporate Restructuring in American Industry* (Baltimore, MD: Johns Hopkins University Press, 1993), pp. 176–201.

8. See John Rawls, *Political Liberalism* (New York: Columbia University Press, 1993).

9. According to Michael S. Gordon, who participated in drafting ERISA, the termination insurance provisions were enacted independent of tax concerns. The authors of ERISA instead focused on a concept of *minimal decency*. Once defined-benefit pension plans had been set up, legislators wanted them to be sound and not cause problems for workers. The metaphor of auto safety standards apparently had some influence: nobody must buy a car, but government was considered to have an

obligation to those who purchased them. These legislators believed that the government's role was to make sure that such products are safe.

10. James H. Smalhout, "Retirement Woes: Pension Saving Short of the Mark," *The Wall Street Journal,* February 4, 1993, sec. A, p. 18.

11. The National Labor Relations Board (NLRB) made pension and health insurance benefits mandatory subjects for collective bargaining in the 1940s. In *Inland Steel v. NLRB* (1948), a federal court affirmed the NLRB's position. The Supreme Court subsequently refused to review and overturn the lower court ruling.

12. Michael S. Gordon, a Washington attorney who helped draft ERISA as a Senate aide, has pointed out that legislators considered the possibility of guaranteeing the assets in defined-benefit plans. However, Congress rejected the idea because it appeared to entail extensive investment regulation and involved potentially far-reaching insurance of stock market performance.

13. See The World Bank, *Averting the Old Age Crisis,* pp. 3–4.

14. See Steven Sass, "The Heyday of US Collectively Bargained Pension Agreements," in Paul Johnson, Christoph Conrad, and David Thompson, eds., *Workers versus Pensioners: Intergenerational Justice in an Aging World* (Manchester, U.K.: Manchester University Press, 1989), p. 109.

15. R. C. Kryvicky, "The Funding of Negotiated Pension Plans," *Transactions of the Society of Actuaries* 33 (1981), pp. 405–72.

16. See David Thompson, "The Welfare State and Generation Conflict: Winners and Losers," in *Workers versus Pensioners,* p. 36.

17. Ibid., pp. 33–56.

18. I am indebted to Michael S. Gordon, formerly a legislative aide to Senator Jacob Javits, for calling this point to my attention.

19. Backloading results from benefit formulas that provide larger pension accruals as the worker ages or serves the same employer for additional time.

20. Within this framework, people are granted "lifetime prudential accounts." These accounts contain the resources that allow owners the same opportunities typical of their age group, but not necessarily the same opportunities typical of other age groups. See Norman Daniels, *Am I My Parents' Keeper?* (New York: Oxford University Press, 1988).

21. For a discussion of the need to include such an approach in the context of the national economic accounts, see Laurence J. Kotlikoff, *Generational Accounting* (New York: Free Press, 1992).

22. Although some economists consider the obligations of a pension plan to provide a more accurate measure of retirement saving by households, the national income and product accounts compiled by the U.S. Department of Commerce as well as the flow of funds accounts published by the Federal Reserve Board measure pension saving in terms of contributions.

23. The number of active participants declined by less than 10 percent from 23.6 million to 21.4 million. See U.S. Department of Labor, *Private Pension Plan Bulletin,* no. 2, (Summer 1993), p. 24; and John A. Turner and Daniel J. Beller, eds., *Trends in Pensions* (Washington, DC: U.S. Department of Labor, 1992), p. 84.

24. See Alicia H. Munnell, "Explaining the Postwar Pattern of Personal Saving," *The New England Economic Review,* November–December 1991, pp. 17–28.

25. See U.S. Department of Labor, "Abstract of 1990 Form 5500 Annual Reports," *Private Pension Plan Bulletin* 2 (Summer 1993), p. 81.

26. See Edward P. Lazear, "Why Is There Mandatory Retirement?" *Journal of Political Economy* 87 (December 1979), pp. 1261–84.

27. See John A. Turner, *Pension Policy for a Mobile Labor Force* (Kalamazoo, MI: W.E. Upjohn Institute for Employment Research, 1993), p. 142.

7

ALTERNATIVES FOR REFORM

In view of the considerable array of shortcomings associated with the ERISA termination insurance concept, any worthy reform initiative should seek to accomplish a substantial number of goals. At the top of the list, future taxpayers need effective protection against significant potential losses from the program. Although policymakers seem to have become more sensitive to the political consequences of problems with federal insurance programs in the wake of the S&L debacle, a massive bailout of the defined-benefit pension system still isn't sufficiently imminent to make taxpayer protection uppermost in their minds. Instead, there is a compelling political incentive to respond to the well-organized groups that derive more immediate benefit from the program. The S&L crisis demonstrated, however, that a lack of prompt action to limit taxpayer losses in this type of situation eventually can produce catastrophic results.

A second vitally important reform objective should be to restructure the program in ways that resolve the classic insurance problems of adverse selection and moral hazard. As a corollary, steps should be taken to introduce market discipline by bringing insurance values into line with premiums. This implies that a credit analysis should be performed before any employer is allowed to use a pension plan as a vehicle for borrowing from employees. The decision to offer pension insurance and the price of that insurance should then be based on this credit judgment. Unfortunately, credit analysis does not play a role in the current benefit accrual process. One of the implications of market discipline would therefore be to eliminate the hidden subsidy to sponsors of certain defined-benefit plans in the form of underpriced insurance.

In view of the pressures that originally led to adoption of the ERISA pension insurance program, any reforms that could be sustained over time must impose equitable benefit allocation rules on terminating plans as well as those plans that would be temporarily frozen. The pre-ERISA approach, which allowed one group of participants to emerge from a termination completely unscathed while another was forced to give up all of its pension saving, would not be acceptable. Certainly, reform would have far greater appeal if it measurably improved the lot of those younger participants who gain little from PBGC insurance as it is currently structured. Equitable allocation of pension assets upon termination also has a major role to play in eliminating adverse selection and moral hazard.

A third priority for reform should be to avoid adverse employment effects. Clearly, some of the proposals that have been suggested for reducing the PBGC's projected deficit are capable of producing a credit crunch and substantial losses in economic output. Similarly, taxpayers would be unlikely to recover much value as a result of policies designed to foreclose on financially weak sponsors of previously underfunded plans. Requiring these firms to reduce and eventually to eliminate previous unfunded liabilities assumes that they will sell their products in markets where prices can be held above marginal costs. However, most markets are "contestable" in the sense that new firms that aren't similarly burdened will enter them if prices increase to this level. Simply the threat of new competition in most cases will prevent prices from rising sufficiently to amortize unfunded liabilities. The effect of imposing this burden, where such conditions exist, would be to force many firms with unfunded liabilities into liquidation. Misguided policies that have tolerated the buildup of large unfunded liabilities have produced "sunk costs." Only a wrongheaded approach would attempt to recover them, as any attempt to do so could impose even greater costs on the economy.

In less desperate cases involving a financially viable sponsor with substantial unfunded liabilities, many would argue for a requirement that the company fund the previous shortfall over some designated period of time. Although this approach has great intuitive appeal, it is unsound in many cases from a social point of view. Consider Bethlehem Steel. As noted in Chapter 3, employment at the company fell from 117,434 in 1975 to 24,900 in 1992: a decline of 79 percent. As for the unfunded pension liability, it had grown to $2.4 billion by 1977: almost exactly the same level as at the end of 1992. In fact, Bethlehem contributed $1.5 billion from 1987 to 1991 just to prevent this shortfall from growing even larger. If a large group of workers and possibly the company's stockholders reaped a windfall due to poorly conceived funding standards many years ago, the first and best solution would be to return to those groups for the resources to make the plan whole. Today, however, such an approach would be impossible to implement. After more than 15 years and drastic reductions in the labor force, the overwhelming majority of those workers no longer work for the company and the shareholder population undoubtedly has changed substantially as well. Most of the burden for extravagant benefits granted in the 1970s therefore has fallen on very different groups and, at least in the case of workers, that burden would be distributed over a much smaller base.

As a final goal for reform, conflicts among the competing objectives that public officials attempted to serve by establishing the program need to be resolved explicitly in new legislation. Bodie and Merton have suggested that the program in part was motivated to revitalize depressed industries, by assuming some of the cost of providing retirement benefits to workers.[1] Others who participated in drafting ERISA report that lawmakers instead aimed to preserve industries that found themselves threatened in the 1970s, and to protect the employment practices on which those industries had grown dependent.[2] In addition, the PBGC has interpreted its ERISA mandate for encouraging the growth of the private pension system as a justification for promoting defined-benefit pension plans, despite a well-established trend to replace these with defined-contribution plans.

The private pension system does not represent an efficient instrument for stimulating growth in depressed regions and industries; it could do so only at substantial unnecessary cost in the form of a deadweight loss. In fact, the fictitious actuarial and accounting practices that are widespread in this area combine with the guarantee to give managers, owners, and unions an incentive to extract more dividends, inflated salaries, and other emoluments from their firms than they are worth—in essence, to bankrupt them for a profit. The IRS even encourages this destructive behavior, perhaps unawares, by requiring that many pension obligations be undervalued or not reported at all.[3]

Furthermore, many firms face compelling incentives to make the switch to defined-contribution plans in order to attract or retain essential workers. Although the PBGC is understandably concerned about the resulting erosion of its premium base, distorting the sponsor's choice between offering a defined-benefit plan instead of a defined-contribution plan can impose potentially large efficiency costs on the economy. One aspect of this final priority for reform therefore should be the clear and unequivocal delineation of program objectives. If there is to be a government program or simply government-mandated insurance provided by private carriers, then its sole purpose should be to provide appropriate levels of security for promised pension benefits against the risk of default.

Figure 7–1 outlines seven generic approaches to reforming pension insurance in the United States. Those approaches comprise preparation by saving more for the future, correction of perverse price incentives, containment of contingent taxpayer liabilities, and various responses that can be characterized as redistribution (to underscore the fact that they can impose significant costs on groups that failed to benefit from the earlier buildup of unfunded pension liabilities). These generic approaches also include conversion to alternative forms of retirement saving, and reorganization to eliminate the secrecy and blatant conflict of interest that ERISA sanctions in the operation of the official PBGC advisory committee. Reorganization also could involve transferring administrative responsibility for the PBGC to the U.S. Treasury. Finally, some have suggested that accrual accounting for the program in the federal budget would produce a more

F I G U R E 7-1

A Taxonomy of Pension Insurance Reform

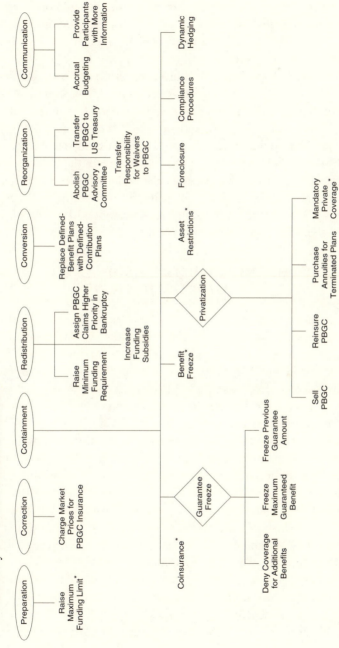

*Indicates a recommended reform if implemented in combination with others.

accurate impression of the distribution of the program's costs and
benefits, and that participants would respond to more information
about the condition of their pension plans. Figure 7–1 therefore iden-
tifies communication as a final generic approach.

Since 1976, legislative proposals from every administration
have brought these approaches together in various combinations and
permutations with, at best, only slightly beneficial effects. To some
extent, the lack of progress has resulted from simple political constraints imposed by well-organized interest groups that stand to lose
subsidies following effective reform. However, the failure to resolve
these problems at an earlier stage also reflects widespread confusion,
even among policymakers, about the ultimate effects of these measures. The remainder of this chapter therefore will review the impact
of the generic approaches we have identified in Figure 7–1.

PROPOSALS FROM THE BUSH AND CLINTON ADMINISTRATIONS

Less than a year before the 1992 presidential election, the Bush administration belatedly produced a multifaceted legislative package
featuring more stringent minimum funding requirements. In addition, President Bush proposed a cap on the guarantee in cases of
underfunded plans, a series of changes in the Bankruptcy Code that
would have improved PBGC's status relative to other creditors, and
a shift to accrual accounting for the PBGC in the federal budget.
These proposals came as a response to conditions that were rapidly
eroding, despite the adoption of the risk-adjusted premium in 1986
and new funding rules that were part of the Omnibus Budget Reconciliation Act of 1987 (OBRA '87). However, Congress declined to
act on these changes before the Bush administration left office.

The Bush administration's proposals suffered from major defects. They ignored the need to bring insurance values into alignment
with premiums. The Administration's emphasis on more stringent
minimum funding requirements was a red herring. The requirements
could have encouraged many financially weak companies to use
the additional pension assets to make high-risk investments and then
liquidate. Risks to the insurance fund could have actually increased

in some cases. In addition, withholding the guarantee from new benefit improvements without freezing all accruals of seriously underfunded plans represented a throwback to the pre-ERISA period.

The Bush administration's proposed bankruptcy changes also were conceptually flawed, because the PBGC could only gain at the expense of other creditors like banks. Although one focal point of the bankruptcy initiatives was simply to obtain clarification of the PBGC's "employer liability" claims, a credit crunch still might have resulted, producing a recession and placing other federal insurance programs at greater risk.[4] When proposing changes along these lines, it is vitally important to distinguish between the treatment of sunk costs associated with the previous buildup of unfunded liabilities and the need for adequate funding of benefits that will be earned in the future. The Bush administration's approach did not make that distinction. As a result, banks and other lenders might have become concerned enough about the status of their existing loans, vis à vis the enhanced PBGC claims, to reduce their exposure to companies responsible for substantial employment around the country. Another problem the Bush proposals failed to address is the severe erosion in corporate net worth shortly before any bankruptcy; this process can all but eliminate any residual value left to pay PBGC claims. Finally, the Bush administration proposed to implement accrual accounting for the program in a manner that would have produced budgetary windfalls. These phantom savings would have occurred because the proposal called for changes in the budget procedures before PBGC cost-saving reforms were implemented. On the whole, the credibility of the Bush package suffered because the purported cost savings would have been used for new spending initiatives instead of for reducing the federal budget deficit.

In late 1993, the Clinton administration released a proposal that emphasized accelerated funding of both previous unfunded liabilities and new benefit improvements. The proposal also called for removal of the cap on the risk-adjusted component of the PBGC premium. (Under previous law, sponsors with underfunded plans paid a variable rate charge of $9 for every $1,000 of unfunded liabilities up to a limit of $53 per participant.) A third aspect of the proposal would assign the PBGC greater enforcement powers to compel funding after mergers, acquisitions, and other corporate restructurings. The agency could also require sponsors of underfunded plans to provide more information to participants about the financial condition of their plan. Finally, the proposal permitted the PBGC to make special exceptions and allowances where the effects of these changes would be "a little too harsh."

Although the Clinton proposal suffered from fewer conceptual defects than the one that came immediately before it, this package also was deeply flawed. The U.S. General Accounting Office estimated that 50 percent of underfunded plan sponsors would initially make no additional contributions under the proposal.[5] This initial weakness became more serious after the legislation was revised and attached to the GATT legislation. Even so, Congress had a powerful incentive to pass the bill. It generated an estimated $1.1 billion in additional PBGC premiums that could be used to offset tariff revenues lost as a result of the GATT agreement. Unfortunately, the version of the bill that Congress ultimately adopted may not prevent further increases in underfunding. That version included a variety of permanent and transitional provisions that exempts some plans from more stringent funding rules or reduces the immediate impact of the rules. Companies will be able to remove "surplus" pension assets—which in most cases are not surplus—to pay for retiree health benefits. "Volatility relief" will be granted to plans when they become less than 90 percent funded.[6] The previous cutoff had been 100 percent. The range of interest rate assumptions that the Clinton administration originally proposed was also extended, allowing plan sponsors to report lower values for benefit obligations.[7] All this, together with the earlier attempts to resolve the PBGC's problems, were fundamentally misguided for the reasons we discuss next.

THE GENERIC APPROACHES

Preparation

A first generic approach to reform would permit employers to make additional tax-deductible contributions to their defined-benefit pension plans. The current limit, set by the OBRA '87, prohibits all contributions to defined-benefit pension plans if assets exceed 150 percent of "current" liabilities, valued on a quasi-termination basis or 100 percent of the PBO, whichever is lower.[8] The motivation for the provision was to reduce the cost of the tax preference for pension contributions. However, it created additional risks for the PBGC because the value of plan obligations on an ongoing basis can greatly exceed their corresponding value on a termination basis, depending on the distribution of participants according to their age and length of service.[9] As Bodie points out, these two valuations of the same pension liabilities coincide at just two points: the beginning of employment, and much later, when the worker retires.

Other countries that rely on prefunded private pensions permit considerably higher funding levels compared to the OBRA '87 maximum limit. For example, the United Kingdom permits funding to a level of 5 percent beyond the going-concern measures of either the PBO or the IBO.[10] In Ontario, plans also are funded on a going-concern basis, including projected salary increases, in a manner that is roughly tantamount to the PBO. Canada, however, prohibits book reserve financing and requires any unfunded liabilities to be amortized over 15 years. The Netherlands has a minimum funding requirement that appears to well exceed the OBRA '87 maximum. The rate of interest used for discounting the liabilities of Dutch pension plans cannot exceed 4 percent. Beyond that, the plans also must maintain excess funding of between 3 and 10 percent of total liabilities.[11]

Figure 7–2 reports benchmark contribution rates with and without the OBRA '87 full funding limit, assuming the "projected unit credit" method for allocating the cost of a given dollar of benefits to each year in the worker's career.[12] This method has become increasingly popular since 1987 as a result of the implementation of a new accounting standard that requires its use in corporate financial reports to shareholders. It involves substantial backloading of pension costs (i.e., postponing more of the burden for funding benefits until late in a worker's career), but is optional under IRS regulations for determining the plan's legal funding requirements.

The OBRA '87 maximum funding limit represents a problem from the PBGC's point of view, because it places severe limits on

F I G U R E   7–2

Effects of the OBRA '87 Full Funding Limits
(Contribution Rates by Age)

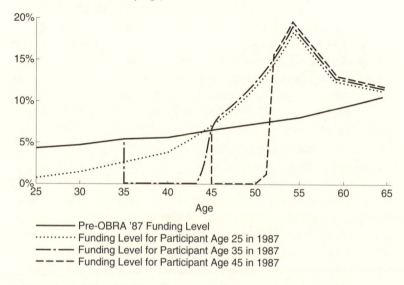

──────── Pre-OBRA '87 Funding Level
· · · · · · · · · · Funding Level for Participant Age 25 in 1987
── · ── Funding Level for Participant Age 35 in 1987
── ── ── Funding Level for Participant Age 45 in 1987

the ability of plan sponsors to fund their pension plans with a stable
and affordable level of contributions. As a result, contributions on
behalf of substantial numbers of workers—particularly members of
the demographic bulge known as the *baby boom generation*—will
be eliminated entirely in some years before rising to more than 18
percent of pay later. One possible result of this constraint could be a
shift in the age distribution of workers covered by pension plans affected by the OBRA '87 limit. Employers generally would prefer to
terminate workers covered by these plans before contribution burdens begin to rise precipitously. In industries and companies that
will rely heavily on workers born after 1952, pressures could grow
to alter radically the terms of these plans or to terminate them altogether by the turn of the century.

Alternatively, the sponsor could elect to use an actuarial cost
method that loads more of the cost of each dollar of benefits onto the
early years of a worker's career. This, however, would entail additional costs for sponsors that have issued publicly traded securities.

Those companies still would need to comply with generally accepted accounting principles when reporting to shareholders. As a result, the value of plan liabilities and the associated amortization charges would have to be computed in two different ways: once using the projected unit credit method; and a second time using the more conservative approach to estimating the current actuarial cost of the plan.

Many of the financially stronger employers undoubtedly will recognize the advantages of converting their defined-benefit pension plans to defined-contribution plans when funding requirements begin to rise.[13] Other companies will inevitably find themselves in dire straits. The best strategy for those sponsors will conform with the familiar pattern of defunding observed today among declining firms, as they take maximum advantage of the subsidy implicit in the ERISA guarantee. Within these parameters, the demographic influence of the aging baby boom generation will determine the increased funding requirements in many of these cases. The PBGC therefore could face reduced premium revenues. These forces could induce many healthy plan–sponsor combinations to convert to defined-contribution plans just when many increasingly underfunded defined-benefit plans begin placing new demands on the insurance fund.

Removing the OBRA '87 maximum funding limit would permit the buildup of additional surplus pension assets in advance of the peak funding requirements attributable to the baby boom generation. However, this approach is no panacea. Increasing the maximum funding limit will not change the incentive to defund a defined-benefit plan when the sponsor goes into a corporate death spiral and then liquidates.

Correction

A second generic approach to reform consists of correcting the perverse behavioral incentives that result from subsidized insurance by setting PBGC premiums to reflect their full market value. Both the Reagan and Clinton administrations took limited steps in this direction. However, no risk-adjusted premium proposed before now comes close to reflecting the market value of the insurance, and the classic insurance problem of moral hazard continues to encourage undesirable behavior. Moreover, the value of the insurance is so large that charging market premiums would cause a massive buildup of the PBGC trust fund reserves.

Such a buildup would raise many of the same issues that apply to the growing trust fund reserves currently being accumulated by the social security system. If such a buildup were used to increase national saving, it would add to the nation's capital stock and increase future production. Future workers therefore would be in a better position to absorb added burdens associated with the termination of large and poorly funded pension plans in the distant future. On the other hand, the additional economic output needed to support the future cost of the program will not materialize if the excess of current premiums over immediate outlays instead is used to support more spending for consumption elsewhere in the federal budget. This, of course, is exactly how the current PBGC budgetary surpluses are used. Merely correcting the adverse behavioral incentives created by the program therefore may not eliminate many of its undesirable consequences for taxpayers in the future.

Containment

As Figure 7–1 indicates, a substantial array of alternatives have been identified to contain future program costs. Four of them, implemented in combination, are essential for bringing this problem under control. In fact, they represent the core of any effective reform proposal. Those recommended measures, together with others that have been suggested as ways of containing PBGC losses, are evaluated here.

Coinsurance

Coinsurance is an essential feature of any sound insurance arrangement. One of the highest priorities for PBGC reform should be ensuring that each pension plan participant faces an effective but equitable level of coinsurance. Maintaining a consistent level of coinsurance across the participant age distribution and in the presence of interest rate changes becomes possible when benefits are insured in real terms.

Today, guaranteed benefits are frozen in nominal terms on the date of plan termination as described in Chapter 1. This feature of the ERISA program imposes the greatest termination losses on younger workers, because inflation erodes the value of expected benefits between the termination date and their retirement. Those expectations, in part, are based on the assumption that pre-retirement earnings will grow by at least the rate of inflation. In most defined-benefit plans, pension income either is linked to the participant's final salary or it is negotiated by a labor union to reflect some fraction of wage levels prevailing at the time of retirement. For their part, retirees tend to receive only partial inflation adjustments, which the sponsor grants voluntarily. The insured benefit therefore could not reflect complete indexation following retirement, for the coinsurance feature to be fully effective.

To see how an effective coinsurance system might work, consider the example of a pension plan that terminates with assets sufficient to cover only 40 percent of projected liabilities after recoveries on all bankruptcy claims.[14] At a 50 percent rate from the first dollar of loss, coinsurance therefore would expose 30 percent of each participant's expected benefits. In contrast with the present system, where some workers lose 90 percent of expected benefits while others lose only 10 percent, participants in each terminating plan would lose by the same proportion. Payments from the insurance fund—when considered with available plan assets—therefore would allow all plan participants to emerge from the termination in this example with 70 percent of their expected benefits.

Freezing the Guarantee
Capping the guarantee can be done in at least three different ways with very different effects on plan participants. Prospects that lawmakers would sustain these changes over an extended period of time also vary substantially. First, Congress could eliminate the guarantee for additional benefit accruals in cases of seriously underfunded plans. After the remaining guaranteed benefits were paid, future workers would then be forced to absorb the full unfunded liability when the plan finally terminated. In fact, the Bush administration included this approach in legislation proposed in early 1992. Although

this throwback to the pre-ERISA period could provide taxpayers increasing protection with the passage of time, it probably would not be sustained, for the same reasons that initially led to ERISA two decades ago.

Second, Congress could freeze the maximum guaranteed benefit for 1995 of $30,886 per year. Unfortunately, this type of freeze would have very little effect on the magnitude of the problem for years to come, as relatively few plan participants have earned guaranteed benefits approaching the current maximum. In the meantime, the condition of many seriously underfunded plans would continue to erode.

Third, Congress simply could freeze the unfunded guaranteed amount, with new accruals becoming guaranteed as old guaranteed benefit obligations were paid. Although tremendous complexities could develop during implementation, this last approach is probably the most sustainable, from a long-term political point of view, because no group of future workers would be left completely without guaranteed benefits.

To conclude, a freeze on the guarantee could provide taxpayers with additional protection. Unfortunately, it fails to address many of the incentive problems that became conspicuous in this area before ERISA was enacted as well as after. This shortcoming would leave certain groups of workers more exposed to termination losses than necessary, in order to contain the costs of the program.

Freezing the Benefits

A freeze on benefits, both on additional accruals and improvements, would reflect an entirely different view of government's role in protecting worker rights. A benefit freeze—in contrast to a freeze on the guarantee—would protect workers in the future from being forced to absorb the cost of additional unfunded liabilities that had been allowed to accumulate without a guarantee. If implemented in conjunction with an effective stop-loss mechanism, a benefit freeze would prevent companies from making false promises to their employees that could be kept only at the expense of the insurance fund. It also would send a clear signal to workers affected by the freeze that adequate preparations were not being made for their retirement. Workers then would know to set aside more funds on their own or to renegotiate compensation with their employer so that the pension plan could be restored to financial health. Some companies, together with their workers, might prefer to replace a frozen defined-benefit plan with a defined-contribution plan or to purchase deferred group annuities from an independent insurance company. In this context, it is interesting to note that several private companies with poorly funded defined-benefit plans have voluntarily imposed freezes on benefit accruals. Pan Am was among them. One of the lessons from the Pan Am termination was that the PBGC's losses can grow even following such a freeze, although at a reduced pace. A benefit freeze has much to recommend it but would need to be augmented by other reforms.

Privatization

Privatization represents an indispensable facet of any plan to halt the growth of risks to taxpayers. The arguments used to support federal deposit insurance clearly don't apply in the case of the pension program. In banking, federal insurance has been seen as a means to prevent panics, the resulting "runs" on banks rumored to be insolvent, and a general breakdown in the payments system. These events often had negative and far-reaching consequences for the broader economy before federal deposit insurance. However, the consensus in support of having government retain the power to intervene in a financial panic does not extend to a belief that risk prevention should take the form of a deposit insurance guarantee.[15]

Similar panics would be virtually impossible among the participants of defined-benefit pension plans. Pension obligations are far less liquid than bank deposits. Participants cannot line up at the door to the plan administrator's office demanding their money in one payment. No payments typically are made to active workers. Furthermore, retirees receive regular monthly checks, thus providing the plan with much more effective control over the rate of cash disbursements compared to that retained by a typical bank or savings and loan. Single payments to plan participants are made only to those eligible for lump-sum distributions at the time that they retire.

Even in the unlikely event that a panic were to develop in the pension system and large numbers of participants somehow tried to withdraw their accumulated retirement saving at almost the same time, the consequences for the economy as a whole would be much less severe. The banking system's ability to process payments would not be affected. As a result, commerce would continue as before, and there would be no loss of output. Furthermore, there is no "market failure" that would prevent private insurance companies from offering pension insurance if the federal government adopted a plan to withdraw or curtail its involvement in this area. How, then, should privatization be introduced if federal pension insurance is, at best, superfluous to a well-functioning economy and prone to high costs of political interference?

Sell the PBGC   A first option would be divestiture. State-owned enterprises are frequently inefficient and overstaffed, largely due to the high cost of political interference. As a result of the increasing pressure on government budgets worldwide, divestiture now has many precedents. The sale of British Steel in 1953 is one example. Korean Airlines was privatized in 1968. More recently, the transfer of state enterprises to private owners has accelerated with the sale of the Mexican telephone company and wholesale privatization programs in formerly socialist economies. Most unprofitable state-owned enterprises need to be radically restructured before they can be sold to private investors; or, at least, a plan must exist to reorganize them shortly after privatization. One observer summed up the political realities of these situations in the following couplet:

> If a public enterprise is making money,
>   the government won't sell it;
> If it's losing money,
>   the private sector won't buy it.[16]

Oddly, these conditions simultaneously apply in the case of the PBGC. For the government, the agency's revenues soon will exceed benefit payments to current retirees by approximately $1 billion per year. Under budget agreements since 1990, this positive cash flow makes additional spending possible for programs within the jurisdiction of congressional education and labor committees. Powerful political interests therefore face incentives to oppose divestiture for this reason alone. At the same time, there is widespread recognition that the PBGC has been insolvent from the day it was established. So, the agency would need radical restructuring in order to make the sale possible from a buyer's point of view. On balance, this alternative appears unlikely to succeed.

Reinsure the PBGC   A second approach to privatization would be to reinsure the PBGC. Established reinsurance companies could do business with the PBGC using contracts similar to those developed for dealing with private financial guarantors.[17] There are two broad categories of reinsurance arrangements in use today: *treaty reinsurance* and *facultative reinsurance.*

In a treaty relationship, the reinsurer assumes a specified portion of all policies written by the primary underwriter during a designated time period. Two types of treaty agreements have become common: a *proportional treaty* and an *excess of loss treaty.* In a proportional treaty, the reinsurer reimburses the primary insurer based on either a fixed or variable share of the exposure and starting with the first dollar of loss. In an excess of loss treaty, the reinsurer does not pay claims until losses exceed a specified amount. Some pension plan participants already provide a form of excess of loss protection to the PBGC under the current coinsurance arrangement, because they absorb any unfunded liabilities for benefits exceeding the guaranteed amount.[18] In bond insurance, the terms of a treaty arrangement typically are negotiated annually. One advantage of a treaty relationship is its lower cost per transaction when compared to facultative reinsurance.

In a facultative arrangement, the reinsurer conducts a separate credit analysis for each insured risk, and then negotiates individual terms based on this assessment. Given the added expense attributable to these tasks, facultative reinsurance tends to be used primarily in cases of large bond issues where the primary insurer is capacity constrained. In other words, it otherwise would exceed limits on the insurance that can be provided to a single enterprise or jurisdiction. Given the government's relatively large exposure to unfunded liabilities generated by plans with more than 1,000 participants, a facultative arrangement involving the PBGC and established reinsurers could be an effective tool for limiting taxpayer losses, particularly as part of a transition to a mandatory but completely private guarantee system. Of course, the facultative approach involves slightly higher administrative costs than the treaty approach, as a result of the company-specific credit analysis.

If this alternative were adopted, the PBGC would need to monitor the financial condition of those reinsurers participating in the arrangement. This much is standard practice when reinsurance is used today. Primary insurers in the private financial guarantee industry face powerful incentives to select financially strong reinsurers and then to monitor their strength carefully, because the primary insurers themselves retain ultimate responsibility for any future claims. Some rating agencies also consider the strength of the reinsurers when evaluating the capital adequacy of the primary insurers. In turn, the reinsurers themselves often reinsure their own risk exposure by "retroceding" a portion of it to still other insurance companies.

Under this arrangement, insurance companies would absorb the PBGC's losses above a specified amount or on a proportional basis from the first dollar of loss. However, private insurance providers almost certainly would insist on periodic renewal options. As a result, the terms and cost of the additional protection would be subject to frequent change. If conditions seriously deteriorated, reinsurance might not be available at all. In Finland, reinsurance was effectively discontinued after it had been used for many years to back up a similar guarantee provided by an agency of the government. The situation in Finland raises the question of whether the PBGC would be capable of developing stable, long-term relationships with reinsurers. On the other hand, even if reinsurance could be used to protect the PBGC from catastrophic losses, there still would be no effective mechanism to control the growth of unfunded liabilities once plans became insolvent. And, too, reinsurance would have little impact on the overall solvency of the program. The mandatory private coverage, which represents the basis for the market-based solvency test discussed shortly, would be preferable for these reasons.

Purchase Private Annuities for Terminated Plans   This alternative would transfer much of the administrative work which the PBGC now performs (maintaining participant records, making benefit payments, managing investments, etc.) to private life insurance companies. Certainly private insurance carriers are at least as capable of performing these functions as a government agency. This alternative would also result in more accurate scorekeeping compared to current accounting for the cost of the program under federal budget procedures. The cost of the annuities would appear in the federal budget for the year during which it was incurred. Unfortunately, this alternative would not address the fundamental insurance problems of the current program that we reviewed in Chapter 1: adverse selection and moral hazard.

Mandate Private Coverage   Mandatory private coverage could effectively secure long-term benefit obligations while internalizing the market price of risk taking within the plan–sponsor combination. Properly designed, it could resolve the moral hazard problem that has plagued the ERISA termination insurance program since its inception. Although private carriers already offer pension termination insurance on a very limited scale,[19] the private financial guarantee industry would need to undergo substantial change in order to meet the demand if termination insurance were mandated for all private tax-qualified defined-benefit pension plans. The industry would, for instance, need to assemble substantial new human resources in order to conduct the necessary credit and actuarial analysis. It would also need to raise large amounts of capital funds in an orderly fashion. Is the private market for financial guarantees capable of assuming major responsibility for securing private pension benefits? The background concerning the industry is as follows.

On a very fundamental level, the companies already active in this market are established, going concerns, complying fully with legal requirements in the states that allow only monoline financial guarantee companies to provide this type of insurance. In addition, the companies have attracted significant equity capital; they count among their shareholders some of the nation's most important financial institutions. Equity participants include GE Capital Corporation, US WEST Capital Corporation, and a variety of well-known foreign and domestic multiline insurance companies. Public shareholders also own substantial positions in four of the seven primary bond insurance companies that serve this market. In turn, most of the primary bond insurance companies also make substantial use of reinsurance.

Beginning in the early 1980s, this entirely new industry has sprung up to provide financial guarantees for publicly traded bonds, most of which are issued by state and local political subdivisions borrowing funds in the tax-exempt municipal bond market. A closely related insurance product is known as a *surety*.[20] Before California passed a municipal bond insurance statute in 1985, most states regulated bond insurance and other financial guarantees as sureties. As of December 31, 1992, seven insurers with approximately $4.3 billion in stockholders' equity were writing bond insurance contracts. These primary insurers can either retain their entire exposure or cede a portion of it and the corresponding premiums to a reinsurer, using methods described in the preceding section. The effect of reinsurance is to increase the primary insurer's underwriting capacity without adding to capital requirements that are set by regulators and the major credit rating agencies. Although reinsurance and other forms of "soft capital" are viewed less favorably by the rating agencies, Standard & Poor's reported that the primaries still rely on it for a weighted average of 15.8 percent of base capital.[21] S&P has established a 33 percent usage limitation for maximum prudent reliance on soft capital.

The act of providing a financial guarantee is often referred to as *credit enhancement* because it represents an "upgrade" in credit quality.[22] In credit enhancement, an insured bond receives a higher credit rating than it otherwise would, thereby improving the issue's marketability and enabling the issuer to obtain the use of funds at lower interest costs. By purchasing a financial guarantee, the borrower in effect rents a higher credit rating from a stronger credit. Financial guarantees can also be used to protect against losses resulting from changes in the level of interest rates, changes in foreign exchange rates, changes in the value of specific commodities, even the movement of general price indices.

In 1980, companies previously had insured a cumulative $1.7 billion in tax-exempt bonds. Less than 5 percent of the new-issue market was guaranteed. By 1992, however, the total cumulative insured volume had grown dramatically, to $320 billion, and 33 percent of the new-issue market was being insured. Observers have cited a number of reasons for this dramatic growth: the increasing need for funds on the part of states and municipalities; a shift in the ownership of tax-exempt bonds from institutional investors, particularly banks, to individuals; financial weakness on the part of some of the largest municipal borrowers; and the traumatic $2.25 billion default by the Washington Public Power Supply System in 1983.

To help control risk, bond insurance companies have developed credit surveillance capabilities. These activities consist of periodic reviews designed to detect a deterioration in credit quality at an early stage as well as to permit the insurance company to intervene promptly in order to prevent or minimize losses. The process begins shortly after the initial sale of the bond issue in question. At that point, the staff of the financial guarantee company prepares a detailed report concerning the events and concerns that deserve scrutiny in the future. The bond insurance company's surveillance staff then develops ongoing procedures for monitoring the credit.

Existing bond insurance companies would be indispensable participants in a possible future market for private pension guarantees. The development of this market beyond its current embryonic state would create the conditions necessary for stable risk sharing among plan participants, their employers, and insurance providers. However, the current group of primary financial guarantee firms is not likely to be capable of meeting all of the demand, even with extensive reliance on coinsurance, reinsurance, and new capital. Large multiline insurance companies not currently involved in the financial guarantee industry therefore would be logical candidates to form new monoline subsidiaries to participate in this market.

Asset Restrictions

Within the containment approach to pension reform, another essential option (for use in combination with others) would restrict the investments of poorly funded plans sponsored by financially weak employers. Ironically, the risk of the combined enterprise can actually increase as this type of company makes additional contributions to its pension plans. This counterintuitive result can arise from the fact that each additional dollar contributed to the plans puts the company closer to bankruptcy. Meanwhile, the new pension assets more likely than not will be invested in stocks which, by definition, are riskier than bonds. In effect, the sponsor borrows additional capital, thereby reducing its equity cushion in order to make risky pension investments. An essential method for controlling risk therefore would limit portfolios of poorly funded plans to investment grade bonds.[23] This would prevent firms from engaging in the familiar practice of "gambling for redemption," which became widespread in the savings and loan industry.

Foreclosure

As noted in Figure 7–1, another option proposed for containing the cost of the program is foreclosure. As Americans learned from the savings and loan crisis, timely foreclosure on insolvent financial institutions can be vital for protecting the insurance fund and, ultimately, taxpayers as well. Sadly, powerful political forces prevented public officials from acting soon enough to prevent the savings and loan debacle. The process of widespread foreclosure began long after hundreds of institutions had accumulated massive losses.

A very similar process now is at work in the pension field. The PBGC has the authority to terminate any pension plan that represents an "unreasonable risk" to the insurance fund. Yet, it has not used this authority in many years, despite large and growing unfunded liabilities in plans sponsored by financially vulnerable companies. Some in government even prefer to postpone termination until the last possible moment, when the damage is greatest, because the delay enables them to maximize the value of subsidies provided to politically important constituencies.

Still, there are important distinctions relative to the problems of the S&L crisis. In the context of pension insurance, the combined financial strength of the sponsor and the pension plan will determine the need for foreclosure. Where the combined enterprise remains solvent despite a large unfunded pension liability, a benefit freeze— together with investment restrictions—represent a more appropriate approach to containing losses. Under those conditions, outright foreclosure on the pension plan could precipitate a liquidity crisis for the sponsor, resulting in the liquidation of a viable enterprise. If these outcomes became widespread, the economy could experience significant unnecessary costs in the form of higher unemployment and lost production. The case for foreclosure is compelling in a limited number of situations, but politically motivated managers in government are most unlikely to resort to this approach until long after insolvency occurs. Furthermore, foreclosure by the insurance fund would represent the most appropriate outcome in fewer cases if less drastic measures were used to contain costs at earlier stages of financial decline.

Compliance Procedures

Another approach to containing the insurance fund's future losses consists of stronger compliance procedures. In this area, the Clinton administration proposed a series of nine reforms that would expand the PBGC's powers to induce more pension funding following corporate transactions such as the divestiture of businesses with poorly funded pension plans. The agency complained that its only recourse in these situations is the termination of the plan before the transaction is completed. While many of these expanded powers are entirely reasonable and appropriate, it would be folly to assume that regulators would exercise them diligently where the political will to do so is lacking. In the end, Congress either dropped the most important of these proposals from the Retirement Protection Act of 1994 or weakened them significantly.[24]

Dynamic Hedging

A final approach to containing the PBGC's future losses has been suggested by Professor Zvi Bodie. As Professor Bodie correctly points out:

> When a pension plan sponsor invests the pension assets in stocks, the actuarial present value cost to the PBGC of providing a guarantee against a shortfall increases rather than decreases with the length of the time horizon, even for plans that are fully funded.[25]

Bodie continues by noting that the PBGC is exposed to two types of risk: interest rate risk and stock market risk. The insurance fund could hedge its exposure to interest rate risk through immunization, and could hedge its stock market risk through a short position in stock index futures.

Although the exposure to both risks is large and would be fully hedged in an ideal world, this proposal is not a panacea either. The PBGC is exposed to other sources of risk, including credit risk, adverse selection, moral hazard, and a variety of political risks. Dynamic hedging therefore could protect against only some of the threats facing the PBGC. Should these problems be resolved as a result of a more comprehensive approach to restructuring the ERISA pension guarantee, private financial guarantors would no doubt use hedging strategies for the reasons cited by Bodie. For its part, the PBGC presently lacks the trading and supervisory skills necessary to manage a containment strategy involving this level of sophistication. Trading losses incurred by the Treasurer of Orange County, California, underscore the importance of adequate management safeguards and supervision. Even major financial institutions such as Baring Securities and others have stumbled in this area.[26] Outside the Federal Reserve Bank of New York, it would not be realistic to expect that an operational group with the required skills could be assembled and maintained within the Federal Government. One more unresolved question relative to the PBGC involves the impact on the Federal budget of potentially sizable trading gains in some years and losses in others.

Redistribution

Another generic category of reforms consists of two alternatives that have appeared repeatedly in legislation proposed by various administrations. These approaches can be characterized in many ways. However, the potentially sizable transfers that could result—and their adverse effects on groups that did not benefit from the previous buildup of unfunded pension liabilities—represent a particularly important source of concern. These approaches are therefore referred to as *redistribution.*

Almost every administration has attempted to find some way to raise the minimum funding requirement. However, requiring more pension contributions from financially weak sponsors only increases the probability of default on the unfunded pension obligations. As noted above, this argues for the imposition of investment restrictions, together with a freeze on benefit accruals that both the Clinton and Bush administrations overlooked. Otherwise, the additional pension assets will, more likely than not, be invested in riskier investments and contingent claims against the insurance fund could actually increase. The adoption of a more stringent minimum funding standard therefore does not represent an effective way of controlling the cost of the termination insurance program—at least, not without a benefit freeze and contingent immunization. Inequities associated with the cost of funding previous unfunded liabilities were discussed in Chapter 6.

A second redistributive approach for addressing the PBGC's problems involves additional funding subsidies. The federal government currently provides tax incentives to promote the use of employer-sponsored pension plans. These provisions include an immediate deduction for contributions as well as an exemption from tax on investment returns from plan assets. This tax treatment allows workers to defer pay until retirement and to defer the resulting income tax over the same period. These incentives are among the costliest tax expenditures for the federal government, involving estimated annual revenue losses of more than $60 billion.

A recent example of an *ad hoc* increase in tax subsidies beyond this level involved GM's contribution of 173,163,187 shares of Class E stock to its pension plan for members of the United Auto Workers Union. GM's Class E stock pays dividends from the earnings of its subsidiary: Electronic Data Systems. GM originally bought EDS from Ross Perot for $2.6 billion in 1984 and it was worth an estimated $22 billion by 1995. The company previously reported that its UAW plan was underfunded by $19.5 billion.

ERISA prohibits this type of transaction, but the company applied to the PBGC and the Department of Labor for a special exemption. When it received the exemption, GM avoided paying an excise tax of 10 percent on the value of Class E shares that exceeded the party-in-interest investment limitation. In addition, the company avoided capital gains taxes on part of its investment in EDS because it contributed GM stock instead of stock in a GM subsidiary. However, the IRS subsequently authorized a tax-free exchange of all GM Class E stock for newly issued shares in EDS. The combined effect could be described as allowing GM to make a special one-time contribution of the stock and then having the government top it up by another $2 billion or $3 billion. This additional subsidy amounted to about $4,000 per participant. The true cost, however, never appeared in the federal budget. Numerous commentators and economists criticize the use of tax expenditures in general for exactly this lack of transparency.

The case for increasing tax subsidies, either on an *ad hoc* basis or across the board, is weak. As the Congressional Budget Office noted concerning their application to retirement saving:

> though these advantages boost retirement incomes, they probably do not significantly raise personal saving rates. In addition, the retirement income gains traceable to these advantages are skewed to highly paid workers and, even more so, to workers who spend 20 years or more under one pension plan. Yet all other taxpayers—including workers who are never covered by a plan or who change jobs relatively often—bear the costs . . . in the form of higher tax rates, lower government spending, or increased federal debt.[27]

Another misunderstood but frequently proposed form of redistribution consists of assigning PBGC claims higher priority in bankruptcy. Proponents of this approach explain it as a de facto form of privatization that would transfer the surveillance function from government regulators to banks and other private creditors. They argue that by subordinating other bankruptcy claims to those of the PBGC, the terms of private lending would become more reflective of the sponsor's financial condition inclusive of the pension plan. This approach is conceptually flawed because the agency could only gain at the expense of other creditors, such as commercial banks. The sunk costs associated with unfunded pension liabilities that were allowed to accumulate in the past would be shifted unfairly to other constituencies. As one economist put it, "Widows and orphans own bonds, too."[28]

To the extent that banks and other private creditors could expect to suffer, they would become more reluctant to lend to corporations that sponsored defined-benefit pension plans. A "credit crunch" might result that could even cause a recession. And other federal insurance programs (e.g., deposit insurance) could be placed at greater risk. This pessimistic scenario might be avoided if the bankruptcy changes were introduced early during a recovery stage in the business cycle, when the demand for credit is low. However, the likelihood that government would adeptly time the implementation of this reform does not seem great in view of the well-known difficulty of Congress and the executive branch to administer a successful countercyclical fiscal policy.

Conversion

A fifth generic approach would emphasize conversion from defined-benefit plans to defined-contribution plans. Conversion would represent a method for reducing the PBGC's exposure to new unfunded liabilities that might develop in the future. Clearly, defined-contribution plans have much to recommend them for other reasons. As highly skilled workers begin to retire in greater numbers, companies will need to offer benefits capable of attracting trained younger workers while keeping older workers on the job longer. Defined-contribution plans are generally better equipped to offer these incentives because they don't penalize job hopping or working past the normal retirement age.[29] Meanwhile, other researchers have found that defined-contribution plans yield a higher average return for most workers and reduce income inequality among the elderly. In addition, they appear to match or exceed the implied retirement income from defined-benefit plans, notwithstanding the tendency for younger workers to spend the lump-sum distributions when changing jobs.[30]

Despite these attractive characteristics of defined-contribution plans, the PBGC has tried to promote defined-benefit plans out of a perceived necessity to preserve its premium income. The mere presence of highly subsidized termination insurance no doubt has dissuaded many firms from joining the trend toward defined-contribution plans. However, there is no economic reason for public policy to favor one type of pension plan over the other.[31] Both plan types have advantages and disadvantages. For their part, defined-benefit plans reduce postretirement uncertainty for workers by providing a specified monthly benefit for life. The goal for public policy should be to create an environment in which sponsors can choose between the two plan types based on the suitability of their respective features. This need for neutrality argues for eliminating the insurance subsidy. However, it does not support a case for using the PBGC's problems to justify measures designed to precipitate defined-benefit conversions.

Reorganization

The sixth generic approach to reform consists of reorganizing the PBGC. One possibility would involve the abolition of the PBGC board of directors and the advisory committee. These peculiar bodies are a product of a political compromise forged when ERISA was drafted. Some members of Congress were deeply suspicious of placing responsibility for the insurance program in the hands of political appointees. They argued for the creation of a large board of directors that would include several nonpolitical pension experts. Other members debated whether the Secretary of Labor or the Secretary of the Treasury should chair a group composed entirely of government officials. The two sides resolved the problem by agreeing to create two groups: a board of directors chaired by the Secretary of Labor, with the Secretary of the Treasury and the Secretary of Commerce serving as the other members; and an advisory committee, consisting of seven members from outside government.

This arrangement has been criticized elsewhere for diluting administrative responsibility for the PBGC and denying it the degree of operating and financial flexibility essential for effective business activity. Another study concluded that the board of directors should be abolished for this reason and that the PBGC should be placed under the "policy direction and supervision" of the Secretary of Labor. The same study also recommended that administrative responsibility for the agency should reside there in the hands of a chief executive officer. It further suggested that the CEO should have the authority to appoint members of an advisory committee based on the needs of the agency. Members currently are appointed by the President. The appointment process has not always been satisfactory for the agency, because it often involves long delays and a reluctance on the part of potential members to subject themselves to the demands necessary to obtain clearance.[32]

The advisory committee consistently has been composed of individuals with a very substantial stake in the insurance program. Even the one member currently charged with responsibility for representing the public interest comes from an organization that depends on the defined-benefit community for much of its funding. The fact that ERISA exempts this group from the requirements of the Federal Advisory Committee Act enables it to operate in complete secrecy. The principle of allowing those who are regulated by a federal agency to advise it with no public scrutiny whatsoever creates blatant conflicts of interest and the opportunity for abuse. The PBGC advisory committee therefore should be abolished.

Another version of reorganization would transfer supervisory responsibility for the PBGC from the U.S. Department of Labor (DOL) to the U.S. Treasury. Proponents of this approach argue that DOL is the most likely agency within the government to adopt an accommodating posture with respect to the interests of organized labor. As a result, the cost of the program is likely to be higher than if the PBGC executive director reported to another department. Of all departments, the Treasury is most likely to be concerned with keeping program costs in line with premium income.

Unfortunately, these arguments ignore the Treasury's well-established role in reducing the maximum limit on pension contributions as noted in connection with the first generic approach, preparation, discussed earlier. By working to restrict the flexibility of plan sponsors to fund their reasonably predictable obligations in advance, the Treasury's influence has created additional risks for the insurance program. Even following such a transfer, the priorities at Treasury would strongly influence a continuation in this direction. On balance, the arguments for transferring supervision of the PBGC to the Treasury are less than persuasive.

A final organizational option would transfer the authority for granting minimum funding waivers from the Internal Revenue Service to the PBGC. During the mid-1980s, the IRS granted many of these waivers to companies that ultimately liquidated. Many of these waivers resulted in additional losses for the insurance fund. PBGC officials complained at the time that they lacked sufficient control over government decisions that were producing significant adverse effects on the program. The upshot of these complaints was that the agency, in 1987, was successful in obtaining a statutory advisory role in the waiver process. As a result of this and other changes related to minimum funding waivers, losses that can be traced to this source apparently have been reduced. However, waivers still have been granted on occasion. In reality, it is difficult to see how this transfer would produce better decisions on a consistent basis, in view of the well-known vulnerability of both agencies to political intervention and the greater risks that such meddling produces.

Communication

Changes in the way pension insurance conditions are communicated have appeared in proposals put forward by various administrations. However, they do not represent reforms per se. In early 1992, President Bush proposed to shift the budgetary accounting for the PBGC to an accrual basis. The Clinton administration, however, failed to include a similar feature in the legislation it sent to Congress 20 months later. Although there were serious flaws in the logic used to support the government position in both cases, the fact remains that the cash flow accounting method currently used in the federal budget produces a very distorted view of the program. These distortions hide both the value of insurance subsidies and growth in liabilities to taxpayers.

Under cash flow accounting, the fact that the PBGC uses a "revolving fund" to receive premium payments and to pay benefits leads to an understatement of the effects on the budget. In budgeting parlance, the cash flows into and out of the revolving fund are reflected in the federal budget on a "net basis." For many years, these cash flows have produced an offset against other spending in the federal budget of several hundred million dollars. Now, following enactment of the Retirement Protection Act of 1994, government officials currently expect premiums to rise by more than $500 million per year. The PBGC therefore has been cast in the unlikely role of deficit reducer. In a very perverse way, it apparently will be contributing to deficit reduction efforts for some time to come. Even though the budget and accounting conventions create exactly the opposite impression, the agency's financial prospects ultimately will have the effect of increasing federal indebtedness over an extended time horizon.

So far, the Clinton administration has failed to confront this reality. The Bush administration, on the other hand, faced it in a way that would have resulted in new and undesirable effects. It wanted to implement accrual budgeting before the programmatic reforms. This meant that large savings would have been recorded in the federal budget. These savings then could have been spent on other initiatives. In fact, the timing of the change to accrual budgeting that the Bush administration proposed would have produced phantom cost reductions on the order of $22 billion over five years. In the end, this intergenerational entitlement program, like the build-up of Social Security reserves,[33] should not be used to finance more spending for consumption elsewhere in the federal budget, regardless of whether the offsetting surpluses are calculated using cash flow or accrual accounting principles.

Another approach that can be classified as communication soon will require that employers with underfunded plans provide information to participants every year, in a simple format specified by the PBGC. This could be a very useful change, depending on how the condition of affected plans is reported in practice. However, it is unlikely to have a major effect on future losses the agency incurs.

CONCLUSION

Between 1977 and 1993, the PBGC proposed a series of six legislative initiatives to address major problems with the single-employer termination insurance program. Congress enacted four of these proposals, including a modified version of the latest one requested by the Clinton administration. Although taxpayer protection has been a recurring theme in all these proposals, the proposed remedies failed to match the rhetoric that accompanied them in virtually every case. Earlier in U.S. political history, the constraints on risk shifting were more compelling than they have been since the middle of this century. A prerequisite for avoiding the gathering crisis that faces the pension insurance program is a recognition of the scale of risk shifting that the program enables, and the need to end it.[34] According to the U.S. Department of Labor, the number of active workers covered by single-employer, defined-benefit plans has declined from 23.7 million in 1980 to 20.8 million in 1991. Meanwhile, the number of active workers covered by defined-contribution plans almost doubled from 18.4 million to 34.2 million during the same period, and the trend in favor of defined-contribution plans shows no sign of abating. So, arguments in favor of supporting a declining share of the labor force with a hidden subsidy embedded in the ERISA insurance program seem bound to grow weaker over time.

Confusion and misunderstanding also have led to proposals that have actually increased the risks to the insurance fund. The proposal recommended in Chapter 8 represents a clear break with this established pattern. It also recognizes the growth and development that have taken place in the private market for financial guarantees. Clearly, private financial guarantors are now capable of assuming major responsibilities for securing retirement promises made to workers outside the main federal entitlements of Social Security, Medicare, and the retirement systems for federal employees. With time, they can be expected to assemble all of the resources necessary to do the work that the PBGC now does and do it far more effectively. The ultimate effect of this change, together with the more effective credit analysis and surveillance that would ensue, would be to prevent companies from making promises to their workers that could only be kept at the expense of the insurance fund. America's pension insurance system needs to be redesigned to manage risk, not simply to shift risks that have been allowed to grow in the absence of effective controls.

SUMMARY

Public officials attempted to serve a variety of objectives—some in conflict with each other—by establishing the ERISA termination insurance program. The program was poorly designed in many areas, but the undesirable effects of its various shortcomings unfortunately have not offset each other. Any effective reform initiative therefore must aim to achieve multiple goals. Three objectives for reform have become conspicuous for their importance. First, taxpayers should receive effective protection against additional losses. Second, the classic insurance problems of adverse selection and moral hazard should be resolved. Finally, adverse employment effects associated with the reform initiatives themselves should be avoided.

Previous reform proposals can be characterized according to a taxonomy of seven categories: better preparation to meet future retirement costs, correction of perverse incentives, containment of pension insurance losses, redistribution, conversion to alternative forms of retirement saving, reorganization of the PBGC, and communication. No single panacea exists for dealing with the problems we have. However, raising the maximum funding limit would permit plan sponsors the flexibility to provide for future retirement needs at times when that is affordable. At the same time, containment of potential taxpayer losses from the PBGC would be greatly improved by a redistribution of the exposure to coinsurance; mandatory private termination insurance; a freeze on subsequent benefit accruals, as well as on increases, when plans do not qualify for private insurance; and investment restrictions in the form of contingent immunization. Finally, Congress should abolish the PBGC advisory committee.

ENDNOTES

1. Zvi Bodie and Robert C. Merton, "Pension Benefit Guarantees in the United States: A Functional Analysis," Ray Schmitt (ed.), *The Future of Pensions in the United States.* (Philadelphia, PA: The Pension Research Council of the Wharton School of the University of Pennsylvania, 1993), p. 209.

2. See Michael S. Gordon, "Introduction: The Social Policy Origins of ERISA," in American Bar Association Section of Labor and Employment Law, eds., *Employee Benefits Law,* (Washington, DC: Bureau of National Affiars, 1991) p. lxviii.

3. See George A. Akerlof and Paul M. Romer, "Looting: The Economic Underworld of Bankruptcy for Profit," in *Brookings Papers on Economic Activity* 2 (1993), pp. 1–73.

4. A lengthy phase-in period could have reduced the threat of a credit crunch. However, the beneficial effects for the insurance fund also would have been diminished. For a sympathetic discussion of these proposals as well as the possibility of shifting the market price of risk taking back to plan sponsors by according PBGC bankruptcy claims "superpriority" in bankruptcy, see David C. Lindeman, "Pensions' Plagues and the PBGC," *The American Enterprise,* March–April 1993, pp. 72–80.

5. See "Private Pensions: Funding Rule Change Needed to Reduce PBGC's Multibillion Dollar Exposure," (GAO/HEHS-95-5 Washington, DC: U.S. General Accounting Office, October 1994), p. 7.

6. See Mark J. Warshawsky, "Funding of Defined Benefit Plans: The Implications of Minimum Funding Requirements and Financial Accounting Standards," July 1995, pp. 12–13.

7. The interest rate corridor established by OBRA '87 ranged from 90 percent to 110 percent of the four-year moving-average yield on 30-year Treasury bonds. The high end of this range will decline by 1 percent per year in five steps beginning in 1995.

8. The current liability does not reflect the official PBGC termination assumptions. However, it doesn't reflect the effects of future inflation and salary increases either. See Richard A. Ippolito, *The Economics of Pension Insurance,* (Philadelphia: Pension Research Council of the Wharton School at the University of Pennsylvania, 1989), pp. 144–50.

9. See Zvi Bodie, "Managing Pension and Retirement Assets: An International Perspective," in *International Competitiveness in Financial Services: A Special Issue* of the *Journal of Financial Services Research,* Marvin H. Kosters and Allan H. Meltzer, eds., pp. 419–60.

10. See E. Philip Davis, "An International Comparison of the Financing of Occupational Pensions," Paper presented at the Pension Research Council Conference, "Securing Employer-Based Pensions: An International Perspective" at the Wharton School of the University of Pennsylvania, May 5–6, 1994.

11. C. Zweekhorst, "Development of Private Pension Plans in the Netherlands," in *Pension Policy: An International Perspective* (Washington, DC: U.S. Government Printing Office, 1990), pp. 174–75.

12. Figure 7–2 assumes that all workers begin their careers at age 25 with a salary of $25,000 per year. Compensation rises by 5.5 percent each year, and the pension plan pays a benefit of 1.25 percent of final average salary for every year of service at age 65. The rate of return on

plan assets was assumed to be 8 percent annually. For the data used to develop this figure, see Sylvester J. Schieber and John B. Shoven, "The Consequences of Population Aging on Private Pension Fund Saving and Asset Markets," Paper presented at a conference on "The Economics of Retirement in the 21st Century" in Washington, DC organized by the Center for Economic Policy and Research at Stanford University and the Association of Private Pension and Welfare Plans. September 1993, p. 10.

13. See James H. Smalhout, "Retirement Woes: Pension Saving Short of the Mark," *The Wall Street Journal,* February 4, 1993, sec. A, p. 18.

14. This extent of underfunding would be unlikely in a world with market participants determining the allocation of termination insurance and effective monitoring of plan condition. By way of contrast, terminating plans transferred to the PBGC on average were 42 percent funded relative to guaranteed benefits during recent years. See the Pension Benefit Guaranty Corporation, *Annual Report,* various years.

15. See Robert C. Merton and Zvi Bodie, "The Management of Financial Guarantees," *Financial Management,* Winter 1992, p. 103.

16. Leroy P. Jones, Pankaj Tandon, and Ingo Vogelsang, *Selling Public Enterprises* (Cambridge, MA: MIT Press, 1990), p. 3.

17. For the most part, the private financial guarantee industry currently insures timely payment of interest and the repayment of principal in connection with state and municipal bond obligations.

18. As noted previously, the coinsurance aspect of the PBGC program is suboptimal.

19. Recently, the American International Group, Inc., began selling private insurance for benefits not guaranteed by the PBGC. The AIG product is designed to secure the deferred retirement income of highly paid corporate executives. In addition, one member of the financial guarantee industry filed a request for regulatory approval in 1991 with the New York State Insurance Department to offer termination insurance coverage for a defined-benefit pension plan that was not tax exempt.

20. A form of insurance, frequently used to bond contract performance, whereby the insurer agrees to indemnify the beneficiary against default.

21. *Standard & Poor's Creditweek,* May 17, 1993, p. 13.

22. Another aspect of credit enhancement is that it is underwritten and priced to a *no loss standard.* This means that, at the time the policy is issued, no losses are anticipated during the life of the policy. The

largest bond insurance company (MBIA, Inc.) has guaranteed approximately 46,000 bond issues and experienced only three defaults.

23. The suitability standard for bond investments would also need to recognize the risk of downgrading. Protection against this possibility can depend on appropriate terms in the indenture agreement for each bond in the portfolio.

24. See "Compromise PBGC Reforms in Trade Bill Hit Underfunded Plans, Ease PBGC Power," in *BNA Pension & Benefits Reporter* 21 (September 26, 1994), pp. 1803–04.

25. Zvi Bodie, "On the Risks of Stocks in the Long Run," Working Paper 95-013 (Boston, MA: Harvard Business School Division of Research August 1994), p. 9.

26. See Sylvia Nasar, "The Oil-Futures Bloodbath: Is the Bank the Culprit?" *New York Times,* October 16, 1994, sec. 3, p. 5.

27. U.S. Congress, Congressional Budget Office. *Tax Policy for Pensions and Other Retirement Saving.* (Washington, DC: U.S. Government Printing Office, 1987), p. xviii.

28. I am indebted to Barry Bosworth for this comment.

29. See Smalhout, "Retirement Woes."

30. See Andrew A. Samwick and Jonathan Skinner, "How Will Defined Contribution Pension Plans Affect Retirement Income?" Paper presented at a conference on "The Economics of Retirement in the 21st Century" in Washington, DC organized by the Center for Economic Policy and Research at Stanford University and The Association of Private Pension and Welfare Plans, 1993.

31. See Bodie and Merton, "Pension Benefit Guarantees in the United States.

32. See the National Academy of Public Administration, "Study of the Pension Benefit Guaranty Corporation's Corporate Status," April 1991, pp. 23–4.

33. See Henry J. Aaron, Barry P. Bosworth, and Gary Burtless, *Can America Afford to Grow Old?* (Washington, DC: The Brookings Institution, 1989), p. 126.

34. See Yair Aharoni, *The No-Risk Society* (Chatham House, 1981), pp. 46–50.

8.

A ROADMAP INTO THE FUTURE

The U.S. government has responded to the occasional crises facing the PBGC by promoting a series of fads and fashions that it described as capable of putting the program on a sound footing. Each of these initiatives fell far short of the mark, and unfunded pension liabilities continued to grow. From the outset, there was an urgent need to repeal the Contingent Employer Liability Insurance (CELI) provisions in ERISA, as they were completely unworkable.[1] CELI represented a political artifice with no serious legislative intent, according to those who participated in drafting the law. It was included, just before ERISA was enacted, as a concession to members of the Senate Finance Committee who wanted to soften the effect of the employer liability claims proposed for the PBGC.[2]

Congress amended ERISA to remove the CELI provisions in 1980. Shortly thereafter, officials began pointing out that premiums were inadequate to support the cost of the program. Then, they told Congress that the introduction of a risk-related premium was the one effective way to discourage undesirable risk taking on the part of plan sponsors and investment managers; this followed two major bankruptcies in the steel industry during the mid-1980s.[3] Under President Bush, changes in the Bankruptcy Code received primary attention. More recently, members of the Clinton administration have stressed a need for more extensive regulation.

The problem for policymakers, however, is not to select one approach that will become the centerpiece for the next round of pension legislation. Instead, it is to identify an effective combination of reforms that complement each other and that will be capable of addressing the needs of taxpayers as well as those groups of pension plan participants that previously received short shrift. Most of the previous approaches relied on the use of law, regulation, or ad hoc suasion by government officials to improve pension funding. These approaches have clearly failed. The possibility of harnessing market forces to produce better outcomes has not, until now, received serious consideration. From the alternatives discussed in Chapter 7, three tools are available that, in combination, would stop companies from making promises that send misleading signals to workers and can only be kept at the expense of the insurance fund. These tools consist of a stop-loss mechanism for inadequately funded pension plans, a market-based solvency test involving mandatory private insurance, and effectively distributed exposure to coinsurance.

Unreasonable risks to the insurance fund could be avoided if benefits simply are frozen when asset values become inadequate to cover them. However, pension liabilities aren't like bank loans for specific amounts. They are imprecise quantities that can be estimated only within a wide range of probability. Making this situation even less tractable, confusion is rampant within the pension community concerning proper assumptions to use for measuring a benefit obligation. The controversy that would surround virtually any reasonable set of actuarial assumptions one uses to estimate these obligations therefore would make it difficult, if not impossible, to implement a benefit freeze by itself.

An effective stop-loss mechanism thus would require use of a second tool: a market-based solvency test. A reasonable test would require sponsors of unsecured private defined-benefit pension plans to maintain AAA or AA credit ratings from at least two of the three major rating agencies (i.e., Standard & Poor's, Moody's, and Fitch). Lower-rated sponsors under this test would need to secure their pension obligations by means of a guarantee from an insurance company that consistently met the AAA standard of creditworthiness. If the combined creditworthiness of a pension plan and its sponsor were so weak that pension insurance could not be obtained, then benefits would be frozen.

By relying on the collective financial and actuarial judgments of the insurance industry among others, this approach would relieve public officials of the responsibility—one which they have not been able to perform effectively—for defining precise funding standards. Requiring plan sponsors to purchase private credit insurance in this way would effectively internalize, within firms, reasonable pension-funding rules. Those rules would not depend on the Internal Revenue Service and the vagaries of the political process to which the IRS is subject. They would, however, reflect the market price of risk.

The third tool, coinsurance at effective levels,[4] is essential to resolve the problem of moral hazard. Coinsurance is necessary but not sufficient to put a reformed termination insurance system on a sound financial footing. Taken together, the stop-loss mechanism and the market-based solvency test would produce a triage system for defined-benefit pension plans. A first group of healthy plans would immediately exit the government-run program to enter new private insurance arrangements. Meanwhile, a second group of less healthy plans eventually would become creditworthy enough to enter the private system, after their urge to make false promises had been thwarted by a temporary freeze on benefits. However, the investments of any plan in this category should be restricted to investment grade bonds until the plan qualifies for private insurance. At that point, the system would allow equity investment only if the projected-benefit obligation (PBO) is hedged, using a well-established method known as *contingent immunization.* So long as plan assets exceeded the PBO, equity investment could continue. However, if the value of assets ever fell to the point where it merely equaled the PBO, all equities would be sold and a portfolio of investment-grade bonds purchased to match the duration of plan liabilities.[5] For all of this to be feasible, Congress also would need to increase the OBRA '87 maximum funding limit because, in some cases, the PBO could exceed the current limit of 150 percent of the ABO.

The third group of plans probably would never satisfy a market-based solvency test. For plans in this group, the approach outlined here would amount to a "termination without termination." Although the PBGC would not actually trustee these plans before the sponsor liquidated, benefits would remain permanently frozen. Contributions could continue at past levels and pension investments would be restricted to investment-grade bonds.

For their part, plan sponsors and their employees would need time to adjust to the new arrangement. Certainly, union negotiators and their corporate counterparts in the collective bargaining process would start making allowances for the new constraints and costs. A phase-in period therefore would be required to permit renegotiation of previous collective bargaining agreements. Implementation should begin no sooner than three years following passage of the legislation for this reason. In addition, the transformation of the financial guarantee industry discussed below strongly suggests that complete implementation might require five years beyond that.

MULTIDIRECTIONAL RISK SHARING

Implementing any approach that features a significant role for private insurance contracts would not involve a single "big-bang" type of event, for additional reasons. Private carriers initially could be tapped to assume only a minor share, perhaps just 5 percent or 10 percent, of the government's exposure to the very largest "insurable" plans under a facultative type of relationship.[6] Yet, the effectiveness of credit judgments and pricing decisions would not be compromised even with this relatively limited exposure. As additional capital and human resources flowed into the new private pension guarantee industry, government exposure to the largest plans gradually could be eliminated. All other privately insurable plans meanwhile could be included in the new arrangement. This approach would offer taxpayers stop-loss protection from the outset, as long as the accrual of additional benefits was contingent on the purchase of a private guarantee, even for a small initial share of plan liabilities.

Moreover, the potentially large capital requirements necessary for this type of insurance operation suggest that both reinsurance and coinsurance would play extraordinarily important roles, particularly at the outset. Given that the private financial guarantee industry currently has less than $5 billion in equity, increasing capacity by the necessary amount would clearly involve a major transformation. For insight concerning how private carriers would price the insurance, as well as the magnitude of the related capital requirements, consider the following generic calculations.

I. Average accrued vested-benefit obligation (ABO)
       = $40,000/participant

   This benchmark reflects two illustrative facts. According to estimates based on the PBGC's "PAI" model presented in Chapter 3, the average ABO for participants in U.S. pension plans sponsored by General Motors was $57,869 ($47.7 billion in total adjusted liabilities divided by 824,277 participants) as of October 1, 1991. In addition, the Department of Labor reports that private defined-benefit pension plans covered 38.8 million participants and had accumulated assets of $961.9 million in 1990. If assets can be considered as a proxy for liabilities, the DOL tabulation would imply an ABO in the $25,000 range.[7]

II. Average projected benefit obligation (PBO)
       = 110% × Average accrued benefit obligation
           ($40,000/ participant)
       = $44,000/participant

   The ABO will differ from the PBO only with respect to benefits promised to active workers. The ABO represents the present value of benefits earned to date without taking account of future inflation or salary increases. For its part, the PBO reflects the same benefits earned to date but includes expected compensation increases during the balance of a worker's career. Insofar as retirees account for the greatest proportion of the ABO in a typical defined-benefit plan, even substantial differences between accrued benefits and projected benefits promised to current workers would have a relatively minor effect on total plan liabilities. Consider the

General Motors Retirement Program for Salaried Employees. Of $13.4 billion in vested benefits reported on the 1991 Form 5500 Schedule B, approximately $3.2 billion was attributable to active workers. If the PBO is 25 percent higher than the ABO for this group, projected liabilities for the entire plan would exceed the ABO by only 5.6 percent. However, the distribution of liabilities between retirees and active workers may be less extreme in the typical case. Hence, the assumption that the PBO will exceed the ABO by 10 percent.

III. Average insured premium base
  = 50% × Average projected benefit obligation
      ($44,000/participant)
  = $22,000/participant

To address serious inequities and efficiency problems resulting from the distribution of coinsurance implied by PBGC coverage, the insured premium base would be expanded to include the projected benefit obligation. After a pro rata distribution of plan assets, this uniform coinsurance rate of 50 percent would apply to every participant from the first dollar of loss. Currently, coinsurance can range from 10 percent for some older participants to 90 percent for some younger participants.

IV. Assumed market value of pension assets
    = $44,000/participant

This assumes that the typical plan is fully funded on a PBO basis. Based on 1987 data, the estimated ratio of pension assets to accrued vested benefits reported in Chapter 2 was 1.28.[8]

V. Average risk-adjusted equivalent value of pension assets
    = 75% × Assumed market value of pension assets
        ($44,000/participant)
    = $33,000/participant

Sources in and close to the private financial guarantee industry believe that an adjustment in this neighborhood would be typical. However, the actual adjustments in practice could range from 2 percent to 50 percent of the portfolio's market value depending on the risk characteristics of plan assets as well as any mismatch between the duration of those assets and the plan's benefit obligations.

VI. Average risk exposure

= Average projected benefit obligation ($44,000/ participant) – Average risk-adjusted equivalent value of pension assets ($33,000/participant)

= $11,000/participant

The average risk exposure reflects the potential for loss on the part of plan participants in the absence of any backup guarantee.

VII. Average par value of the insurance contract

= Coinsurance rate (50%) × Average risk exposure

= $5,500/participant

With the recommended 50% coinsurance rate discussed in Section III, the average net risk exposure would be the same for plan participants and the insurance carriers.

VIII. Insurance carrier capital requirement

= 6% × Average par value ($5,500/participant)

= $330/participant

Credit analysts at Standard & Poor's report that the capital requirement applicable to corporate credit risks would be 6 percent of par value.

IX. Insurance carrier cost of reserve capital

= 23% × Capital requirement ($330/participant)

= $75.90/participant

(a.) Return on reserve capital

= 8.25% × Capital requirement ($330/participant)

= $27.23/participant

(b.) Reserve-related premium requirement

= Insurance carrier cost of capital ($75.90/participant)

– Return on reserve capital ($27.23/participant)

= $48.68/participant

To raise the necessary equity capital, the insurance carrier would need to provide shareholders with a competitive after-tax return on their investment of approximately 15 percent. Assuming a 35 percent tax rate, insurance carriers would set premiums based on a pre-tax hurdle rate of 23 percent. However, the carriers in turn would reinvest shareholder equity in high-quality securities (e.g., tax-free municipal bonds with after-tax yields equivalent to those available from AAA-rated corporate bonds). The initial 23 percent cost of capital therefore would be offset in part by a return on investment.

X. Insurance carrier operating costs
   = 0.3% × Par value ($5,500/participant)
   = $16.50/participant

Analysts at Fitch Investors Service, Inc. estimate that the above rate is typical for the private financial guarantee industry in the United States.

XI. Expected losses
   = Default rate × Average recovery rate (55% per claim)
      × Average insured premium base ($22,000/
      participant)

   Case I: The AA-rated sponsor
      = .7% × 55% × $22,000/participant
      = $84.70/participant

   Case II: The A-rated sponsor
      = .93% × 55% × $22,000/participant
      = $112.53/participant

   Case III: The BBB-rated sponsor
      = 2.66% × 55% × $22,000/participant
      = $321.86/participant

These default rates assume a five-year term for the insurance contract. The case of AAA-rated sponsors was not calculated because insurance carriers with equivalent credit ratings would not be capable of enhancing the pension promises of companies in that group. Costs that might be involved with sponsors rated below the BBB-level also were not calculated, because private financial guarantors generally do not insure credits that are not investment grade. Standard

& Poor's provided five-year average default rates from its 1993 "Corporate Default and Rating Transition Study." They cover the period 1981–1993.

XII. Annual premium supplement for expected losses
$$= 26.4\% \times \text{Expected losses}$$
    Case I: The AA-rated sponsor
    = $22.34/participant
    Case II: The A-rated sponsor
    = $29.68/participant
    Case III: The BBB-rated sponsor
    = $84.91/participant

The annual premium supplement for expected losses was estimated here by amortizing the expected losses over the five-year term of the insurance contract using a discount rate of 10 percent.

XIII. Annual premium range
= Insurance carrier cost of reserve capital
    + Insurance carrier operating costs
    + Annual premium supplement for expected losses
    Case I: The AA-rated sponsor
    = $87.52/participant
    Case II: The A-rated sponsor
    = $94.86/participant
    Case III: The BBB-rated sponsor
    = $150.09/participant

The resulting premium range suggests that for fully funded plans, AA-rated sponsors would face annual premium costs amounting to approximately 0.4 percent of the average insured premium base. This compares with the shadow-price estimate from Chapter 4 of approximately 0.6 percent for PBGC insurance based on 1987 sample data. Otherwise similar plans sponsored by BBB-rated companies would face annual premium costs of almost 0.7 percent of the average insured premium base. The 1987 shadow price estimate for annual PBGC insurance premiums was more than three times that rate, or about 2.3 percent.

For an example involving both high benefit levels and substantial unfunded liabilities, consider the case of General Motors.[9]

I. Average accrued vested-benefit obligation
   = $47.7 billion/824,277 participants
   = $57,869/participant

II. Average projected benefit obligation
   = 110% × Accrued benefit obligation ($57,869/
      participant)
   = $63,656/participant

III. Average insured premium base
   = 50% × Average projected benefit obligation
      ($63,656/participant)
   = $31,828/participant

IV. Average market value of pension assets
   = $34 billion/824,277 participants
   = $41,248/participant

V. Average risk-adjusted equivalent value of pension assets
   = 75% × Average market value of pension assets
      ($41,248/participant)
   = $30,936/participant

VI. Average risk exposure
   = Average projected benefit obligation ($63,656/
      participant) – Average risk-adjusted equivalent
      value of pension assets ($30,936/participant)
   = $32,720/participant

VII. Average par value of the insurance contract
   = Coinsurance rate (50%) × Average risk exposure
   = $16,360/participant

VIII. Insurance carrier capital requirement
   = 6% × Average net risk exposure ($16,360/
      participant)
   = $982/participant

IX. Insurance carrier cost of capital
 = 23% × Capital requirement ($982/participant)
 = $225.86/participant

   (a.) Return on reserve capital
 = 8.25% × Capital requirement ($982/participant)
 = $81.02/participant

   (b.) Reserve-related premium requirement
 = Insurance carrier cost of capital ($225.86/
 participant) – Return on reserve capital
 ($81.02/participant)
 = $144.85/participant

X. Insurance carrier operating costs
 = .3% × Par value ($31,828/participant)
 = $49.08 / Participant

XI. Annual premium supplement for expected losses
 = 0.4% × Insured premium base
 = $126.28/participant

XII. Total annual premium
 = Insurance carrier cost of reserve capital
 + Insurance carrier operating costs
 + Annual premium supplement for expected
 losses
 = $320.21/participant

Given the substantial unfunded liabilities associated with the GM plans, this calculation shows that private insurance can represent an alternative even in cases where the credit quality does not seem particularly attractive. Assume that 50 percent of all plans would require a private backup guarantee in such a system, and that 38 million participants would remain covered by private defined-benefit plans. If $330 per participant reasonably approximates the insurance company capital requirement, then the carriers would need to raise approximately $6.3 billion in new equity. This clearly is a very substantial figure compared to their current net worth. However, the industry should be able to attract it, particularly if it makes effective use of reinsurance, and/or if new firms enter the market.

Assembling the human resources necessary to conduct this business would require an equally important transformation. In contrast with their commitment to the tax-exempt municipal market, bond insurers clearly have very limited and specialized staffs involved in guaranteeing corporate risks. Private financial guarantors therefore would need time to assemble teams with good general skills in the field of corporate credit analysis and with an in-depth understanding of specific industries. Although private carriers have considered offering this type of insurance as early as 1991,[10] senior management at these firms would likewise need time to become more acclimated to the somewhat different environment of corporate credit risk.

AIG's recently introduced "executive deferred income insurance" provides another pricing benchmark. This product secures pension benefits from loss in cases of employer bankruptcies, mergers, acquisitions, and changes in management policy. It provides covered benefits under so-called supplemental or "top hat" plans that do not qualify for the same favorable tax treatment accorded plans covering lower-paid corporate employees. This type of insurance is advantageous from the employer's point of view because it reduces the pressure to incur high funding costs in the absence of better tax treatment. In contrast with tax-qualified defined-benefit plans, companies typically don't fund the pension benefits that this type of insurance covers beforehand.

. A five-year policy from AIG costs between 1.25 and 2.5 percent, depending on the employer's credit rating and assuming no decline in its financial strength. AIG requires a minimum triple-B credit rating from Standard & Poor's. While this premium structure is much higher than the one discussed above, several factors could lead to lower costs if private insurance were phased in to replace PBGC coverage. First, the AIG product is designed to serve a very small, elite group within the labor force. However, premiums could be reduced if selling and administrative costs were spread over a much larger base of covered benefits. Second, AIG has introduced an innovative product in a market of relatively limited but unknown size. So far, it faces no direct competition. In a more mature and competitive market, insurance prices would reflect the carriers' marginal costs. Third, the AIG premium schedule reflects risks associated with benefits that are not funded in advance. Exposure to loss would be much less severe, even in cases of the most poorly funded pension plans that the PBGC now covers, due to the presence of substantial pension assets. Finally, giving insurance providers greater powers to intervene in cases of deteriorating credit quality would undoubtedly reduce costs.

INTERVENTION RIGHTS

Adequate rights for insurance providers to intervene are essential, because so much can change between the time that a worker earns a given dollar of benefits and the time when that money is actually paid as a pension. The fortunes of the sponsor will ebb and flow. Mergers, acquisitions, leveraged buyouts, and other types of financial restructurings can dramatically alter the company's credit quality. The courts may determine that malfeasance on the part of corporate officials justifies large damage awards to outsiders. Product liability claims (e.g., the Manville Corporation) and the cost of cleaning up decades of environmental damage can, in rare cases, even bankrupt sponsors.

Each of these factors can impair the sponsor's ability to pay future benefits and thus increase the risk to insurance providers. Yet, outright cancellation of coverage would defeat the purpose of the insurance and therefore should not be an option to the carriers. Short of cancellation, however, the right simply to terminate the plan would be among the most important remedies available to private insurers. In the most desperate situations, this has proven effective in Sweden. The Swedish system also teaches that losses can be reduced if guarantors have the right to require that a company's entire pension liability be eliminated over a period as short as five years. As noted in Chapter 5, this is accomplished when the sponsor purchases deferred group annuities from the SPP insurance company.

In cases of serious mismanagement, private insurance companies in the United States almost certainly would exercise these prerogatives. These rights, however, would not be particularly valuable in the context of the current government program. Elected officials and their agents throughout the executive branch would find confronting the politically influential groups associated with a troubled sponsor far too daunting. More often than not, government officials would tend to be negligent in requiring such changes when they were needed. In fact, the PBGC already has the authority to terminate a pension plan that represents an "unreasonable" threat to the insurance program. But, predictably, the agency has not used this provision in many years for political reasons.

Other forms of intervention also might be useful. The insurance companies, for example, could be given the right to replace pension plan trustees, the plan administrator, the enrolled actuary, and the outside auditor, as well as staff employees of the pension plan. The ultimate cost of coverage also could be reduced if carriers received the right to demand a change in investment policy, the right to seize plan assets, and the right to secure additional collateral from plan sponsors. However, such a system clearly would not be effective in achieving its objectives if private guarantors had the right to return any plan that subsequently became insolvent to the PBGC.

Clearly, these essential intervention powers could significantly reduce risks facing the insurance companies. The carriers could be given other rights that would reduce these risks further. For example, insurance providers could be given the power to veto merger and acquisition activity. They also could be authorized to replace the plan sponsor's senior management as well as its board of directors. These last possibilities, if they ever were used, almost certainly would result in complex and protracted litigation. Their value to the insurance carriers would be doubtful for this reason.

REGULATION

Government would need to take on some new responsibilities in such a system. It would be necessary to monitor the financial strength of the private insurance carriers to ensure that promised retirement benefits ultimately would be paid. But if government has repeatedly failed to institute effective solvency regulation in the pension field, what justification is there for supposing that it could monitor the safety and soundness of insurance providers? To be sure, government supervision of any financial institution can be a difficult task, particularly in this age of arcane investment strategies that rely on complex, difficult-to-value assets. To gauge the condition of a major financial institution accurately, regulators today must be prepared to intrude to the extent of installing a "shadow management," with access to all the information necessary for evaluating the numerous sources of risk facing the enterprise.

Even this degree of involvement in the affairs of the institution, however, does not assure financial soundness. Ill-conceived approaches to regulation and backup guarantee arrangements have been destabilizing in cases where massive resources were committed to auditing and data collection. Certainly, federal regulation of the S&L industry in the 1980s provides a conspicuous example of such an outcome. Just as lessons from the S&L debacle shed important light on how regulation of the pension industry should not be conducted, the experience of the life insurance industry offers some insight concerning ways of avoiding widespread financial disaster. While it is true that a vastly different system of state regulation of the life insurance industry produced a few highly publicized insolvencies in the 1980s, these have proven to be isolated incidents in retrospect.

What factors protected taxpayers and policyholders from a systemwide crisis in the life insurance industry, and how did they differ from the corresponding aspects of savings and loan regulation?[11] First, federal guarantees inspire virtually universal confidence among lenders. Guarantees provided by state governments enjoy considerably less credibility. As a result, insurance companies were more sensitive to the impact of deteriorating financial health on their ability to raise funds. Today, replacing a federal guarantee that secures pension benefits with a private one (even from a carrier with the very highest credit rating) is likely to produce a similar effect.

Second, a smaller portion of life insurance company liabilities were secured by government guarantees. In 1981, Congress increased deposit insurance coverage to $100,000 per depositor in any single institution. In addition, some of the growth at weaker S&Ls during the 1980s was facilitated by access to deposits in a national market (i.e., brokered deposits), which also received coverage from the federal deposit insurance fund. For their part, life insurance companies used guaranteed investment contracts (GICs)[12] and single-premium deferred annuities (SPDAs) to achieve growth during the same period. However, government guarantees secured these instruments to a much lesser extent compared with brokered S&L deposits.[13]

Third, monitoring will be more effective if other institutions in the system realistically expect to absorb the losses resulting from future insolvencies. In support of this point, Calomiris found that self-regulating mutual liability deposit insurance achieved stability and survived financial panics after the Civil War.[14]

The experience of life insurance companies also has shown that insiders can be motivated to create the conditions necessary for maintaining financial stability within the industry. In particular, life insurance companies hold safer portfolios in states where they do not receive tax credits for payments to the guarantee fund.[15] In these states, the surviving carriers absorb the full costs of resolving other insurance company failures. Regulators therefore find themselves under more pressure to enforce effective standards. Unfortunately, pension plan sponsors understand that they are not likely to bear the full cost of any financial debacle in the pension system, with U.S. taxpayers standing behind the PBGC.

Fourth, large government insurance systems face greater free-riding problems, leading to less monitoring and weaker enforcement of regulations. This is the logical consequence of spreading the cost of failure resolution over a much larger base of firms covered by the insurance fund. Thus, individual firms have more at stake in smaller insurance arrangements organized at the state level than they would in a national system set up by the federal government.

The mere existence of a guarantee fund reduces the incentives for pension plan participants and their representatives to exercise market discipline. In the absence of a guarantee fund, insurance company policyholders have an incentive to buy from sound insurance companies or to demand lower premiums from risky carriers. One study found that the growth of state guarantee funds contributed to the increased number and cost of insurance company insolvencies.[16] Certainly, an interesting feature of the private financial guarantee industry is that it has maintained a high level of confidence throughout the financial community, despite the absence of a collective fund to absorb losses from the default of one of the companies in that market.

Turning to the practical issue of how government might regulate a restructured pension insurance system consisting of private carriers, few believed until recently that Congress would cede this activity to private firms while leaving the entire responsibility for regulating the firms in the hands of state governments. One plausible alternative would assign a federal agency the task of approving specific carriers before they can offer the product. The Treasury Department already performs a similar activity before allowing private insurance companies to provide surety bonds for government contracts. Beyond this initial certification, state insurance departments might retain regulatory authority over the companies, or they might share that responsibility with federal and state authorities and with private credit rating firms like Moody's and Standard & Poor's.

Following the Executive Life default, current state regulation has been criticized for ineffectively monitoring the solvency of the insurance industry. By way of response, some of its defenders have pointed out that, with 53 state-level insurance departments monitoring these companies, the probability that a major problem will go undetected is substantially less than if just one agency were responsible. The same defenders have also suggested that the legislative branch may be much weaker at the state level, thus producing lower costs of political interference. At this point, legislation authorizing the federal government to regulate insurance companies has been proposed by Rep. John Dingell. However, the issue does not have a high priority on the domestic agenda. Assuming for a moment that the Dingell proposal or one like it is not adopted, pension insurance would probably be treated as a special case featuring limited federal oversight combined with additional supervision from authorities at the state level.

Another unusual feature of the regulatory terrain in this area is the role played by the three principal bond rating agencies: Fitch Investors Service, Inc., Moody's, and Standard & Poor's. Insofar as bond insurance companies perform a function that improves the credit ratings of municipal bond issues from at least the triple-B level to their own triple-A ratings, they have nothing to sell if their own creditworthiness were downgraded below the very highest level. A prerequisite for remaining in that business therefore requires that they maintain extremely stringent standards for managing the risks reflected on their own balance sheets. The three principal rating agencies not only subject the bond insurance companies to the usual rating criteria related to portfolio quality, management, ownership and the use of reinsurance, but they also examine whether these companies could withstand the losses that would occur in a worst-case scenario similar to the Great Depression of the 1930s.

To summarize, the combined scrutiny of credit rating agencies, state and federal regulators, and properly motivated premium payers could obviate the need for yet another backup guarantee fund to protect against losses resulting from insurance company insolvencies. Indeed, they could provide perfectly adequate safeguards in a system lacking this feature, thereby avoiding many of the incentive problems that otherwise would develop.

CONCLUSION

This book has argued that retirement income security, properly defined, is a concept quite different from the measure of benefits that is guaranteed by the ERISA termination insurance program. Although ERISA provides workers and retirees with maximum guaranteed benefits of about $30,000 per year (i.e., a figure permanently set for pension plans terminating in 1995 but that will rise for future terminations), participants in terminating underfunded plans can be treated substantially better or worse than the ERISA maximum appears to suggest. Retirees with pension benefits greatly exceeding the guaranteed amount may receive unreduced payments from the

PBGC insurance fund as a result of the allocation rules for distributing the remaining plan assets. On the other hand, large numbers of workers—particularly those who are not yet close to retirement age—remain exposed to substantial losses when their pension plans terminate, because benefits are frozen in nominal terms at that point.

This same problem confronts many more plan participants, even those with vested benefits, when making routine employment changes anytime before their last years at work. These participants can lose as much as 90 percent of the value of promised benefits when coverage stops, due either to termination of the plan or merely to a job change. An important goal for retirement income policy should be to protect workers from such losses, particularly in view of continuing structural change in the economy and the resulting mobility among the labor force. This objective can be achieved if employers are obligated to provide a reasonable measure of projected benefits secured by a guarantee from a properly designed termination insurance fund.

Having established this as a first principle, it is important to recognize that currently accepted accounting and actuarial practices often seriously understate the employer's ultimate pension liability. This situation is dangerous for workers because they can make inappropriate choices between saving and consumption in response to the misleading signals communicated to them by both employers and the government. If workers are rational and want to avoid the risks associated with poorly funded pension plans, they need to take the necessary steps to avoid them. In fact, workers can achieve additional protection against this source of risk by negotiating a greater proportion of total compensation in the form of cash to be contributed to an underfunded pension plan or, alternatively, to a defined-contribution plan.

By marking pension asset and liability data to market values using sample data for 1981, 1986, and 1987, large discrepancies became apparent between the actual and reported condition of most plans. At the beginning of the 1980s, the actual condition of private defined-benefit pension plans was considerably better than most sponsors were reporting, because interest rates had risen to unprecedented levels. This situation was reversed by the middle of the decade, however, in a pattern of change that extended to union and nonunion plans alike, and in both the manufacturing and service sectors.

These results are consistent with the belief that the condition of a typical defined-benefit plan erodes as interest rates decline. With respect to the termination insurance program operated by the PBGC, the findings strongly suggest that, in addition to major credit risks, substantial interest rate risk also represents a long-term threat to taxpayers. This risk will persist regardless of the value of the unfunded liabilities at any particular moment, and/or the current state of the economy.

Besides these gaping holes in the safety net and major weaknesses in financial reporting, another reason for advocating fundamental reform is the destabilizing effects of incentive problems created by the ERISA termination insurance program. Can benefit security be improved without exposing taxpayers to major new risks? Here there are grounds for optimism. Protecting workers against post-termination erosion of pension wealth represents the linchpin of a sound approach to coinsurance. In turn, adequate coinsurance represents an essential safeguard against some of the more destabilizing influences created by this poorly designed insurance system.

One measure of insurance value—the shadow price—suggests that the PBGC is providing coverage at a cost that would require annual premiums averaging 2 percent of guaranteed benefits. A reasonable goal for reform would be to secure the projected benefit obligation for premiums of no more than approximately one-third of that amount. As the case of Sweden demonstrates, this could be achieved by limiting the term of the insurance; granting private financial guarantors effective intervention rights in deteriorating situations; and requiring less creditworthy sponsors to replace their existing defined-benefit pension plans with deferred group annuities, which they would purchase from financially solid insurance companies.

The ERISA termination insurance program clearly has the potential to impose major budgetary costs on the federal government sometime during the first quarter of the next century. Unfortunately, denial and a reluctance to confront powerful interest groups are reactions that come naturally to many of the policymakers who can bring about the necessary changes now, when they would be most effective. ERISA should never have allowed companies to make false pension promises to their workers, promises that could be kept only at the expense of the insurance fund. The incrementalist approach to reform demonstrated so far by the government is still far from the point of stopping this in the future.

Before ERISA, benefit security could have been delivered by severing the link between the sponsor's financial health and the condition of the pension plan. To accomplish that objective, unfunded pension liabilities simply could have been prohibited. Those insurance companies, mutual-fund managers, and bank trust departments that could meet the highest standards of financial soundness could have been entrusted with operating our retirement institutions in a truly independent fashion. Instead, ERISA introduced a bankruptcy-for-profit scheme. Its perverse incentives for managers and workers alike have encouraged continuing financial mayhem in the back alleys of the nation's capital markets. Restoring some semblance of order will now require a slightly more complicated framework. Unfortunately, the cost of past mistakes cannot be avoided. Better policies, however, can prevent those costs from growing larger. For that to happen, policymakers must be willing to break with past approaches and focus in a serious way on this important issue.

SUMMARY

A combination of methods from among the reform alternatives discussed in Chapter 7 yields a three-pronged approach for producing more secure pension promises. That approach consists of a stop-loss mechanism for inadequately funded pension plans, a market-based solvency test involving mandatory private insurance, and effectively distributed exposure to coinsurance. Successful implementation would involve an extended transition period to permit necessary adjustment on the part of plan sponsors, their employees, and labor unions, as well as the private financial guarantee industry.

Plan sponsors with investment-grade credit ratings would qualify for private insurance. However, companies meeting the highest credit-quality standards (i.e., those rated triple or double A by Moody's and Standard & Poor's) can make highly credible long-term retirement promises to their workers unassisted by a third-party backup guarantee. Firms in this group therefore would be exempted from the new requirement. At the other end of the spectrum, companies without investment-grade credit ratings would be unable to obtain the mandatory private guarantees. Instead, they would retain PBGC insurance until their financial health improved sufficiently so that they could meet the new requirement. Companies in this group could make no additional retirement promises without private guarantees. In effect, their plans would remain frozen until that time.

Private insurance carriers would be required to maintain a triple A credit rating from at least two of the three recognized rating agencies (Fitch Investors Service, Moody's Investors Service, and Standard & Poor's) in order to provide this type of cover. These insurance carriers would perform periodic credit surveillance to determine whether employers, together with their pension plans, remain solvent. The private guarantors would be accorded enhanced intervention rights in cases of deteriorating credit quality.

ENDNOTES

1. CELI would have greatly reduced if not eliminated altogether the value of PBGC bankruptcy claims against plan sponsors. With CELI, the agency would have been able to recover the lesser of the face value of the pension claims or the sum of the sponsor's corporate equity plus all pension assets. In one section, ERISA had made plan sponsors fully liable for their pension promises but the CELI provision then provided the means for escaping this new liability. CELI originally was scheduled for implementation as of September 1977. See Pension Benefit Guaranty Corporation, *Contingent Employer Liability Insurance: Status Report to the Congress*, July 1, 1978.

2. Employers had complained about the proposed PBGC bankruptcy claim for as much as 30 percent of the sponsor's net worth. The author is indebted to John N. Erlenborn and Michael S. Gordon for this background concerning CELI.

3. Those steel companies were Wheeling-Pittsburgh and LTV.

4. For a discussion of coinsurance, see Chapter 7.

5. Using the PBO as the funding target assumes that the employer is required to provide PBO-based benefits—as in the United Kingdom—and that the insurance fund guarantees them at this level. As noted above, such a guarantee represents an important aspect of a sound approach to coinsurance. However, requiring employers to provide some measure of projected benefits would represent a fundamental reform of the U.S. pension system in its own right. The market-based solvency test described above still would produce major improvements in funding practices, even without such a reform. In the context of the present system with its more limited guarantee, others have argued that only the accumulated-benefit obligation (ABO) should be hedged. Hedging the PBO in conjunction with the three-part approach recommended here should be regarded as both consistent with and an extension of the previous literature. See Robert C. Merton and Zvi Bodie, "On the Management of Financial Guarantees," *Financial Management,* Winter 1992, pp. 87–109.

6. At this time, the single risk limit (i.e., the maximum legal exposure to any one borrowing group) of the financial guarantee industry amounts to $500 million. This amount would increase if more equity capital were raised by these companies, if new carriers entered the industry, or if reinsurance were used. The succeeding calculation suggests that the General Motors pension plans involve more than $13 billion of exposure net of coinsurance.

7. See U.S. Department of Labor, *Private Pension Plan Bulletin* 2 (Summer 1993), p. 5.

8. See Table 2–5.

9. Based on 1992 data provided by the company.

10. In that year, one member of the financial guarantee industry filed a request for regulatory approval with the New York State Insurance Department to offer termination insurance coverage for a defined-benefit pension plan that was not tax-exempt. However, the proposal was dropped after the plan sponsor chose not to pursue it.

11. See Elijah Brewer III, Thomas H. Mondschean, and Philip E. Strahan, "Why the Life Insurance Industry Did Not Face an S&L-type Crisis," *Economic Perspectives, Federal Reserve Bank of Chicago,* September–October 1993, pp. 12–24.

12. GICs are not guaranteed by a U.S. government insurance program.

13. See Richard M. Todd and Neil Wallace, "SPDAs and GICs: Like Money in the Bank?" *Quarterly Review, Federal Reserve Bank of Minneapolis,* Spring 1992, pp. 2–17.

14. See Charles W. Calomiris, "Deposit Insurance: Lessons from the Record," *Economic Perspectives, Federal Reserve Bank of Chicago,* May–June 1989, pp. 10–30.

15. See Elijah Brewer III, Thomas H. Mondschean, and Philip E. Strahan, "The Effect of Capital on Portfolio Risk at Life Insurance Companies," *Federal Reserve Bank of Chicago, Working Paper Series, Issues in Financial Regulation* (WP 92–29), 1992.

16. See Scott E. Harrington, "Should the Feds Regulate Insurance Company Insolvency?" *Regulation,* Spring 1991, pp. 53–61.

INDEX